Renewing Black Intellectual History

Renewing Black Intellectual History

The Ideological and Material Foundations of African American Thought

Adolph Reed Jr.
and Kenneth W. Warren

Madhu Dubey
William P. Jones
Michele Mitchell
Touré F. Reed
Dean E. Robinson
Preston H. Smith II
Judith Stein

Routledge
Taylor & Francis Group
LONDON AND NEW YORK

Chapter 1 is reprinted from Eric J. Sundquist, ed., *Frederick Douglass: New Literary and Historical Essays.* Copyright @ 1990 Cambridge University Press. Reprinted with permission of Cambridge University Press. Chapter 2 is reprinted from *Science and Society* 38 (Winter 1974–1975): 422–463. Chapter 4 is reprinted from *boundary 2* 27, no. 3 (2000): 153–169. Copyright © 2000 Duke University Press, all rights reserved. Used by permission of the publisher. Portions of Chapter 5 are reprinted from Touré F. Reed, *Not Alms but Opportunity: The Urban League and the Politics of Racial Uplift, 1910–1950.* Copyright © 2008 University of North Carolina Press. Used by permission of the publisher. Chapter 7 is reprinted from Michele Mitchell, *Righteous Propagation: African Americans and the Politics of Racial Destiny after Reconstruction.* Copyright © 2004 University of North Carolina Press. Used by permission of the publisher. Chapter 8 is adapted from Dean E. Robinson, *Black Nationalism in American Politics and Thought.* Copyright 2001 Dean E. Robinson. Reprinted with permission of Cambridge University Press. Chapter 9 is adapted from Madhu Dubey, *Signs and Cities: Black Literary Postmodernism.* Copyright © 2003 University of Chicago. Used by permission of the University of Chicago.

First published 2010 by Paradigm Publishers

Published 2016 by Routledge
2 Park Square, Milton Park, Abingdon, Oxon OX14 4RN
711 Third Avenue, New York, NY 10017, USA

Routledge is an imprint of the Taylor & Francis Group, an informa business

Library of Congress Cataloging-in-Publication Data

Renewing Black intellectual history : the ideological and material foundations of African American thought / edited by Adolph Reed, Jr. and Kenneth W. Warren.
p. cm.
Includes bibliographical references and index.
ISBN 978-1-59451-665-8 (hardcover : alk. paper)
ISBN 978-1-59451-666-5 (paperback: alk. paper)
1. African Americans—Intellectual life. 2. African American intellectuals. 3. African American philosophy. 4. African Americans—Politics and government. 5. African Americans—Civil rights—History. 6. African Americans—Social conditions. 7. United States—Intellectual life. 8. United States—Race relations. I. Reed, Adolph L., 1947– II. Warren, Kenneth W. (Kenneth Wayne)
E185.R45 2010
305.896'073—dc22

2009025509

Designed and Typeset by Straight Creek Bookmakers.

ISBN 13: 978-1-59451-665-8 (hbk)
ISBN 13: 978-1-59451-666-5 (pbk)

Contents

Introduction

Adolph Reed Jr. and Kenneth W. Warren

This volume coheres around a presumption that African American studies and its subject matter are both nested within and partly constitutive of broader currents of American history and thought and, therefore, that making sense of the black American experience requires situating it fundamentally within the larger cultural, political-economic, and ideological dynamics that shape American life in general. Specifically, we stress this view against the tendency to attempt to reposition the field within putatively "diasporic" frames of reference. Although such perspectives have attracted considerable interest over the past two decades, their appeal stems more substantially from their privileging of racial commonality as the fulcrum of inquiry than from the quality of the accounts they render of black American life. We should be clear that our objection is not to transatlantic inquiry in principle. However, much of the discursive strain associated with the frame of the African diaspora, particularly that lying outside the nonverbal arts, relies on exceedingly thin intellectual or cultural history, naive textual interpretation, nimble yet facile cultural analysis, or other forms of metonymic fallacy to justify a claim that black Americans' beliefs and practices are most authentically understood as nodes in a supraterritorial world of African descent. This objective is rooted in the unproblematized conflation of scholarly and political legitimations that besets the field, including the presumptive posture that black studies scholarship articulates needs, concerns, and perspectives for the race.

Rather than succumb to the temptation to attempt to speak on behalf of the political and social needs of some "black community" outside the academy, we argue that the study of the evolving discourses of politically articulate black Americans has provided an important conceptual anchor for the black studies field for most of its own history. These discourses have shaped the main lines of public debate of political, social, and cultural ideas and strategies through which dominant notions of common black American identity and agendas have been constructed and pursued. To that extent they also undergird the black studies field's definition of its subject matter and its interpretive frameworks.

Inattentiveness to historiographical and interpretive frameworks in favor of an effort to get inside the minds and to read the vernaculars and quotidian practices of "everyday" folk ironically has an effect precisely opposite of that intended in the shift away from focus on elite discourse. Because the sedimented premises of elite debates are no longer scrutinized systematically, they have become too easily naturalized among the background assumptions that guide African American studies as a field of scholarship. The embrace of vernacular modes, instead of transcending those elite frames of reference, has tacitly reinforced them. Much black studies scholarship remains unreflectively moored to notions such as race leadership, unitary racial interest, as well as an intellectually and politically naive rhetoric of racial authenticity on which those notions rest. Yet these notions—all of which emerged within the patterns of elite discourse that evolved between the second half of the nineteenth century and the middle of the twentieth—have become increasingly problematic as frames for interpreting black American experience. An active critical scholarship on black American intellectual history may not be sufficient to prompt general interrogation of these and other similarly problematic notions that organize the black studies field's commonsense assumptions, but it certainly could contribute toward that goal.

To be clear, our objection is not that African American studies has sacrificed intellectual integrity in pursuit of a political agenda. No scholarly endeavor can be innocent of the ideological matrices and controversies of its historical moment, least of all scholarship on human affairs. The problems with the turn in African-Americanist discourse dating all the way back to the Reagan era stem from the *way* that it links political and intellectual concerns. The presumption that the goal of scholarly intervention is to speak for a black collectivity in effect posits a primary audience that lies outside the universe of fellow practitioners.

Thus literature produced in this vein typically resolves down to almost ritualistic assertion of familiar conclusions embedded in a pro forma narrative: that racism has been and remains a potent force constraining the black American experience, that black American agency has been propelled by pursuit of an ensemble of abstract goals such as autonomy, community, and family and performance of a comparably generic "resistance" to racial or other forms of oppression. The responses by African-Americanist scholars to the presidency of Barack Obama helpfully illustrate this dynamic. In one breath these scholars proclaim Obama's election as the culmination of centuries'-old black collective hopes; in the next they warn that his presidency does not signal the waning force of racism on American social life. By failing to interrogate the grounds on which they assert black political consensus both past and present, and by failing to define just what they mean by racism, these scholars merely express the anxieties of their position as putative interpreters of a black experience changing in ways they hadn't anticipated because it had never corresponded to the scripts they had imposed on it.

As a result they resort to a potted punch line that does not contribute to our understanding of black Americans' thinking and activity because it is a conceptual shorthand that ventriloquizes them to make a reductivist political point. Real people do not organize or narrate their lives and pursuits consciously around such gross, clichéd abstractions. That is, notwithstanding the primacy this discourse assigns to representing nonelite black Americans' suppressed or marginalized agency, its interpretive practice tends to do exactly the opposite. It imposes a summary normative script onto behavior and aspirations that are certainly more complex and various.

This move has been naturalized as an interpretive norm in black studies discourse. No one even notices it for what it is because it is the coin of the realm. As a well-embedded, commonsense form of narrative for making claims about black collective *mentalité,* it predates the emergence of contemporary black studies discourse. Although its deepest roots lie in the rhetorical style of race spokesmanship and brokerage that emerged in the context of the Jim Crow regime, it is most proximately a vestige of the naive hermeneutic of post–black power radicalism, which overlapped academic black studies. This hermeneutic was naive in that it failed to distinguish inquiry from the taxonomic enterprise of reading black Americans' beliefs and practices as summary affirmations of one or another strain of the ideological enthusiasms of the day—pan-Africanism, cultural nationalism, third worldist Marxism-Leninism. More recently this failure has been enabled, or at least papered over, by a substantivist claim that hinges on appropriation of phraseology associated with the linguistic turn in cultural studies. Characterizing black people's everyday practices and aspirations as "strategies" exploits an ambiguous conflation of the word's meanings. In common usage, strategy implies intentional behavior. In the discourse grafted from poststructuralism, strategy has no such connotation. In that context—following from the premise that texts, or actions that may be read as texts, have meanings of their own quite apart from the people who produce or embody them—claims that agents enact rhetorical strategies carry no requirement for argument or evidence of their intention to do so. Evocation of this latter meaning of strategy finesses what is in fact a dubious contention: that black agents' thinking and practices *in effect* are impelled by pursuit of the broad, idealized objectives that African American studies scholars impute to them. But on its face this contention is circular. The putative evidence and argument plausibly demonstrate the claim only if we believe it from the outset; only appeal to personal, esoteric knowledge is available to sway the skeptic.

Nor does this perspective help advance a practical political program or critique. Its hortatory message fails to go beyond hollow calls to combat racism, and, often enough, the burden of its monotonic narrative is to reinforce the notion that no significant political change is possible. This is particularly true to the extent that this tendency insists that authentically black forms of expression lie outside the realm of public and institutional action.

And we do not maintain that the field's problematic characteristics arose entirely de novo in the Reagan era, as a decline from an original, authentic black studies. The tendency to confound the scholarly and political warrants of black studies has haunted the field since its institutionalization. Nor do we contend that the limitations of currently popular approaches to African American studies, and much less their solutions, are primarily technical or procedural. In fact, as the chapters here illustrate, the task of reflecting critically on the discipline of African American studies cannot be boiled down to a single theoretical formula. Rather, what we have looked for in constructing this volume are essays that define historically and conceptually discrete problems affecting black Americans as these problems have been shaped by specific regimes of the study of black America over the previous century. That is, in some way or other, the several authors here understand their various objects of inquiry not only as, say, the cultural production of blues singers in the early 1920s or the gender and reproductive politics of the Garvey movement, but also as the intellectual, institutional, and conceptual frames that gave these practices their social and political salience. In bringing together new pieces with previously published work we have been guided by the sense that the critical stance we are advocating has been an ongoing posture, albeit one overshadowed by the disciplinary paradigms under critique here. Our act of collecting is meant to amplify, consolidate, and advance this critique primarily by showcasing the interpretive payoff represented by each of the essays published here.

We have grouped the chapters in this volume in such a way as to reflect the changing conditions of black political practice from Emancipation to the consolidation of the recent black studies regime. The divisions here are both a matter of convenience, in the way that periodizations always are, and an argument for interpretive significance. That is, we don't feel the need to insist that these divisions are the only sensible way of approaching the history of black political and intellectual practices. Nor do we insist that the chapters grouped in each section exhaust the possible concerns raised during a particular historical moment. We do assert, though, that these pieces address crucial and often overlooked features of these periods and that these features can be grasped only by acknowledging and engaging the often profound changes that have occurred over some 125 years and counting.

The first set of chapters comes in Part I under the heading "Emancipation, Reconstruction, and Retrenchment." These essays work implicitly to expose the explanatory insufficiency of the recent tendency to adduce the historical fact of slavery and the legacy of slavery as a way of understanding fully the course of events contributing to the subordination of the black population as a group for much of the twentieth century. It should go without saying that we regard the institution of slavery as one of the major factors in understanding the history of the United States and the West more generally. Our objection, though, is to the use of slavery as an a priori to account for, or insist upon, the essential distinctiveness of black Americans' political concerns and beliefs. The entries in Part I demonstrate that political emancipation and the various interventions of Reconstruction figured prominently in black writers' and thinkers' calculations of efficacy of strategies for realizing visions of how a society without slaves ought to look. These pieces also help reveal that the period of retrenchment following the era of reconstruction was not foreordained by the history of the slave era that preceded it but occurred as the result of a convergence of intentions, mistakes, and limitations—not all predictable and certainly not all inevitable.

In many ways, Part II, "The Jim Crow Era," which covers the roughly half-century-long period of constitutionally sanctioned segregation, constitutes the heart of this volume. Most of the chapters in this book engage aspects of this crucial period. It was during the Jim Crow era that the sensibility that continues to undergird much of contemporary black intellectual and cultural life was established. The chapters here address and examine the major streams of thinking that issued from and shaped this era, particularly those that reinforced notions of cultural particularity, group identity, and group unity. In varying ways these works reveal that these emphases, which were at the outset largely tactical responses to the regime of racial segregation, have subsequently been fused, centered, and naturalized as the raison d'etre of black literary and political inquiry.

Our sense of the importance of the Jim Crow era for understanding the shape of black political and intellectual practice determined our decision to title Part III "The Post–Jim Crow Era" rather than some other term to describe the period following the demise of de jure segregation. This label, as illustrated through the chapters in Part III, marks both the significance of the ending of legal segregation and the persistence of strategies and habits of mind deriving from the Jim Crow era. The work here reflects critically on the often-expressed sentiment that despite the political gains of these decades, some crucial element of black life was lost with the end of Jim Crow. These chapters demonstrate that what crucially defines this period is the failure—intellectually and politically—to come to terms with the changing terrain of American life in the wake of the major civil rights court decisions and legislative acts.

Acknowledgments

That this volume is a collaborative project goes without saying. Nonetheless we would be remiss in not acknowledging the contributions of several people in addition to the authors of these essays. We are grateful to Paradigm Publishers, especially Jennifer Knerr, Jessica Priest, and Melanie Stafford, for shepherding this volume through the editorial process. Our discussions with graduate students from Northwestern, the New School of Social Research, and the University of Chicago in our "Rethinking African American Studies" seminars were crucial in helping us recognize the need for this volume. Additional thanks are due the Andrew W. Mellon Foundation for funding two of these seminars. Last, and certainly not least, we owe a debt of gratitude to Maria M. Warren for helping us prepare many of these essays for editing and revision—we couldn't have done this without her gracious commitment of technical expertise and time.

Part I

Emancipation, Reconstruction, and Retrenchment

The first part of this book takes up the various tendencies and dynamics—intellectual and political, as well as national and regional—out of which the segregationist order took shape. Understanding the emergence of Jim Crow and gauging the full effect of its consolidation on black life at the turn of the twentieth century requires seeing blacks as political actors who, during and subsequent to Reconstruction, pursued a range of ends that cannot be distilled into a single, corporate racial-group interest. Indeed, the payoff of one of this volume's interpretive assumptions—namely that black intellectual and political life is embedded within and continuous with American life generally—is crucial to making sense of this period, when black political activity was part of the calculus of elites and popular groups, both black and white, as they sought to achieve or hold power during the decades between Reconstruction and the rise of disfranchisement.

Attempts to account for the emergence of Booker T. Washington solely in terms of whether blacks should have contested more vigorously, or instead have made the best of, the wave of disfranchisement that swept through much of the South at the turn of the century leave unexamined fundamental questions. For example, why did segments of the southern elite turn toward disfranchisement in the late 1890s, after a period of almost two decades of operating with some level of black voting as a feature of the political landscape? Moreover, such approaches tend myopically to view Washington, the pivotal figure of the segregation era, as merely reacting to white political initiatives rather than having himself played a role in shaping the political terms in which he operated. Such a view produces errors of the sort committed in Robert J. Norrell's recent biography of Washington, *Up From History: The Life and Times of Booker T. Washington,* which, though correctly noting that an "accommodation-protest binary" is inadequate to any assessment of Washington's role during the period, nonetheless concludes that the course taken by Washington in the 1890s was the only reasonable one available to blacks during this period.[1]

By contrast, the two essays here acknowledge the ways in which the expectations of the former slaves about their role in the polity—indeed the shape of the polity—sometimes conflicted with the strategies and rhetoric of those who purported to represent their interests. Kenneth Warren's "Frederick Douglass's *Life and Times:* Progressive Rhetoric and the Problem of Constituency" analyzes Douglass's difficulties in trying to harmonize the terms of his effectiveness within the Republican Party and among northern progressive audiences with the shifting assessments that black freedmen were making during this period about how best to protect the rights they had gained as a result of emancipation, as well as about which individuals were best suited to represent their interests. Judith Stein's "'Of Mr. Booker T. Washington and Others': The Political Economy of Racism in the United States" is a foundational text for the strain of historicist interpretation represented in this volume. It remains as timely now as when it was first published in the mid-1970s. Stein makes clear that understanding the rise of Booker T. Washington requires examining "the whole pattern of social forces affecting blacks after the Civil War, not only the racial manifestations," including "early political events, such as the Compromise of 1877 and the establishment of the 'White Democracies' in the South, the popular movements, and finally the disfranchisement and Jim Crow system at the beginning of the twentieth century." Stein demonstrates that in 1895, when Washington delivered his famous "Address to the Atlanta Cotton States Exposition" (which came to be known as the "Atlanta Compromise"), "the most effective means to struggle against discriminatory practices, disfranchisement, and racism" was populism, which at that moment enjoyed significant interracial support among the South's rural and urban proletariat. Washington's program was proposed and supported largely on the basis of its promise as a means of meeting the challenge of black and white political insurgency. That is, rather than merely navigating within narrow political straits, certain black political elites—and Washington especially—actively sought to channel black political activity in certain directions rather than others.

NOTE

1. Robert J. Norrell, *Up From History: The Life and Times of Booker T. Washington* (Cambridge, MA: Harvard University Press, 2009), 439.

1
Frederick Douglass's Life and Times

Progressive Rhetoric and the Problem of Constituency

Kenneth W. Warren

As Frederick Douglass, in his autobiographical *Life and Times of Frederick Douglass,* accounts for his decision not to move to the South and seek elective office following the Civil War, he recalls having considered three prominent reasons. First, he remembers his sense that a move south would involve a degree of impropriety: "The idea did not square well with my better judgment and sense of propriety. The thought of going to live among a people in order to gain their votes and acquire official honors was repugnant to my self-respect."[1] Second, he claims to have been beset by self-doubt: "I had small faith in my aptitude as a politician, and could not hope to cope with rival aspirants" (398). And third, he refers to his belief that he could be more effective in the politically powerful North: "The loyal North, with its advanced civilization, must dictate the policy and control the destiny of the republic" (399).

It is the second claim, the claim of self-doubt, that chiefly concerns me here, for the vision of Douglass—who had gone toe-to-toe with plantation overseers, Garrisonian abolitionists, and a U.S. president quailing—before potential opposition is not readily credible. Indeed, upon further inquiry, it seems clear that Douglass's self-deprecatory pose is highly ironic. Though he discounts his own ability, he does so in a way that places the burden of blame elsewhere. He explains:

> I could not have readily adapted myself to the peculiar oratory found to be most effective with the newly enfranchised class. In the New England and northern atmosphere I had acquired a style of speaking which in the South would have been considered tame and spiritless, and consequently he who "could tear a passion to tatters and split the ear of groundlings" had far better chance of success with the masses there than one so little boisterous as myself. (398)

Again, Douglass's self-deprecation demands suspicion. "Tame" is hardly the word for Douglass, who was experienced in tailoring his addresses to the needs of his audiences and whose oratory has been characterized as "bold, emphatic, and aggressive."[2] What Douglass seems bent on is not characterizing his own style accurately but in drawing a contrast between his style and that of his rivals.

As Douglass describes the southern political climate, the freedmen, like the groundlings at an Elizabethan theater "who for the most part are capable of nothing but inexplicable dumb shows and noise,"[3] lack the ability to understand and appreciate the oratorical style that Douglass had honed in the "advanced civilization" of the North. As the references to *Hamlet* make plain, Douglass felt that the speakers who could appeal directly to the newly enfranchised class were not merely endowed with different oratorical skills, but with lesser ones of bombast and passion.[4] Yet these lesser skills were no barrier to popularity. In fact, during this period the popularity of what were perceived to be inferior literary styles and forms proved a considerable challenge to those writers or public figures who styled themselves as progressive, democratic spokesmen but employed oratorical and literary styles that often seemed out of sync with popular tastes. It was not that progressive intellectuals were never well received. Many achieved or maintained a great deal of prominence during the 1880s and 1890s, Douglass being arguably one of the three or four most famous Americans of the nineteenth century. His prominence, however, did not exempt him from challenges, and the nature of these challenges prompted him to examine and reexamine the validity of his claim to a democratic idiom.

In the pages that follow, I argue that in *Life and Times* Douglass, like other social reformers, among whom one can number realist and naturalist novelists, explores the boundary between a democratic style on the one hand and a popular style on the other. Just as the realistic novel staged "a debate ... with competing modes of representation," chief among which were "the emergent forms of mass media,"[5] so Douglass's autobiography engages a variety of competing forms in seeking to speak on behalf of the true interests of African Americans. And in recognizing his prospective audience's receptiveness to competing forms, Douglass, like many of his contemporaries, mobilized a democratic apologetic that first located and then spoke on behalf of silenced but sympathetic constituencies. By stressing the strategic nature of this mobilization, I do not mean to suggest that Douglass made these gestures cynically or that there were not disfranchised, silenced communities in need of representation. Rather, I mean to suggest that in having dismissed elective office and pulpit rhetoric as avenues to democratic representation, Douglass, like novelists who downplayed mass market appeal as an indicator of democratic appeal, consistently reinvented means through which popular disregard or disapprobation might be met with implicit democratic assent.

For example, when the southern progressive author George Washington Cable found that his writings on civil justice for black Americans evoked a storm of protest, he endeavored to create and appeal to a "Silent South," that part of southern society that he saw as constituting "our whole South's better self; that finer part which the world not always sees; unaggressive, but brave, calm, thoughtful, broad-minded, dispassionate, sincere, and in the din of boisterous error round about it, all too mute."[6] This Silent South was not merely fictional. Cable's views had indeed met with some favor during his visits to the South. The term, however, functioned less as a demographic designation than as a rhetorical warrant that Cable, a southerner himself, spoke not as an individual but on behalf of other southerners. Similarly, the editor, novelist, and Christian socialist William Dean Howells often represented himself as speaking for American writers who as a group were estranged from their natural constituency. According to Howells, the writer "is really of the masses, but they do not know it, and what is worse, they do not hear him; as yet the common people do not hear him gladly or hear him at all."[7] In Howells's conception, the novelists' natural constituents responded with hostility if they responded at all, leaving the novelist unable to communicate with those who needed most to hear him. Thus, as editor of *Harper's,* Howells took it upon himself to champion the cause of realistic fiction, both to his fellow writers and to the American public.

For most of his career, of course, Douglass deemed African Americans "a people long dumb, not allowed to speak for themselves, yet much misunderstood and deeply wronged" (511), his silent constituency. But he did not play this role without encountering significant difficulty. His various public and personal decisions—from opposing black migration to the North, to staying on as recorder of deeds in the District of Columbia following the election of Grover Cleveland, to marrying Helen Pitts, a white woman, some seventeen months after the death of his first wife, to serving as the U.S. minister resident and consul general to the Republic of Haiti—at one time or another enraged his black as well as his white supporters. In his *Life and Times,* Douglass uses these unpopular stands as opportunities to locate other silenced communities—opportunities that would make his unpopular stances if not popular, then, in their own way, democratic.

For example, in responding to his "Afro-American critics," who had chided him when he did not immediately resign his post as recorder of deeds for the District of Columbia after the election of Grover Cleveland, a Democrat, Douglass invokes the anomalous status of the people of the District of Columbia:

> Then again I saw that there was less reason for resigning because of the election of a President of a different party from my own, when the political status of the people of the District of Columbia was considered. These people are outside of the United States. They occupy neutral ground and have no political existence. They have neither voice nor vote in all the practical politics of the United States. They are hardly to be called citizens of the United States. Practically they are aliens—not

> citizens, but subjects. The District of Columbia is the one spot where there is no government for the people, of the people, and by the people. Its citizens submit to rulers whom they have had no choice in selecting. They obey laws which they had no voice in making. They have a plenty of taxation, but no representation. In the great question of politics in the country they can march with neither army, but are relegated to the position of neuters.
>
> I have nothing to say in favor of this anomalous condition of the people of the District of Columbia, and hardly think it ought to be or will be much longer endured, but while it exists it does not appear that the election of a President of the United States should make it the duty of a purely local officer, holding an office supported, not by the United States, but by the disfranchised people of the District of Columbia, to resign such office. (533)

I quote this passage at length to underscore how willfully Douglass echoes the arguments used in justifying both the American Revolution and the abolition of slavery. He even employs the exclusion of the disfranchised from military service (an issue he had pressed before Abraham Lincoln in the 1860s) as a metaphor. Central for Douglass is the way the real political needs of a mute constituency with which he is associated can be mobilized to deflect the criticism that he has placed his private interests above the interests of party or race.

Although Douglass's brief on behalf of the District of Columbia seems remarkably significant and prescient in light of the recent efforts of African American spokesmen to take up the cause of the inhabitants of our nation's capital, other issues are more pertinent here. Douglass's dependence upon mute communities to justify his public stances has a troubling side to it. Recent studies of American realist and naturalist fiction of this period have illuminated the way in which the textual strategies of novelists tended to merge with the managerial and authoritarian aspects of social reform movements. In her study of the naturalist novel, June Howard has argued that "it is a very short step . . . from the sympathy of the naturalist spectator to the altruistic and ultimately authoritarian benevolence of the progressive reformer."[8] The intelligent, articulate spectator, while attempting to reveal the details of these mute, silenced lives, distances himself from those he represents, making them other than himself, and confines them to a realm outside of that inhabited by the spectator. The condition of representation seems to be alienation.

Waldo E. Martin Jr. has also observed that on occasion Douglass himself characterized other blacks in ways that "separated himself . . . in an important sense from them," attributing to his fellow blacks qualities he himself did not possess.[9] Martin also places Douglass's sometimes problematic relationships with other African Americans within the larger sphere of the conflicts of nineteenth-century American reform movements.[10] What I would like to add to Martin's perceptive analysis of Douglass's reformism is a discussion of how many of the problems that surface in *Life and Times* are constitutive of the problems of realistic representation during the latter part of the century. Though it would take a more lengthy argument to work out fully the mechanics of reading *Life and Times* as a realist or naturalist fiction, these recent studies offer some tentative help in sorting out Douglass's textual and political strategies.

As a former slave and as a black man subject to discrimination following emancipation, Douglass remained intimately tied to the constituency he most consistently represented. And yet Peter F. Walker has provocatively speculated that Douglass's embrace of the abolitionist cause involved a degree of distancing himself from the race of his mother. Analyzing Douglass's reflections on his speaking debut—"For a time I was made to forget that my skin was dark and my hair crisped"—Walker asserts that during the period before his rupture with the Garrisonians, in 1847, Douglass felt himself "divested of his dark skin and crisped hair. He had ceased to be a Negro. The agency, the 'good cause,' was the literal escape from his physical features and from everything that tied him to his black mother."[11] Whether or not Douglass wished to "escape from his physical features," Walker's observations may point to a troubling liability that one may incur when speaking for the silenced: a tendency to underwrite difference in a way that "reinforces the hierarchy between classes" or groups.[12] Significantly, when Douglass speaks out against black migration to the North, he does so in a way that figures his southern constituents as other than himself:

> The Negro, as already intimated, is preeminently a southern man. He is so both in constitution and habits, in body as well as mind. He will not only take with him to the North southern modes of labor, but southern modes of life. The careless and improvident habits of the South cannot be set aside in a generation. If they are adhered to in the North, in the fierce winds and snows of Kansas and Nebraska the migration must be large to keep up their numbers. (438)

In enumerating the impediments to the successful emigration of the freedmen, Douglass seems to forget his own story, his own rise from an "unthrifty district ... among slaves who, in point of ignorance and indolence, were fully in accord with their surroundings" (27). And in intimating that the inability of blacks to cope with northern climates would prevent them from sustaining their numbers in their new environment, Douglass succumbs to a Social Darwinist rhetoric that he castigates elsewhere in his story. Despite his commitment to the cause of equality and justice for black Americans, Douglass, throughout his career, but especially in the decades following the Civil War, found himself both empowered by and limited by the rhetoric of reform that was available to him.[13]

One such limitation may have been Douglass's inability to appreciate and to understand fully the voices lifted in answer to his own. Although his autobiographical enterprise had come to be regarded as the work of a "self-made man," Douglass voices from time to time the belief that others would assist in the completion of the "Life" that he had begun. As he neared the end of the 1881 edition, Douglass conjectured that "what may remain of life to me ... will probably be told by others when I have passed from the busy stage of life" (478). He had not, however, finished writing the story, and as he took up the pen again, there was an air of both pride and pathos in the realization that "the unity and completeness of the work require that it shall be finished by the hand by which it was begun" (514):

> When the first part of this book was written, I was, as before intimated, already looking toward the sunset of human life and thinking that my children would probably finish the recital of my life, or that possibly some other persons outside of family ties to whom I am known might think it worth while to tell what he or she might know of the remainder of my story. I considered, as I have said, that my work was done. (513)

Having angered his children by his marriage to Helen Pitts in 1882, and having suffered criticism from erstwhile supporters for reasons already mentioned, Douglass may have felt, in addition to the potential financial gain to be enjoyed by the publication of another edition of his life's story, that the only voice fully in harmony with the story he had already told was his own. Additionally, Douglass's position on social reform, which inclined him to identify his cause with the values of reason, thrift, self-reliance, and self-control, while identifying the forces of opposition with passion, extravagance, and indolence, confirmed him in his belief that the voice most in evidence among his black constituents was a voice in discord with his own: that of the black preacher.

Douglass's disapproval of black Protestant oratory is well known. As he explains his rhetorical style to his white readers, Douglass claims:

> In my communication with colored people I have endeavored to deliver them from the power of superstition, bigotry, and priestcraft. In theology I have found them strutting about in the old clothes of the masters, just as the masters strut about in the old clothes of the past. The falling power remains among them long since it has ceased to be the religious fashion in our refined and elegant white churches. (479–480)

Treating religion as style or fashion, and fashion as being of the utmost importance, Douglass views black and white southern Protestantism as if they were one. And as the possessive pronoun "our" indicates, he locates himself within the fashion of white congregations. The path of progress is clearly marked, with Douglass leading the way; equally well marked is the path leading backward:

> Thus the forces against us are passion and prejudice, which are transient, and those for us are principles, self-acting, self-sustaining, and permanent. My hope for the future of my race is further supported by the rapid decline of an emotional, shouting, and thoughtless religion. Scarcely in any direction can there be found a less favorable field for mind or morals than where such a religion prevails. It abounds in the wildest hopes and fears, and in blind unreasoning faith. Instead of adding to faith virtue, its tendency is to substitute faith for virtue, and is a deadly enemy to our progress. (508)

With religion and progress clearly at odds, Douglass's influence over a people still under the sway of old fashions was questionable. Thus, as he presses his criticism of the black church, Douglass admits to his reader, "My views at this point receive but limited endorsement among my people" (480). And as is evident from his previous remarks, Douglass's only hope lies in his belief that passion is "transient" and that this religion will naturally die out.

Douglass, of course, was not alone among black leaders in decrying the supposed counterproductive role of black religion in the cause of black progress. W. E. B. Du Bois concurred with Douglass's belief in the need to supplant the old-style preacher with enlightened leaders. Writing in "The Talented Tenth," Du Bois argued, "The preacher was, even before the war, the group leader of the Negroes, and the church their greatest social institution. Naturally this preacher was ignorant and often immoral, and the problem of replacing the older type by better educated men has been a difficult one."[14] Just how difficult this task was is made evident in Du Bois's treatment of the issue in chapter 13 of *The Souls of Black Folk,* titled "Of the Coming of John." In that chapter, Du Bois chronicles the career of John Jones, a "loud and boisterous" young black man who leaves the small southern town of Altamaha to attend a school called the Wells Institute. Although the white people of Altamaha view John's prospective education with foreboding, the black inhabitants invest his departure and eventual return with messianic hopes strong enough to sustain them during what turns out to be a seven-year absence. "'When John comes,'" the black townsfolk intone, "then what parties were to be, and what speakings in the churches; what new furniture in the front room—perhaps even a new front room; and there would be a new schoolhouse, with John as teacher; and then perhaps a big wedding; all this and more."[15] The refrain "When John comes" captures the anticipatory anxiety that pervades the early portion of the chapter.

This anticipation, however, is only partly fulfilled. John does return, and the black citizens of Altamaha plan great festivities. Their celebration, however, falls flat:

> The meeting of welcome at the Baptist Church was a failure. Rain spoiled the barbecue, and thunder turned the milk in the ice cream. When the speaking came at night, the house was crowded to overflowing. The three preachers had especially prepared themselves, but somehow John's manner seemed to throw a blanket over everything,—he seemed so cold and preoccupied, and had so strange an air of restraint that the Methodist brother could not warm up to his theme and elicited not a single "Amen"; the Presbyterian prayer was but feebly responded to, and even the Baptist preacher, though he wakened faint enthusiasm, got so mixed up in his favorite sentence that he had to close it by stopping fully fifteen minutes sooner than he meant. (529)

As Du Bois describes it, not only the weather conspires against the success of the welcome; John's "manner" itself blunts the speaking style of the three preachers. They are ineffective and unable to stir the crowd. The usual call and response fails to materialize, and the well-rehearsed sentences become garbled in their delivery. In fact, the traditional oratory is cut short, setting the stage, it would seem, for a new style of address.

Accordingly, John rises and speaks to the congregation (529). The boisterous boy who had left Altamaha seven years prior has been transformed into a "tall, grave man" who preaches a gospel of social progress to the townspeople, speaking "of the rise of charity and popular education, and particularly of the spread of wealth and work" (529). He concludes by enjoining them to embrace social, economic, and political progress while eschewing sectarianism, asking, "What difference does it make whether a man be baptized in river or washbowl, or not at all? Let's leave all that littleness, and look higher" (530). Predictably, the message fails miserably. He is speaking in a Baptist church to a combined Presbyterian, Methodist, and Baptist congregation that might heed the ecumenical call but would not tolerate out-and-out atheism. John's failure, however, stems not only from his perceived sacrilege but also from the inability of the crowd to comprehend him: "Little had they understood of what he said, for he spoke an unknown tongue, save the last word about baptism" (530).

And though the incomprehensibility of John's "unknown tongue" might derive from the words he uses, Du Bois draws equal attention to the style in which John delivers his address. He speaks "slowly and methodically," "reflectively," and "in detail" (527). His manner, which had proved so crippling to the efforts of the three preachers, also disables his own message, and he evokes not assent but "a painful hush" (530).

The hush, however, is only short-lived. After a few moments an outraged man rises from the Amen Corner, raises a bible, "and then fairly burst into the words, with rude and awful eloquence. He quivered, swayed, and bent; then rose aloft in perfect majesty, till the people moaned and wept, wailed and shouted, and a wild shrieking arose from the corners where all the pent-up feeling of the hour gathered itself and rushed into the air" (530). The physical power of the old man's eloquence contrasts starkly with John's "air of restraint." Freed from the task of honoring John by John's own sacrilege, the old man awakens the assemblage with his rhetoric, and now, ironically, it is John who does not fully understand the message. He cannot, however, mistake the implications of the speaker's rhetorical style: "John never knew clearly what the old man said; he only felt himself held up to scorn and scathing denunciation for trampling on the true Religion" (530).

The clash of rhetorical styles in "The Coming of John" seems quite similar to the problem Douglass alluded to in deciding not to seek elective office in the South during Reconstruction: There would be no community between speaker and audience. Similarly, Douglass's denunciation of black religion, which includes no detailed critique of its content, suggests that Douglass, like Du Bois's John, "never knew clearly" what was being said.

Du Bois's story ends tragically. Young John is lynched when he kills his white counterpart of the same name for sexually accosting his sister. Earlier in the story, however, Du Bois has told us that John opens a school for the black residents of Altamaha. Significantly, the only lesson the story narrates is a lesson on style: "Now, Mandy," he said cheerfully, "that's better; but you mustn't chop your words up so:

'If—the—man—goes.' Why, your little brother even wouldn't tell a story that way, now would he?" (533).

Immediately following this lesson, the school is closed as a result of rumors that John is also teaching about the "French Revolution, equality, and such like" (532). Yet as I have said, the only lesson that the tale narrates is a lesson on speaking and reading. The closing of John's school, John's tragic fate, and the ambivalent note sounded throughout *The Souls of Black Folk* testifies to the breadth of the gulf that black leaders perceived between them and their intended audiences, both black and white. But John's endeavor to teach a lesson in style, like Douglass's persistence in publishing his story into the 1890s, attests to a continued belief in the missionary potential of the educated voice.

This belief was not specific to the cause of African American civil rights but pervaded the thinking of many of Douglass's contemporaries in their preoccupation with other social and literary concerns. In fact, this belief in the power of the educated voice was carried to an almost absurd extreme by Henry James in a commencement address he delivered at Bryn Mawr College in Pennsylvania on June 8, 1905. And though James did not have in mind the particular plight of black Americans, his remarks bear reference here, both in terms of seeing how much weight some writers placed on conversational style and in seeing how the conflict in which Douglass's text is embroiled did not lend itself to an easy conclusion.

James's address to the Bryn Mawr graduates is at once a lesson in elocution, a social commentary, and a xenophobic tirade against American ethnic minorities. Proclaiming to his audience that "of the degree in which a society is civilized the vocal form, the vocal tone, the personal, social accent and sound of its intercourse, have always been held to give a direct reflection,"[16] James not only outlines the threat to American civilization deriving from the lack of a "tone standard" but also describes examples of improper speech and enjoins the young women to embark upon life "sounding the clearer notes of intercourse as only women can, become yourselves models and missionaries, perhaps a little even martyrs, of the good cause."[17]

Attributing the lack of an American tone standard to popular education, mass culture, and American ethnic groups—"to the American common school, to the American newspaper, and to the American Dutchman and Dago, as the voice of the people describes them"[18]—James defines the threat to American society as a dire one indeed:

> The conservative interest is really as indispensable for the institution of speech as for the institution of matrimony. Abate a jot of the quantity, of the consecration required, and we practically find ourselves emulating the beasts, who prosper as well without a vocabulary as without a marriage service. It is easier to overlook any question of speech than to trouble about it, but then it is also easier to snort or neigh, to growl or to "meaow," than to articulate and intonate.[19]

James's mingling of mass culture, ethnicity, social dissolution, and a brutish state signals clearly his almost hysterical reaction to the country that he found on his return to his homeland in 1904 after an absence of twenty years. The attack on American vernaculars is unmistakable here, just as the attack on the black pulpit voice is unmistakable in Douglass's *Life and Times*. Douglass, too, shared James's view of mass culture as vulgar and brutish, lamenting at one point in *Life and Times*:

> There is, however, enough of the wild beast left in our modern human life to modify the pride of our enlightenment and humanity.... In this respect our newspapers tell us a sad story. They would not be filled with the details of prize fights, and discussions of the brutal perfections of prize fighters, if such things did not please the brutal proclivities of a large class of readers. (567)

And yet it would be erroneous to see James's and Douglass's texts solely in the context of their antagonism toward mass culture and the spoken vernacular.

James's attacks, unlike the English-only movements of the present day, are directed less at the presence of other languages in American public discourse than at what America itself does with these other languages. A polyglot, James was quite ready to address American immigrants in their native tongues. What he discovers, however, as he writes in *The American Scene,* is that his fluency in Italian is no guarantee of communication with the Italian laborers he confronts in New York; conversely, the failure in Italian ensures no necessary success in English. "It was as if contact were out of the question."[20] James confronts a simple failure to communicate.

Although this qualification does not exempt James from a charge of ethnic prejudice, one should not ignore the fact that in repeating the ethnic slur "Dago" and the imprecise term "Dutchman" James attributes them to "the voice of the people." The popular voice, the vernacular voice, is identified not merely with the aliens themselves but likewise with the social intolerance of aliens, as exemplified in ethnic and racial epithets. Staunchly Anglocentric though James's voice may be, it is a voice conscious of itself in relation to other voices. As he laments the absence of an American tone standard, James utters his concern for America's representation "in the international concert of culture," noting that "the French, the Germans, the Italians, the English perhaps in particular, and many other people, Occidental and Oriental, I surmise, not excluding the Turks and the Chinese, have for the symbol of education, of civility, a tone standard."[21] The international note struck here provides a gloss on both James's remarks and Douglass's *Life and Times.* Concerned with the vulgarity that they thought they saw destroying the fiber of American public life, both men sought to play the role of social missionary or popular prophet while speaking in tones dignified and reasonable. They sought to have the effect of popular media without employing the styles of these media. And their belief in the success of that mission, whether through the agency of the female voices of the upper-class graduates of Bryn Mawr or the sonorous utterances of Douglass himself, is as poignant as it is unrealistic.

Thus, in assessing Douglass's *Life and Times,* one must keep in mind its attempt to play the prophet without "tearing a passion to tatters." Of the last six chapters of Douglass's life's story, the first two are devoted to the European journey he took in the company of his second wife, the last two are a vindication of his role as minister resident and consul general to the Republic of Haiti, and the other two describe Douglass's role in the election of 1888, which led to his appointment by President Benjamin Harrison as consul to Haiti.

The first of his European chapters sounds an *ubi sunt* theme. Returning to England some forty years after his first stay there, Douglass expresses a desire to see again "England's great men" whom he had known and seen before: "There were Sir Robert Peel, Daniel O'Connell, Richard Cobden, John Bright, Lord John Russell, Sir James Graham, Benjamin Disreali, Lord Morpeth, and others, but except Mr. Gladstone, not one who was there then is there now" (557). The melancholy litany of absent faces is not meant to distance Douglass from his past. Rather, the chapter serves to distinguish Douglass as one of the few remaining representatives of a heroic age, an age whose speakers spoke in cadences unequaled in the present day. As he describes the abilities of each of these worthies, Douglass rolls out paragraphs of complimentary prose, presenting his reader with a laudatory encyclopedia of the oratorical styles of the great men he had heard years before. And when he reaches the end of the chapter, Douglass need not say, though the point is clear, that his style is a continuing example of that grand oratory of the past.

In the second chapter treating his European travels (Chapter 9 of Part Three), Douglass adopts the more conventional pose of the "American tourist" commenting on the sights and customs in France, Italy, and Egypt: "When once the American tourist has quitted Rome ... he is generally seized with an ardent desire to wander still farther eastward and southward" (579). This pose for Douglass, however, is fraught with significance. He recalls that on his first trip to England he was refused a passport to visit the continent by George M. Dallas, the minister to England, "on the ground that I was not and could not be an American citizen" (587). Contrasting his current privileges to his past restrictions, Douglass exults that "this man [Dallas] is now dead and generally forgotten, as I shall be, but I have lived to see myself everywhere recognized as an American citizen" (587). The trip abroad is an affirmation of his American citizenship—he tours the world as an American.

Douglass, however, mentions another purpose behind his visit:

> an ethnological purpose in the pursuit of which I hope to turn my visit to some account in combating American prejudice against the darker colored races of mankind, and at the same time to raise colored people somewhat in their own estimation and thus stimulate them to higher endeavors. I had a theory for which I wanted the support of facts in the range of my own knowledge. But more of this in another place. (579)

Although Douglass had written and lectured extensively on race and ethnology, that "other place" is not found within the *Life and Times* but was taken up elsewhere.[22] Douglass does not allude again to this "theory" in his text, but he leaves hints as to what he was about. Remarking earlier in the chapter upon the women he sees carrying burdens on top of their heads, Douglass comments that "I was glad to see, both in Italy and the south of France, that this custom is about as common there as it is among the dusky daughters of the Nile" (563). He continues:

> Even if it was originated by the Negro, it has been well copied by some of the best types of the Caucasian. In any case it may be welcomed as a proof of a common brotherhood.
>
> In other respects I saw in France and Italy evidences of a common identity with the African. In Africa the people congregate at night in their towns and villages, while their living is made by tilling the soil outside. We saw few farmhouses in the south of France. Beautiful fields and vineyards are there, but few farmhouses. The village has taken the place of the farmhouse, and the peasants sometimes go several miles from their villages to work their vineyards. (563)

Having identified this region as the "cradle in which the civilization of Western Europe and our own country was rocked and developed," Douglass proceeds to note the similarities to be found between European and African cultures: communal life, the bearing of burdens, the participation of women in fieldwork, and the carefree attitudes of the inhabitants. Africans need not feel themselves strangers to the civilization of the West; they are indeed a part of it.

In going to Egypt, Douglass perhaps wanted to carry this observation one step further. Egypt was more venerable than Europe, boasting a "civilization which existed when these countries of Europe [France and Italy] were inhabited by barbarians" (579). And as he chronicles his travels on the Suez Canal and the Nile, Douglass does comment sporadically upon the racial similarities between black Americans and the peoples of the Mideast. The comparisons, however, are limited and amount to very little. Douglass spends a great deal of time musing upon the landscape of biblical history as well as upon the wonders of Egyptian history, but no grand theory materializes. Instead, Douglass recounts his return to Rome, where he meditates on the vanity of human wishes. The chapter then ends with Douglass visiting the tomb of fellow abolitionist Theodore Parker and with Douglass marveling at the contrast between his former status as a slave and his present state, "when I could and did walk the world unquestioned, a man among men" (590).

What Douglass may have been intending to do before he changed direction was to link black America more securely to Egyptian civilization by finding concrete evidence for his long-held belief "that a strong affinity and a direct relationship may be claimed by the Negro Race to *that grandest of all the nations of antiquity, the builders of the pyramids.*"[23] Additionally, Douglass's scheme may have had a personal note. Peter Walker has commented at length on Douglass's claim that his mother resembled a figure in James Prichard's *Natural History of Man.* Walker notes that the head is supposed to be a likeness of Rameses, and that the likeness, "as far as the picture showed, may have been white." Douglass's fascination with the image suggests for Walker his "continuing conflict" over his racial identity.[24]

As strong as these ethnographic and personal motives may have been, their full articulation in *Life and Times* seems to have been derailed by the progressive dynamic within realistic representation. Douglass's foreign travels had allowed him to see that religious zeal and emotionalism were not the peculiar property of southern blacks. In Rome he marveled that "fanaticism is encouraged by a church so worldly wise as that of Rome" (575), and in Cairo he noted:

> If Rome has its unwashed monks, Cairo has its howling and dancing dervishes, and both seem equally deaf to the dictates of reason. The dancing and howling dervishes often spin around in their religious transports till their heads lose control and they fall to the floor sighing, groaning, and foaming at the mouth like madmen, reminding one of the scenes that sometimes occur at our own old-fashioned camp meetings. (587)

Finding in the cradle of civilization evidence of the religious spirit he had derided among the freedmen of the South, Douglass seems to have stumbled upon the keys for striking a harmonious chord with his voice and that of the southern black preacher. In Rome and Cairo were both passion and reason in the form of religious fanaticism and civilized achievement. The peoples responsible for civilization were also responsible for promoting "irrational" practices of faith.

But Douglass cannot long entertain a coexistence of passion and reason other than as a contradiction. In Rome, struck by the aspect of the young seminarians from around the world, Douglass remarks that "on the surface these dear young people ... are beautiful to look upon, but when you reflect that they are being trained to defend dogmas and superstitions contrary to the progress and enlightenment of the age, the spectacle becomes sad indeed" (575). The outward beauty of the young is belied by the superstitions that they are imbibing through their studies. The apparent harmony is spurious. And though Douglass is willing to admit that in his censures he "may be less wise than the Church" (575), the rest of his travels seem to support his criticism.

It is not that he does not give religion its due. In fact, as he tours the Holy Land, he indulges in lengthy meditations on the significance of these holy places. The settings of these meditations, however, make it clear that the religious spirit is alien to the world of progress. Douglass affirms that humanity is closer to the religious spirit in the lonely wilderness than "in the noise and bustle of the towns and men-crowded cities" (583). Then, while reflecting upon the divine revelations to the apostle Paul and the prophet Mohammed, he finds himself brought up short: "Such speculations were for me ended by the startling whistle of the locomotive and the sound of the rushing train—things which put an end to religious reveries and fix attention upon the things of this busy world" (583–584). The shrill whistle of a train, the note of progress, shakes Douglass from his reveries, reminding him that though the religious world may be beautiful and moving, it is not a world on the move. Even in Rome, "where the longer one stays the longer one wants to stay" and where one desires "to withdraw ... from the noise and bustle of modern life and fill one's soul with solemn reflections and thrilling sensations" (588), Douglass finds the ruins of a great civilization a scene inimical to human progress, a scene that underscores "the vanity of all things" (588).

The failed reconciliation of reason and passion on Douglass's European tour can be seen as emblematic of the dilemma that American reformers, whether as novelists or as social activists, never resolved. The voice of reason that they adopted seemed necessarily to draw a circle around themselves, separating them from those whose interests they proposed to represent. The Howellsian realistic novelist had to acknowledge that "by far the greatest number of people in the world, even the civilized world, are people of weak and childish imagination, pleased with gross fables, fond of prodigies, heroes, heroines, portents and improbabilities, without self-knowledge, and without the wish for it."[25] And as minister to Haiti, Douglass found that his unwillingness to represent what he believed were selfish and ignoble interests led to his being rhetorically divested of his American citizenship. Accused by a South Carolinian agent of a New York mercantile firm of being "more a Haitian than an American," Douglass "soon saw myself so characterized in American journals" (616). His critics charged that Douglass's sympathy for the Haitians rendered him unable to represent American interests, and though Douglass maintained otherwise, the voice in which he sought to speak was held to represent nothing in the country from which he derived his citizenship.

Ironically, Douglass saw his rhetorical exile made literal in an unexpected way. He was selected by Haiti to represent that country at the World Columbian Exposition of 1893. And in the final sentence of *Life and Times,* he mentions that selection and his ministry to Haiti as the "crowning honors to my long career and a fitting and happy close to my whole public life" (620). Given Douglass's account of the difficulties that beset him in Haiti, along with the fact that the organizers of the World Columbian Exposition, which was held in Chicago, barred African Americans from any substantive participation in the U.S. portion of the celebration, Douglass's crown seemed an uncomfortable one to wear.[26] In Haiti he was charged with representing a nation other than his own; in Chicago he had to represent a nation other than his own in order to walk "among all the civilized nations of the globe" (620). In both cases, although it may be clear to whom Douglass speaks, Douglass's dilemma leaves the reader wondering just whom the writer represents.

NOTES

1. Frederick Douglass, *The Life and Times of Frederick Douglass: Written by Himself* (New York: Collier, 1962 [1892]), p. 398. Subsequent references will appear parenthetically in the text.

2. John W. Blassingame, "Introduction," *The Frederick Douglass Papers, Series One: Speeches, Debates, and Interviews,* ed. John W. Blassingame, vol. 1: 1841–1846 (New Haven: Yale University Press, 1979), xxxi.

3. William Shakespeare, *Hamlet,* act 3, sc. 2, ll. 10–12.

4. Donald B. Gibson has argued that *Hamlet* plays a key role in Douglass's *1845 Narrative,* providing Douglass with a means of objectifying and making public his private experience.

Hamlet's inability to "reconcile thought and action" (563) reflects a similar dilemma within Douglass. Gibson's reading is helpful in revealing Douglass's strategies for reconciling "the tension between the social definition that he feels a white audience places on him and his own markedly different, private sense of who he is" (569). Douglass's use of Hamlet here, however, suggests that the tensions between Douglass and his audience did not correspond solely to racial divisions and that the tensions between his public and private selves might be more provocatively explored as an interplay between various public selves. See "Reconciling Public and Private in Frederick Douglass' *Narrative*," *American Literature* 57, no. 4 (December 1985): 549–569.

5. Amy Kaplan, *The Social Construction of American Realism* (Chicago: University of Chicago Press, 1988), 13.

6. George Washington Cable, "The Silent South," *Century Magazine* (September 1885), rpt., George Washington Cable, *The Negro Question: A Selection of Writings on Civil Rights in the South,* ed. Arlin Turner (New York: Doubleday, 1958), 78.

7. William Dean Howells, "The Man of Letters as a Man of Business," in *Literature and Life* (New York: Harper and Brothers, 1902), 35.

8. June Howard, *Form and History in American Literary Naturalism* (Chapel Hill: University of North Carolina Press, 1985), 131.

9. Waldo E. Martin Jr., *The Mind of Frederick Douglass* (Chapel Hill: University of North Carolina Press, 1984), 200.

10. Ibid., 136–193.

11. Peter F. Walker, *Moral Choices: Memory, Desire, and Imagination in Nineteenth-Century American Abolition* (Baton Rouge: Louisiana University Press, 1978), 244.

12. Kaplan, *American Realism,* 55.

13. Cf. Martin, *Mind of Frederick Douglass,* 167.

14. W. E. B. Du Bois, "The Talented Tenth," in *Writings* (New York: Library of America, 1986), 852.

15. W. E. B. Du Bois, *The Souls of Black Folk,* in *Writings,* 522. Subsequent references will appear parenthetically in the text.

16. Henry James, "The Question of Our Speech," in *The Question of Our Speech/The Lesson of Balzac: Two Lectures by Henry James* (New York: Houghton Mifflin, 1905), 11.

17. Ibid., 52.

18. Ibid., 41.

19. Ibid., 47.

20. Henry James, *The American Scene* (Bloomington: Indiana University Press, 1968), 119.

21. James, "The Question of Our Speech," 12.

22. See, e.g., Douglass's 1854 lecture, "The Claims of the Negro Ethnologically Considered," in *The Life and Writings of Frederick Douglass,* ed. Philip S. Foner, vol. 2 (New York: International Publishers, 1950–1975), 289–309.

23. Ibid., 301. See also Martin, *Mind of Frederick Douglass,* 202–213.

24. Walker, *Moral Choices,* 253–254.

25. William Dean Howells, "Novel-Writing and Novel-Reading: An Impersonal Explanation," ed. William M. Gibson, *Bulletin of the New York Public Library* 62, no. 1 (1958): 28.

26. Significantly, Douglass's efforts to speak on behalf of American blacks during the exposition also encountered what I have termed the "problem of constituency." For example, the publication and distribution of *The Reason Why the Colored American Is Not in the World's Columbian Exposition,* a pamphlet written and compiled by Douglass and Ida B. Wells, was "condemned scathingly by many Negro editors"; see Elliot Rudwick and August Meier, "Black Men in the White City: Negroes and the Columbian Exposition, 1893," *Phylon* 26,

no. 4 (1965): 356. Similarly, Douglass's support of, and decision to speak at, the "Colored Jubilee Day" occasioned controversy as well; see again Rudwick and Meier, "Black Men in the White City," 357–361, and Robert Rydell, "The World's Columbian Exposition of 1893: Racist Underpinnings of a Utopian Artifact," *Journal of American Culture* 1, no. 2 (1978): 253–275.

2
"Of Mr. Booker T. Washington and Others"

The Political Economy of Racism in the United States

Judith Stein

The research stimulated by the black politics of the 1960s has made Afro-American history more widely known and better documented.[1] Yet some of the findings are contradictory while others are isolated from larger meanings; crucial areas have been ignored even while the quantity of data has increased. Gaps exist because many writers have concentrated on seeking historical antecedents for the culture and politics of the 1960s. As a result, examination of black culture has often been narrowed to nonpolitical, slowly changing facets, like family life, religion, music, and folklore, and the study of black politics has been largely limited to men and movements seeking purely racial goals—the forerunners of the civil rights and nationalist movements of the past decade [the 1960s]. The root of the problem is that most historians possess the disconnected ideology characteristic of the dominant intellectual traditions of their class and era. Thus while the social and cultural historians have found that black community life was rich and vital, the political historians have treated the popular resources of black political leaders as passive, needing either massive exhortation or opportunistic compromise. These contradictions and others coexist because analyses are frequently limited to one oversimplified explanation—racism.

I

To demonstrate how the historians' use of racism excluded important areas of black culture and politics and mystified central dynamics in black history, I propose to examine a central period in Afro-American history—from the formal end of Reconstruction in 1877 through the creation of the legal structure of Jim Crow during the first decade of the twentieth century. Sometimes called the Era of Booker T. Washington, the period has been well explored by historians. The literature contains an interpretation of the South by C. Vann Woodward, a comprehensive examination of black thought by August Meier, the first volume of Louis Harlan's definitive two-part biography of Booker T. Washington, the first three volumes of Washington's papers, as well as many local studies that echo the major ideas of these three writers.[2]

Woodward, Meier, and Harlan see Washington as the embodiment of the central tendencies of black life in his time. Harlan's biography reinforces the popular belief that while Washington opportunistically accommodated black politics to the racism of his era, he had no alternative, and Southern blacks shared his situation and solution. According to this tradition, Washington's career was formed by the accelerating racism and vanishing political alternatives of the late nineteenth century, which gave rise to black ideologies embracing self-help, nationalism, and emigration. Because the political struggles for integration during the Reconstruction period became futile by the 1880s, Washington tried to build black institutions like Tuskegee and to encourage others, like black businesses. Racial self-help, not racial protest, he believed, would achieve the material basis for black equality in the South. The "better whites," by blunting the racism of poor whites, financially aiding black institutions, and recognizing the successful Negro, would provide the environment in which blacks could prosper.

The dominant American historians have used formal categories—accommodation and militance, self-help and protest—to describe the course of black history. But viewing black movements as mechanical successions of protests against racism and withdrawal into self-help only mystifies the historical process. Why did protests fail? The answer given is—racism. In essence, the explanation is advanced before the investigation is conducted. Racism is reified, divorced from the concrete and complex experiences of social groups in particular circumstances.

This framework was first fully elaborated by August Meier, whose work has added to our knowledge of Afro-American movements even while it has excluded important areas and has failed to examine black politics within the larger society. Meier's approach essentially limits significant Afro-American activity to movements that defined and reacted to the oppression of black people primarily in racial terms, even when the movements included whites. Thus, W. E. B. Du Bois's NAACP and Marcus Garvey's UNIA are seen to have conducted *racial* struggles. A movement to include black workers in a discriminatory union was a racial movement, whereas black unionists on strike, according to this thesis, were not engaging in racial struggle. Within the spectrum of racial movements, Meier finds that black ideologies moved regularly between integration and nationalism. The first approach tried to change particular laws or institutional practices that sanctioned or prescribed overt racial barriers, like segregated public facilities. The second sought equality through organizations of racial unity, without directly confronting basic social and political institutions.

This restriction of black politics distorts the content of Afro-American history by excluding actions that encompassed but transcended racial goals, and at the same time it misrepresents the racial movements themselves because of the abstractions that lie at the base of the theory. Meier's formalistic definitions of racism and integration transform legislators' attempts to pass civil rights bills, black laborers' entrance into unions, and social workers' negotiations to find jobs into equivalent acts. Although these three initiatives, perhaps, formally sought integration, the basis of the actions and their relationships with other forces in society were very different. Similarly, the formation of the Colored Farmers Alliance (CFA) and the creation of black professional organizations shared formal attributes of nationalism. But defining them solely in this way distorts the dynamics of the organizations—their class origins, the future course of their actions, and their impact on the social order.

Just as Meier limits black actions to those seeking racial goals, he similarly explains the white society's reactions to black movements in terms of its racial attitudes. He does not examine how attitudes developed to affect popular and institutional behavior. Instead, increasing and decreasing racism become mechanical explanations of change. Meier writes:

> The outlook of the Reconstruction period was primarily integrationist, for it was a period *when there was much sympathy and support among whites* for the Negro cause and the passage of concrete legislation assuring Negroes of their citizenship rights. Later, *as conditions took a turn for the worse,* the theme of self-help and solidarity again assumed a major role.[3]

While Meier acknowledges that alterations in racial attitudes were related to larger social changes, he obscures these crucial relationships. This is how he explains how "the conditions took a turn for the worse" (a reference to the national government's failure to protect formal rights during the late 1870s and 1880s):

> *Correlated* with the changes in the status of Negroes, and *to a large extent causing them,* were larger economic and social issues.... Northern capitalists, allied with and dominating Southern industry, not only found Negro votes unnecessary, but were interested in securing a stable, semi-skilled labor force with which to exploit Southern resources and develop Southern industry rather than in securing justice and social reform for the benefit of the ex-slaves and their descendants.[4]

But what precisely had been the capitalist position earlier, during Reconstruction? Had northern capitalists then been interested in "securing justice and social reform"? Were they the whites mentioned as allies of the Negroes during Reconstruction? Without providing a larger and clearly formulated framework to explain facts, Meier tells us only that "conditions took a turn for the worse," that there were "correlating" changes, and that economic phenomena "to a large extent" caused them.

Similarly, social changes seemed to affect blacks only as they affected the racial attitudes of whites. Noting the rising labor and agrarian opposition to industrial capitalism, Meier observes, "The Negroes appeared to be among the losers."[5] Were they or were they not? If they were, how? Meier examines the impact of industrial capitalism not on black lives but on the racial attitudes of the reform movements, which held "contradictory tendencies" with respect to blacks. "The rise of the lower class whites to political consciousness and power was *related directly and indirectly* to the disfranchisement and oppression of Negroes and final codification of the Southern race system."[6] Further, he does not examine the significant relationship between two important events, the rise of popular insurgency and the proscriptions against blacks, which occurred at approximately the same time. Meier concludes that it was the lower-class whites who protested, achieved power, and caused the disfranchisement of blacks. Finding that poor whites held racist attitudes, he assumes that their racial views were decisive in their actions and that their power was the determining factor in the Jim Crow era.

To understand black history, one must examine the principal social forces affecting black people concretely and in historical time. Because blacks interacted with other workers and other social classes, the historian must analyze specific social and class relationships and not be satisfied with general statements about broad social changes as backdrops for Afro-American history. To understand the era of Booker T. Washington, one must first examine the whole pattern of social forces affecting blacks after the Civil War, not only the racial manifestations. A discussion of these forces will elucidate the early political events, such as the Compromise of 1877 and the establishment of the "White Democracies" in the South, the popular movements, and finally the disfranchisement and Jim Crow system at the beginning of the twentieth century. It will also explain how these forces interacted with black aspirations and produced a variety of responses—one of which was that associated with Booker T. Washington.[7]

II

The dynamic northern business class, fearing a return of a southern party in alliance with agrarian interests in the West and antagonistic to the legislation and institutions favorable to industrial capitalism, initially embraced black voting as the means of securing Republican rule in the South and, thus, in the nation. Financiers, merchants, and railroad executives joined with the Radical politicians, representing principally northern abolitionists, some sections of labor, and some manufacturers. The Radicals envisioned transforming the South into a replica of northern society.[8]

To prevent a resurgence of the planter class, northern capitalists were willing to endorse elements of the Radical program—the ballot, property rights, wage labor, and education—during Reconstruction.

Having established its national hegemony, the capitalist class modified its reluctant commitment to bourgeois democracy in the South, which had launched the period known as the "New South." Farmer and labor opposition to the tariffs, the railroad subsidies, the financial burdens, and monetary instability became a threat to the new political structure. Therefore, northern capitalists renewed their antebellum Whig alliance by formally acknowledging the impoverished and capital-hungry southern elite.[9] This was the political basis of the Compromise of 1877, so called by historians because it removed the last federal troops from three southern states while southern Democrats accepted the Republican candidate in the disputed presidential election of 1876. The political order of Reconstruction, which had been based upon Republican rule through black voting, was replaced by Democratic hegemony, reflecting planter and capitalist interests in the South. Because the new regimes represented a minority of the population, they were able to remain in power only through demagoguery, fraud, violence, and laws designed to restrict the electorate.

The removal of the army and the political agreements, however, only gave sanction to a social process that Reconstruction had not successfully confronted. Men dedicated to the goals of even the minimum Reconstruction program—the ballot, citizenship rights, wage labor, free education—never controlled the state governments and never advocated the revolutionary means necessary to implement them. The more astute white southerners had recognized that the federal government would not underwrite a social revolution in the South, which the minimum Reconstruction program would have necessitated. President Ulysses Grant's Reconstruction measures, Virginia conservatives observed in 1870, had "recognized the political enfranchisement of the negro" but gave the whites "the opportunity to secure for themselves the control of the State forever."[10]

White men's rule after the Civil War signified a particular form of domination stemming from the prevailing pattern of the southern economy. Even southerners who wanted to industrialize their region saw that their programs were dependent upon the reinvigoration of the plantation, which in turn depended upon a secure and cheap labor supply. Southerners agreed that the "labor upon which the planter has to rely must be subject to his control."[11] Political mechanisms were required to ensure an adequate labor supply and an agricultural surplus. The kind of marriage between planters and industrialists necessary to achieve this goal resembled that of the German Junkers rather than the northern alliance of industrialists and farmers.

In the early days of Reconstruction, the black search for alternatives to the mode of life under slavery made the labor supply of the plantation uncertain. Some planters sought an imported laboring population. But unlike the former slaveholders in some of the Caribbean islands, southerners did not control the national government, which refused to use capital resources to subsidize their labor needs. Without aid, the planters were too poor to compete for Chinese labor. Yet despite the South's initial fears, the limited availability of land and the absence of alternative employment (encouraged by the planters themselves) drove blacks to resume plantation labor. To make the labor force secure required overt and covert restrictions on labor's mobility. To profit from cash crops, particularly cotton, in a period of declining prices and capital shortage required a labor system—sharecropping—in which the worker was forced to share the risks of capital. Southern labor relations differed, therefore, from those of northern agriculture. The maintenance of the plantation's labor relations, the basis of postbellum racism, resulted in other elements dissimilar to those of the social system in the North. Just as wage labor was transformed into sharecropping and convict labor, the free ballot became dependent and clientage politics, and free education degenerated to minimal literacy, at best.

Although the withdrawal of the federal commitment to bourgeois democracy was phrased in regional terms—"southern home rule" (in racial terms, "white supremacy")—the essential content of the Compromise of 1877 was the North's acceptance of the planters' regulation of the black labor force without federal hindrance, along with those white farmers who increasingly found themselves drawn into the plantation economy in competition with blacks and each other. The nationalization of the southern stereotype of blacks reflected the Compromise of 1877 and aided its workings. After 1877, the dominant bourgeois image of blacks became that of a people happy only in the rural South, working for their old masters.[12] The prevalence of this view explains in part the northern industrialists' reluctance to hire blacks except in labor emergencies. The holding of the stereotype and the refusal to hire blacks was irrational from the perspective of the individual employer, but not in terms of the functioning of the national political economy, which needed the black labor force in the South.

The strengthening of the southern system of racial and labor subordination stimulated northern investment in southern plantation and extractive industries, which yielded raw commodities for capitalist mills and markets. At the same time, the South provided votes for the maintenance of bourgeois hegemony in the nation. The Democratic rule of the planter, now allied with industrial interests, no longer threatened the nation, as it had in 1861 and again in 1867.

The Compromise of 1877 weakened the dominant mode of black struggle—Republican politics. Blacks and southern whites, principally outside the plantation areas, had fashioned an uneasy coalition, which was held together by men—black and white, northern and southern—eager for northern capital to reestablish the plantations and build new industry. Because the party's political victories were consolidated by the overwhelming Republican allegiance of blacks, the GOP attempted to establish some institutions of bourgeois democracy in the South—free labor, the ballot, education. But the conflicts in the system of labor relations were reproduced in the politics of Reconstruction.

The intellectual basis of black politics was Radical ideology, which assumed that a community of equal men could be created by allying labor (blacks) and capital to produce material progress and enlightenment. The ideology, a reflection of the coalition that had ended slavery, was reinforced by the personal experiences of many black leaders. The programs reflecting Radicalism varied. The black New Orleans *Tribune* urged a reinvigorated plantation system fueled by "new capital and new proprietorship [northerners]."[13] Some black Republicans in the South Carolina Reconstruction convention sought capital for land for the freedmen. F. L. Cardozo urged Congress to appropriate $1 million for state land purchases to be resold cheaply to the freedmen. He assumed favorable congressional action because of the common interest of the North and the black man against the "rebels." His colleague, W. F. Whipper, opposed the memorialization, but on grounds consistent with Radical ideology. Whipper wanted to use the resources of the state to secure rights for the laborer. "Protect labor and secure the laborer in all his right, and with their own strong arms and willing hands the people will accumulate property for themselves, and purchase homesteads with the result of honest industry."[14] Whether relying upon the direct investment of capitalists, the indirect appropriation of the nation's resources through Congress, or the political power of blacks to protect the value the plantation laborer produced, black Radicals assumed that the interests of capital and labor would harmonize.

But capital performed differently. New capital investment in plantations strengthened the powers of their owners. As Sea Island black laborers learned during the war, northern capital went south in competition with, not in support of, popular land desires.[15] Congress did not appropriate the money to subsidize land purchases for freedmen. Although South Carolina sold $200,000 in bonds for that purpose and attempted to use its tax policies to force land onto the market, the amount of land available was insignificant and of poor quality, as Whipper had predicted. Radical politics failed to protect black agricultural labor, too. South Carolina rice workers struck in 1876 against payment of wages in scrip redeemable only in company stores, a practice prohibited by law. Black Congressman Robert Smalls personally led the militia to put down the insurgency. Although he temporarily succeeded in redressing the grievance for the particular plantation by appealing to the Republican governor, the practice remained widespread in South Carolina.[16]

The actual conditions of labor and capital eroded the ideology of Radicalism before the formal end of Reconstruction. Grant's support of some of the works of Radicalism—the southern Republican regimes and black voting rights—became a defense of partisan power, not an instrument of social transformation. Black Republicans, however, continued to channel black opposition to southern conditions into the GOP. Frederick Douglass dissuaded black workers in the National Negro Labor Union from supporting an independent Labor Party. Black trade unions passed under the control of Republican politicians and lost their potential class power.

In the plantation counties, the party faced more profound problems because there independent black action that seemed to challenge planter power met with intimidation and violence.[17] Where black workers outnumbered white planters, Republicanism meant labor control of local governments. Despite national

Republican policy, when black Republicans threatened the precarious local control of the plantation economy, they were intimidated into either living with the white democracy by managing the black vote to gain some black appointments and the "good will" of the planters, or leaving the party or region.

In other areas of the South, notably in urban and rural communities of small and medium-sized farms composed of mixed black and white populations, black Republicans continued to exercise some independence on the local level and protected some Radical gains in education, self-government, and safety. Historically, the political economy of these regions had provided the social basis for what democracy there was in the South. But blacks in these areas were affected by the political economy of the plantation. Because the majority of blacks lived in the Black Belt, the GOP's voting base diminished as all black workers came under the domination of the planter.

Increasingly dependent upon federal appointments, not black votes, black Republicans defined black interests in terms of patronage, not the interests of workers.[18] But by narrowing their measure of influence to a few patronage positions for themselves and friends, they limited their appeal to the masses. Nevertheless, they continued to argue that they merited more patronage on the basis of black votes that they no longer controlled. Thus, black Republicans, and the middle class they represented, found themselves inextricably tied to the lot of the black masses even when they no longer articulated their interests. It became increasingly apparent that for the black petit-bourgeoisie traditional political methods could not win conventional partisan goals. To gain more patronage, they would have to challenge the planters for control of the black worker. But to do that in the New South required a new ideology, a new party, and new allies.

The invasion of industrial capital challenged the remaining Republican strength outside the plantation area and completed the disintegration of Radical theory. Especially after 1877, huge areas in the timber and mineral regions of the lower South were opened, accompanied by the construction of railroads and improvement of gulf harbors to transport raw materials.[19] The rapidly growing new cities, like Birmingham and Anniston in the mineral region, and the lumber towns in the "wiregrass" region of Alabama became bailiwicks of the corporations, which combined railroad, commodity, manufacturing, and real estate operations. Industrial development brought areas of subsistence farming into the boom-bust cycles of capitalism. The political domination of these areas by capitalist interests produced new centers of power that joined with the planters to dominate the Democratic party and ensure Democratic hegemony.

The decisive events of the 1880s were the solidification of planter control over the Black Belt[20] in all the southern states and the intensive capital investment in raw materials and railroad construction. Having achieved political hegemony earlier, the Democrats used state resources for plantation and industrial interests, taxing the peasant sector through regressive capitation and land taxes and facilitating the extraction of surpluses from the sharecropper through the lien system and local political domination.[21]

III

Prodded by the popular opposition of plantation workers, industrial workers, and farmers to the events of the 1880s, black leaders began to search for ways to meet the new conditions emerging in the South. Some of the petit-bourgeoisie opposed the new order by joining with workers engaged in strikes or by building cooperatives and third parties. Especially in areas directly experiencing capital investment, like northern Alabama, black and white dissidents joined in the various Greenback-Labor and Independent third parties, as well as the fledgling unions created by farmers and workers.[22] In Alabama, the resistance to industrial capitalism was greater than in many other southern states because of the intensive development of industry in the northern part of the state. The consolidation of smaller operations by powerful corporations like the Tennessee Coal, Iron, and Railroad Company increased industrial power over workers. These events produced bitter proletarian challenges to capital, culminating in the protracted miners' strike in 1894. At the same time, they intensified the farmers' alienation from the New South.[23]

The major political challenge to the planters and industrialists—Populism—grew out of the farmers' condition, even though it included urban and industrial workers. In 1900, almost 90 percent of Alabama's people were rural; the state's total population of 1,828,697 included only 52,902 wage-earners. The major expression of agrarian opposition to the new order was the Southern Alliance. Beginning in Texas and spreading eastward, the Alliance gathered up many of the local groups that had mushroomed in the late 1880s. It attempted to confront the monopolies of capital, transportation, and marketing by forms of collective self-help—cooperatives, boycotts, newspapers. The Alliance, and even more its successor, the Populist Party, represented more than interest politics. While agrarian protest by itself did not necessarily challenge the established social and political order, the creation of alternative institutions mobilizing excluded popular elements represented potential social revolution. In 1891, for instance, Bourbon senator John Morgan of Alabama expressed his sympathy with the farmers' problems in an article, "The Dangers of the Farmers' Alliance," in the *Forum.* The danger, of the movement, as he saw it, was that

> almost every man in the United States who had earned any character as a statesman or a legislator, jurist, or financier, was excluded from the Alliance, and as such abilities are essential to safe government, their places are assumed ... by men of imperfect education and of little experience in government, and too often by mere charlatans and demagogues.

Morgan feared that the displacement of the "better people" would produce a movement that could challenge class rule. It had already formulated a "corrupt and destructive policy of using taxing power to collect money from one man to lend it to another."[24] While some members of the ruling class favored forms of inflation, they feared that the Alliance's subtreasury plan to use the nation's capital resources to advance and cheapen agrarian credit would both break the crop-lien system and the social order that it supported. Making the subtreasury plan the litmus test of acceptability dramatized the social division that the movement represented. By 1891, the Alliance became more militant when farmers who owned more land and commanded more satisfactory credit arrangements dropped out of the order, opposing the subtreasury plan and independent politics. More new men—blacks and urban laborers—entered and broadened the order's social base.[25] More suballiances endorsed the subtreasury plan and the Populist Party. In the period 1887–1891, the Alliance movement used various collective, nonpolitical techniques. As these measures failed to solve agrarian problems and the major parties opposed its evolving demands, the Alliance chose to contest state power by proposing to substitute popular rule for the rule of capital.

Paralleling the development of the Southern Alliance and encouraged by it, the Colored Farmers Alliance by 1890 grew to more than a million black farmers. In 1889, Alabama had more than 1,600 black suballiances composed of 50,000 farmers. Although we do not have a precise map of its geographical distribution, the sheer size of the organization and the frequent mention of the movement in Black Belt newspapers clearly implies an existence in plantation areas.[26] Although the Bourbon Montgomery *Advertiser* criticized the white Alliance's support of the black organization, the CFA was initially tolerated (probably because, like the white Alliance, it declared its intention to avoid politics and used rhetoric consistent with southern nationalism). CFA's opposition to northern and European capital and monopolies did not immediately threaten the planters. Nor did the Alliances' joint, successful boycott of the jute trust.

Like the white local groups, CFA's suballiances were simultaneously fraternal organizations, which helped sick and disabled members and purveyed advice on farming, raising families, and other problems of interest to rural people; they also taught the order's principles of political economy. Quickly expanding its activities, the Alabama CFA created a marketing exchange in Mobile, united against the cottonseed mills to obtain higher prices for seed, and cooperated with the Southern Alliance in other areas affecting farmers.[27]

The black and white Alliances began as distinct organizations, reflecting the texture of Southern social life. As they expanded their actions, the Alliances began to provide structures for joint action and fusion. In 1890, at Ocala, Florida, the CFA and the Alliance confederated, on the same basis as the Alliance had previously united with other farmer organizations and the Knights of Labor.[28]

The refusal of the two major parties to accept the subtreasury plan was the dramatic event that made Populists out of Democratic and Republican Alliancemen. The major parties' bipartisan campaign against Alliance programs and their attempt to infiltrate and dominate the order convinced radical Alliancemen that they must have a new political organization to reflect the social base and ideology of the movement. The Reverend J. L. Moore, a black Methodist minister of Crescent City, Florida, and County Superintendent of his local CFA, asked in February 1890:

> Can we do anything while the present parties have control of the ballot-box, and we [the Alliance] have no protection? The greatest mistake, I see, the farmers are now making, is this: The wily politicians see and know that they have to do something, therefore they are slipping into the Alliance, and the farmers in many instances are accepting them as leaders; and if we are to have the same leaders, we need not expect anything but the same results.[29]

The break with the past signified by joining the Populist Party was obvious to blacks and whites. R. H. Hayes, a black Populist from Texas, denied that blacks were married to the party of Lincoln and said, "The colored people in the rural districts will affiliate with any party that is against monopolies, in the interest of the poor men."[30] A white Populist argued along the same lines:

> We are not looking to men of the past but to men of the present. The time has passed when an American citizen especially among the working classes will before he gives the hand of fellowship ask whether the man wore the blue or the gray, or whether the man came from Maine or Florida. Our swords are rusted and we are now preparing for war again. We feel that we have been sadly neglected by both parties. The colored man said that the Negroes are naturally Republicans. I do not blame them. I was a natural Democrat. The attention of the colored brother has been called to what that grand old Moses Abraham Lincoln said in announcing their freedom, but they are not told that the labor of this country is in slavery.[31]

The break with the past involved more than sentiment. In the Black Belt, third party politics, encouraging social rebellion, immediately came into conflict with the institutions of the counties. There, most suballiances, black and white, had to be cautious. By 1891 the planters became alert to the social implications of the Alliance and tried to discourage its growth. Many white farmers in the Black Belt expediently accepted planter power, which after all was real, and eschewed the third party. One white Populist editor, I. L. Brock, of a safer hill county, after being praised for the vigor of his indictments of the ruling class of Alabama, responded that credit should not go to him but to the editor of the *Alabama Populist,* who survived for a while in the Black Belt.[32] For black leaders in the plantation *regions,* political action was even more difficult. Some of them were landowners, whose very purchase of land had been accomplished only with the tolerance of the planters. But the black tenants who composed the alliances were not under the same restraints. Earlier in 1889, the Montgomery *Advertiser* announced that the head of the CFA in Alabama was "Frank Davis, a solvent and successful negro farmer," who was not interested in politics. The Bourbon newspaper further noted that some blacks at the meeting wanted to go into politics immediately but had been expelled from the meeting.[33] We know no more about this particular meeting. Yet the action of those expelled blacks was consistent with the fact that where the black Alliancemen were not subject to constraint and could freely vote, they overwhelmingly sought radical political action. They were not free to do so in the Black Belt. In Union Springs,

Bullock County, Frank Davis's home, a newspaper threatened to print the name of *any* person who voted for a Populist in 1892.[34]

Populists expected blacks to seek third party action and initially seemed optimistic about their success, even in the Black Belt. While one Populist predicted that planters would try to stop their black sharecroppers from joining the new party, he also expressed confidence that the obstacle "would be attended to at the proper time." How this was to be done was unclear. Populists advised blacks to carry guns when they voted; many times they formed protective groups. The Bourbon press in Alabama spoke of Gideon's Band, a secret organization that functioned during elections.[35] We do not know very much about these groups, but it appears that at times the party was able to protect its members.

The third party won the support of southern labor organizations. If it is true that northern labor resisted Populism because its leadership was committed solely to trade union organization, the same cannot be said for southern labor. The depression of the 1890s had seriously weakened the southern unions. Declining wages and failing strikes made radical politics an attractive alternative. Farmer-labor coalitions had a history in the New South. The Knights of Labor had attempted to organize plantation workers, as well as craftsmen and laborers.[36] In 1889, the Knights joined with the Alliance in support of the farmers' St. Louis platform and, in 1890, confederated with it. In turn, the Alliances added the specific demands of urban workers to their platforms and aided workers in many strikes of the 1880s and 1890s. In 1896 the Alliance openly supported the Knights' Great Southwest Strike against the Gould system, as farmers had previously supported miners in Alabama's 1894 strike. Officials of the Texas State Federation of Labor were among the organizers of the Populist Party.[37] The Southern laboring population was composed of workers who still retained their rural roots. Where Populists were weak in southern cities it was due not to supposed urban-rural divisions but to political opposition. In New Orleans, for instance, Populists won only 71 votes out of the 40,000 ballots reported in 1892. The traditional explanation is unconvincing if one notes that at the first Populist state convention in Louisiana that year one-half of the delegates had come to Alexandria from Orleans Parish. A more reasonable explanation would be that in no precinct in the city were the Populists allowed to have election commissioners.[38]

Black Populists led farmers and workers who had a long and varied history of lost causes. They now had white allies, whose political movement paralleled their own. Together they were capable of winning majorities at the ballot box.

Other black leaders, those with institutional power within the southern Republican parties, optimistically insisted that the GOP would continue to be the black man's vehicle. Their hopes were fueled by the Republican introduction of the "Force Bill"—congressional legislation designed to guarantee black voting in the South. But the economic bonds between the southern and northern economies were too strong to permit the repeal of the Compromise of 1877. To be sure, some northern Republicans continued to pay homage to the Reconstruction commitment, but their voices were stilled by those whose racial views reflected the current North-South connections.

Although the political promises proved valueless, there was a social basis for black Republicanism within the South of the 1890s. While the movement of capital into the South impoverished most black farmers and workers, industrialization and urbanization produced a small black petit-bourgeoisie of businessmen and professionals. Although they were Republicans, many had the necessary ties to the white Democratic elite, an essential prerequisite for success in southern cities. Many others did not engage directly in politics, but the black officeholders in the Republican Party reflected their needs and offered potential employment to them and their children.[39] The birth of the Populist Party in the 1890s allowed black Republicans to bargain with politicians from the other parties.[40] They collaborated with Populists on patronage and election reform in North Carolina.[41] In Alabama, black GOP leader William Stevens, after toying with Populism, supported conservative Stephen Oates for governor.[42] In Texas, Norris Cuney went over to the Bourbons.[43] The varieties of political behavior should not obscure the common element in the actions. Black Republicans, presuming harmony between capital and labor, never challenged the foundation of Southern racism. After disfranchisement, when the hopes of marshalling black votes disappeared, they merged easily with the Washingtonians.

IV

Booker T. Washington, like others of his generation, was compelled to respond to the events of the 1890s, which he found to be eroding his position with blacks and whites as he reached for broader influence. The creation and operation of Tuskegee during the 1880s had assumed that the interests of blacks, planters, and capitalists could be harmonized. Within the Black Belt of the 1880s, an ambitious teacher or school principal needed good relations with the local community, with the state legislature, and with northern businessmen who could supplement meager public funds.

While ambitious and capable black Republicans frequently left the Black Belt,[44] institutions like Tuskegee grew in the vacuum of black politics and, in their sponsors' imagination, assumed large proportions. Their supporters identified the existence of their institutions with racial survival and their operations as the basis of black liberation. Spurred by Washington's ambition, Tuskegee became for those of his outlook the symbol of racial progress. The school's program—formal training in the values and skills necessary for bourgeois success—was viewed as the beginning of mass liberation.

Washington was aware that other—specifically, political—action was a necessary complement to self-help and that the masses had a role to play in politics. But he hoped that the masses would accept the dominant, and ultimately benevolent, forces in society. When black voters in increasing numbers opposed the Democrats in the 1890s, Washington publicly denigrated the importance of politics. Meanwhile, he, who understood what the masses did not, tried to manipulate the political system to speed the process of advancement by offering the Tuskegee way to the ruling elite. Recognition of Washington's conception of the different roles of leaders and followers dissolves the apparent contradiction between Washington's extensive private political actions and his public statements disclaiming the significance of black politics.

According to Washington, the majority of black farmers needed education to make their labor profitable. But while the poor had always desired education, they rarely made education their principal strategy for survival. During Reconstruction, the demand for education expressed the desire to produce an informed citizenry capable of participating in community life and work. Individual efforts, strengthened by mass political power, was to be the engine of black progress. Whatever the limitations of Reconstruction politicians, all understood that blacks could have a voice in the allocation of public resources only by political organization independent of their employers.

The new theory of education was an ideology that stemmed from a part of the black petit-bourgeoisie, not the masses. The daily lives of plantation workers and the occupational structure of the South made mobility through education an aspiration possible at best for their children, not themselves. But where the labor of children was necessary for family survival, minimal literacy was the most children could attain. The fact that the majority of the students at Tuskegee were teachers reveals how far the institution was from the expectations of plantation workers. The student population also revealed how removed Washington's strategy was from the material needs of the black poor. Tuskegee, Washington believed, would produce leaders who would then proceed to uplift the working masses. Writing to the *Southern Workman* in 1881, he said: "If there is any place where a good Normal School is needed it is right here. What an influence for good, first on the teachers, and from them on the children and parents."[45]

Washington's conception of education left undisturbed the planters' needs for black cheap labor by deferring change to some time in the future. His early links with and dependence on the leading citizens of the town ensured that the school would not jeopardize the social relations of Macon County. His definition of the educational needs of blacks in terms of proper training, not state financial support, harmonized with Bourbon definitions of economy. Because the graduates of Tuskegee generally migrated from plantation areas, the school had the effect of removing potentially unruly elements of the laboring population.[46]

The urgency of farmers' needs and the response of black farmers to the politics of the 1890s forced Washington to address agrarian problems more directly than in the previous decade. Perhaps it was the black response to Populism in 1892 that led Washington to think of setting up a summer school in Union Springs, the home of black Alliance leader Frank Davis.[47] Washington's principal effort, the 1892 farmers' conference at Tuskegee, placed him at the extreme right wing of the agrarian movement. Farmers were urged to buy land, raise more food, build houses, go to school, keep out of debt, avoid lawsuits, and treat women better. The fact that Macon County gave the Populists 63 percent of the vote later that year indicates that black farmers were beyond that message even in Tuskegee's surrounding area. Washington's conferences occurred regularly after 1892. The Montgomery *Advertiser* found them "in the right direction" and predicted that if Negroes followed Tuskegee's leaders, they were "sure to be prosperous and happy and live in peace and harmony with all mankind." Conference speakers urged blacks to "keep out of politics, make any concession consistent with manhood. Let the white men know you are glad you are a Negro. Don't push but be proud of your blood."[48]

The growing attention that Tuskegee won from white leaders coincided with the rise of Populism. It was in this period that Washington began speaking to white elite groups on his theory of race relations, a theory that had immediate practical uses. His reputation grew, and he was invited to speak at the Atlanta Exposition in 1895. Because the speech launched Washington into the period of his greatest political influence, it is useful to examine not only what he said but also why it brought him prestige. Merely showing that his ideas reflected those of the ruling class of the South and the nation, as Harlan, Meier, and Woodward do, is insufficient because ideological coincidence cannot explain why those forces needed to elevate a black leader.

At Atlanta, Washington spoke of blacks prospering in proportion to their willingness to "dignify and glorify common labor," to "put brains and skill into the common occupations of life," and to refuse to "permit . . . grievances to overshadow opportunities." While publicly endorsing the New South's role for the Negro, he rejected the alternative of the "agitation of questions of social equality."[49] During the mid-1890s, the term "social equality" was frequently used to describe the unnamed but harmful results of black political power. Thus, Democrats in Louisiana referred to their opponents in 1896 as "John N(igger) Pharr" and the "Populist-negro social equality ticket."[50] But who were the black "agitators" who articulated "grievances"? On the basis of Harlan's survey of black reactions to the speech, it would appear that they were primarily northern professionals, scholars, and journalists. Harlan cites only two black southern reactions—a negative comment from African Methodist Episcopal bishop Henry Turner of Georgia, an emigrationist, and a mocking criticism from a black newspaper in Atlanta.[51]

Harlan and most historians have incorrectly imposed the later Washington–Du Bois controversy on the South of 1895. At this time, Du Bois was in basic agreement with Washington[52] while the few northern blacks who criticized Washington's speech were marginal in the North and without an organizational vehicle in the South.

In 1895 the most effective means to struggle against discriminatory practices, disfranchisement, and racism—all of which affected prosperous black southerners as well as the poor—was Populism.[53] Where black Republicans succeeded in challenging racial practices, it was through alliance with the Populists. In general, human rights could be won only by joining or allying with the party challenging capital.[54]

Without understanding the fear engendered by Populism, we cannot understand why the ruling class elevated Washington and tried to strengthen his power among blacks.[55] The Atlanta *Constitution,* the principal exponent of New South ideology, wrote of Washington's speech: "Beginning from today let the Negro register an oath in heaven that from henceforth he will cast his lot materially, civilly, and morally with the best people of the South; that he will cultivate the closest friendship with the Southern white man, that when he can he will vote with and for the Southern white man."[56]

The editor and Georgian Democrats had particular reason for lauding the politics of Washington's speech. Just a few weeks after Washington's speech there was to be a runoff election between Populist Tom Watson and his Democratic opponent. A runoff became necessary because Democratic fraud and intimidation, especially against black voters, had been so blatant that the Democratic winner was forced to agree to Populist demands to repeat the election.[57] In the runoff the black vote was crucial.

Watson was the nation's best known Populist. Most other Populists had little national visibility because few of them were elected to national office. One historian recently estimated that between 1892 and 1894 at least twenty Populist congressmen had been denied election through ballot-stuffing alone.[58] Watson had been elected in 1890 as a Democrat and subsequently became a Populist, provoking particular rage among his former colleagues. When Watson ran in 1892, northern capitalists raised $40,000 to help defeat him. President Grover Cleveland announced that he was as interested in the congressman's defeat as he was in his own election. Watson's popularity in a district that included Black Belt and industrial areas directly challenged the ruling coalition. While New South leaders were alarmed by Populist victories in white hill counties, successful penetration of the Black Belt and industrial areas would create majorities capable of challenging their state power.

Washington offered southern leaders a way to combat black insurgency. Meier and Harlan's explanation that the Bourbons needed a black leader to "express Negro accommodation to the social conditions implicit"[59] in the Compromise of 1877 does not violate the facts so much as the dynamics of history. In 1895, while southern rulers were combating other blacks and whites whose politics challenged the 1877 compromise and the social system it embodied, some men reached out for a symbol that would deny that reality and preserve their ideology and self-conception. Then as now, however, the encouragement of moderate men was not the principal weapon used against radical movements. The history of Populism demonstrates that violence and intimidation were the primary weapons used to combat its challenge to the prevailing order.

While planters and industrialists generally agreed upon naked force as the weapon against black militancy, it was the capitalists who pioneered in the encouragement of the Tuskegee approach because they had greater need for it. Washington's promises of industrial peace were welcomed by capitalists throughout the country and by the beleaguered President Cleveland, who sent Washington his congratulations. While the planters' labor supply was secured by cruder forms of domination, industrialists sought Tuskegee graduates to man schools and manage black labor within the corporations. This was not, as Washington argued, because blacks needed to learn the values of work or even technical skills. The corporations, like the plantations, needed cheap unskilled labor. They also needed Tuskegee's trained men and women to confront the militancy of an industrial proletariat.[60] Capitalists did not immediately perceive the varied uses of Tuskegee. They, like the planters, combated popular militancy in the depression years of the 1890s principally by force and the substitution of convict labor. But the returning industrial expansion and consolidation of smaller companies by the giant corporations at the turn of the century allowed industrialists to fashion more permanent institutional networks.

Washington, too, did not immediately perceive the varied uses of his school. During the 1890s, he forged personal ties and solicited financial support from capitalists with immediate interests in Alabama's industry. New Englander William H. Baldwin Jr., vice president and general manager of the Southern Railroad, was on Tuskegee's board of trustees from 1895.[61] As early as 1887, Washington secured summer employment for Tuskegee's students in the Pratt mines, owned by Tennessee Coal and Iron. They remained aloof from other workers, strikes, and unions, but sometimes they became the teachers of the miners' children.[62] At the turn of the century, however, corporate needs expanded, and new roles for the school's graduates strengthened earlier relationships. Public officials and corporate leaders initiated requests for graduates to become principals and teachers in the new schools in industrial areas and for social workers within the corporations.

V

The historians' restricted conception of black movements and their consequent neglect of black Populism leaves undisturbed the traditional theory of the source of racism.[63] Their theory is Washington's: The poor whites were the source of proscriptions against the blacks; the "better whites," even when they disappointed Washington, were the allies of black people. If a ruling group governs benevolently or paternalistically, then it follows that the lower orders should accept its hegemony. But if black opposition during the 1890s was a dominant, if unsuccessful, factor, one must modify their description of class rule. In fact, Harlan's conception of the paternalistic upper class rests on isolated statements from those who encouraged Washington's accommodating approach. Viewing a very small sample, Harlan and other historians have the attitudes of the paternalists toward Washington, but not their larger conceptions of moral economy.

The "better whites" were the planters and industrialists of the New South, plus the political and intellectual elite who articulated their values. They justified the laws that placed the burden of taxation on small landed property while industrial assets were largely tax-exempt. They placed sharecroppers under the control of planters by forbidding tenants to take liens.[64] They shackled rural wage-earners by making ordinary forms of labor association illegal. During the 1880s, when the Knights of Labor was organizing in the South, states invoked conspiracy laws to prevent the formation of local assemblies and at the same time increased the militia. Newspapers openly called for murder, and the "best people" followed their advice. When the black Washington *Bee* warned that black South Carolinians were losing their rights, it referred to the rights of laborers to organize to obtain decent wages and treatment.[65] Gerrymandering, the appointment of local officials, and complex election laws neutralized local black majorities. In the occasional city that possessed an active black majority, charter revisions, making local government responsive to white businessmen, effectively removed black political power and officers.[66] These institutionalized means of class and racial oppression, backed by violence, secured state power and control. The laws, by debasing the poor and giving the rulers immense power over their subjects, encouraged contempt for and fear of the masses. These feelings were readily translated into personal cruelty in daily affairs, and violence against organized opposition was openly sanctioned.

Washington's white friends were very clear about their primary allegiance. Governor Oates, the inveterate foe of the Alliance and Populism, spoke at the Tuskegee commencement of 1896 in the midst of a bitter political campaign. Fusion forces had united behind a Populist gubernatorial candidate who, while a congressman, had voted in the House to seat a black over a white Democrat. The party of Governor Oates (who was not running for reelection) tried to use that issue as the basis of its white supremacy campaign. Oates's speech followed one by John C. Dancy, a conservative black Republican from North Carolina. Dancy had praised the role of New Englanders in the establishment of black educational institutions like Hampton and Tuskegee. The audience warmly applauded his talk. Evidently, Oates became agitated at Dancy's talk or at the audience's response, and to the surprise of his listeners, he ignored his prepared speech and said:

> I want to give you niggers a few words of plain talk and advice. No such address as you have just listened to is going to do you any good; it's going to spoil you. You had better not listen to such speeches. You might as well understand that this is a white man's country, as far as the South is concerned, and we are going to make you keep your place. Understand that. I have nothing more to say to you.[67]

Oates's undelivered speech was probably of benevolent intent toward blacks. By citing such speeches and addresses, historians have placed Oates and others like him in the category of "Southerners of the older generation,"[68] paternalists who were friendly toward their former slaves. But to do this ignores the function of paternalist rhetoric and the social behavior of the men who used it. The myth of the friendly class, sustained by this fragmented view of the paternalists and an equally erroneous analysis of the popular forces, pervades the historical literature of the South.

Poor whites, unlike the planters and industrialists, did not depend for their livelihood upon the exploitation of black labor. Many poor whites undoubtedly held racist attitudes, which they absorbed from their society's ideological apparatus[69]—the schools, the newspapers, the churches—but popular attitudes divorced from power are politically insignificant.[70] Reflecting their social experiences, poor whites did not advance racial legislation as a means of confronting their poverty. Sometimes, however, legislation motivated by the social conditions of poor whites came to have racial results in the course of the political bargaining of the Bourbon era. During the 1880s, for example, rural whites outside the plantation areas continually tried to obtain common school education for their children. In 1889, after failing to win

Black Belt support for greater taxation and school funds, politicians representing white counties won from the Alabama legislature an additional appropriation for schools in return for their acceptance of greater local discretion in the allocation of funds in the counties. County distribution of educational funds was a demand of the Black Belt, whose leaders, in control of local government, then proceeded to starve their black schools. The leadership of the white counties, pressing for more education for their children, accommodated to the white planters' opposition to black education. But the bargain of 1889 did not produce better education in the white counties. Ensuring sufficient money for the white schools in the Black Belt by diverting funds from black schools, the new law allowed the white elite to oppose in the future new taxation and appropriations for schools.[71]

During the height of the Alliance period, from 1887 to 1891, when the organization initiated various measures of collective self-help, suballiances set up their own schools or supplemented the funds of existing schools. But self-help was no more a solution to education than it was to credit. The patent inadequacy of old leaders, old methods, and old ideas led the whites of the hill counties to seek an alternative explanation of events and to find a new political praxis, which transcended the racial ideas of the Bourbon era as well as its political and economic practices. Whites who had been geographically, politically, and socially apart from blacks moved toward them, not for humanitarian reasons but because they required their support.[72]

Commonality of need among all parts of the laboring classes was basic to the Populist view of the world. It taught that both whites and blacks were oppressed, and it promised to "wipe out the color line" in the South. The means of achieving racial equality, however, did not typically include racial legislation, as was to be the case in the twentieth-century civil rights movements. As the leader of the CFA in Florida said, "Especially is this true in the South [that] anything that can be brought about to benefit the working man will benefit the Negro more than any other legislation that can be enacted."[73]

Central to the enactment of legislation in the interest of "the working man," the Alliance program asserted, was ensuring the right to vote. This was considered by both blacks and whites to be the major civil right because political power was viewed as the essential means to solve the people's problems. Unlike other social rights, the free ballot had been consistently under attack after 1877. In the 1890s, the campaign for voting rights enjoyed mass support because it was rooted in a popular movement with specific programs. Since political participation was central to the protection of the ballot, most Populist parties had blacks on state, county, and district executive committees, elected them as delegate's to national conventions, and proposed them as candidates on party tickets.[74]

Populists rarely sought specific legislation in race relations, probably because they were suspicious of the administration of the laws in a state they did not control. Since most of the purely racist practices were in fact against the law and occurred because the Democrats controlled the process of government, Populist political power was deemed the means to end those practices. Where Populists controlled local governments (they never controlled a state), blacks had political representation, their lives were protected, they held government jobs, they served on juries, and they were part of the life of the community. Populist newspapers recognized and reported black achievements.[75] That is why politics and political rights were considered so important by black communities.

While Democrats tried to devise a system of race relations consistent with white supremacy, Populists measured race relations by the standard of equality. Results followed from this assumption, even when initially white Populists were insensitive to racial discrimination. For instance, at the first Populist convention in Texas, there were no blacks on the state executive committee. When reminded of that fact by a black delegate, the convention applauded him and unanimously voted to place blacks on all committees from the state to local levels. When two whites suggested some form of separation, they were quickly rebuked by the convention.[76] This is not to say that no white Populist held racist ideas, any more than no Populist held other ideas of the dominant culture. But the collective practices flowing from the party countered prejudice. There were, of course, differences among blacks, among whites, and between blacks and whites, about the means of addressing and resolving problems. But that was not unique to Populists.

Populists did not conduct campaigns against the idea of racism, a word not used at that time. In part, this stemmed from the fact that the full institutionalization of racism in law and practice occurred in the first decade of the twentieth century, after the defeat of Populism.[77] Also, the elaborate rationalizations and theories of race differences written by intellectuals were unknown to the average white Populist. Populist treatment of race came principally from their own analysis of their past actions. In their view, former white Democrats had opposed black Republicans because they had not understood the world, not because of racism. The corollary of racism, black powerlessness, was a view white Populists did not hold. Populism was not the politics of guilt. Blacks and whites needed political education, not moral uplift. A white Populist could well have echoed these words of a black Populist leader: "The time I have craved for has come. The people's eyes are open and farewell to the political lash."[78] Explanations for the defeat of Populism lie outside the area of Populist race relations.

Harlan ignores the changing social and political behavior of blacks and whites during the Populist era when he identifies Reuben Kolb, the anti-Bourbon candidate for governor of Alabama in 1892, as merely a "spokesman for the agrarian faction of white small farmers."[79] It is true that Kolb was nominated by white farmers in the Jeffersonian Democratic Party (a halfway house between the Democratic Party and the Populist Party) to oppose the Democratic corporation lawyer Thomas G. Jones. But the major organizations of black opposition endorsed Kolb: the Populist Party, the Alliance, the Knights of Labor, the United Mine Workers, and the Republican Party.[80]

To safeguard the black and white vote, Jeffersonians and Populists formed the Southern Ballot Rights League. The free exercise of the ballot among all people was at stake. A Jeffersonian editor warned voters that the Democratic Party's platform urged a restricted electorate: "If college graduates are alone permitted to vote, it will keep the aristocratic, autocratic and plutocratic Jonesocrats in power worlds without end.... Under it every poor man, white and colored, in Alabama could be disfranchised."[81]

Populists, not Republicans, braved the Black Belt to protect the ballot. The chairman of the Populist Party's state executive committee told his black audience there: "I had rather see Mobile Bay filled with Pinkerton's detectives, the banks of every river and creek in Alabama lined with Federal bayonets and crimson with blood, rather than see you deprived of the privilege of voting.... Let the colored man stand up for his race and vote for a free ballot and civil liberty."[82]

Kolb narrowly lost the election. Fraud in the Black Belt, publicly admitted by Democratic leaders, defeated the insurgents. The Sayre Election Law, adopted during the next legislative session and designed to restrict the Populist electorate, confirmed campaign predictions. New legislation was passed aimed at punishing tenant farmers who broke their contracts, a useful disfranchising device.[83] Having little faith in the federal government, some Populists proposed that the people should not pay their taxes until Alabama had a republican government. At least one recommended force.

Populism was stronger in 1894, but so was the determination of the planters, strengthened by industrial support. Northern Alabama capitalists, in the midst of a protracted coal strike, knew that the planters' control in the Black Belt was vital to their battle to subdue miners and Populists. Once again, Populism could not find the organization and ideological strength to harness the widespread anger and suffering of the New South. The small farmer's mode of production, individualistic and isolated, made cohesive social and political organization difficult and unstable. But this is the historian's judgment. The rulers of the New South, closer to the threat of Populist victories, acted vigorously to destroy the popular challenge to their control.[84] The mobilization of the Tuskegee apparatus, the appointment of a few Populist leaders to government jobs, and financial contributions to some hard-pressed newspaper editors supplemented direct fraud and violence.[85] But to safeguard the future, structural changes were necessary: Disfranchisement followed on the heels of the defeat of Populism.

VI

Writing about disfranchisement, Harlan says: "Disfranchisement did not come with the single force of a tidal wave but more like the ordinary rising tide, the breakers of each successive election or legislative session rolling higher until only vestiges of the black vote of Reconstruction were left." Metaphor, however, does not elucidate the process. Neither does a multicausation theory. The "disfranchisement movement," Harlan concludes, "grew because of mounting racism, fear of Populist radicalism and even Progressive reformism." Whose mounting racism? Harlan explains that Washington, "privately, with and through whites of good will ... sought to moderate the politics of the more inimical whites"[86] (a codeword for the poor whites).

Instead of rolling in waves, efforts to restrict the electorate followed periods of popular opposition. The election law of 1882 succeeded the Greenback-Labor challenge; the Sayre Law followed the bitter Kolb insurgency in 1892. Despite legal and illegal barriers, black and white votes increased as long as the Populist Party could sustain its organization. Even its very existence in the late 1890s, after annual defeats had sapped its strength, raised the specter that a Populist victory would produce new election laws. Planters and industrialists were determined to write restrictions into the constitution where they could not be removed by simple legislative repeal.

In 1892, the Alabama Democratic platform urged a constitutional convention, looking to the Mississippi plan of 1890 as a model.[87] Democrats feared, however, to initiate a convention in 1893 because of the active opposition of the Alliances and the Populist Party. So long as the poor were politically active, constitutional disfranchisement was infeasible. Disfranchisement occurred only after the violent destruction of Populism, when the agrarian poor of both races were intimidated and left without effective organization.

Although the greatest support for constitutional revision came from the Black Belt, industrialists held the key positions in the 1901 Alabama convention that achieved constitutional disfranchisement. The chairman, John Knox, a lawyer for the dominant Louisville and Nashville Railroad, was from Anniston, a new industrial town in Calhoun County, a center of Populism and strikes. He wrote in *The Outlook* a few years after the convention: "The true philosophy of the movement was to establish restricted suffrage and to place the power of the government in the hands of the intelligent and virtuous." The language was almost identical to the words the Black Belt's Selma *Times* had used to celebrate the virtues of the 1892 Sayre Law, which had placed "authority in the hands of those best qualified to serve the people and promote their interests." To Knox, restriction was justified because "to say that those whose participation in the affairs of the state would endanger and imperil the good of the state have nevertheless the right to participate, is not only fallow in itself, but it is to set the individual above it."[88]

While the Black Belt registered its traditional fear of black domination, Frank S. White, a Birmingham industrialist, demonstrated that the capitalists, too, could speak the language of the plantation areas. "Time has demonstrated," he said, "that the negro has not capacity to rule, but a great capacity to ruin."[89]

The period 1897–1903 represented years of renewed working-class organization in Birmingham. The State Federation of Labor, formed in 1900, with black unionists in executive positions, was a major vehicle of racial cooperation. During 1899 and 1900, when the convention was being discussed, unskilled black miners and coke and steel workers had organized locals that engaged in militant, extended strikes, belying Birmingham's claims that it offered industrialists a cheap, docile, and divided labor force.[90] Workers in Birmingham, although in opposition to disfranchisement, were fighting for their organizations' legitimacy at the time of the convention. Although disfranchisement would ultimately make that work more difficult, the labor movement in Alabama was too weak and its potential numbers too small to mobilize a statewide opposition to disfranchisement.

The main opposition to disfranchisement came predictably from the "wire-grass" section of southeastern Alabama, the hill country, the older mining towns—areas of former or current Populist strength. But although Populists opposed disfranchisement,[91] the small number who voted for their delegates testifies to the demoralization of the old organization after years of struggle and defeat.[92] The ability to arouse people to defend voting rights in 1892 had been based on the union of formal rights and a party and program that promised changes in state policy. Events of the later 1890s eroded that hope. It was difficult to mobilize a defeated people to preserve rights that had not helped them gain their substantive ends. One black editor wrote: "It is good bye with poor white folks and niggers now, for the train of disfranchisement is on the rail and will come thundering upon us alike an avalanche, there is no use crying, we have got to shute the shute."[93]

The twentieth-century decline in voting revealed the success of the upper class in 1901. The most complete disfranchisement, of course, occurred among blacks. As always, the greatest fear of the laboring classes showed itself in Black Belt areas. Disfranchisement secured the labor and political needs of the Black Belt ruling class, which continued until the mechanization of cotton-picking after World War II made the plantations less dependent upon black labor.[94] It also allowed the industrialists to rule Alabama. The reduction of the number of black and white lower-class votes and the elite's tight control of the machinery of elections made popular challenges to the southern system impossible.

To see disfranchisement purely in terms of race, therefore, is inaccurate in several ways. Poor whites and white Populists were targets, too. But more important, to ignore Alabama's need to control the lower classes obscures the fact that racial controls were forms of class control and had identical roots. Periods of increasing racism, like the first decade of the twentieth century, also showed increasing labor exploitation. The nature of these controls changed, given the historical patterns of black and white labor. In the New South of the nineteenth century, blacks were the principal source of labor exploitation within the plantation belt, while many whites, although poor, were outside the cash-crop economy. This situation was modified in the late nineteenth century when formerly independent white farmers were drawn into the plantation economy as sharecroppers and tenants or joined blacks as part of the industrial proletariat. Yet the richest planters (and they were the ones who dominated the Democratic Party) used and preferred black laborers. Their domination of blacks served others, too. The racial controls that functioned to extract surplus value from black labor did this for all farm labor, which in turn produced the manpower for cheap industrial labor.

The varieties of forms of control used for black and white labor and the usefulness of the physical attributes of race as a means of exploitation only underscored the historicity of the labor systems and labor relations in the United States. Constitutional disfranchisement was tailored to disfranchise plantation workers by requiring literacy, cash payments, and the absence of a criminal record. The wide discretion given registrars provided the extra insurance to deny the determined voter. The early-twentieth-century political devices developed to neutralize the voters of the urban working class in northern cities (through city manager plans, nonpartisan tickets, etc.) were obviously different from southern disfranchisement, yet the two phenomena must be seen as having similar purposes.

By removing the lower class from politics, disfranchisement had enormous effects upon subsequent black and white political movements. It encouraged among northern blacks petit-bourgeois notions like Du Bois's "talented tenth." Although northern black leaders personally possessed more rights, they were basically proposing solutions for all the black people, nine-tenths of whom were southern. The prevalent northern ideologies, like the southern, were based upon appeals to the ruling elements of society. Whereas Washington tried to persuade whites of their self-interest, Du Bois appealed to their sense of justice and morality. Although Washington urged blacks to build up racial enterprises and Du Bois to fight for constitutional rights, both positions fused in practice. The two leaders perceived their roles as elevating a passive population.

Within the South, constitutional disfranchisement had more effect on the forms of black opposition than it did on the actions of the ruling class, whose behavior had merely been reinforced by the constitutional changes. Without the potential of mass politics, the militancy of black workers and farmers remained local. They were denied the possibility of linking up with other groups and deprived of the hope of participating in state governments.

Disfranchisement permitted the passage of Jim Crow laws. Since racial separation in major areas of social life was written into law, interracial action among the South's poor could be attempted only by heroes, not ordinary men. The condition that allowed blacks and whites to cooperate during the period of the Colored Farmers Alliance and the Southern Alliance had disappeared, and a mass Populist movement was unthinkable. Instead, black efforts to improve the conditions of black people were channeled into Tuskegee-like institutions, or else black militants migrated.

Black businessmen frequently became community leaders in the cities. Learning from Washington that politics was an essential supplement to economic activity, the business elite attempted to influence the politics of the South, but with nonpolitical organizations dedicated to purely racial goals. Where black Populists had believed the race's particular burdens could be removed only by popular power, the black petit-bourgeoisie of the twentieth century attempted to bargain with those who ruled. Because disfranchisement immunized them from black mass pressure, they initially conducted single-issue campaigns against the new racial laws and created ad hoc organizations unconnected with the tradition of mass Populism. Without support from either the white elite or the black majorities, their struggles against the new Jim Crow laws collapsed. After boycotting failed to remove laws mandating Jim Crow streetcars in some Southern cities, they attempted to establish transportation companies of their own, but their efforts to provide the first-class service the laws proscribed failed.[95]

For poor whites, cut off from the black working and agricultural classes by disfranchisement and Jim Crow, mass politics became impossible. They drifted into apathy and individual quest for survival, which sometimes involved opportunistic practices against blacks. Southern politicians proclaimed a white solidarity and ritually attacked "the interests," as well as other alien forces, but countenanced the domination of their society by the owners of capital.

After the destruction of Populism, therefore, one by one the institutions of the South erected barriers, making it difficult to challenge southern society from within. Disfranchisement and Jim Crow institutionalized modes of black protest that had previously existed only as tendencies. Now they were reinforced by social forces affecting all southern classes. This pattern survived as the basis of the southern order until after World War II. This was the era of Booker T. Washington.

To understand the development of black leadership and movements, the language of mechanical oscillations between protest and withdrawal, integration and nationalism, is inadequate. I have tried to suggest a framework that makes intelligible the facts that are known and to point to areas that need to be investigated. The form and content of black politics depended on the experiences of the various classes that composed the society in which it operated. The resulting black culture included the development of a number of strategies. Implicit in the view I have tried to present is that one cannot understand the development of culture and politics from within the black community alone. Most historians accept this in the abstract. In practice, the dialectic operating between blacks and whites is ignored, and racism is given as the explanation of behavior. While racism has been present in American history, it has not been causal. To understand the behavior of various white groups toward blacks, and blacks toward whites, one must understand the larger forces at work and the structures of power in the society. By reifying and isolating race consciousness and racism, these relationships are ignored, with the result that the function of racism in maintaining the power of the bourgeoisie is distorted, and we are led to believe that men make history according to their racial likes and dislikes.

NOTES

1. The title of this chapter, of course, is the title of W. E. B. DuBois's initial criticism of Washington in *The Souls of Black Folk* (Chicago: McClurg, 1903).

2. C. Vann Woodward, *Origins of the New South, 1877–1913* (Baton Rouge: Louisiana State University Press, 1951); August Meier, *Negro Thought in America, 1880–1915* (Ann Arbor: University of Michigan Press, 1963); Louis R. Harlan, *Booker T. Washington: The Making of a Black Leader, 1856–1901* (Oxford: Oxford University Press 1972); Louis Harlan, ed., *Booker T. Washington Papers* (Urbana: University of Illinois Press, 1972–1974).

3. Meier, *Negro Thought in America,* 8 (emphasis added).

4. Ibid., 22 (emphasis added).

5. Ibid., 23.

6. Ibid.

7. A good beginning and overview of this subject is Harold M. Baron's "Demand for Black Labor: Historical Notes on the Political Economy of Racism," *Radical America* 5 (March–April 1971): 1–46.

8. The most obvious means of breaking the planters' power—land confiscation—was espoused by a few individuals. That proposal collided with the capitalist notion of property.

Despite its expedient use during the war, reflecting the army's need to defeat the Confederacy, maintain order in conquered areas, and recruit blacks for armed service, after the war was over land division was not the goal of any social class in the society—except, of course, the former slaves.

9. Woodward, *Origins of the New South,* 23–24; Vincent P. De Santis, *Republicans Face the Southern Question—The New Departure Years, 1877–1897* (Baltimore: Johns Hopkins University Press, 1959), 23.

10. *Conservative Address,* 1870, 4, cited in Jack P. Maddex Jr., *The Virginia Conservatives, 1867–1879: A Study in Reconstruction Politics* (Chapel Hill: University of North Carolina Press, 1970), 194.

11. *Alabama Beacon,* December 7, 1867, cited in Peter Kolchin, *First Freedom: The Response of Alabama's Blacks to Emancipation and Reconstruction* (Westport, CT: Greenwood, 1972), 54.

12. George R. Lamplugh examined the black image in the fiction of magazines like *Atlantic Monthly, Harper's, Scribner's Magazine,* and the *Century* in "Image of the Negro in Popular Magazine Fiction, 1875–1900," *Journal of Negro History* 57 (April 1972): 177–189.

13. Cited in Howard A. White, *Freedmen's Bureau in Louisiana* (Baton Rouge: Louisiana State University Press, 1970), 107. Because most poor whites were outside the plantation economy, the terms *labor* and *blacks* were used interchangeably.

14. John H. Bracey Jr., August Meier, and Elliott M. Rudwick, eds., *The Afro-Americans: Selected Documents* (Boston: Beacon, 1972), 239–241.

15. Willie Lee Rose, *Rehearsal for Reconstruction: The Port Royal Experiment* (Oxford: Oxford University Press, 1964), esp. chaps. 10 and 13 and Epilogue.

16. Okon Edet Uya, *From Slavery to Public Service: Robert Smalls, 1839–1915* (Oxford: Oxford University Press, 1971), 87–89; George B. Tindall, *South Carolina Negroes, 1877–1900* (Columbia: University of South Carolina Press, 1952), 99–100. A simultaneous erosion of Radical ideology occurred in the North. Although working-class pressure on Radical politicians won an eight-hour day in the legislatures of several northern states, capitalist resistance made the laws inoperative. When workers struck, the courts and public opinion upheld the capitalists' prerogatives. David Montgomery, *Beyond Equality: Labor and Radical Republicans, 1862–1872* (New York: Knopf, 1967), chap. 8. The implications of Montgomery's work have not yet been absorbed into the literature of southern radicalism.

17. A good example of this phenomenon was the career of Jack Turner, black Republican leader in Choctaw County, Alabama. The story of this former slave is told by William Warren Rogers and Robert David Ward in *August Reckoning: Jack Turner and Racism in Post–Civil War Alabama* (Baton Rouge: Louisiana State University Press, 1973).

18. The declining numbers of black votes set the stage for the rise of the lily-white faction of the Republican Party. Throughout this period, black Republican leaders complained of their winning fewer appointments from the federal government and their declining influence in the southern Republican parties. Historians have again used the general rubric of increasing racism to explain the rise of the lily-whites. It was unlikely, however, that white Republican leaders suddenly altered their opinions of their former black colleagues. Rather, in the struggles for patronage, black leaders could safely be ignored when they no longer performed their function—bringing out the black vote—or when that function was no longer necessary.

19. Woodward, *Origins of the New South,* chap. 5.

20. De Santis, *Republicans Face the Southern Question,* 178–180, 191. A good example of this power was the gerrymandering of Alabama in 1891. So secure were the white Democrats of their control in the plantation areas that whereas in the 1875 apportionment all Black Belt counties were grouped together so that they would yield only one seat, in 1891 they attached one or two Black Belt counties to each surrounding congressional district so that by manipulating the totals the Democrats could win them all. Malcolm Cook McMillan, *Constitutional Development in*

Alabama, 1798–1901: A Study in Politics, the Negro, and Sectionalism (Chapel Hill: University of North Carolina Press, 1955), 22.

21. Although at times there was conflict between plantation and industrial interests, each needed the other to discipline and rule the majority of black and white laborers and farmers in the South. This need overshadowed the continuous competition for labor and capital resources. Over time, the planters merged with merchant and financial interests, an early social development of the postbellum South produced by the crop-lien system. Unlike other forms of agrarian credit, this system required the farmer to pledge his unplanted crop to pay for loans and supplies necessary to produce the crop. Not only did the crop-lien system extract high rates of interest, but it also gave the merchants control over the production process itself while encouraging the planting of cash crops. Merchants either gained control of the plantations or prosperous planters moved to town and became merchants themselves (Woodward, *Origins of the New South,* 180–184). This process only narrowed the credit resources of small farmers and sharecroppers. Therefore, even though agricultural interests were subordinate to northern capital, the larger planters, with capital and political power, survived and prospered.

22. A fascinating account of the response of black and white coal miners in the late 1870s can be found in Herbert Gutman's collection of letters, "Black Coal Miners and the Greenback-Labor Party in Redeemer, Alabama, 1878–1879," *Labor History* 10 (Summer 1969): 506–535. See also William Rogers and Robert Ward, *Labor Revolt in Alabama: The Great Strike of 1894* (Tuscaloosa: University of Alabama Press, 1965), 23, 35, 37.

23. Capital penetration affected, directly and indirectly, all aspects of the farmer's life. For instance, railroad construction was primarily for the purpose of capital investment, particularly in minerals. The new railroad networks did not help the farmer. Frequently, by introducing western competition, they harmed him. Always his transportation needs were secondary and, in many cases, unfulfilled.

24. John T. Morgan, "The Danger of the Farmers' Alliances," *Forum* 12 (November 1891): 407.

25. William W. Rogers, *The One-Gallused Rebellion: Agrarianism in Alabama, 1865–1896* (Baton RougeL Louisiana State University Press, 1970), 140–141.

26. Rogers, "The Negro Alliance in Alabama," *Journal of Negro History* 45 (January 1960): 38–44; Rogers, *The One-Gallused Rebellion,* 131, 141–146. It is very difficult to obtain data on the black Alliances—in part because historians have not sought them. Even if they have the incentive, however, students will experience difficulties because surviving black Alliance newspapers are practically nonexistent. Although some Populist newspapers are to be found, they represent a tiny proportion of those published. It is difficult to find personal papers of Alliance leaders because they were not of the class that kept records. Probably the best source is the local Bourbon newspapers. Obviously, these must be read with great care because of their bias. Some surviving black urban papers also reported on the Alliance.

27. Rogers, "Negro Alliance in Alabama," 42.

28. N. A. Dunning, *The Farmers' Alliance History and Agricultural Digest* (Washington, DC: N.p., 1891), 162–163.

29. Cited in Dunning, *The Farmers' Alliance,* 275.

30. Lawrence C. Goodwyn, "Origins and Development of Populism," unpub. Ph.D. diss., University of Texas, 1971, 342. It would seem that the black Republicans found the Alliances more threatening, initially, than the Democratic Party did. Black Republican boss Norris Cuney of Texas actively discouraged blacks from joining. Goodwyn, "Origins and Development of Populism," 281.

31. Ibid., 343.

32. Cited in Rogers, *The One-Gallused Rebellion,* 263.

33. Ibid., 142.

34. Ibid., 219–220.

35. Ibid., 218.

36. Sidney H. Kessler, "The Organization of Negroes in the Knights of Labor," *Journal of Negro History* 37 (July 1952): 248–275.

37. Woodward, *Origins of the New South,* 253–254.

38. William Ivy Hair, *Bourbonism and Agrarian Protest: Louisiana Politics, 1877–1900* (Baton Rouge: Louisiana State University Press, 1969), 255.

39. President Harrison speeded that process by appointing black men to positions in the larger southern cities. This reflected the demographic shift of black Republicans out of the Black Belt and encouraged the movement by giving black politicians strong ties to the national GOP. Because their positions frequently threw them into contact with the local business class, it established bonds here, too. De Santis, *Republicans Face the Southern Question,* 223.

40. Many historians have mistaken the black Republican elite's opposition to Populism for black people's opposition. See William Chafe, "The Negro and Populism: A Kansas Case Study," *Journal of Southern History* 34 (1968): 402–419. Because much of the evidence on black attitudes in this period comes from the urban black press, published by the small business and professional classes, and frequently subsidized by the GOP, historians have concluded that blacks were not interested in the radical economic doctrines of Populism. Chafe is partly correct when he says that some individuals had reason to support the Bourbons, and some eventually did. For example, Norris Cuney, by supporting the Democrats, advanced his own labor contracting business in Galveston, and William Stevens furthered his newly incorporated Afro-Americans Mill Company. But to argue that the Bourbons could offer anything to the masses of black people is to misunderstand Democratic rule in the South.

41. Helen Grew Edmonds, *The Negro and Fusion Politics in North Carolina, 1894–1901* (Chapel Hill: University of North Carolina Press 1951), 34–64.

42. *Booker T. Washington Papers,* vol. 2, 351.

43. Lawrence D. Rice, *The Negro in Texas, 1874–1900* (Baton Rouge: Louisiana State University Press, 1971), 71–73.

44. In Alabama, for instance, William Stevens, a former legislator from Selma, head of the Black and Tan faction of the Republican Party, moved to Anniston, an industrial town in the new mineral region, in 1887.

45. July 14, 1881. *Booker T. Washington Papers,* vol. 2, 140. Much of the response of Washington and Tuskegee's teachers to the rural blacks of Macon County conveyed this missionary attitude. When Olivia A. Davidson, Washington's second wife, observed a camp meeting thirteen miles from Tuskegee, she wrote: "Their strange costumes, customs, wild religious services, songs and shoutings . . . made up a scene . . . which is utterly indescribable." Olivia Davidson to Mary Berry, September 12, 1881, ibid., 148.

46. Washington to James Fowler Baldwin Marshall, March 4, 1883, ibid., 221; Washington to *Southern Workman,* September 10, 1881, ibid., 146.

47. Washington to John Gideon Harris, February 20, 1822, ibid., vol. 3, 215.

48. Cited in Harlan, *Booker T. Washington,* 200–201.

49. Washington, "Atlanta Exposition Address," in *Negro Social and Political Thought, 1850–1920,* Howard Brotz, ed. (New York: Basic Books, 1966), 356–362.

50. Baton Rouge *Daily Advocate,* March 1, 1896, cited in Hair, *Bourbonism,* 256.

51. Harlan, *Booker T. Washington,* 224–228.

52. DuBois sent Washington enthusiastic congratulations for "a word fitly spoken." DuBois to Washington, September 24, 1895, in *The Correspondence of W. E. B. DuBois,* vol. 1, ed. Herbert Aptheker (Amherst: University of Massachusetts Press, 1973), 39. DuBois urged black self-help during this period of his career. He told Negroes "that they must not expect to have things done for them—they MUST DO FOR THEMSELVES; that they have on their hands a vast work

of self-reformation to do, and that a little less complaint and whining, and a little more dogged work and manly striving would do us more credit and benefit than a thousand Force or Civil Rights bills." "The Conservation of the Races" (1897), in *Negro and Social Political Thought,* 490. DuBois, like Washington, did not object to literacy tests, as long as they made no racial distinctions. This agreement illustrated how he, like Washington, saw no political role for black masses.

53. Charles A. Roxborough, a former black Republican politician and lawyer, was a good example of one of these prosperous blacks. He left the old party because in Louisiana both major parties tended "towards that same goal—white supremacy." Roxborough to J. S. Davidson, July 31, 1890. Cited in Hair, *Bourbonism,* 223. The presence of former black Republicans who were attracted to Populism for its civil rights position weakened Populism's radical thrust. Some, principally urban, petit-bourgeois leaders, eschewed economic radicalism. See Chafe, "The Negro and Populism." Yet other members of this class did able organizing work. John Raynor of East Texas, a former school principal and Republican, braved the Black Belt of Texas to organize and educate blacks. The black petit-bourgeoisie as a class took a variety of positions. With popular pressure in this period many chose to work with the masses. Without that possibility after disfranchisement, many migrated (Roxborough moved to Detroit in the late 1890s) or opted for Washington's solution. John Raynor, after a period of chastisement, won good standing with the Texas Democrats and, by advocating vocational education, became principal of a school. Jack Abramowitz, "John B. Raynor—A Grass Roots Leader," *Journal of Negro History* (April 1951): 160–193.

54. This made the Populist approach to constitutional rights different from Du Bois's subsequent position, embodied in the Niagara movement in 1905 and then the NAACP in 1909. Despite some of the rhetoric in the Niagara movement, the praxis of both organizations—the appeal to the courts and politicians of the major parties—assumed that a part of the ruling class had an interest in the preservation of black rights. The position emerged among northern black leaders when the Jim Crow era had definitively created a system that rendered black achievement insignificant. If blacks acquired education and wealth but were Jim Crowed, Du Bois's earlier stress on self-improvement was inadequate.

55. While wooing some black leaders, the Bourbons attempted to convince white agrarian leaders that their home was in the Democratic Party. These appeals took the form of rhetorical expressions of sympathy for farmers and the creation of nonpolitical farmers' organizations dominated by larger planters. Sometimes, too, as in the case of some blacks, money was given to prominent leaders.

56. Atlanta *Constitution,* September 20, 1895, cited in Robert Factor, *The Black Response to America: Men, Ideals, and Organization from Frederick Douglass to NAACP* (Reading, MA: Addison-Wesley, 1970), 169.

57. C. Vann Woodward, *Tom Watson: Agrarian Rebel* (Oxford: Oxford University Press 1963), 270–277.

58. Goodwyn, "Origins and Development of Populism," 429, 395–398.

59. Harlan, *Booker T. Washington,* 227–228; Meier, *Negro Thought in America,* 25.

60. Although most blacks were agricultural workers, Afro-Americans were the principal source of unskilled labor in the new industries of the South, analogous to the immigrants in the North. In Alabama at the time of the coal strike of 1894, blacks were 46 percent of the workers in the struck mines. By 1910, 55 percent of the coal miners and 80 percent of the iron-ore miners in Alabama were black. They held the majority of unskilled jobs as well in the new iron and steel industry in Alabama. In other southern states the pattern was similar in shipbuilding, dock work, tobacco, as well as in some of the traditional crafts. Paul B. Worthman and James R. Green, "Black Workers in the New South, 1865–1915," in Nathan Huggins, *Key Issues in the Afro-American Experience,* (Belmont, CA: Wadsworth, 1971), vol. 2, 52–53.

61. Factor, *The Black Response to America,* 197.

62. For examples of a student's response to the mines see two letters from David Lee Johnson to Washington, May 31, July 19, 1887, in *Washington Papers,* vol. 2, 356–357, 371–373.

63. C. Vann Woodward's recent statement on the origins of Jim Crow was basically the result of his ignoring black militancy in the 1890s. *American Counterpoint: Slavery and Racism in North-South Dialogue* (Boston: Little, Brown, 1971), 253, 258–259. It perpetuated the notion of upper-class paternalism and the determining role of popular racism. The Jim Crow system became "modified paternalism," while "the escalation of lynching, disfranchisement, and proscription reflected concessions to the white lower class." To Woodward, the new system was shaped by the upper class's desire to continue its personal and paternal relationships with blacks. Thus, ruling-class behavior was determined by desires for personal relationships with subordinates. Written by a former Beardian, this is truly a strange history of Jim Crow.

64. Allen Johnston Going, *Bourbon Democracy in Alabama, 1874–1890* (Tuscaloosa: University of Alabama Press, 1951), 93–95, 118. In Alabama, where the Reconstruction Constitution of 1868 had exempted $500 worth of property, the new Constitution of 1875 exempted individual items on farms. Small farmers, mechanics, and laboring men could no longer deduct $500 worth of property, whereas the large planters could write off thousands.

65. Kessler, "The Organization of Negroes in the Knights of Labor," 265–266.

66. Maddex, *The Virginia Conservatives,* 200–202.

67. Harlan, *Booker T. Washington,* 231.

68. Woodward, *Origins of the New South,* 352.

69. Even in this area, the historian should be cautious. In the Populist era, many farmer and labor groups had their own newspapers. One should not assume the same ideological hegemony that exists in mid-twentieth century sources of information.

70. There is little written on the attitudes of poor whites, most of whom are "anonymous." In most cases the attitudes of the group—which included small farmers, "dirt" farmers, and skilled or unskilled workers—have been inferred from incidents of racial conflict. Sometimes they are read into a period, using evidence from earlier or later periods. One racist politician frequently serves as evidence for the whole group. The demon of race is easily invoked and becomes a facile substitute for serious analysis.

71. Horace Mann Bond, *Negro Education in Alabama* (Washington DC: Associated Publishers, 1939), 148–163.

72. Blacks and whites moved together in other ways. In many parts of the southern Black Belt, especially in the older cotton-growing states, there was black movement out of the old cotton areas and into the previously all-white counties. This movement came about at the time of the growth of a white tenantry, which made the economic positions of the two groups more similar than they had been. See Monroe H. Work, "Racial Factors and Economic Forces in Land Tenure in the South," *Social Forces* 15, no. 2 (December 1936): 208.

73. Goodwyn, "Origins of Populism," 272.

74. Ibid., 373–374.

75. See, for example, Lawrence Goodwyn, "Populist Dreams and Negro Rights: East Texas as a Case Study," *American Historical Review* 76 (December 1971): 1435–1456.

76. Goodwyn, "Origins of Populism," 373–374.

77. Hackney, *Populism to Progressivism in Alabama,* 181–84; see also Charles Wynes, *Race Relations in Virginia, 1870–1902* (Charlottesville: University Press of Virginia. 1961), and Henry C. Dethloff and Robert R. Jones, "Race Relations in Louisiana, 1877–1898," *Louisiana History* 9 (Fall 1968): 305–317. Another indication of the novelty of the Jim Crow system was the reaction of the urban black middle class at the turn of the century. August Meier and Elliot Rudwick wrote that for them "the new order was startling, even shocking." "The Boycott

Movement Against Jim Crow Streetcars in the South, 1900–1906," *Journal of American History* 55 (March 1969): 756–775.

78. Goodwyn, "Origins of Populism," 374. The depression of the 1890s also produced racist practices among other whites. Sometimes "whitecapping," terrorism against blacks, and Populism occurred in the same county. (Clay County, Alabama, produced both the leading Alabama Populist, William Manning, and the future head of the new Ku Klux Klan of the 1920s, Hirman Evans.) The racist response among poor whites seemed to have been most common in areas where planters and merchants took over the land of independent white farmers while bringing in a black labor supply. William F. Holmes, "Whitecapping in Mississippi: Agrarian Violence in the Populist Era," *Mid-America* 55 (April 1973): 134–148, and his "Whitecapping: Agrarian Violence in Mississippi, 1902–1906," *Journal of Southern History* 25 (1969): 165–185. Without an instrument or ideology to combat the planters and merchants, opposition in these areas sometimes took the form of violence against the blacks, frequently organized by local political aspirants. In the older Black Belt counties, the political and economic power and racist ideology of the planter class created a social atmosphere that encouraged whites, rich or poor, to translate personal and social conflicts with blacks into violence.

79. Harlan, *Booker T. Washington,* 255.

80. Rogers, *One-Gallused Rebellion,* 220–227.

81. Ibid., 219.

82. Ibid.

83. Going, *Bourbon Democracy in Alabama,* 33.

84. A leading spokesman of the Louisiana oligarchy put it bluntly during the fusion campaign of 1896: "It is the religious duty of Democrats to rob Populists and Republicans of their votes whenever and wherever the opportunity presents it self. . . . The Populists and Republicans are our legitimate political prey. Rob them! You bet! What are we here for?" Shreveport *Evening Judge,* December 15, 1895. Cited in Hair, *Bourbonism,* 260.

85. Hackney, *Populism to Progressivism in Alabama,* 119.

86. Harlan, *Booker T. Washington,* 289, 292. Harlan's effort to preserve the notion of "whites of good will" becomes absurd when he characterizes the espousal of the repeal of the Fifteenth Amendment by the Reverend Edgar Gardner Murphy, a friend of Washington, as "muddled." Ibid., 292.

87. Hackney, *Populism to Progressivism in Alabama,* 149.

88. John B. Knox, "Reduction of Representation in the South," *Outlook* 79 (1905): 171.

89. Montgomery *Advertiser,* March 15, 1901. Cited in Hackney, *Populism to Progressivism in Alabama,* 175.

90. See Paul B. Worthman, "Black Workers and Labor Unions in Birmingham, Alabama, 1897–1904," *Labor History* 10 (Summer 1969): 375–407.

91. Horace Mann Bond concluded that there "had not been a development of anti-Negro sentiment in the counties almost entirely populated by white persons. The most virulent anti-Negro speakers were from the Black Belt or from counties bordering on the Black Belt; and from counties where the new industrialization was developing." Bond, *Negro Education in Alabama,* 168. Representatives from poor white counties voted against the general disfranchisement article. They also opposed Alabama's "Fighting Grandfather Clause," which was supposed to offer poor whites with a military record a temporary loophole. This infamous clause has been used to show that poor whites supported the disfranchisement of blacks. It has been used also to demonstrate that the "better whites" were not hostile to blacks because a few leaders opposed the clause. But because those who supported it stressed the fact that it was temporary, the debate was really about the tactics of achieving ratification. To argue that the opponents of the clause were southern paternalists, friendly to blacks, necessitates ignoring the context of the debates. The majority of planters, bosses, and industrialists supported the clause. If the intention of

its insertion was to sweeten disfranchisement for the poor whites, it failed to work. Hackney, *Populism to Progressivism in Alabama,* 357.

92. Ibid., 153.

93. Huntsville *Journal,* April 20, 1900. Cited in ibid., 157.

94. These changes were the social basis for the southern civil rights movement of the 1950s and 1960s. Harry C. Dillingham and David F. Sly, "The Mechanical Cotton-Picker, Negro Migration, and the Integration Movement," in *Black Society in the New World,* ed. Richard Frucht (New York: Random House, 1971), 115–126.

95. Meier and Rudwick, "The Boycott Movement."

Part II

The Jim Crow Era

What we typically recognize today as black American politics and thought emerged most crucially in relation to the regime of codified white supremacy that was imposed in all of the American South and in modified forms in border states and elsewhere in the decade or so on either side of the turn of the twentieth century. The Jim Crow regime and the struggle against it was a central problematic shaping forms and expressions of black Americans' race-conscious activity—strategic action, reflection, and debate—for at least two-thirds of the twentieth century. It was within the segregation era that the black American population became primarily urban and spread outside the South. Put perhaps more dramatically, it was in this era that a great deal of what most of us recognize, or imagine we do, about black Americans came into existence. From this perspective, it is not surprising that Part II is the largest section of this book.

The chapters in Part I consider the intellectual and political tendencies and dynamics—national and regional—out of which the segregationist social order took shape and examine black Americans' interpretive and programmatic responses to them. The chapters in Part II explore different moments of black thought and practice during the long Jim Crow era. William Jones's "How Black 'Folk' Survived in the Modern South" explores Zora Neale Hurston's development of a dialectical approach to the study of black cultural and economic transformation in the industrializing South of the 1920s and 1930s, noting how her own perceptions evolved as she confronted the complexity and fluidity of cultural practices that challenged static notions of racial authenticity. Kenneth Warren's "An Inevitable Drift?" explores, through a reading of the 1928 novel *Dark Princess,* tensions within W. E. B. Du Bois's elaboration of race-conscious politics and his ambivalent commitments to democracy and oligarchy in the 1920s. Touré Reed, in "The Educational Alliance and the Urban League in New York," examines some similar tensions through comparison of black and Jewish group advocacy and uplift organizations and the class character of their constructions of the mission of group uplift. Preston Smith, in "The Chicago School of Human Ecology and the Ideology of Black Civic Elites," demonstrates that a central strain in race-conscious black elites' critiques and programs for racial advancement in the 1940s and 1950s was significantly informed by the social theories associated with the University of Chicago sociology department.

Michele Mitchell's "'What a Pure, Healthy, Unified Race Can Accomplish'" focuses on the confluence of contemporary race theory and very conventional gender ideology in underwriting the Garvey movement's formulations of the role of women in the Universal Negro Improvement Association as well as Garveyite commitments to notions of racial purity and the control of black women's sexuality. This analysis sets the stage as well for consideration of the evolution of black political thought into the 1960s, as the Jim Crow era was defeated finally. Dean Robinson's "Black Power Nationalism as Ethnic Pluralism" demonstrates the extent to which the forms of ostensible black nationalism that emerged in the mid-1960s were embedded in patterns of discourse and practice of conventional social science and frameworks of ethnic pluralism and race relations.

3
How Black "Folk" Survived in the Modern South

Industrialization, Popular Culture, and the Transformation of Black Working-Class Leisure in the Jim Crow South

William P. Jones

> *Much is forever being made of the deleterious effects of slavery on the generations of black Americans that followed. But for some curious reason, nothing at all is ever made of the possibility that the legacy left by the enslaved ancestors of blues-oriented contemporary U.S. Negroes includes a disposition to confront the most unpromising circumstances and make the most of what little there is to go on, regardless of the odds—and not without finding delight in the process or forgetting mortality at the height of ecstasy. Still, there is a lot of admittedly infectious exuberance, elegance and nonsense to be accounted for.*
>
> —Albert Murray, *Stomping the Blues*[1]

When anthropologist Zora Neale Hurston arrived in Loughman, Florida, in 1927, she discovered a society in transition. Loughman was owned by the Everglades Cypress Lumber Company, one of more than 150 firms that operated at least 300 industrial sawmills along the Atlantic and Gulf Coasts of the southern United States.[2] Having leveled more than 150 million acres of southern forestland during the wasteful "cut-out-and-get-out" era between 1880 and 1920, Everglades and other firms were attempting to convert to a sustainable policy based on forest conservation and more efficient logging and milling. Such a strategy required a steady and experienced workforce, unlike the seasonal farm labor that had sustained early southern lumber production. To attract such a workforce, lumber firms turned primarily to African American men, many of them former seasonal employees. These black men were also searching for a new way of life. Since the Civil War, most African Americans had struggled to make a living through family farming, often piecing together income from their own plots, sharecropping, and seasonal wage work. Thousands of black men moved permanently into southern sawmill towns in the 1920s and 1930s, making a full-time occupation out of a previously supplementary pastime. Like other southern sawmill towns, Loughman was shaped by the sometimes parallel, often conflicting, and always changing interests of lumber companies and their employees.

Ironically, Hurston entered Loughman in search of a static and isolated "Negro folk culture." As a participant in the New Negro literary movement and a student of anthropologist Franz Boas, Hurston believed that rural southerners had preserved an authentic form of African American culture created by slavery and lost to herself and other participants in the Great Migration.[3] She sought this "old stuff" initially in the southern city of Jacksonville, but she left in dismay as the locals' "Negroness had been rubbed off by close contact with white culture."[4] Her next destination was Eatonville, the all-black agricultural village where she had spent her childhood and a place that she remembered as "the crib of negroism."[5] After a few days in her hometown, Hurston learned from locals that better sources of folklore were the sawmill towns and railroad camps surrounding Loughman. It is there that she gathered most of the material published in *Mules and Men,* which remains perhaps the most highly regarded collection of African American folklore. By the time she published that volume in 1935, Hurston had begun to revise her view of black culture to account for the changes that she observed in Loughman and also to understand better the relationship between black southerners and the broader popular culture of the modern United States in the 1920s and 1930s.

In this chapter, I read Hurston's writing in the context of the transformation of the southern lumber industry in the late 1920s and early 1930s. In contrast to previous scholars who have evaluated Hurston according to her ability to penetrate the barriers between "folk" and "mainstream" culture, I demonstrate that the culture documented in *Mules and Men* was a product not of isolation but of African Americans' participation in the process of modernization that transformed the Jim Crow South in the early twentieth century. Hurston's observation of that participation caused her to rethink the folklore model, and she eventually developed pieces of a more historical and dialectical approach to the study of African American culture. By overlooking this transformation in Hurston's thinking, current scholars fail to appreciate the insights that her writing offers for contemporary scholarship on black working-class history in the Jim Crow South.

Hurston was first attracted to Loughman by a romantic discourse concerning southern sawmill towns that was common in both popular music and scholarly writing in the 1920s. She wrote of hearing this discourse "set to music passed over the guitar strings" of Eatonville musicians in 1927. That experience sparked memories of earlier encounters. "Seems like when Ah was a child 'round here Ah heard de folks pickin' de guitar and singin' songs to dat effect," she wrote in *Mules and Men.*[6] Given their sources and their subjects, these songs were most likely adaptations of barrelhouse blues songs, which were among the earliest recorded black musical forms and which were products of southern sawmill towns. Blues is widely believed to have originated in the plantation South.[7] The country or Delta blues that became popular in the early 1930s was in many ways derivative, however, of a piano style developed by musicians who traveled among the sawmill towns and industrial work camps of the Gulf Coast in the 1910s and 1920s. Vaudeville performer Gertrude "Ma" Rainey brought national attention to barrelhouse music and culture through recordings such as her 1923 "Barrelhouse Blues" and the 1928 "Log Camp Blues," which she coauthored with composer Thomas Dorsey.[8] The legendary Robert Johnson, who is revered today as the prototypical wandering country blues man, learned the blues from older musicians in the southern Mississippi lumber town of Hazelhurst. Only after he developed a reputation and considerable skill did Johnson return to his home in the Delta. Johnson acknowledged his relationship to sawmill town culture when he sang "we still can barrelhouse" in his classic "Traveling Riverside Blues."[9]

While Rainey, Dorsey, and Johnson are not likely to have worked in the lumber industry, they brought national attention to a musical tradition that emerged primarily as entertainment for black industrial workers. Named for the company-operated saloons that one scholar described as "the social centers of every work camp," barrelhouse blues songs were composed to appeal to men who were temporarily separated from homes and communities in the plantation region.[10] Joseph Pleasant's "Sawmill Man Blues," for example, expressed the fears of a man forced to leave his lover in search of work. "An' when I'm on my job mama," the musician sang, "I don't want no man hangin' around." Like many blues artists, Pleasant offered his audience a positive interpretation of an otherwise lonely situation. "Yes, I'm workin' on the sawmill, sleepin' in a shack six feet wide. I see my gal every payday and I'm perfectly satisfied."[11] Lewis Black's "Gravel Camp Blues" also related the story of a man longing to return home after seasonal work; "ain't gonna be long, hey pretty mama ain't gonna be long." Black ended with an optimistic note about the possibilities for industrial employment in the rural South: "If I don't find no log camp, I'll find a gravel camp sure."[12]

Not all the characters in barrelhouse songs lamented their separation from agricultural homes. In fact, many songs related the possibilities for freedom and adventure that young African Americans saw in industrial settings. Joe Dean sang of being "so glad I'm twenty one years old today." Implying that maturity gave him independence to work away from home, Dean's character rejoiced that his "baby" could not longer "make no fool" out of him.[13] In "Evil Woman Blues," James Wiggins sang about a young man who woke up "every morning with leaving" on his mind: "Cause my momma's so evil, and she treats me so unkind." Wiggins ends the song with his character seeking to escape to Bogalusa, one the South's largest sawmill towns:

> Mr. conductor man, I wanna talk with you,
> I wanna ride your train from here to Bogalu.
> I wanna leave here this morning and I haven't got my fare,
> I want'a see if I can find my good girl there.[14]

Composed initially for rural African American men, barrelhouse blues popularized a romantic and yet partially accurate testimony to the hardships and possibilities offered by short-term industrial wage work.

While the promise of adventure and wages may have tempered separation from home during seasonal employment, plantations remained the centers of black family and community life through the 1920s. For that reason, barrelhouse musicians performed primarily to young men who were desperate for a break from the isolation and tedium of camp life. "Poor" Joe Williams, who performed in Mississippi and Alabama barrelhouses in the 1910s, described such an audience in an interview. "When somebody like me went through there it was like the President coming there," he recalled. "They'd come from all over—they hear of a man coming there with a guitar. They'd get real rough on Saturday night."[15] According to Texas pianist Robert Shaw, the few women who lived in sawmill towns were prostitutes hired to work in the barrelhouses where he performed: "Sheds lined with barrels of chock beer and raw whiskey, an open floor, a piano on a raised platform in the corner, a back door opening on a line of rooms, each with a woman and a bed."[16]

In these interviews, Williams and Shaw testified to a kernel of truth at the core of barrelhouse songs' descriptions of a "rough" sawmill town culture in the early-twentieth-century South. Distorted in their narrow focus on the leisure lives of men temporarily isolated from agricultural households and communities, these descriptions nevertheless reflected some reality about the heavy drinking, prostitution, and violence that often characterized leisure culture in transient industrial work camps. By disseminating these images through popular culture, musicians stripped them from their social and historical context, thereby allowing them to be interpreted as representative of rural African American culture in general. Historian Benjamin Filene has argued that early commercial recordings predated scholarly collection of African American folklore, providing many scholars with their initial introduction to what they assumed to be an undifferentiated and timeless "Negro folk culture." Even as they aimed to collect more "authentic" material than that available through commercial catalogues, these early folklorists accepted the categories created by producers of commercial popular music.[17]

A pioneer in the scholarly study of "Negro folklore," Howard W. Odum introduced barrelhouse blues as a lens through which to examine African American culture. A generation older than Hurston, Odum interpreted black men's seasonal labor migration initially as an inherited biological trait. "The Negro has little home conscience or love of home, no local attachment of the better sort," Odum wrote in

The Social and Mental Traits of the Negro, a 1910 study based on research in Mississippi. "He does not know in many cases for months or years the whereabouts of his brother and sister or even parents, nor does he concern himself about their welfare."[18] After studying under Franz Boas at Columbia University and particularly after reading the work of Hurston and other New Negroes, Odum began to investigate the social and historical roots of what he believed was the essential African American culture. This study culminated in a series of popular publications including his 1926 *Negro Workaday Songs* and a trilogy devoted to the life and songs of Black Ulysses, a wandering musician and wage worker who Odum described as "perhaps more representative of the Negro common man than any other."[19]

Framing the "bad men" and "black sirens" of barrelhouse blues as representative of black working-class southerners, Odum initiated a scholarly debate over the roots of black men and women's reputed "Ramblin' Minds." For his part, Odum attributed African Americans' failure to establish families and communities to the difficulty of being a "primitive man in a modern world."[20] Odum refused to "sentimentalize the Negro" but hoped that readers would find beauty in the "finer points of humor, pathos, and poignancy" that characterized black southerners' "native quests for satisfaction, adventure and sex love."[21] Historian Carter G. Woodson made a similar argument that "present-day troubles" such as "drinking and sexual indulgence" were a "natural consequence of passing through a transition period" from traditional to modern society. Due to the increased availability of radios, moving pictures, and automobiles, Woodson explained, even those black people who remained in agricultural communities had begun to reject what he believed were more traditional leisure activities such as barn raisings, harvest festivals, hunting, and "the popular picnic in the nearby woods." "Let us have recreation like that in the city," Woodson lampooned the calls of rural people. "Let it come from without rather than as formerly from within."[22]

Odum, Woodson, and other scholars were convinced that Jim Crow excluded African Americans from active participation in American society, and they portrayed black southerners as helpless victims of a foreign culture.[23] Forrester B. Washington, a National Urban League official who headed the Atlanta University School of Social Work, charged "industrial firms and railroads" with "forcing upon the Negro a taste for degraded forms of leisure time activities." By "deliberately setting up gambling games" and other seemingly unhealthy activities "as part of a recreational program" for their black employees, Washington explained, employers produced the "social pathology" that he believed plagued rural African Americans.[24] "Recreation among Negroes in the rural districts is a problem," Woodson agreed. "These people have such difficulty in making a living and must spend so much of their time in this important effort at self-preservation that little or no time is left for organized or directed recreation as it exists in urban centers." After all, the historian reasoned, "it does not require very much time for a man to get a drink and be happy with his dulcina."[25]

Both black and white scholars viewed the spread of commercial popular music as part of a broader process of cultural breakdown. The "universal constant" of rural life, in Odum's words, gave way to the modern "world of variables."[26] Whereas Odum interpreted barrelhouse recordings as simple reflections of that breakdown, Forrester Washington argued that record companies facilitated cultural disintegration by "almost forcing on the Negro race records that are distinctly immoral in their title and content." The social worker implied that white consumers had more discriminating tastes, charging record companies with taking advantage of black consumers' reputed inability to distinguish between moral and immoral culture: "Some of these records are so obscene that the companies have not the courage to advertise them in their regular catalogues, but issue special booklets for Negroes. Not content with issuing these booklets to Negroes, these companies also flaunt the suggesting titles of these records, accompanied by obscene pictures, in the Negro newspapers."[27]

From this perspective, the onslaught of modernization seemed so powerful that some sociologists became convinced that black people's only hope was to abandon their southern folkways for the modern urban culture of the North.[28] E. Franklin Frazier argued in a 1927 essay that slavery had destroyed black peoples' African heritage, presenting "the Negro masses" with a stark choice between "assimilation of American civilization" and "the disorganization of the past."[29] Restricted by segregation, Frazier argued in *The New Negro,* black people were capable of "absorbing the typical spirit and push of modern industrialism" only through wealth, formal education, or migration to the urban North.[30] "In ten years, Negroes have been actually transplanted from one culture to another," Charles S. Johnson rejoiced in reference to the Great Migration.[31] This thinking culminated in Frazier's 1939 study *The Negro Family in the United States,* which cited Odum's Black Ulysses as "a composite picture of the impulsive behavior of this group compressed into a single fictional character." Urban sociologists would later cite Frazier's study to justify their claim that that only dramatic federal intervention could address the "dense tangle of pathology" that black southerners had reputedly carried with them to the urban North.[32] Subsequent scholars have rejected the language of "pathology," but they retain the model of cultural competition that informed scholarly debates over black culture in the late 1920s.

Zora Neale Hurston traveled to Florida in 1927 with the explicit goal of correcting what she saw as Odum's condescending view of black "folk" culture.[33] Initially, she did not challenge the white scholar's basic premise that black industrial communities were both isolated from white culture and representative of the "Negro South" in general.[34] After spending nearly three years in Loughman and other southern lumber towns, and particularly after returning to Florida with the Federal Writers Project in 1934, however, Hurston began to acknowledge the extent to which African American leisure culture in these towns was part of the broader biracial popular culture of the modern United States.

Even as she entered Loughman in 1927, the anthropologist's vision of an isolated "folk" world gave way to a "huge smokestack blowing smut against the sky" and a "big sign" that announced her entry into the domain of the Everglades Cypress Lumber Company. Shortly after arriving in Loughman, she discovered that institutions such as jook joints, which she had seen as essentially black cultural spaces, were in fact products of social contestation between black workers and their white employers. She also found more diverse black communities than she had expected, populated by black women and children who had begun to settle in what were previously male-dominated, seasonal work camps. This diversity was reflected in the variety of leisure activities that she observed, which included barrelhouses but also included parties in private homes, organized baseball games, and swing dances that demonstrated these towns' participation in the evolution of mass popular culture in the 1920s and 1930s.

Over the next three years on the Gulf Coast, and then in Florida as a researcher for the Federal Writers Project, Hurston adapted her analysis to account for the dynamic and cosmopolitan nature of southern leisure culture. After spending two months in Florida she continued her fieldwork in the "locale of sawmills, lumber camps and fishermen" surrounding Mobile, Alabama. She then traveled to New Orleans and finally to Bogalusa, Louisiana, which she described as a "huge industrial center, [with] sawmills, paper mills, chicken hatcheries and reforestation nurseries."[35] Rejecting a cultural pluralism inspired by Odum and the New Negro movement, Hurston began to acknowledge modern influences within southern African American culture. "Negro folklore is not a thing of the past," she wrote in 1934. "It is still in the making. Its great variety shows the adaptability of the black man: nothing is too old or too new, domestic or foreign, high or low for his use."[36]

Subsequent scholars have ignored this evolution of Hurston's thinking, therefore evaluating *Mules and Men* according to the author's initial goal of penetrating the cultural barriers between "Negro folk" and the white or interracial "mainstream" of modern America. Historian Robin D.G. Kelley, for example, cites Hurston's work as a model for historians who seek entry into the "unmonitored, unauthorized social sites in which black workers could freely articulate" a cultural critique of "the prevailing class-conscious, individualist ideology of the white ruling classes."[37] Literary critic Hazel Carby is more critical of *Mules and Men,* but not because it portrayed Loughman as isolated from modern culture. Repeating the criticism of Hurston's contemporaries Richard Wright and Arna Bontemps, Carby charges the anthropologist with a "nostalgic attempt to preserve a disappearing form of folk culture." By essentializing black people as "primarily rural and oral," Carby argues that "Hurston did not take seriously the possibility that African American culture was being transformed as African American peoples migrated from rural to urban areas."[38] Kelley and Carby echo opposing sides of the 1920s' debate, assuming that black people faced a choice between black tradition and white modernity.[39]

As Hurston discovered, neither position could account for the degree to which the changes that she observed in Loughman articulated transformations that occurred within southern society. Industrialization had shaped southern society since before the Civil War, but the 1920s brought a particularly dramatic change. The collapse of southern agriculture, accompanied by the expansion of industrial employment in both the North and the South, sparked a mass exodus from the plantation regions where the majority of African Americans remained after the end of slavery. While textile mills and many urban employers reserved industrial jobs for whites, southern lumber firms recruited black men with offers of steady work and wages far higher than they had earned in agriculture. Many of these men brought skills and experience accumulated through years of seasonal employment in sawmill towns and logging camps. Starting in the 1920s, they began to settle permanently in those places, either bringing families with them or building new ones in the black working-class communities that began to appear in mill towns.

When Hurston traveled to southern sawmill towns in the late 1920s, they exhibited characteristics of this transition. The songs that first enticed the anthropologist to Loughman related stories of male industrial workers such as John Henry, single women (or "jook lights"), and "sawmill and turpentine bosses and prison camp 'cap'ns.'" Such images reflected a popular view of the rural South as filled with transient black men, black women who were employed to entertain them, and white authorities who were charged with keeping them at work and well-behaved. This was a partially accurate description of black working-class leisure culture in sawmill towns during the "cut-out-and-get-out" period, when lumber firms provided seasonal employment to men whose families most often remained in plantation regions. Upon her arrival in Loughman, however, Hurston also discovered features of a more age- and gender-balanced leisure culture, one rooted in black working-class households and communities that began to appear in southern sawmill towns in the 1920s and 1930s. These two cultures were not distinct but represented extremes on a continuum of industrialization in the South. Neither were they isolated from modern, mainstream, or white culture. They both expressed African American southerners' participation in the industrial transformation of the region.

Hurston's first indications that she was not leaving "white culture" when she drove into Loughman were "signs all over that this was private property and that no one could enter without the consent of the company." She avoided detection by white authorities only because a black woman named Mrs. Allen, who "ran the boardinghouse under patronage of the company," took her in. When a fight broke out at the town's barrelhouse, Hurston noted that the "only thing that could have stopped the killing occurred [when the] Quarter Boss stepped in the door with a .45 in his hand and another on his hip." His timing led her to "expect he had been eavesdropping as usual." She discovered that company officials used vagrancy laws to secure particular employees and that they allowed unemployed women to live in Loughman on the condition that they did not carry guns or kill more than "their quota" of black men. Parties and dances were timed not by "folk" traditions in Loughman but by pay schedules at the sawmills: "They paid off twice a month and pay night was big doings."[40]

While they differed from other scholarly depictions of an isolated black culture, Hurston's observations of Loughman parallel those provided in interviews with barrelhouse musicians. Danny Barker, an African American musician from New Orleans, recalled that local officials played an important role shaping black leisure in the Mississippi and Louisiana towns that he visited in the early 1920s. When Barker and his mentor Eureal "Little Brother" Montgomery arrived in Crystal Springs, Mississippi, they arranged to play a "jook dance" in the rear of a local cafe. After the pair played "a couple of dances," Barker was terrified to see a white sheriff enter the room. He assumed that the dance would be shut down, until he noticed that the officer was "followed by two colored men who carried gallon jugs of 'smoke'—that's what they called moonshine whiskey." After the men made their delivery, the sheriff sat near the door eating chicken and biscuits while the dancing continued. Barker watched nervously as the white man "took off his two large ugly looking pistols and placed them on the table." After that, he added, "the place really jumped."[41]

Joseph E. McCaffrey, the white manager of a logging camp near Savannah, Georgia, in the 1920s, explained that lumber companies countenanced drinking and gambling among black workers, even in the midst of Prohibition, because they believed that it attracted young black men to their towns. Whereas white workers frequented bars in nearby towns, segregation left black workers with fewer options for leisure. At a time when thousands of rural blacks were heading for large northern cities, lumber companies worked to ensure that some of the Great Migration headed their way. "We always had places for entertainment, commonly known as jooks," McCaffrey explained. On Saturday nights, the company hired local deputies to keep outsiders off the premises and to maintain "reasonable control over liquid refreshments and disturbances."

Barrelhouses had the added advantage of keeping black workers within the legal jurisdiction of their employers. "When we established a camp," McCaffrey continued, "we'd go to the sheriff and say, 'We're going to set up a log camp and sawmill here. We've got a quarter boss and we'd like to have him deputized." McCaffrey asked the local sheriff to check with them before arresting any employee charged with a crime outside company property. "They always cooperated with us," he claimed. "We never had any trouble in that respect."[42] By providing spaces for drinking and sex, employers created an environment that they believed would attract a steady supply of young black men.

As efforts toward social engineering, barrelhouses were in some respects analogous to the "welfare" programs that other industrial employers developed to attract steady and reliable labor supplies in the early twentieth century.[43] Because barrelhouses were constructed exclusively for black employees, they in fact complemented reform strategies that lumber firms directed toward white workers by emphasizing the contrast between white and black working-class leisure. Alabama mill owner John Kaul called for a "new welfare emphasis in the southern lumber industry" in his 1914 presidential address to the Yellow Pine Manufacturer's Association. When the *American Lumberman* described the health and educational programs that Kaul developed to inspire this initiative, the trade journal noted "a separate passage" to the "Negro quarters" among the facilities that contributed to the "home and community spirit" enjoyed by white employees.[44] Great Southern Lumber Company encouraged a similar spirit in Bogalusa by housing white workers on Pleasant Hill, separated from the noise and pollution of the mill and the "Negro Quarter," a fifteen-block triangle squeezed between the mill and the Columbia Street commercial district. By restricting barrelhouses to Columbia Street, Great Southern maintained the spatial association between vice and black workers.[45] Employers' cooperation with local law enforcement reinforced this association, by allowing white workers to drink and dance in surrounding communities while restricting black leisure to the jurisdiction of their employers.[46]

Such details appear to support Washington's and Woodson's contention that barrelhouse culture was a white invention imposed on black people. What both scholars overlooked, however, was the extent to which lumber company managers acted within limits set by their black employees. Sociologist Abraham Berglund conducted a survey among managers of the region's largest firms in the late 1920s, seeking to explain "why the greater percentage of the southern lumber camps are far from being model villages." One manager responded that "the sawmill Negro is rather shiftless, and is not inclined to stay long in one location."

While Berglund and other scholars accepted these cultural or even biological theories—"not as excuses for some of the conditions found, but as explanations, very well presented"—black men provided more rational explanations for their resistance to long-term employment in lumber mills.[47] Ned Cobb, who took seasonal lumber jobs throughout his career as a sharecropper in Alabama, explained that industrial wage work was more lucrative, but less reliable, than agriculture before the 1920s. He therefore went to the mills with a definite goal in mind, such as saving for his wedding, buying a mule, or, as he put it, "to make a speck if I could and then go back to my farm." As long as he "didn't know definitely at the time 'bout what the sawmills would bring," he "absolutely had [his] heart in farming."[48] Cobb was typical of many southern men of his generation, who viewed industrial wage employment as a supplement to their primary goal of becoming independent family farmers. This calculation, and not some biological or cultural defect, created what Berglund described as a "notoriously itinerant" labor supply.[49] Because married men insisted on spending weekends at home, one employer wrote to Berglund, "which makes it extremely inconvenient to me," he preferred to hire men with no "family in the neighborhood."[50]

When Hurston arrived in Loughman, both workers and employers were abandoning the employment practices designed in the context of the "cut-out-and-get-out" era of southern lumber production. Just as barrelhouse blues expressed the tensions between black workers and white employers during the early periods of southern industrialization, new cultural forms began to appear in southern sawmill towns and other industrial work camps as both blacks and whites adapted to the economic and social conditions that emerged after World War I. Southern farm income collapsed after the war and inflation of land and livestock prices made family farming nearly impossible, particularly for African Americans. During that same period, timber shortages compelled large southern lumber firms to experiment with tree farming and more efficient logging and milling. Invested in regrowth and more costly machinery, lumber firms became interested in attracting more stable and more experienced workforces. At the same time, black men began to seek alternatives to farming. By 1927, more than 200,000 southern men considered lumber manufacturing their primary occupation. Two-thirds of them were African Americans.[51]

With more stable male employment, black families and communities began to move into southern sawmill towns in the late 1920s. Zora Neale Hurston noted this transformation in Loughman, where black families hosted house parties that rivaled the company-operated barrelhouse as the social center of the sawmill town. Hosts lit bonfires outside the doors of rented cottages to advertise dance parties. They provided free drinks to musicians and to "ole square dance" callers, and they sold roasted peanuts and fried rabbit, chicken, fish, and chitterlings to supplement the family income.[52] Residents of other sawmill towns described similar leisure activities. W. T. Smith Lumber Company prohibited drinking in the center of Chapman, a company town in southern Alabama. Managers allowed black families to operate cafés and jook joints, however, out of the rental homes that lay across Rocky Creek Swamp, still within company property but a safe distance from the homes of white managers and skilled workers. Hosts charged admission and hired musicians from nearby Greenville or Georgiana and, occasionally, Montgomery.[53]

In addition to house parties, African Americans began to transform sawmill town leisure culture to cater to more age- and gender-diverse working-class communities. Great Southern Lumber Company, a pioneer in the shift toward conservation and stabilized production, boasted in 1924 that African Americans attended three schools and "churches of every denomination" in Bogalusa.[54] Smaller towns changed at a slower rate, but even the tiny logging camps that surrounded Bogalusa began to attract rural African Americans to church services, schools, and athletic events in the 1930s. Hogan Chappelle lived on his father's farm in the 1930s, but he would ride the log trains to a Great Southern camp to meet young women on the weekends.[55]

Black churches and schools developed initially in southern sawmill towns with little support from lumber company management. In contrast to textile employers who launched elaborate welfare programs for their employees in the 1910s, Abraham Berglund found "very few cases" where lumber companies supported religious or educational activities among their employees. One employer told Berglund that "a large labor turnover ... principally among Negroes or common laborers" provided employers with "little incentive" to support "welfare work in any extensive manner."[56] Even as they employed a more stable workforce, many employers retained the belief that black workers were culturally or biologically incapable of building stable family and community lives. When Cary Miles Cartwright, a black minister, moved to a North Carolina sawmill town in the late 1920s, the mill owner refused to help him establish a church on the grounds that workers had stolen the supplies that he previously donated to build a church. "You have come to preach to the triflingest set of damn niggers I have ever seen," he insisted. "You can't help them; nobody can help them." It may be that workers did not support earlier church-building efforts because they attended church in agricultural communities. Whatever the reason, they helped Cartwright build one in less than one year with no support from their employer.[57] The owners of W. T. Smith Lumber Company donated money to operate a church and a school operated by black workers in Chapman, but they provided only a building with a leaky roof and gaping holes in the walls.[58] Great Southern praised the black institutions in Bogalusa, but the company neglected to mention that the churches and at least one of the schools had been erected and maintained by black workers with no support from their employer.[59] As black workers did in many southern sawmill towns, African American employees left Elizabethtown, North Carolina, each Sunday to attend services in the nearby black village of Newtown.[60]

That religious activity in these towns reflected the initiative of African American communities is further reflected in the nonchalant tone with which one employer described two buildings that he provided for the use of his black employees: "One for the pious folks, whose chief amusement is the lodge and revival meetings, and another at the other side of the 'quarters' for those Negroes who wish to dance, shoot craps, and carry on in a lighter vein than that offered by the brethren of the cloth."[61] Another employer took little interest in his workers' religious lives, other than to urge black preachers to "impress upon their flocks the fact that the company expected six days of work from each employee."[62]

Only after African Americans began to establish more permanent communities in sawmill towns did employers begin to involve themselves in the leisure activities of those communities. A few large southern lumber firms followed John Kaul's initiative toward welfare programs in 1914, but these recreational, educational, and sanitary efforts were designed to encourage skilled white workers to settle in sawmill towns.[63] Great Southern Lumber Company expanded its welfare program after crushing an interracial union movement in Bogalusa during World War I and slowly developed a parallel program aimed to generate loyalty and steady employment among black workers. The focal point of this effort became Bogalusa's "Colored Y," which was constructed "along the lines of an army 'Y'" and administered under the direction of the general secretary of the town's white YMCA.[64] A new "Colored Section" in the company newsletter, *The Mill Whistle,* announced in 1923 that "the colored race has awakened to the advantages of education." Indicating the motivations behind Great Southern's newfound interest in African American welfare, the newsletter included articles extolling the "Dignity of Labor" and reported on the racist violence and poverty faced by recent migrants to the urban North.[65]

Rejecting their previous strategy of attracting single men for seasonal employment, Great Southern began to support African Americans' attempts to build families and communities in the camps and towns that surrounded their mills. "It has been rumored that Dan Cupid will tie a number of love knots in June and July," *The Mill Whistle* speculated in 1923. The company pledged to support these developments: "The houses are ready for you girls; the G.S.L. Company is waiting for you, young men—don't put it off for fear of work. Your job is ready for you." Company officials praised black parents for sending their children to school, not only to "be taught to read and write, but to be clean, honest, respectful and better citizens for the communities in which they live." *The Mill Whistle* reported that Colored Y director D. L. Smith had been counseling young black men on starting families and encouraged older men to "stop by the 'Y' and hear him talk to the young men—he has good advice for you."[66]

Smaller companies followed the model set by Great Southern. W. T. Smith Lumber Company launched an ambitious campaign after World War I to renovate its company town of Chapman, Alabama. In addition to improving housing, religious, and educational facilities, the company built a health clinic in 1924 and hired a second doctor to care for workers and their families. With one of the doctors, a female cousin of the owners started the Chapman Welfare Association, which distributed food baskets to poor families and in other ways took "care of charity" in the mill town and surrounding communities.[67] After commuting for twenty years from his home in Brewton, Alabama, owner Greeley McGowin finally moved into a mansion built just outside the mill town in 1926. In 1932, the company rebuilt black and white school buildings in Chapman and erected an additional white school in East Chapman, a growing community just outside the company gates.[68] After McGowin's death in 1934, his sons Julian, Earl, and Nicholas completed W. T. Smith's shift toward sustainability. The younger McGowins paved Chapman's streets and improved drainage to alleviate the floods that in previous years had covered the town in several feet of mud and water. By 1947, the mill employed more than 800 workers and was "considered one of the finest of its sort east of the Mississippi." Chapman contained 250 homes, two schools, several churches, a community house, and a hotel—all essential parts of what the company considered "a modern industrial town."[69]

Just as southern lumber companies viewed barrelhouses as complementary to their employment strategies before World War I, they also extended modernization efforts beyond housing, health care, and education to encompass support for working-class recreation. The most obvious example of this shift was company support for organized baseball leagues. After a rocky start in 1922, limited primarily by local church opposition to games on Sunday, baseball skyrocketed in popularity to become the single most important recreational activity in Bogalusa.[70] Demonstrating how quickly the community adapted to the new pastime, several Protestant congregations organized an all-white Church League in 1923 that included teams representing the Catholic Church, the Bogalusa Shrine Club, the Blue Lodge Masons, city officials, two groups of office workers from Great Southern, and the official "G.S.L. Plant Team." Company officials applauded the league, hoping it would "bring individuals, families, churches and other organizations and communities into closer friendly relationships and truer sportsman-like methods" in their personal, business, and political lives.[71]

While Great Southern provided support initially only to white baseball, managers reacted enthusiastically when workers organized a team out of the Colored Y. *The Mill Whistle* celebrated "one of the best baseball games ever played in Bogalusa," reporting on the July 17, 1923, showdown between the Giants, of nearby Bissant, and Bogalusa's black team, the Kelly Tigers. After tying the Giants in three consecutive games, the Tigers had a "good chance" of entering the Louisiana championship that fall. The company newsletter predicted that Bogalusa's "colored" team was on its way to becoming the "strongest club in the South."[72] According to Larry Powe, a black worker whose father pitched for the Tigers from the 1920s into the 1950s, "ball games were one of your basic activities" in Bogalusa. The company erected a Colored Athletic Park near the Y, which hosted doubleheaders on Sundays and single games after work on Mondays. The field had no lights, so evening games would continue until the players "couldn't see anymore."[73] Great Southern also supported baseball teams organized by workers and managers at the logging camps that surrounded Bogalusa. Camp superintendents hired local African American baseball stars and assigned them to work as brakemen on the log trains, or "some other easy job," in order to build up his team. The most hotly contested games occurred when the Tigers rode the log trains from Bogalusa to play the camp teams. [74] One migrant from Mississippi described Bogalusa as a "sawmill and baseball town" when he moved there in 1945.[75]

Whereas barrelhouses reflected and in some respects reinforced the separation between white and black leisure in mill communities, baseball had the contradictory effect of bringing white and black workers together in parallel, but segregated, leisure activities. Both blacks and whites enjoyed baseball, at times even watching each other's games and taking pleasure in the successes and failures of each other's teams. At the same time, teams and leagues remained strictly segregated, reinforcing racial identities within towns and providing avenues for both players and spectators to identify with broader regional and even national racial communities. In Great Southern's log camps, where few white workers lived, the company reinforced segregation by transporting whites into Bogalusa to participate in their own ballgames.[76] The Bogalusa Tigers traveled and hosted black industrial league teams from as far away as Mobile, New Orleans, and Laurel, Mississippi. Professional clubs also barnstormed though Bogalusa, among them the Baltimore Elite Giants, the Chicago Brown Bombers, and the New York Cubans. Fans from Bogalusa and the surrounding communities flocked to the colored Athletic Park to catch a glimpse of Negro League heroes and future major league stars like Satchel Paige and Roy Campanella.[77]

Smaller firms were less willing to devote the significant resources that Great Southern spent to maintain segregated recreational facilities, narrowing even further the distance between black and white working-class leisure. W. T. Smith Lumber Company bought uniforms and equipment for both black and white teams in Chapman and they granted players two weeks off for summer tournaments. Unlike in Bogalusa, however, Chapman's black and white teams played on the same field. George Cheatham, who played on the black W. T. Smith team, remembers the "whole town" coming out to watch Sunday afternoon matches.[78] According to Marvin Mantel, who was superintendent of education in Butler County in the 1940s, company-sponsored baseball games helped knit together the "geographical, social, and business contact area" surrounding Chapman. In nearby Brewton, the T. R. Miller Lumber Company sponsored both the (white) Millers and the Black Millers. While they never played each other, the Brewton teams also played on the same field, with black and white fans watching both teams from segregated grandstands.[79]

Because baseball was so clearly cosmopolitan, it is not surprising that Hurston made no reference to the sport in *Mules and Men*. It may be that baseball had not made its way to Loughman in 1927, but a film that Hurston made there in the early 1930s shows black men and women gathering in the bleachers of a stadium. Hurston also omitted from *Mules and Men* scenes of schoolchildren and of men working with heavy machinery, both significant portions of her film, indicating that she edited references to social change and modernization from her published account of the sawmill town. Further support for this supposition is the fact that those gathered at Loughman's baseball stadium were entertained by a musician playing a saxophone, rather than a guitar. In order to market *Mules and* Men as a window into a static and isolated folk society, Hurston seems to have omitted indications that Loughman was part of modern America.[80]

More than any other cultural practice, music and dance provided a venue through which southern African Americans participated in the creation of modern American culture in the 1920s and 1930s. As historian Lizabeth Cohen has pointed out, black consumers were generally more receptive toward "mass consumption trends" than other working-class Americans in the 1920s. In the case of commercial music however, "the trend setting went the other way. Black folk culture, black inventiveness, and black talent gave the twenties its distinctive image as the *jazz age* and dictated the character of mainstream American popular music for many years to come." In much the same way that baseball facilitated communication between black communities, "race records helped unify black musical styles across regions, creating an increasingly national black sound" according to Cohen.[81]

Cohen implies that this national sound disseminated from Chicago, "the jazz capital of the nation," but the growth of jazz bands in southern sawmill towns and their relationship to older blues styles indicates a multidirectional process. The Colored Y began organizing Saturday night swing dances at Bogalusa's Colored Athletic Park, according to Larry Powe, shortly after the baseball stadium became "the center of cultural activity in Bogalusa."[82] Henry Sims, who moved to Bogalusa with his family in 1923, signed up with a YMCA Jazz Band organized by A. M. "Appie" Wadell, an older black man who worked as a chauffeur for the general manager of Great Southern. Sales manager A. C. Long bought instruments and the white YMCA superintendent Harry Hoppen provided additional financial support for a musical group for young black men. With Willie "Hump" Manning and two other young men, Sims formed the Rhythm Aces, a swing band that dominated Bogalusa's music scene in the 1930s.[83]

The Rhythm Aces performed some of the same blues songs played by barrelhouse musicians, but they became famous for renditions of the swing hits that they copied off Count Basie, Duke Ellington, and Harry James records. Sims had taken formal music classes in school, but most of the band members' training came from older musicians who taught them to read and write music. The young men first bought sheet music at Wurliner's Music Store, and Manning learned to transpose each of their parts directly from a record. "When we get through with it," Sims claimed, "you couldn't tell it was, you know, just off of the record."[84] By the late 1930s, the band traveled regularly between Jackson, Mobile, New Orleans, and Baton Rouge. Sims kept his job at the sawmill commissary throughout this period, but John "Duke" Oatis, who moved from Jackson to play with the Aces in 1945, supported himself completely off of his earnings as a musician.[85] The Rhythm Aces rode the wave of popularity for swing music that swept through the South and the nation in the 1930s. Fans came from all over Washington Parish to see the Rhythm Aces at the Athletic Park, and the swing band commanded an annual gig at the Washington Parish Fair. The band cut a record for the Decca label in 1940, released under the name of Lorenzer "Good" Lewis, a drummer who sat in with them for the New Orleans recording session. Manning's transposing skills allowed the Aces to keep up with new styles. The Aces began playing bebop in the 1940s and conceded reluctantly to rock 'n' roll requests in the 1950s, but their passion was the early swing tunes of their youth. Sims admitted that by the time the band stopped playing in 1964 he was playing with cotton in his ears.[86]

Swing music also became popular in Chapman, Alabama, where the W. T. Smith Lumber Company sponsored dances at Chapman's African American school in the mid-1920s. The company donated land near the company gate for a Civilian Conservation Corps (CCC) Camp, which erected a dancehall for the black men who lived there. Marie Cobb, a black woman who grew up in Chapman, remembers lying on her front porch at night, listening to the music playing at the schoolhouse. When she grew older, she started going to dances at the CCC Camp. Cobb's husband, Jack Rudolph, played piano at a few of these affairs, but more often the school paid for big bands from Montgomery.[87]

Again, Forrester Washington and Carter Woodson were not unreasonable to interpret popular music as a foreign imposition on rural African Americans. It was true, as Washington charged, that record companies worked aggressively to create a market for recorded music among southern African Americans in the 1920s. Following the Okeh label's successful marketing of two Mamie Smith recordings in 1920, labels specializing in "race" music began searching for ways to extend sales into the South, where the majority of African Americans still lived. "We want live agents everywhere," declared Black Swan, the black-owned New York label that in 1923 began advertising for representatives in southern drug stores, furniture shops, hair salons, and cafés. Agents for Black Swan and other companies peddled records at bars and workplaces or through mail order.[88] Describing the impact of such marketing after a 1935 research trip to Florida, Hurston wrote that commercial jukebox music was "greatly affecting the originality of the Negro songs" in even "the farthest-removed places," such as "remote turpentine, logging, phosphate, and other camps."[89]

Just as she found little to support the notion of an isolated folk culture, however, Hurston discovered that rural southerners had influenced mass culture as much as they had been shaped by the companies who distributed it. "Traditional singing" had not disappeared, she wrote in 1936, particularly where "gangs of men work at the same jobs." Visiting docks, sawmills, turpentine stills, and logging operations, Hurston heard "many of the old melodies that have at one time been so prevalent in the state." She marveled at workers' ability to adapt songs to meet the particular conditions of each job, noting that in sawmills songs were "frequently punctuated by the whine of the huge circular saws, while in logging operations they were pitched to carry long distances through the forests."[90]

As significant as the survival of local traditions was the dissemination of local sounds through popular culture. One of many blues musicians raised in southern sawmill towns, "Mississippi" Matilda Witherspoon settled in Bogalusa when her father went there to work for Great Southern in 1919. She learned to sing in the Mt. Zion Church choir and performed in the Columbia Street bars and dancehalls. In 1936 she traveled with her husband, Eugene "Sonny Boy" Nelson, to record four tracks at the Bluebird Record studio in New Orleans. "Peel Your Banana" and "A&V Blues" were barrelhouse standards and were never distributed commercially. "Hard Working Women Blues" and "Happy Home Blues," which were released as a single, provided an autobiographical account of one black woman's life in a mill town. Contradicting the image that women were in these towns only to entertain men, Witherspoon claimed she provided housing for a man who "had no place to go." Growing tired of supporting that man, she threatened "I'm a hard working woman, but I'm becoming a rolling stone." Witherspoon did indeed leave her first husband when she moved from Bogalusa to the Mississippi Delta shortly after the recording session.[91]

Music became a vehicle through which black southerners shaped modern popular culture. Record companies combed the South for new artists, paying musicians to travel from small towns to Paramount's studios in Wisconsin, Bluebird's Indiana headquarters, and scores of other studios in New York and Chicago. Before the Great Depression curtailed their operations, several "race" labels also set up temporary studios in Atlanta, New Orleans, and Dallas.[92] Musicologist John Fehey observes that "by 1931, the companies had been performing for three or four years the function of passively allowing hundreds of Southern Negroes to sit in their studios and record the songs which they had been singing for decades." Hardly passive consumers, black record buyers succeeded in imposing their "own tastes upon" record company executives who, according to historian Lawrence Levine, "understood the music they were recording imperfectly enough so that they extended a great deal of freedom to the singers they were recording."[93] Implying that local place-names indicated consumers' preference for local artists, Hurston wrote in 1936 that "for some time one of the best known phonograph singers has been a man known as Tampa Red; Tampa Slim is another favorite."[94]

Even when black musicians adopted new forms such as swing, most audience members welcomed them as additional options for leisure activity rather than competitors in a struggle between traditional and modern cultural forms. Some residents preferred one type of leisure over another, according to their individual tastes. Marie Cobb recalled that school dances in Chapman were more elegant than the house parties "across the creek," stating that he dressed up in "crazy hats" and danced popular steps such as the Charleston and the Jitterbug that would have been out of place in the more informal jooks.[95] Ire Abrams, a black man who worked at the W. T. Smith mill in the 1940s, countered the house parties were "more fun" than school dances because they served alcohol and were open most nights of the week. "The school dances were run by the company," explained black worker Mate Montgomery, "and they didn't want people dancing all night before work."[96]

By adapting local traditions to an increasingly commercialized and national popular culture, sawmill town musicians succeeded in preserving and extending the reach of their art form. According to Hurston, rather than cover jukebox or radio hits exactly, sawmill town musicians altered the form and content of songs "to satisfy the taste of the communities' own singers." Contradicting Forrester Washington's charge that record companies forced "immoral" material on black consumers, Hurston found that local versions of popular songs were "not always mentionable in polite company; in the cases of some records they are unprintably vulgar." [97] Howard Odum and coauthor Guy Benton Johnson also noted that blues lyrics sung outside of studios were more sexually explicit than those recorded by commercial studios, leading the folklorists to argue that record labels had "whitewashed" the cultural form.[98] When singing before white audiences, according to Daphne Duval Harrison, black singers also tempered sexual or overtly political lyrics, using "snappy repartee to tone down the dirty lyrics, or sly looks with fancy nods and body movements that were implicit rather than explicit."[99]

The recording process did change black popular music. Musicologist Mac McCormick points out that studio managers passed over "the strongest part" of the barrelhouse blues tradition when they discouraged extended instrumental solos in commercial recordings. Because they were recorded "theater style," while standing in front of the microphone, the records of many female performers featured only their vocals and not their virtuoso piano lines that were an integral part of their live performances. McCormick finds "little in the early records" of popular female blues singers Victoria Spivey, Hociel Thomas, or Sippie Wallace to indicate that they "had developed their own versions" of popular songs.[100] Even these limitations inspired innovation, however, as musicians brought the technical and aesthetic peculiarities of studio sessions home with them when they returned to live performance. Solo pianists, according to Hurston, played "loudly and insistently" to replicate amplified jukeboxes, and they pounded the foot pedals "to give the effect of a drum." Musicians who were unsure of the lyrics of a popular song could expect "frequent cheerful volunteer vocal assistance" from the audience. "There is little need for other instruments if he knows his 'jook' music well."[101] An appreciation for live music developed side by side with records and jukeboxes. As late as 1936, Hurston found that "the nickel phonograph" had "not yet entirely displaced the traditional piano player always found wherever groups of Negroes live in the State, and the often-improvised jazz-band."[102]

In addition to blurring the lines between northern and southern, rural and urban, popular music also challenged the distinction between white and black leisure. In small towns, where racial boundaries were less formal and more porous than larger towns, cultural changes lent new degrees of respectability to interracial cultural exchange. Black and white neighborhoods were separated by only a few hundred feet in Chapman, allowing for frequent interracial exchange on the streets, at baseball games and in the mills. Even in larger towns like Bogalusa, commercialization often blurred the racial divisions that had been central to Great Southern's early social policy. While barrelhouses retained a reputation among white working people as male-dominated and rowdy, swing dances catered to the men and women who moved into southern sawmill towns in the 1930s. The growing popularity of black popular music in the towns allowed white working-class women to listen to black musicians in a more socially respectable environment.[103] "We played for everybody, white, colored, whatever," recalled Rhythm Aces member Henry Sims. Hank Williams, who's father drove a log train for W. T. Smith, learned to play guitar from Connie "Big Day" McKee, Rufus "Tee Tot" Payne, and other black musicians who played at house parties and barrelhouses in Chapman. Even after he emerged as a Hillbilly music star in the 1940s, Williams retained a large following among black southerners. None other than blues legend B. B. King testified to Williams's ability to "carry me back to my same old blues."[104]

A shared popular culture set the stage for increased interactions between whites and blacks in the South. One observer claimed that jazzman Duke Ellington "erased the color line" when he toured the South in 1933.[105] Jim Crow laws typically prohibited black and white audiences from dancing in the same hall, but black and white crowds danced the same steps and demanded the same songs. In Bogalusa, white musicians frequently sat in with the Rhythm Aces at both black and white shows. In most southern towns, whites were allowed to listen at black dances, as long as they did not dance. Bogalusa music fans occasionally violated these rules against interracial dancing although, according to Sims, the "police would come in there and close it down, run everybody out of there and bust some heads."[106]

Employers struggled to control this shifting biracial culture. Continuing an older policy of restricting vice to black neighborhoods, managers at Great Southern attempted to "suppress the gambling houses that catered to white people and to more strictly enforce the prohibition acts relating to the sale of intoxicating liquors." After that focused strategy failed, the city council authorized a more "general clean-up of the City," which included crackdowns on barrelhouses and strict segregation of sporting events and alcohol consumption. Finally abandoning its support for distinct black and white leisure, Great Southern attempted to control what had become segregated versions of the same popular culture.[107] W. T. Smith attempted a similar suppression of drinking and "rude or indecent" behavior in Chapman in the early 1930s. While baseball games and swing dances remained strictly segregated, nearby roadhouses and honky-tonks continued to serve alcohol to black and white workers, occasionally violating local laws barring integrated leisure.[108]

Hurston and other early twentieth-century anthropologists assumed a clear distinction between rural "folk" cultures that they studied and the urban, industrial societies in which they were trained. Even as anthropologists have rejected such dichotomies, social historians have retained their conceptual trappings.[109] Robin Kelley's appreciation of Hurston, for example, is based on his adaptation of political scientist James Scott's concept of a "hidden transcript," which Scott defines as "a discourse that takes place 'offstage,' beyond direct observation by powerholders" in societies that allow for no public dissent. Scott developed this model through his study of Malaysian peasant society, and he suggests that scholars apply it to "structurally similar forms of domination" such as "slavery, serfdom and caste subordination."[110] Jim Crow restricted black social and political influence in sawmill towns, but segregation does not seem to have circumscribed African American cultural expression to the extent that it retreated to a "hidden transcript." Historian Tera Hunter invoked Scott in an early publication, but her study of Atlanta suggests that urban black working-class leisure also diverged from his model.[111] Black and white middle-class Atlantans condemned the public nature of dancehalls, "where anyone may go in and take part for a price," while working-class women and men turned these "melting pot[s] of Dixie" into crucibles of "broader African American working-class self-understandings in the modern world."[112] In both industrial towns and cities, southern culture was transformed by the geographic mobility associated with wage employment and with black participation in commercial popular culture, two qualities that distinguished the Jim Crow South from slave and serf societies.[113]

Whereas Kelley conflates Jim Crow and slavery, Hazel Carby and other scholars maintain an equally essentialist conception that modernization spread unilaterally from the urban North. In place of the "mythical rural folk existence" that included both slavery and Jim Crow, Carby describes twentieth-century black cultural forms such as the blues simply as products of an "urban environment," produced for "urban consumption."[114] Historian Joe William Trotter describes black mining communities in West Virginia as part of a "rural periphery" that "witnessed the increasing onslaught of industrial capitalism" in the early twentieth century.[115] Both scholars overlook the possibility that African Americans could have created a modern culture within the Jim Crow South, one related to the modern society of the urban North but also informed by racial and economic relationships that were specific to southern society. Barrelhouse blues was one expression of such a culture, reflecting the movement of young men between agricultural communities and the industrial worksites that became critical to the viability of family farming before World War I. Baseball and swing indicated a turn away from that oscillation, but it represented a transformation of southern society rather than an invasion from the urban North.

The failure to recognize African Americans' participation in the modern culture of the South is remarkable in light of the large body of scholarship devoted to the role that southern textile workers, who were similar in number to lumber workers but nearly entirely white, had in "creating the modern South."[116] Inattention to the significance of black industrial employment is a venerable feature of southern studies, stretching back to Abraham Berglund's argument that slavery created a legacy of dependency that prevented African Americans from taking advantage of "progressive industrialization" in the 1920s.[117] From C. Vann Woodward to Leon Litwack, few historians have challenged the belief that industrialization allowed the white South to "pull itself up by its bootstraps and gain the respect, recognition, and investment capital of a rapidly industrializing America," while black workers found only a "fleeting" foothold in industry before being "forced back into agricultural labor."[118] Such statements overlook the reality of black industrial employment in the South and rely upon a mechanical theory of modernization long since rejected by scholars of other industrializing societies.[119]

It is equally notable that literary scholars such as Paul Gilroy and Houston Baker identify northern black artists and intellectuals, many of them originally southerners, among the vanguard of American modernism. According to Gilroy, black modernity stems from participation in an international "Black Atlantic" culture that was centered in the port cities of the United States, Great Britain, and the Caribbean. Rather than recognizing Hurston's fascination with southern culture as a reflection of her embrace of current anthropological theory, Gilroy charges her with fabricating "an essentially invariant, anti-historical notion of black particularity" as part of a cynical bid for scholarly authority.[120] Gilroy associates black modernity with the transcendence of nationalism, but Baker argues that black people become modern by transcending the South. Only through the Great Migration, which Baker compares to the escape from slavery, did black people escape Jim Crow's "world of murderous exclusion" and enter the "Afro-American field of possibilities." Overlooking Hurston's ambivalent stance toward urbanization, Baker claims that the New Negro movement, as the ultimate expression of black modernism, sought its "inspiration in the very flight, or marronage, to the urban North of millions of black folk."[121]

This chapter has demonstrated that African Americans became central actors in the creation of modern American culture—without leaving the South. Even as white textile workers remained skeptical of social transformation, black lumber workers embraced the improved transportation and communication networks, permanent reliance on wages, and participation in commercial popular culture that were central to the experience of modernity.[122] Southern lumber communities cannot be understood as outposts of urban or northern culture in an essentially rural land. Neither can they be understood as intersections between the white or interracial mainstream and an authentic African American folk tradition. Southern industrialization was a product of the South, a biracial and dynamic society. It was shaped by both race and class tensions within southern society, and it reflected attempts by blacks and whites, workers and employers, to shape that society toward their economic and political advantage.

During her extended study of southern lumber towns between 1927 and 1936, Zora Neale Hurston developed pieces of an intellectual model for understanding the process of cultural creation within the modern South.[123] Her thinking was informed during this period by collaboration with B. A. Botkin and other functionalist anthropologists who became critical of the Boasian tendency to "emphasize the anachronistic and static, the useless and meaningless aspects of folklore to the neglect of its living and dynamic phases." By paying attention to the contemporary social and economic conditions that shaped black leisure in the South, according to Benjamin Filene, Hurston and other "New Deal folklorists shifted the profession's mission from preserving cultural relics to exploring the process by which culture was created and transmitted."[124] That contemporary scholars continue to criticize Hurston according to her previous position indicates the degree to which they have not followed her in making that shift. Contrary to Robin Kelley, the "crucial lesson" to be learned from *Mules and Men* is not that black people turned inward in the face of an unyielding "white culture" but that they succeeded in shaping, in some ways even controlling, cultural production in the South.[125] They did so not by abandoning their ancestral home or, as Hurston feared initially, rejecting their "negroness." By embracing the opportunities offered by industrialization, black lumber workers and their families helped to create a modern culture in the Jim Crow South. Until we recognize their ingenuity, as Albert Murray has noted in reference to the blues, "there is a lot of admittedly infectious exuberance, elegance and nonsense to be accounted for."[126]

NOTES

1. Albert Murray, *Stomping the Blues* (New York: McGraw Hill, 1976), 69–70.

2. I distinguish industrial sawmills from the "peckerwood" or "ground" mills that southern farmers used to process wood cut to clear fields. Larger in number than industrial mills, the smaller mills produced lumber below market grade and employed mostly farmworkers, therefore not contributing significantly to the rate of industrialization in the rural South. For more on this distinction see William P. Jones, *The Tribe of Black Ulysses: African American Lumber Workers in the Jim Crow South* (Urbana: University of Illinois Press, 2005).

3. George Hutchinson, *The Harlem Renaissance in Black and White* (Cambridge, MA: Harvard University Press, 1995), 62–78.

4. Robert E. Hemenway, *Zora Neal Hurston: A Literary Biography* (Urbana: University of Illinois Press 1977), 91.

5. Zora Neal Hurston, *Mules and Men* (New York: HarperPerennial, 1990 [orig. 1935]), 1.

6. Ibid., 55.

7. Clyde Woods, for example, argues that "the Mississippi Delta is the home of the blues tradition." His contention that Blues reflected black southerners' response to social relations on the plantation, however, leads him to minimize the influence that nonplantation experiences had on blues performers. He describes barrelhouse blues, for example, as an "offshoot of the blues" that "emerged in the late nineteenth century" and implies that plantation musicians invented it when they transplanted the blues to "isolated lumber and turpentine camps" and then to Chicago in the 1920s. Clyde Woods, *Development Arrested: The Blues and Plantation Power in the Mississippi Delta* (New York: Verso, 1998), 25, 308, n. 90.

8. Paul Oliver, ed., *The Blackwell Guide to Recorded Blues* (Cambridge, MA: Blackwell, 1991), 103; *Ma Rainey: The Complete 1928 Sessions in Chronological Order* (compact disc; Document Records, DOCD-5156).

9. Steven C. LaVere, liner notes to *Robert Johnson: The Complete Recordings* (compact disc; Columbia 46222).

10. Mike Rowe, "Piano Blues and Boogie-Woogie," in *The Blackwell Guide,* 112–138. Francis Davis, *The History of the Blues: The Roots, the Music, the People, from Charley Patton to Robert Cray* (New York: Da Capo, 1995), 148–150.

11. Pleasant Joseph, "Sawmill Man Blues," quoted in Paul Oliver, *Blues Fell This Morning: The Meaning of the Blues* (Cambridge: Cambridge University Press, 1990).

12. *Next Week Sometime: A Compilation of 'Pre-War' Blues, 1927–1940* (LP recording; Nugrape CBR-001).

13. *Barrelhouse Blues, 1927–1936* (LP recording; Yazoo L-1028).

14. *Barrelhouse Blues and Boogie Piano, 1927–1930* (LP recording; RST BD-2033).

15. Karl Gert zur Heide, *Deep South Piano: The Story of Little Brother Montgomery* (London: Studio Vista, 1970), 12.

16. Mac McCormick, liner notes for Robert Shaw, *The Ma Grinder: Texas Barrelhouse Piano* (Compact disc; Arhoolie).

17. Benjamin Filene, *Romancing the Folk: Public Memory and American Roots Music* (Chapel Hill: University of North Carolina Press, 2000), 35–39.

18. Quoted in Daniel Joseph Singal, *The War Within: From Victorian to Modernist Thought in the South, 1919–1945* (Chapel Hill: University of North Carolina Press, 1982), 141–142.

19. Howard W. Odum and Guy B. Johnson, *Negro Workaday Songs* (Chapel Hill: University of North Carolina Press, 1926), 1–4.

20. Quoted in Singal, *The War Within,* 143.

21. Odum quoted in Morton Sosna, *In Search of the Silent South: Southern Liberals and the Race Issue* (Chapel Hill: University of North Carolina Press, 1977), 50–51; and Howard W. Odum, *Rainbow "Round My Shoulder: The Blue Trail of Black Ulysses* (Indianapolis, IN: Bobbs-Merrill, 1928), 127.

22. Carter G. Woodson, *The Rural Negro* (New York: Russell and Russell, 1930), 132–136.

23. For a history of such "damage imagery," see Daryl Michael Scott, *Contempt and Pity: Social Policy and the Image of the Damaged Black Psyche, 1880–1998* (Chapel Hill: University of North Carolina Press, 1997).

24. Forrester B. Washington, "Recreation Facilities for the Negro," *Annals of the American Academy of Political and Social Sciences* 140 (November 1928): 279.

25. Woodson, *The Rural Negro,* 132–136.

26. Odum quoted in Allen Tullos, *Habits of Industry: White Culture and the Transformation of the Carolina Piedmont* (Chapel Hill: University of North Carolina Press, 1989), 298.

27. Washington, "Recreation Facilities for the Negro," 279.

28. See Lee D. Baker, *From Savage to Negro: Anthropology and the Construction of Race, 1896–1954* (Berkeley: University of California Press, 1998), 176–179.

29. E. Franklin Frazier, "Is the Negro Family a Unique Sociological Unit?" *Opportunity: Journal of Negro Life* 5 (June 1927): 165–166.

30. E. Franklin Frazier, "Durham: Capital of the Black Middle Class," in *The New Negro: Voices of the Harlem Renaissance,* ed. Alain Locke (New York: Simon and Schuster, 1997 [orig. 1925]), 285.

31. Charles S. Johnson, "The New Frontage on American Life," in *The New Negro,* 285.

32. E. Franklin Frazier, *The Negro Family in the United States* (Chicago: University of Chicago Press, 1939), 220. On Frazier's influence see Nathan Glazer's forward to the 1966 edition (Chicago: University of Chicago Press) and Nicholas Lemann, *The Promised Land: The Great Migration and How It Changed America* (New York: Vintage Books, 1991), 170–221.

33. Hemenway, *Zora Neal Hurston,* 124–129.

34. See Hurston's Introduction to *Mules and Men,* 1–4.

35. Zora Neal Hurston, *Every Tongue Got to Confess: Negro Folk-Tales from the Gulf States* (New York: HarperCollins, 2001), 257–258.

36. Zora Neal Hurston, "Characteristics of Negro Expression," in *Negro: An Anthology,* ed. Nancy Cunard (New York: Continuum, 1970 [orig. 1934]), 27.

37. Robin D. G. Kelley, "'We Are Not What We Seem': Rethinking Black Working-Class Opposition in the Jim Crow South," *Journal of American History* 80 (June 1993): 75–112.

38. Hazel V. Carby, *Cultures in Babylon: Black Britain and African America* (New York: Versol, 1999), 168–183.

39. Other writers have been even less critical of Hurston's distinction between modern and

folk cultures. One critic writes that "because blacks were isolated ... in sawmills and lumber camps of the deep South, oral tradition remained strongest among them, and most were uninfluenced by standard American paradigms of thinking and acting." Beulah S. Hemingsway, "Through the Prism of Africanity: A Priliminary Investigation of Zora Neal Huston's *Mules and Men,*" in *Zora in Florida,* ed. Steve Glassman and Kathryn Lee Seidel (Gainesville: University Press of Florida, 1991), 38. Hurston's biographer reports uncritically that Hurston's familiarity with southern black culture allowed her to collect more authentic material, ignoring her own observations that expensive clothing, a new car, and her lack of familiarity with industrial working-class communities all alienated her from people in Loughman. Hemenway, *Zora Neal Hurston.* In her introduction to a recently published volume of material not included in *Mules and Men,* Carla Kaplan praises Hurston for "attempting, in spite of constant resistance, to bring authentic black folklore to mainstream, popular audiences." Hurston, *Every Tongue Got to Confess,* xxii.

40. Hurston, *Mules and Men,* 152, 60, 61.

41. Gert zur Heide, *Deep South Piano,* 37–38.

42. Joseph E. McCaffrey, interview by Elwood R. Maunder, February 5, 1964, Forest History Society Oral History Collection, Durham, NC.

43. See Jacquelyn D. Hall, James Leloudis, Robert Korstad, Mary Murphy, Lu Ann Jones, and Christopher B. Daly, *Like a Family: The Making of a Southern Cotton Mill World* (Chapel Hill: University of North Carolina Press, 2000), 131–139.

44. John Kaul, "The New Welfare Emphasis in the Southern Lumber Industry," n.d., Box 3, Folder 41, Kaul Lumber Company Records, Collection 1230, Department of Archives and Manuscripts, Linn-Henley Research Library, Birmingham Public Library, Birmingham, Alabama. George H. Miller, "Kaulton: A Proprietary Village Scientifically Planned to Attain Definite Objectives," *American Lumberman* (November 13, 1915).

45. Jerry L. Myrick, "A History of the Great Southern Lumber Company," (Ph.D. diss., Louisiana State University, 1970). Amy Quick, "The History of Bogalusa, The 'Magic City' of Louisiana," (MA thesis, Louisiana State University, 1942).

46. McCaffrey interview.

47. Abraham Berglund et al., *Labor in the Industrial South: A Survey of Wages and Living Conditions in Three Major Industries of the New Industrial South* (Charlottesville: University Press of Virginia, 1930), 54.

48. Theodore Rosengarten, *All God's Dangers: The Life of Nate Shaw* (New York: Avon, 1974), 182.

49. Berglund et al., *Labor in the Industrial South,* 53.

50. Jeffrey A. Drobney, *Lumbermen and Log Sawyers: Life, Labor, and Culture in the North Florida Timber Industry, 1830–1930* (Macon, GA: Mercer University Press, 1997), 84.

51. Berglund et al., *Labor in the Industrial South.* Vernon H. Jensen, *Lumber and Labor* (New York: J. J. Little and Ives, 1945), 76.

52. Hurston, *Mules and Men,* 141–144.

53. Make Montgomery, interview with author, January 12, 1998. Unless otherwise noted, taped copies of all interviews are available at the Southern Oral History Collection, Wilson Library, University of North Carolina at Chapel Hill.

54. Great Southern Lumber Company, Department of Publicity, "Bogalusa: City of Families and Factories," 1924, Series 3, Folder 16, Great Southern Lumber Company Collection, Louisiana and Lower Mississippi Valley Collections, LSU Libraries, Louisiana State University, Baton Rouge.

55. Talmadge Reeves and Hogan Chapelle, interview with author, February 16, 1998.

56. Berglund et al., *Labor in the Industrial South,* 54.

57. W. O. Saunders, "A Taskmaster in the Vineyard of the Lord," Box 22, Folder 723,

Federal Writers Project Papers, Life Histories, Southern Historical Collection, Wilson Library, University of North Carolina at Chapel Hill.

58. "Chapman People at Work," *Lumbering Along,* October 26, 1951 [company newsletter], W. T. Smith Lumber Company Records, Alabama Department of Archives and History, Montgomery, Alabama.

59. Willie Ginn, interview with author, February 25, 1998.

60. Orie and Louise Tyson, interview with author, September 1, 1996.

61. Berglund et al., *Labor in the Industrial South,* 58.

62. Ibid., 65.

63. Kaul, "The New Welfare Emphasis."

64. GSLC, "Bogalusa: City of Families and Factories."

65. *Mill Whistle* (July 1923), W. T. Smith Lumber Company Records.

66. Ibid.

67. "Form Chapman Welfare Society," April 12, 1924 [unmarked clipping], Newspaper Clippings Surname File, "MGill, J.—McGowin, J." Alabama Department of Archives and History, Montgomery, Alabama.

68. "W. T. Smith Lumber Company, Chapman, Alabama," October 27, 1947, W. T. Smith Lumber Company File, Forest History Society, Durham, NC. J. H. Lehman Audit Co., "Report of Examination of Accounts of W.T. Smith Lumber Company," December 31, 1933, Box B8, W. T. Smith Lumber Company Records.

69. "W. T. Smith Lumber Company."

70. H. E. Hoppen, "The Spirit of Baseball and Good Sportsmanship Is Contagious," *Mill Whistle* (July 1923).

71. Ibid.

72. "Colored Section," *Mill Whistle* (July 1923).

73. Mike Salinero, "Whatever Happened to Claude Green?" *Bogalusa Daily News,* June 14, 1981.

74. Reeves and Chapelle interview.

75. John Oatis, interview with author, March 1, 1998.

76. Reeves and Chapelle interview.

77. Salinero, "Whatever Happened to Claude Green?"

78. George Cheatham, interview with author, January 10, 1998.

79. Charles Peavey [notes], October 29, 1948, Brewton, AL, Subseries 1.2, Field Studies in the Modern Culture of the South Records, Southern Historical Collection.

80. Zora Neale Hurston, n.d., untitled 16mm B&W film, Margaret Mead Film Collection, Library of Congress Motion Picture Collection, Washington, DC.

81. Lizabeth Cohen, *Making a New Deal: Industrial Workers in Chicago, 1919–1939* (Cambridge: Cambridge University Press, 1990), 154–155.

82. Mike Salinero, "Whatever Happened to Lynn Powe?" *Bogalusa Daily News,* May 24, 1981.

83. Al Hansen, "The Aces Who Were Bogalusa's Kings of Swing." *Bogalusa Daily News,* June 7, 1981, A-9.

84. Henry Sims, interview with author, February 19, 1998.

85. John Oatis interview.

86. Paul Harvey, interview with author, February 17, 1998. Notes in possession of author. Reeves and Chapelle interview. Sims interview.

87. Marie Cobb, interview with author, January 12, 1998.

88. Robert E. Weems Jr., *Desegregating the Dollar: African-American Consumerism in the Twentieth Century* (New York: New York University Press, 1998), 38–41.

89. Zora Neal Hurston, "Florida, Negro Folklore," June 30, 1936, Florida File, Traditional

Folklore, WPA Manuscripts, Folklore Project, Archive of Folk Song, Collections of the Manuscript Division, Library of Congress, Washington, DC.

90. Hurston, "Florida, Negro Folklore."

91. Bob Eagle and Steve LaVere, "Hard Working Woman, Mississippi Matilda," *Living Blues* 8 (March 1972): 7. Paul Garon, "Mississippi" Matilda Witherspoon (Powell), liner notes for *Four Woman Blues: The Victor/Bluebird Recordings of Memphis Minnie, Mississippi Matilda, Kansas City Kitty and Miss Rosie Mae Moore* (compact disc; RCA 07863 66719–2; 1997).

92. Bruce Bastin and John Crowley, "Uncle Art's Logbook Blues," *Blues Unlimited* 108 (June 1974): 12–17. Daphne Duvall Harrison, "'Classic' Blues and Women Singers," in *The Blackwell Guide,* 83. Paul Oliver, "An Introduction to the Recording of Folk Blues in the Twenties," *Jazz Review* 2 (February 1959): 20–25.

93. Levine and Fehey, quoted in Lawrence Levine, *Black Culture and Black Consciousness: Afro-American Folk Thought from Slavery to Freedom* (New York: Oxford University Press, 1977), 225–229.

94. Hurston, "Florida, Negro Folklore."

95. Cobb interview.

96. Ire Abrams, interview with author, January 12, 1998. Make Montgomery, interview with author, January 12, 1998.

97. Hurston, "Florida, Negro Folklore."

98. Odum and Johnson. *Negro Workaday Songs,* 31–32.

99. Harrison, "'Classic' Blues," 83–111. William Ferris Jr., "Racial Repertoires among Blues Performers," *Ethnomusicology* 14 (September 1970): 439–449.

100. Mack McCormick, "Texas Barrelhouse Piano," liner notes for *Robert Shaw: Texas Barrelhouse Piano* (LP recording; Arhoolie, 1010, 1963).

101. Hurston, "Florida, Negro Folklore."

102. Ibid.

103. Evelyn Boyette, interview with author, February 20, 1998.

104. George Lipsitz, *Rainbow at Midnight: Labor and Culture in the 1940s* (Urbana: University of Illinois Press, 1994), 26.

105. John Edward Hasse, *Beyond Category: The Life and Genius of Duke Ellington* (New York: Simon and Schuster, 1993), 176–180.

106. Sims interview.

107. Bogalusa Commission Council, "Regular Meeting Minutes," March 31, 1931–September 4, 1936 (City Hall, Bogalusa, LA). *City of Bogalusa Code: The Charter and General Ordinances of the City* (Tallahassee, FL: Municipal Code Corporation, 1955).

108. "Ordinance Book, Chapman, AL," Box B7, W. T. Smith Lumber Company Records. "Trial Docket Police Court, Town of Chapman, AL," November 8, 1927–February 27, 1965, Box B7, W. T. Smith Lumber Company Records. Cobb interview.

109. Daniel T. Rodgers made a similar, if largely unheeded, criticism of social historian's adoption of outdated anthropological models in "Tradition, Modernity, and the American Industrial Worker," *Journal of Interdisciplinary History* 7 (Spring 1977): 655–681. For an anthropological critique see Johannes Fabian, *Time and the Other: How Anthropology Makes Its Object* (New York: Columbia University Press, 1983).

110. James C. Scott, *Domination and the Arts of Resistance: Hidden Transcripts* (New Haven: Yale University Press, 1990), x, xii. For other attempts to apply Scott's model to the Jim Crow South see Tera W. Hunter, "Domination and Resistance: The Politics of Wage Household Labor in New South Atlanta." *Labor History* 34 (March 1993): 205–220; and Mary L. Wingerd, "Rethinking Paternalism: Power and Parochialism in a Southern Mill Village," *Journal of American History* (December 1996): 872–902.

111. Hunter, "Domination and Resistance."

112. Tera W. Hunter, *To 'Joy My Freedom': Southern Black Women's Lives and Labors After the Civil War* (Cambridge: Cambridge University Press, 1997), 172, 186, 169.

113. On the relationship between industrialization, consumer culture, and the emergence of "modern subjectivity" see James Livingston, *Pragmatism, Feminism, and Democracy: Rethinking the Politics of American History* (New York: Routledge, 2001), 17–33.

114. Carby, *Cultures in Babylon,* 147.

115. Joe William Trotter Jr., *Coal, Class, and Color: Blacks in Southern West Virginia, 1915–1932* (Urbana: University of Illinois Press, 1990), 268. Ronald L. Lewis describes these same communities as a "transitional culture" between the "peasant" of the rural South and the "proletarian" society of the urban North: "From Peasant to Proletarian: The Migration of Southern Blacks to the Central Appalachian Coal Fields," *Journal of Southern History* 55 (February 1989): 231.

116. For a review of this literature see Hall et al., "Afterword," *Like a Family,* 358–363. For a work that relates the story of southern textiles to the development of modern society see Douglas Flamming, *Creating the Modern South: Millhands and Managers in Dalton, Georgia, 1884–1984* (Chapel Hill: University of North Carolina Press, 1992).

117. Berglund et al., *Labor in the Industrial South,* 3. There is a large and growing body of literature on black industrial workers in the South. With the exceptions of Trotter, Lewis, and Kelley, the authors of these works focus narrowly on workplace and union history, ignoring the implications of black industrial employment for the broader social and cultural history of the Jim Crow South. For a review of this literature see Eric Arnesen, "Up From Exclusion: Black and White Workers, Race, and the State of Labor History," *Reviews in American History* 26 (1998): 146–174.

118. Leon F. Litwack, *Trouble in Mind: Black Southerners in the Age of Jim Crow* (New York: Knopf, 1998), 137, 143. C. Vann Woodward, *Origins of the New South* (New York: Knopf, 1951), 221–234.

119. On the application of modernization theory to the southern United States see Alex Lichtenstein, *Twice the Work of Free Labor: The Political Economy of Convict Labor in the New South* (New York: Verso, 1996), 1–16.

120. Paul Gilroy, *The Black Atlantic: Modernity and Double Consciousness* (Cambridge, MA: Harvard University Press, 1993), 91.

121. Houston A. Baker Jr., *Modernism and the Harlem Renaissance* (Chicago: University of Chicago Press, 1987), 77–81.

122. For a discussion of textile workers' ambivalence toward modern culture see Hall et al., *Like a Family,* 237–288.

123. For a reconsideration of Hurston's later work in light of this intellectual model see Ross Posnock, *Color and Culture: Black Writers and the Making of the Modern Intellectual* (Cambridge, MA: Harvard University Press, 1998), 208–215.

124. Filene, *Romancing the Folk,* 137–139.

125. Robin D. G. Kelley, *Race Rebels: Culture, Politics, and the Black Working Class* (New York: Free Press, 1994), 36. Frederick Cooper makes a similar critique in relation to anticolonial politics that "contrary to James Scott's distinction of 'hidden' and 'public transcripts,' effective challenges to colonial authority came not just from groups who had preserved their discrete ideologies and identities and mobilized them at the right moment in the struggle, but from the subtle and ongoing interplay of cooperation and critique, of appropriation and denial." Cooper, *Decolonization and African Society: The Labor Question in French and British Africa* (Cambridge: Cambridge University Press, 1996), 10.

126. Murray, *Stomping the Blues,* 70.

4
An Inevitable Drift?

Oligarchy, Du Bois, and the Prospect of Democracy Between the Wars

Kenneth W. Warren

At a moment that can only be described as a crisis of faith, Matthew Towns, the hero of W. E. B. Du Bois's 1928 novel *Dark Princess,* writes to his lover and soon-to-be wife, Princess Kautilya, saying, "Hitherto I have seen democracy as the corner stone of my new world. But today and with the world, I see myself drifting logically and inevitably toward oligarchy."[1] Occurring late in the novel, Matthew's crisis of faith is particularly acute because the Princess has only just recently rescued him from the quicksand of political cynicism. Arriving in Chicago as Matthew is about to abandon his democratic principles to secure a nomination to the U.S. Congress, the Princess manages to pluck him from the clutches of his scheming wife, Sara, and for a time seems to have restored his faith in democracy. Matthew's salvation, though, is short-lived because the two are again separated, and it is during this subsequent separation that Matthew finds his democratic faith once again waning.

Although Matthew's confession does not constitute *Dark Princess*'s final word on the prospects of global democracy in the late 1920s, his despair is nonetheless illustrative of Du Bois's long-standing preoccupation with reconciling what appeared to be natural hierarchies of talent and ability among human beings with a commitment to democratic principles. Given Matthew's belief that "whether we will or not, some must rule and do for the people what they are too weak and silly to do for themselves" (283–284), the problem of government appears to come down to that of making sure that the "right" people act as rulers in a world in which it is quite possible that some people are more suited for rule than others. How, then, could a democratic form of government that gave equal weight to every individual regardless of intelligence and ability conduce to the larger human good? Of course, Du Bois's baseline assumption in considering these questions was that "natural" hierarchies among humans did not map onto notions of racial hierarchy prevailing in the early twentieth century—races may have been distinguished by the different "gifts" that each had contributed or could contribute to the entirety of the human race, as he argued in "The Conservation of Races," but they were not inferior or superior to one another in terms of their capacity to produce exceptional human beings.[2] Consequently, the rule of "the best" did not mean the rule of the white race. In fact, for Du Bois, to make possible a true "rule of the best" it was necessary to dissolve the rule of one race over another. In *Dark Princess,* which was likely begun as its author was returning from the Soviet Union, he complicated the matter by acknowledging as well that bringing about a more democratic order would require dissolving or attenuating the power of capital over labor.[3] Just how could the rule of "the best" be compatible with a commitment to the rule of "the many," who of necessity labored for their daily bread in pursuits that did not enable them to acquire the learning Du Bois deemed necessary for leadership?

This is the problem that once again shakes Matthew's moral resolve late in *Dark Princess,* precipitating a descent into cynicism that is only one more dramatic dip in the novel's roller-coaster plot, which reads a lot like a boy-meets-girl, boy-gets-girl, boy-loses-girl, boy-gets-girl story freighted with a political thesis. Matthew has left the United States in disgust after being denied an opportunity to take a required course in obstetrics because, according to the medical school dean, "white women patients are [not] going to have a nigger doctor delivering their babies" (4). While in exile in Berlin, Matthew comes to the aid of an attractive Indian woman who is being accosted by a racist American tourist. As he and the woman, who turns out to be the Princess Kautilya of Bwodpur, India, are whisked away in a taxicab, the Princess, upon hearing Matthew's story, takes him with her to a multinational conference representing the darker peoples of the world. Although members of the conference espouse the idea of multiracial unity against white domination, they nonetheless harbor deeply aristocratic sentiments that include racist estimations of the ability of Africans and African Americans to participate in their movement as equals. The Japanese representative admits that "for the larger company we represent, there is a deeper question—that of the ability, qualifications, and real possibilities of the black race in Africa or elsewhere" (21). Matthew, who had just begun to feel at home in this nonwhite atmosphere of refinement and ability, rejects this charge, first, by singing "Go Down, Moses," a song whose aesthetic beauty he sees as vindicating "the black rabble of America," and then by professing his faith in the capacities of the lowly in the United States: "America is teaching the world one thing and only one thing of real value, and that is, that ability and capacity for culture is not the hereditary monopoly of a few, but the widespread possibility for the majority of mankind if they only have a decent chance in life" (26).

Moved by Matthew's passion, the Princess defies the rest of the council by sending Matthew on a mission to assess the likelihood that blacks in the United

States are ready for an insurrection. Matthew eagerly accepts the Princess's charge and returns to the United States, where he sends her regular reports on what he observes. She reads his reports, but her skeptical colleagues intercept the letters she writes him in return, leaving him to believe he has been abandoned. His despair is deepened by several circumstances, including his discovery that Perigua, the leading man in the black revolutionary effort, is something of a crackpot. But the lynching of a friend (for which Matthew feels responsible) and an aborted Pullman Porter strike of a special Ku Klux Klan train lead Matthew not only to countenance Perigua's plan to dynamite the train but also to place himself on board, working as a porter, so that he will be martyred for the cause when Perigua blows up the train. It is only the somewhat improbable reappearance of the Princess as a passenger that leads Matthew to stop the train, saving her and also himself, so that the novel may stage their eventual reunion as husband and wife.

Before this reunion can occur, however, the two are separated twice more, setting the stage for the Princess's timely reappearance as Matthew is about to accept the nomination that will likely make him the first black congressional representative since Reconstruction. Engineered by his wife, Sara, a corrupt Chicago political operative, the nomination has come at a considerable moral price, and Matthew describes himself as having "sold his soul to the Devil" in deciding to accept it (207). So it is nothing less than his soul that the Princess is determined to save when she again returns. Appearing before Matthew as a representative of the Box-Makers Union, she declares to him, "See, I came to save you! I came to save your soul from hell" (209). This rescue of Matthew makes possible a brief reunion during which he and the Princess sexually consummate their relationship, despite his marriage to Sara—a legal and ethical obstacle that the novel keeps in place long enough to gear up the plot's separation/reunion dynamic one more time so that Matthew can slip again into the political slough of despond where oligarchy, rather than democracy, seems to be the future of humanity.

In setting up Matthew's rescue and redemption, *Dark Princess* takes up two lines of skepticism concerning the political prospects for black people. The first, as we have seen, constitutes a response to doubtful assessments of the capacities of the black race generally. The second concerns whether or not it is possible, in light of the world of realpolitik depicted in the novel's third part, "The Chicago Politician," to sustain a belief that black political participation could produces outcomes that Du Bois could characterize as democratic. At the turn of the century when Du Bois had faced skeptical assessments of blacks' capacities and readiness for full participation in the rights and responsibilities of citizenship and higher education he did so in the context of his opposition to Booker T. Washington's program for advancing the black race, objecting to Washington's advice "that black people give up, at least for the present, three things,—First, political power, / Second, insistence on civil rights, /Third, higher education of Negro youth"[4] Against Washington, Du Bois asserted not only the fundamental importance of each of these demands but also the necessity of pressing for all three more or less simultaneously rather than sequentially. The granting of political power could not be made contingent on prior acquisition of education. Elsewhere in *Souls* he observes "that in every state the best arbiters of their own welfare are the persons directly affected; consequently that it is only by arming every hand with a ballot,—with the right to have a voice in the policy of the state,—that the greatest good to the greatest number could be attained." To the extent that any one of these demands could precede the other, it was political power, exercised through the franchise, that could take precedence because universal suffrage would make evident the immediate need for universal education: "The possession of so great power by a great class in the nation would compel their fellows to educate this class to its intelligent use."[5] An intelligent vote was better than an ignorant vote, but an ignorant vote was better than no vote at all, largely because, in Du Bois's reckoning, ignorant votes would not long stay ignorant.

To be sure, as Judith Stein notes, in the late 1890s "Du Bois, as well as Booker T. Washington, accepted southern franchise restrictions" to ensure that as a people developed, its presumed incompetence and weaknesses did not sully the ballot, but that by the time he wrote *Souls* Du Bois had come to oppose such limits after seeing how they "struck at the educated as well as the ignorant."[6] His growing disagreement with Washington was not, however, premised on an opposition to all forms of social hierarchy but stemmed in part from his fear that Washington's program impeded the selection of exceptional men and women from the black populace, as well as from his concerns that Washington's "Tuskegee Machine" was aggressively stifling all critical opposition. Writing in *Dusk of Dawn* about his objections to Washington, Du Bois recalls, "Contrary to most opinion, the controversy as it developed was not entirely against Mr. Washington's ideas, but became the insistence upon the right of other Negroes to have and express other ideas."[7] Du Bois's advocacy for liberal education was crucial to making it possible for those capable of leadership and distinction to have and express ideas. In *Souls* he writes in regard to broadening access to liberal education, "Today we have climbed to heights where we would open at least the outer courts of knowledge to all, display its treasures to many, and select the few to whom its mystery of Truth is revealed, not wholly by birth or the accidents of the stock market, but at least in part according to deftness and aim, talent and character" (426). On this account, the chief problems with Washington's program were that it denied the race necessary opportunities for developing its leadership cadre and insisted on stifling the voices of dissent that already existed within that group. Although Washington had died more than a decade before Du Bois wrote *Dark Princess,* the terms of agreement and disagreement between the two men continued to frame Du Bois's engagement with the problem of equality. Indeed, it is against the backdrop of this dialogue with Washington that *Dark Princess*'s equivocations about democracy are best understood.[8]

Early in the novel Matthew describes himself as having been a young man "firm in my Hampton training" and stalwart in his belief that "desert and hard work were bound to tell."

> Prejudice was a miasma that character burned away. I believed this thoroughly. I had literally pounded my triumphant way through school and life. Of course I

> had met insult and rebuff here and there, but I ignored them, laughed at them, and went my way. Those black people who cringed and cowered, complained of failure and "no chance," I despised—weaklings, cowards, fools! Go to work! Make a way! Compel recognition! (12)

But the bitter irony that creeps into Mathew's description of his early beliefs makes clear his realization that Booker T. Washington's Hampton-Tuskegee model severely misrecognized the nature and effects of racial prejudice and thereby undermined Matthew's capacity to sympathize with the plights of other blacks. Under the sway of his Hampton training Matthew had "covertly sneered at" and "avoided" the two other black students in medical school who were clearly struggling (12). It is only after being denied access to the clinical training necessary to complete his medical career—a rebuff impossible to ignore—that he begins to see the inadequacy of his "life theory" that "character and brains were too much for prejudice" (13). Now seeing "there may have been a dozen reasons why Phillips of Mississippi could neither spell nor read correctly and why Jones of Georgia could not count. They had had no hardworking mother, no Hampton, no happy accidents of fortune to help them on," Matthew comes to understand the difference between himself and Phillips and Jones as merely a matter of circumstance and accident and not one of innate capacity, an understanding that helps set the terms for the ways in which the novel goes about reconciling the problem of class differences within the black race with democracy (12).

Dohra Ahmad, along with other readers of the *Dark Princess,* has argued that the novel's formal oscillations between realism and romance reflect its internal political debate. Ahmad not only maps the story's geography onto the novel's formal divisions by noting that Chicago is rendered realistically while romance is reserved for the U.S. South and India, but she also links the differing representational modes to the contrasts between Washington's and Du Bois's accounts of racial progress. Describing realism as an "aesthetic of limitation coincid[ing] with an era of compromise and palliative reform," the era during which Washington came to power, Ahmad reads *Dark Princess*'s formal structure as one that identifies, in order simultaneously to "unwrite," realism, the ideology of Tuskegee, and the corrupt politics of Chicago.[9] The novel's privileged geographies are "Oriental" and rural, and its privileged mode is romance. Accordingly, Kautilya's final rescue of Matthew involves getting him away from the city. She pleads with him, saying, "You are not free in Chicago nor New York. But here in Virginia you are at the edge of a black world" (286). Although Ahmad's identification of Chicago's political maneuvering with Washington's ideology makes sense to the extent that Du Bois censures both as betrayals of higher ideals, the pairing nonetheless obscures the way that Du Bois's critique of black participation in Chicago's electoral politics, and of black life in Chicago generally, dovetails with some of the reservations both he and Washington had voiced in the 1890s about what they regarded as negative social effects caused by urbanization, too easy access to consumer goods, premature political participation, and the immediate exercise of the franchise by uneducated black masses.

In *Up from Slavery*, Washington expresses alarm at what he describes as the "superficiality" of much of black life in the nation's capitol. He writes,

> I saw young coloured men who were not earning more than four dollars a week spend two dollars or more for a buggy on Sunday to ride up and down Pennsylvania Avenue in order that they might try to convince the world that they were worth thousands. I saw other young men who received seventy-five or one hundred dollars per month from the Government, who were in debt at the end of every month.... Among a large class there seemed to be a dependence upon the Government for every conceivable thing. (63)

Uttering a vilification of black political activity used to justify disfranchisement in the 1890s (a vilification that in various guises has persisted as a mode of antiprogressive critique up to the present moment), Washington then indulges a moment of wishful fantasy—perhaps we might even call it a moment of romance—to imagine how a future for the black denizens of D.C. might look otherwise. He wishes for himself "some power of magic [so] I might remove the great bulk of these people into the country districts and plant them upon the soil, upon the solid and never deceptive foundation of Mother Nature, where all nations and races that have ever succeeded have gotten their start,—a start that at first may be slow and toilsome, but one that nevertheless is real" (63).

Washington's imaginary "repatriation" of D.C.'s black population to southern country districts is mirrored in *Dark Princess* by Matthew's return to the Virginia environs he left before the novel's beginning, suggesting that the move from Chicago to Virginia can be seen as much a move toward aspects of Booker T. Washington's concerns as it is a move away from them. Just as his Hampton education had led Washington to believe in the importance of having his students in the newly founded Tuskegee Institute "erect their own buildings,"[10] Kautilya, who has spent her time away from Matthew learning the virtues of labor, prepares for Matthew's return to Virginia by building a new cabin for the two of them (282). She declares in a letter to him that the cabin will be "a place of worship, of beauty and books" with "a half story for a broad and peaceful chamber—for life with music and color floating in it" (278). By filling this simple rural structure along "Hampton Roads" with a life of books, music, and spirituality the novel virtually rehabilitates the Hampton-Tuskegee model.[11] That is, while Matthew had left Virginia because Hampton had "insisted on making him a farmer," Kautilya, by creating a space for higher things, makes it possible for Matthew to return to the world of the farmer: "the earth yearning for seed" in a place where "men make food and clothes," "the bottom and beginning of things" (11, 278). Indeed Kautilya's words come close to paraphrasing Washington's expressed desire for the "solid and never deceptive foundation of Mother Nature, where all nations and races that have ever succeeded have gotten their start." Of course, in one sense the differences here make all the difference: Kautilya's cabin with its emphasis on art and music is not General Samuel Armstrong's Hampton or

Booker T. Washington's Tuskegee campus where the gospel of industrial training reigned.

Yet one feature making possible a convergence of Kautilya's idyll and Washington's Hampton-Tuskegee model is *Dark Princess*'s persistent commitment to an understanding of human progress as racial group progress, and racial group progress as a matter of cultivating from within each group a leadership cadre. So when Matthew despairs of democracy's prospects in the face of oligarchy, the Princess responds not so much by rescuing democracy but by redeeming oligarchy. She writes to Matthew,

> your oligarchy as you conceive it is not the antithesis of democracy—it is democracy if only the selection of oligarchs is just and true. Birth is the method of blind fools. Wealth is the gambler's method. Only Talent served from the great Reservoir of All Men of All Races, of All Classes, of All Ages, of Both Sexes—this is the real Aristocracy, real Democracy—the only path to that great and final Freedom which you so well call Divine Anarchy. (285)

She adds, "The tyranny of which you dream is the true method which I too envisage. But choose well the Tyrants—there is Eternal Life!" (286). As Arnold Rampersad observes, Matthew's preferred "vision is of an agrarian America, guided into gentility by an oligarchy of excellence" (213). Or to put the matter differently, democracy in *Dark Princess* comes down to a matter of being ruled by the right people. Du Bois's novel, in the words of Lovie N. Gibson, constitutes a search "for positive political activity within the 'veil.'"[12] And given the logic of the novel, the conclusion of this search would also seem to mean replacing the cabal of political operatives who attend Sara Andrews's dinner on the night Matthew is supposed to accept nomination to the U.S. House of Representatives with the more ideal political assemblage of representatives of the darker races convened by Kautilya at the close of the novel.

Democracy, of course, was a constant theme in Du Bois's writings, and in the years leading up to the ratification of the Nineteenth Amendment he advocated staunchly for the measure that would ultimately make a Sara Andrews possible. Writing in the sixth chapter of *Darkwater* (1919), he insists "if America is ever to become a government built on the broadest justice to every citizen, then every citizen must be enfranchised." The only exclusions on the franchise that he was willing to tolerate were temporary ones. All people, he insisted, "must be raised rapidly to a place where they can speak for themselves." Extending in *Darkwater* the line he took in defending the franchise in *Souls* sixteen years earlier, he asserts, "Education is not a prerequisite to political control—political control is the cause of popular education."[13]

Indeed, as he makes the case in *Darkwater* for universal suffrage, Du Bois argues for the pedagogical and "civilizing" effect that voting would have on those newly admitted to the franchise, declaring that in "every modern state there must come to the polls every generation, and indeed every year, men who are inexperienced in the solutions of the political problems that confront them and who must experiment in methods of ruling men. Thus and thus only will civilization grow"

(*Darkwater,* 553). This process of growth, however, would be far from smooth and would entail significant social upheaval. Elaborating this argument in support of the Nineteenth Amendment, Du Bois admits:

> It is not, for a moment, to be assumed that enfranchising women will not cost something. It will for many years confuse our politics. It may even change the present status of family life. It will admit to the ballot thousands of inexperienced persons, unable to vote intelligently. Above all, it will interfere with some of the present prerogatives of men and probably for some time to come annoy them considerably. So, too, Negro enfranchisement meant reconstruction, with its theft and bribery and incompetency as well as its public schools and enlightened, social legislation. (*Darkwater,* 556–557)

That Du Bois in the conclusion of this passage partly acquiesces in a view of Reconstruction politics as roiled by black incompetence—a view that his later book *Black Reconstruction* will help undermine—is telling because it underscores his commitment to the idea of politics as collective, mutual tutelage. Du Bois's unspoken assumption of group knowledge and progress obscures his earlier acknowledgement that human societies are always absorbing inexperienced individuals into political life. What comes to the fore instead is the view that because propertied white men as a group have long wielded the franchise, and women as a group lack comparable experience and history, an individual man voting for the first time will likely do so more intelligently than a woman voting who is doing likewise. *Darkwater*'s vindication of extending the franchise to women rests, in the first instance, on a claim that women are individuals whose knowledge of their own needs as individuals is necessary to successful governing. Du Bois observes that while many "people assume that it was corruption that made such aristocracies fail" in truth, the "best and most effective aristocracy, like the best monarchy, suffered from lack of knowledge. The rulers did not know or understand the needs of the people and they could not find out, for in the last analysis only the man himself, however humble, knows his own condition" (*Darkwater,* 554). Attributing effective governance to the state's knowledge of its citizens, Du Bois proclaims that the "real argument for democracy is, then, that in the people we have the source of that endless life and unbounded wisdom which the rulers of men must have" (*Darkwater,* 554). But in reckoning the cost of keeping women disenfranchised, he marks the specific contributions of women to democracy in terms of their socially gendered roles, writing that "no state can be strong which excludes from its expressed wisdom the knowledge possessed by mothers, wives, and daughters. We have but to view the unsatisfactory relations of the sexes the world over and the problem of children to realize how desperately we need this excluded wisdom" (*Darkwater,* 555).

Accordingly, whatever the initial problems that would follow from the extension of the franchise to women, Du Bois's defense of the Nineteenth Amendment predicted that eventually the nation's political life would benefit greatly from the contributions of women. *Dark Princess,* in which two women figure quite prominently, would appear then to provide the perfect vehicle through which Du Bois could test this proposition. And indeed it does, but the answer the book offers is at best ambivalent. To be sure, Kautilya's influence on Matthew's political life is undeniably uplifting. Late in the novel he tells the Princess the "only thing that was able to lift me from cynical selfishness, organized theft and deception, was that finest thing within me—this love and idealization of you. If I had not followed it at every cost, I should have sunk beneath hell" (263). Yet if Kautilya redeems Matthew politically, her influence cannot be construed to have redeemed franchise extension because Kautilya is not a U.S. citizen and therefore cannot vote. More important, the place "beneath hell" that is Chicago's electoral politics is also the province of another woman, Sara Andrews, Matthew's first wife. As such Sara would seem to refute Du Bois's argument that deeper political wisdom would accrue from the enfranchisement of women. Her effect on political life in Chicago seems far from what Du Bois had in mind when he wrote his essays in *Darkwater.* Sara is described as having "no particular scruples or conscience. Lying, stealing, bribery, gambling, prostitution, were facts that she accepted casually. Personally honest and physically 'pure' almost to prudery, she could put a lie through the typewriter in so adroit a way that it sounded better than the truth and was legally fireproof. She recognized politics as a means of private income" (112). A damning portrait, and yet, as many readers of the novel have noted, the overall depiction of Sara is not entirely unsympathetic. In fact, some have argued that although Du Bois reserved some of his most erotically charged language to portray the Princess, he renders Sara more fully as a fictional character than Kautilya. In his 1928 review of the novel for the *Crisis,* Allison Davis deems Sara "more significant than any character yet drawn from Negro life" and credits the accuracy of her portrait as the work of "an artist in fiction."[14] Ironically, Du Bois's success in creating Sara may have resulted from his decision to place her entirely in the realm of politics. It is as if by removing sexuality, idealism, and even the conventional goals of domesticity from his representational palette, Du Bois was obliged to render a character who was almost nothing more than political calculation. Although lacking idealism or spiritualism, Sara has a sense of self-interest more imaginative and capacious than that of her Chicago associates. On the strength of this self-interest, she is able to elevate the ambitions of those around her beyond small-time political graft. The larger arena represented by the U.S. Congress is nothing more to her than "the greatest market in the land" (156). Du Bois's powerfully effective rendering of Sara's manipulation of Republicans, Progressives, Democrats, and union leaders alike through the machinery of Chicago politics is intended to drive home the fact that while the electoral process can create the facade of representativeness, it does not even approximate the real democracy of which Du Bois wrote in *Darkwater.*

Du Bois's virtual unsexing of Sara (she's "pleasing but a trifle disconcerting to look at. Men always turned to gaze at her, but they did not attempt to flirt—at least not more than once" [109]) underscores the sterility of Chicago politics. Structurally, then, Kautilya's sexuality and fertility are almost demanded of the novel by way of contrast. Likewise demanded, given Sara's rather soulless instrumentalism, is a resolution that involves some form of spirituality. Expectedly then, the salvation of

Matthew and of the narrative's political hopes lies not only in the final reunion of Kautilya and Matthew but in the birth of their child, Madhu, who proves the fertility of their politics. Emphasizing the transcendent quality of Matthew and Kautilya and the global politics they represent, the pageant that announces their marriage also announces their son-to-be, the "Messenger and Messiah to all the Darker Worlds!" (311). The solemn reverence with which Du Bois treats the wedding of Kautilya and Matthew contrasts markedly with his depiction of Matthew's earlier nuptials with Sara, when the bride had punctuated the ceremony with sartorial remonstrances to the groom: "Straighten your tie" and "Be careful of the veil" (143–144).

Yet in the romantic pageantry of the novel's ending it is easy to forget that despite being thwarted in her political ambitions by Matthew's renunciation, Sara is not permanently scapegoated. To be sure, she suffers through public humiliation and voluntarily exiles herself from Chicago for a time after the debacle of the nominating dinner. But she doesn't end the novel wandering in a wilderness outside the political order. That is, *Dark Princess* ends not with one marriage but with two (or at least the immediate prospect of a second). The more prominent of the two of course is the union of Matthew and Kautilya, which is rendered in the idealized language and conventions of romance. The second, which we see as Sara's acceptance of a marriage proposal from her longtime political co-operative, Sammy Scott, is portrayed in the mode of comic realism. The language of the scene is casual if not slangy. Sammy tells Sara, "I'm damned if I am going to lose you to another half-baked guy," and he puts the question to her with a "What d'ya say, kid?" to which Sara responds, "You're on, Sammy" (275, 277). And while Matthew continually views Kautilya through a soft-focus lens that ennobles even apparent flaws, Sara appraises Sammy with an unsentimental eye: "Sammy was no Adonis. He was approaching middle age and was showing signs of wear and tear" (275). Yet if Sara's decision to accept Sammy's offer has about it the air of a ward meeting, business transaction, or merger (not only do the two talk more of Sammy's new wealth and of the political possibilities that will ensue from their marriage than they do of their feelings for each other, but the narrator also observes, "Neither quite trusted the other, and yet they needed each other"), Du Bois does suggest that in its own way this will be a marriage of true minds based on something like genuine feeling. Sara realizes that "between her and Sammy there was a common philosophy, a common humor, and a common understanding." In fact, both she and Sammy recognize a true emotional need for the other: "Sara had missed Sammy more than she dared acknowledge, while without Sara, Sammy felt one-armed." But perhaps the most important indication that Du Bois does not treat this marriage as merely a parody of the true companionate marriage of Matthew and Kautilya is this: Once Sara seals the deal with Sammy, she gives way to an "impulse, a thing she had not done in ten years" and kisses him (275)—a faint indication of the possibility of passion and fertility.[15]

That Du Bois does not completely vilify Sara for denying him an opportunity to demonstrate the political benefits of extending the franchise to women stems partly from his assessment of the progress of democracy at that particular moment. The good that he asserted would ensue from universal suffrage would be realized only if the right to vote truly became universal, which it had not. In a two-part article, "The Possibility of Democracy," published in the September and October 1928 issues of *The Crisis,* Du Bois sets out to assess "how far the policies of this government are going to be controlled by the vote of its citizens."[16] The answer, which Du Bois reaches through an analysis of available statistics, is that the story of the electoral process in the United States during the first decades of the twentieth century has been a story of general disfranchisement effected through the effort to keep black voters off the rolls. Even the Nineteenth Amendment had failed to stem this tide. Looking at the statistics from South Carolina, Du Bois observes that "a hundred and fifty thousand women came to the polls right after the adoption of the woman's suffrage amendment out of a possible two million and 50,000 of these disappeared four years later in spite of a million increase in population."[17] The trend Du Bois discerned was unmistakable, and in light of that trend, he argues, the nation either needed to realize its commitment to universal suffrage or admit its de facto endorsement of limited suffrage. Using language that could have come from *Dark Princess,* he writes, "Possibly we are ready for Italian syndicalistic oligarchy or Spanish dictatorship. But if this is true we must face the change frankly and adopt it logically. We must not drift further as we are doing. For a generation the possibility of any rational consultation of the public will in this country has been fading."[18]

If the possibility of the public's exercising its will over government had been waning for a generation, then Sara Andrews and Sammy Scott could not be solely held responsible for the deplorable state of electoral politics in Chicago. They may be simply as good as their circumstances allow, which also explains the urgency of Kautilya's appeals to Matthew to leave the big cities. *Dark Princess* (at least in its "Chicago Politician" chapter) operates up to a point as a novel that, true to the tenets of realism, withholds some measure of moral judgment of its characters in favor of viewing them as creatures of their environment. This is not to say that Sara escapes judgment entirely—she is clearly not worthy to be Matthew's wife. Nor is it to say that many of the novel's readers haven't seen her as deserving of moral opprobrium. Allison Davis's review of the novel (which appears in the same issue of the *Crisis* as does the second part of Du Bois's assessment of American democracy) describes Sara as a moral mirror revealing the venalities of the "Negro middle class"—a class that is "ignoble" and "killing its dignity and its vision by selfish comfort and detachment."[19] Yet if *Dark Princess* clearly does not enjoin its readers to be like Sara, it certainly helps them understand how a Sara might come to be and to see that becoming as not entirely a matter of moral failure. Like Matthew, she is a refugee from the Jim Crow South, who had "fought her way through school," "forced herself into the local business college," and refused to acquiesce when "the color line appeared, broad and clear, in the town, following the influx of black laborers from the countryside" (110).

Even so, actual black participation in politics by individuals like Sara, a business school graduate, and Sammy, "a super-businessman," presented Du Bois with a problem because the reality did not come close to matching the ideal (110). As Wilson Jeremiah Moses notes, because Du Bois, like many black progressives from

Frederick Douglass onward, shared the distaste of northeastern white intellectual elites for the rough and tumble of city politics, it was "impossible [for him] to view Tammany Hall or the Chicago ward as offering models for black American political organization."[20] On the one hand, during this period the city stood as a "dream of a Black Metropolis" and, in 1928, had elected the first black to the U.S. Congress since 1901. But on the other hand, as St. Clair Drake and Horace Cayton have pointed out, Chicago, for many black Americans, had also come to represent "a makeshift dream, a substitute for the real American Dream of complete integration into American life. To some who watched Negroes inherit the city's slums, crowded together amid squalor and vice, where schemers, white and black, battened on their blood, the dream seemed a fraud and a delusion."[21] These schemers troubled Du Bois's vision. Black Chicago politics was defined by the likes of Jesse Binga, Pullman Porter turned banker, and Oscar DePriest, who, although indicted in 1917 on conspiracy and bribery charges connected with gambling houses and brothels (he was not convicted), had nonetheless managed, by 1928, to win a U.S. congressional seat. DePriest, who, as David Levering Lewis observes, "might be an unscrupulous character strutting out of *Dark Princess,*" received from Du Bois the kind of practical endorsement that characterizes his stance toward Sara in his novel.[22] Asked by a reader to "repudiate" DePriest as an "unethical colored man" in the pages of *The Crisis,* Du Bois refuses to do so, observing that in the current political environment, "the only organized interests in the United States who could be induced to send a colored man to Congress or any man who stands for enforcement of the Reconstruction Amendments, passage of the Dyer Anti-Lynching Bill, abolition of Jim Crow in interstate commerce, and abolition of color segregation and discrimination in the U.S. civil service are the same interests which are allied with the rule of wealth and crime."[23] If, as Rampersad, asserts, *Dark Princess* shows its author to have been "totally aware of the limitations of such political pragmatism," the novel also enacts Du Bois's willingness to countenance a limited political compromise with the politics of DePriest and other machine politicians until such a time as a new leadership group could emerge to take its place.[24]

Dark Princess makes it clear that the realm of electoral politics could not produce the well-chosen tyrants who, in Kautilya's vision, were required if oligarchy were to be transformed into divine anarchy. Those individuals would have to come from elsewhere. Du Bois had insisted from the turn of the century forward, in essays titled "The Talented Tenth" and "Careers Open to College-Bred Negroes," that liberal arts colleges ought to be the places where exceptional men and women could gain a "vision of life" that was "truer and holier and more real than the narrow, sordid views of life which you meet on the streets and in the homes of smaller souls." Yet in *Dark Princess* colleges such as Fisk, where Du Bois delivered these remarks, are conspicuously absent from the novel's romantic resolution.[25] To be sure, Kautilya's new cabin makes a place for liberal learning. But the black liberal arts college as an institution is missing from this setting. Taking its place is the newlyweds' home from which emanates an apparent modification of the idea of elite rule from Du Bois's earlier essays. The Princess observes that while the cry of the moment is "Workers

Unite" the problem is that "thinkers who do not work have tried to unite workers who do not think. Only working thinkers can unite thinking workers" (286). Although Kautilya presents her vision as a bottom-up social order, the artful chiasmus in which she expresses her solution nevertheless keeps intact the distinction of those who rule from those who are ruled, even as it presents workers in terms of their current inadequacies. She asserts plenty of reason for political optimism—"I have seen slaves ruling in Chicago and they did not do nearly as badly as princes in Russia"—but *Dark Princess,* despite the wish-fulfilling license granted to romance, defers the realization of its new social order until the future. Bringing about a society of thinking workers will, according to Kautilya, require the passage of "Time. The slow majestic march of events" (286).

But if the moment when thinking workers will emerge in significant numbers lies somewhere beyond the novel's distant horizon, working thinkers, in the persons of Matthew and the Princess, exist within the novel's present, and the work they are to do does come with a specific timetable: "In 1952, the Dark World goes free," the Princess tells Matthew after informing him of his selection to "The Great Central Committee of Yellow, Brown and Black" (296–297). In its concluding pages the novel summons to Virginia a "representative" body of darker peoples, which, in contrast to the Council of Darker Races encountered by Matthew at the beginning of the novel, includes not only members from "Black America" but also individuals who came "as laborers, as cotton pickers, as peddlers, as fortune tellers, as travelers and tourists, as merchants, as servants" (297–298). Kautilya's phrasing makes it unclear whether those members in nonelite guise were people like her—that is, elites who had voluntarily taken on more humble occupations to learn about life from the bottom up—or whether they represented a select group of talent gleaned from various walks of life. Either way, the Committee, with its plan for liberation, exemplifies what remained central to Du Bois's vision of democratic politics: a talented group of individuals speaking and acting on behalf of those who were not yet able to speak for themselves. Notably, the Committee has already made its decisions and adjourned before Matthew can arrive to take part in its deliberations. Again to quote Reed, notwithstanding his support for socialism, pan-Africanism, and racial pluralism, Du Bois remained, during the period between the wars, consistent "on the importance of the elite's role" and "emphatic about the need for 'trained' leadership."[26] If reading fiction like *Dark Princess* was to be part of this training, one problem with the black political leadership of Chicago is that the novel cannot imagine Sammy or Sara taking out the time to read the kind of book *Dark Princess* represents. When Du Bois commented on the importance of "Negro Art" in 1926 he imagines himself as addressing an audience that recognizes the emptiness of defining life's goals as owning "the most powerful of motor cars" or "the most elaborate estate on the North Shore," or wearing "the most striking clothes" and giving "the richest dinners."[27] Such goals are of course the very things that impress Sara and Sammy, and if the novel holds out little hope for the redemption of the type that these two represent, it also keeps them on the social scene. One of Du Bois's goals in writing the novel was to reveal the "difficulties and realities of race prejudice on many sorts of people—ambitious black American youth, educated Asiatics, selfish colored politicians, ambitious self-seekers of all races."[28] But perhaps, more than he realized, the novel, which he deemed his favorite book, also reveals the difficulties that political reality presents for his vision of racial unity—the Saras and Sammys of the world were not about to disappear. They stay in view in part because of the persistence of racism but also because of the persistence of politics as a realm in which people of competing interests jostle and jockey for gain and advantage.

In conclusion, *Dark Princess* stands as one of Du Bois's periodic messages to a black elite he saw as needing occasional reminders of its higher mission. These reminders, which he delivered in his writings beginning with his turn-of-the-century essays through and beyond his 1940 autobiography, *Dusk of Dawn,* in which he championed bringing "the cultured face to face with the untrained" through Negro consumer cooperatives for the purpose of accomplishing "the acculturation of the many through the few," remained consistent in their emphasis on racial group progress (714). From Du Bois's point of view what was in the best interest of the race was not difficult to discern, but what needed continual attention were the processes by which those individuals best able to express and act according to that interest could come to the fore. *Dark Princess*'s cognizance of the rise of labor power on the world scene demanded greater access to the halls of leadership from the ranks of the hewers of wood and drawers of water—but Du Bois had made similar arguments for decades. At the moment of the writing of *Dark Princess* what he wanted to convey to the would-be Talented Tenth was that their own disdain and contempt for the power of labor threatened to make them parochial and ineffectual in challenging the existing political order. Nonetheless, while the world Du Bois sought to represent in *Dark Princess* had been profoundly shaken from the bottom up, he remained convinced that for the time being its salvation—like Matthew's rescue from political cynicism—would come from the top down.

NOTES

1. W. E. B. Du Bois, *Dark Princess* (Jackson: University of Mississippi Press, 1995), 283. Subsequent references in the text will be cited parenthetically by page number only.

2. W. E. B. Du Bois, "The Conservation of Races," in *Writings* (New York: Library of America, 1986), 817–819.

3. David Levering Lewis writes that Du Bois returned from Russia in 1927 "in first-class comfort ... and very probably writing the first pages of what would become *Dark Princess,* his second novel." Lewis, *W.E.B. Du Bois: The Fight for Equality and the American Century, 1919–1963* (New York: Henry Holt, 2000), 203.

4. W. E. B. Du Bois, *Souls of Black Folk* in *Writings* (New York: Library of America, 1986), 398.

5. Ibid., 481–482.

6. Judith Stein, "Defining the Race, 1890–1930." In *Up From Slavery* Washington writes, "As a rule, I believe in universal, free suffrage, but I believe that in the South we are confronted with peculiar conditions that justify the protection of the ballot in many of the states for a while at least, either by an educational test, property test, or by both combined; but whatever

tests are required, they should be made to apply with equal and exact justice to both races." *Up From Slavery* (New York: Signet, 2000), 165. See also Adolph Reed Jr., *W. E. B. Du Bois and American Political Thought: Fabianism and the Color Line* (New York: Oxford University Press, 1997), 66.

7. Du Bois, *Dusk of Dawn* in *Writings,* 609. Elsewhere in this volume, Adolph Reed's "*The Souls of Black Folk* Revisited: The Context of Black Politics Then and Now" carefully lays out the lines of convergence and difference between Washington and Du Bois over the course of the latter's career.

8. As Stein points out, the necessity of elite stewardship worked out by Du Bois in the early decades of the twentieth century "persisted in his novel *Dark Princess* (1925)."

9. Dohra Ahmad, "More Than Romance: Genre and Geography in *Dark Princess,*" *ELH* 69 (2002): 781.

10. Washington, "Up from Slavery," 103.

11. Rampersad labels the novel's vision "Jeffersonian." See 217.

12. Lovie N. Gibson, "W. E. B. Du Bois as a Propaganda Novelist," *Negro American Literature Forum* 10, no. 3 (Autumn 1976): 79.

13. W. E. B. Du Bois, *Darkwater: Voices from Behind the Veil,* in *The Oxford W. E. B. Du Bois Reader,* ed. Eric Sundquist (New York: Oxford University Press, 1996), 557, 555, 553.

14. Allison Davis, *Dark Princess* (Review), *Crisis* 35, no. 1 (October 2008): 359, 360. For other appreciate assessments of Du Bois's rendering of Sara, see Rampersad, *Art and Imagination,* 211; and Keith E. Byerman, *Seizing the Word: History, Art, and Self in the Work of W. E. B. Du Bois* (Athens: University of Georgia Press, 1994), 131.

15. Rampersad sees no softening in Sara whatsoever, observing, "beneath her cold exterior is a heart of stone"; *Art and Imagination,* 212.

16. Du Bois, "The Possibility of Democracy in America (Part I)," *Crisis* 35, no. 9 (September 1928): 295.

17. Du Bois, "The Possibility of Democracy in America (Part II)," *Crisis* 35, no. 10 (October 1928): 353.

18. Du Bois, "The Possibility of Democracy in America (Part I)," 295.

19. Davis, *Dark Princess* (Review), 339.

20. Wilson Jeremiah Moses, *Afrotopia: The Roots of African American Popular History* (Cambridge: Cambridge University Press, 1998), 130.

21. St. Clair Drake and Horace R. Cayton, *Black Metropolis: A Study of Negro Life in a Northern City* (Chicago: University of Chicago Press, 1993), 81–82.

22. Lewis, *W.E.B. Du Bois,* 238.

23. Du Bois, "DePriest," *Crisis* 36, no. 2 (February 1929): 57.

24. Rampersad, *Art and Imagination,* 212.

25. Du Bois, "On Careers Open to College-Bred Negroes," in *Writings,* 840.

26. Reed, *W. E. B. Du Bois and American Political Thought,* 76.

27. Du Bois, "The Criteria of Negro Art," in *Writings,* 994. Herman Beavers reads *Dark Princess* as exemplifying Du Bois's arguments in "Criteria." See Beavers, "Romancing the Body Politic: Du Bois's Propaganda of the Darker World," in *Annals of the American Academy of Political and Social Science* 568, special issue on the Study of African American Problems: W. E. B. Du Bois's Agenda, Then and Now (March 2000): 256.

28. Quoted in Lewis, *W.E.B. Du Bois,* 220.

5
The Educational Alliance and the Urban League in New York

Ethnic Elites and the Politics of Americanization and Racial Uplift, 1903–1932

Touré F. Reed

Since the 1980s, a growing body of scholarship has explored how the class identities of black Progressive-era activists shaped their visions of group advancement. Few, however, have offered direct comparisons of the aims and tactics pursued by Afro-American and white reformers. As a result, historians have tended to take the parallels and divergences in the class perspectives of black and white ethnic elites for granted, leading to largely speculative accounts of difference. This essay examines the class perspectives and the assimilationist projects of Jewish and black reformers during periods of substantial migration through a comparison of the activities of the Educational Alliance and the Urban League. By treating the Alliance and the League as case studies in Americanization and racial uplift, this essay seeks to place the class visions of Afro-American social activists in the broader frame of Progressive reform. It, moreover, examines not only philosophies but programs created by Jewish and Afro-American elites to assist their poor brethren to fully explore the implications of black self-help ideology.

David L. Lewis's groundbreaking "Parallels and Divergences: Assimilationist Strategies of Afro-American and Jewish Elites from 1910 to the Early 1930s" is one of the few systematic accounts of the similarities in class perspectives between black and Jewish reformers. Focusing largely on ideology, Lewis traces the origins of Jewish philanthropic support for black civil rights to Afro-American and Jewish elites' shared anxieties over a swelling tide of racial antagonism in the early twentieth century.[1] Though Lewis makes clear that ties between these ethnic leaders were further strengthened by a mutual distrust of their unacculturated migrant brethren, he devotes little attention to how such fears influenced specific efforts. Lewis therefore offers few insights into the similarities and differences between the actual reform endeavors pursued by Jewish and black leaders.[2]

Since the publication of Lewis's "Parallels and Divergences," historians of black reform have devoted little attention to the similarities in class perspectives between black and white ethnic reformers.[3] Instead, much of the more recent scholarship on black uplift has presumed that the uniqueness of the black experience imbued Afro-American Progressive-era activists with a class vision that was necessarily distinct from their white ethnic counterparts. Evelyn Brooks Higginbotham[4] and Stephanie Shaw,[5] for example, have each argued that whites' failure to acknowledge class and cultural differences among Afro-Americans led middle-class black women to develop a sense of collective responsibility that generally muted the class tensions shaping other reform movements of the era. While these studies, as well as those by Glenda Gilmore, Paula Giddings, and Kevin Gaines, have certainly advanced our understanding of how black reformers viewed themselves, they have focused on Afro-American activists in isolation from other contemporaneous movements. Consequently, uplift scholarship takes for granted that middle-class Afro-American reformers developed unique perspectives and goals, leading much of this work to gloss over the class fissures shaping black self-help.

To appreciate the parallels in class perspective between Jewish and black reformers, this chapter focuses primarily on the housing, neighborhood improvement, and employment programs initiated by the Educational Alliance and the Urban League. Without question Afro-Americans confronted greater obstacles in housing and job markets than did Jews in the early twentieth century; nevertheless, both groups were victims of what should be understood as racial discrimination.[6] As a result, the Alliance and the League engaged in related assimilation projects. Jewish leaders formed the Educational Alliance in 1891 in order to Americanize the city's growing Jewish immigrant population. Black elites established the National Urban League in 1910 to assist black migrants' adjustment to New York and other cities across the nation. Confronted with growing migrant populations that faced intense discrimination, the Educational Alliance and the Urban League assisted immigrants and migrants in maintaining both community and housing standards and finding decent employment. While such efforts were undoubtedly intended to meet the immediate material needs of poor Jews and Afro-Americans, they nonetheless frequently reflected the class apprehensions and biases of Jewish and black elites.

The Educational Alliance's and the Urban League's efforts to acculturate their poor brothers and sisters were predicated on what Chicago school sociologists called ethnic cycle theory.[7] Alliance and League members believed that immigration and migration freed individuals from constraints imposed by communal organizations, such as religious institutions and the family, resulting in personal demoralization and social disorganization. The Alliance and the League feared that native whites' tendency to associate aberrant behavior with Jewish immigrants and black migrants fueled racial antagonism, which in turn retarded assimilation. Jewish and black leaders therefore hinged their claims to equality on their respective group's ability to demonstrate its assimilability—acceptance of middle-class values. Neither organization desired to destroy the ethnic identities of their migrant brethren. However, the Alliance and the League ultimately attempted to reorganize the lives of Jewish immigrants and black migrants by creating outlets for the frustrations of Jewish immigrants and Afro-American migrants that demonstrated their commitment to the existing political economy. This approach not only assumed the need for elite stewardship over each group; it led both organizations to try to separate the deserving from the undeserving poor. The Alliance and the League would thus call for imparting proper values to some and containing those who threatened each group's progress. In so doing, the activities of the Alliance and the League reflected the marginality of Jewish and black elites as well as the similarities in their class perspectives.

THE EDUCATIONAL ALLIANCE

In the last decades of the nineteenth century European immigration to the United States underwent a considerable transformation. Whereas prior to the mid-1890s Northern and Western Europe supplied the bulk of America's immigrant population, by 1896 immigration from Southern and Eastern Europe surpassed that from accustomed sources—Germany, Great Britain, Scandinavia, France, Switzerland, and the Low Countries.[8] Pogroms in Russia and Romania (1870–1895), tsarist conscription laws, the cholera epidemic (1868), famine (Poland, 1869), and economic and political distress inspired hundreds of thousands of East European Jews to seek refuge abroad. Thus between 1870 and 1914, more than 2 million Jews immigrated to the United States, most of whom settled in New York City.[9] Consequently, between 1870 and 1915, New York City's Jewish population increased from about 80,000 (9 percent) to nearly 1.4 million (28 percent), with the greatest growth occurring in the 15 years before World War I.[10]

The arrival of the East European Jews did not mark the introduction of Jews to the city. Prior to the 1870s, New York's Jewish population was composed primarily of those of German descent. Arriving in comparatively small numbers as part of a larger influx of German immigrants in the 1830s and 1840s, German Jews encountered less anti-Semitism than their Russian counterparts would in America.[11] Furthermore, while the Lower East Side became the center for Jewish clothing and retail shops, laying the foundation for the establishment of later Jewish communities, German

Jews could be found in virtually all quarters of the city, with those who were more prosperous residing uptown. These factors combined with favorable economic conditions and their greater wealth at the time of their arrival to allow German Jews to integrate with relative ease into the city's mainstream. East European Jews, however, would face stiffer obstacles.

New Jewish immigrants brought with them a host of tastes, customs, and problems that would unnerve both native whites and American Jews. Immigrants had little control over their living arrangements. Employed primarily as shop workers, they lived in squalor and poverty.[12] Trapped in cramped, poorly ventilated, unsanitary tenements, they were plagued with disease, high infant mortality, and crime. Compounding the situation was the Lower East Side's high population density. By the late 1880s the Lower East Side was the most densely populated part of the city, with 522 inhabitants per acre in 1890 and more than 700 in 1900.[13]

As the problems confronting the residents of the Lower East Side grew with their numbers, many identified the new immigrants as threats to social order. Economic depressions (1873–1877; 1883–1886; 1893–1897), the rise in labor radicalism, crime, vice, "pauperization," and the birth of "scientific" racism convinced men such as Massachusetts senator Henry Cabot Lodge that immigration restriction was essential to the nation's survival.[14] Others, however, were more optimistic. Believing that these new immigrants needed only to be adjusted to their milieu, a number of Christian missionaries by the mid-1860s descended on the Lower East Side. Men such as Reverend Jacob Freshman, a *meshumed,*[15] and Herman Warszawiak hoped to uplift Jews through conversion.[16] For both East European and the German American Jews, however, Christian efforts to proselytize their "poor cousins" were an affront. Thus in the last decades of the nineteenth century, New York's German Jewry set out on the daunting task of Americanizing their East European brethren.

One of the most important organizations created by German Jews to Americanize New York's East European Jews was the Educational Alliance. Established in 1891, the Alliance's foundation was laid nearly thirty years before it was brought into existence, for it was the product of the merger of three organizations: the Hebrew Free School Association (HFSA), the Young Men's Hebrew Association (YMHA), and the Aguilar Free Library. Each of these groups pursued a different approach to the immigrant problem. The activities of both the HFSA (founded spring 1865) and the YMHA (established in New York City in 1883) were inspired by Christian organizations. Reasoning that the success of the Christian mission school on the Lower East Side could be attributed to the dearth of affordable educational facilities, a committee of ten rabbis, led by Rabbi Samuel Myer Isaac, formed the Hebrew Free School Association to promote Judaism in a fashion that was consistent with American principles.[17] The Young Men's Hebrew Association—like its Christian predecessor, the YMCA—combined athletic activities with intellectual development. The YMHA's emphasis on "physical culture,"[18] its most distinguishing feature, was designed to provide young immigrants socially constructive outlets while introducing them to an important aspect of American culture.[19] At roughly the same time the YMHA opened its doors in New York City, the Aguilar Free Library was formed. The

Library's program likewise centered on the mental development of its beneficiaries. It is the least understood of the three groups, in part because it existed only briefly as an independent organization. In 1886 the Library merged with YMHA, which by 1891 combined with the HFSA to form the Hebrew Institute. The Hebrew Institute was reorganized as the Educational Alliance in 1893.[20]

What led these three organizations to merge was a common desire to combat native Americans' negative perceptions of East European Jews by assisting immigrants in finding a middle ground that combined the strengths of their native culture—including their religion—with the best qualities of American culture. They hoped to smooth the transition from the *shtetl* to life in the big city and believed the most effective means of assuaging natives' concerns was to educate newcomers as to how best to survive in America. Consequently, each hoped to Americanize Jewish immigrants as rapidly as possible and merged, like the three organizations that would form the National Urban League in 1910, to avoid duplication of activity.

In 1890 the Baron de Hirsch fund surveyed some 50,000 Lower East Side residents. To the surveyor's dismay, only about one-third of those interviewed possessed a working knowledge of English, while a comparable number of interviewees had acquired citizenship or were being naturalized. At the same time, anti-Semites/racists and proponents of immigration restriction identified the "strange" customs of the immigrants as proof of their inferiority. Throughout the 1890s popular magazines titillated the imaginations of natives with feature articles that questioned whether Jews could lose "their racial identity" and eventually assimilate. In 1894, the Immigration Restriction League argued that the country was in decline thanks to the unrestricted "invasion" of Jews, Italians, and Slavs, "the beaten members of beaten breeds," who would eventually outnumber their superiors.[21]

Alarmed by these developments, the Alliance stepped up its efforts to Americanize the newcomers. Expressing sentiments overlapping those of the Immigration Restriction League, Isidor Straus, a founding member of the Educational Alliance, argued in 1895 that if action were not taken "to eradicate the innate principles ... of these people [the immigrants], they will, by their superior numbers, in time bring so much injury to our children that I shudder to think of it."[22] Thus the Alliance's charter declared that the scope of its work "shall be of an Americanizing, educational, social, and *humanizing* character" (emphasis added). The potential threat posed by its unacculturated coreligionists ultimately led the Alliance to an assimilationist approach that, like the Urban League's, called for imparting middle-class values to some and relocating and/or containing those who posed a threat to order.

Inheriting the agendas of its parents, the organization attempted to Americanize the newcomers along four basic lines: educational instruction, social work, physical training, and moral guidance. Education, as the Alliance conceived it, was intended to inform immigrants of their rights and duties as American citizens. Social work was "calculated to develop the social instincts through various forms of innocent pleasure ... to be obtained through ... the more elevated and enlightened forms of recreation." Physical work was designed to combat the charge that the "coreligionists" lacked "physical courage" and possessed a "repugnance of physical work." Finally, through the use of lectures and religious guidance, moral work was intended to make the Alliance a "center of sweetness and light, in an oasis in the desert of degradation and despair."[23]

Between 1903 and 1917 these features of the Alliance's program were especially important. The rapid growth of New York's Jewish population between 1900 and 1914, changes in leadership, and the advent of World War I led the Educational Alliance to broaden its activities. While the Alliance's stated aim and objective had always been "to Americanize the recently arrived immigrant and to socialize him in the sense of making him better able to do his share in the work of society,"[24] by the turn of the century it established a number of special committees to directly confront the needs of the Jewish immigrants.

Perhaps no Alliance committee was more important or provided a better window into the organization's ideology and objectives than the Committee on Education. The broad tasks undertaken by this group outline all of the Alliance's major objectives. For the period examined in this chapter, Julia Richman headed the Committee on Education. Richman would eventually become the first woman superintendent of schools in New York City. Richman's committee established classes on citizenship and provided vocational assistance. It also offered courses on American history, politics, and civics and in the winter of 1905 opened classes in "English for Foreigners."[25]

Much of its coursework was designed to address issues ignored by public schools and other existing agencies. English for Foreigners, for example, opened one week after the Board of Education closed its own night schools, at which point the Alliance established four such classes meeting four times per week for four hours.[26] Adult classes were generally scheduled during the evening to accommodate working people, whereas classes for children met during the day. The committee's courses on citizenship also met four evenings per week, with the expectation of assisting some 2,000 students a year. About fifty students attended each session on citizenship, and the courses' instructors—who were all volunteers—distributed literature that explained the rights and duties of American citizens.[27]

Such courses were ultimately intended to adjust immigrants' attitudes to ensure a consonance between newcomers' expectations of America and the realities of their circumstances. According to David Blaustein, the Alliance's superintendent (1898–1907) and a Russian Jew,[28] centuries of persecution engendered in East European Jews "a philosophy of submission and sadness"; in the United States, however, immigrants confronted a new philosophy of optimism and mobility.[29] This mismatch between the immigrant's values and America's (i.e., "maladjustment") often led many newcomers to withdraw from society, a retreat that led some to a life of crime, radicalism, and even vice. Maladjustment and "de-Judaization," according to Blaustein, were responsible for divisions and hostilities between orthodox and reformed, rich and poor, and Russian and German Jews. Thus the Alliance hoped to "restore" the tensionless Jewish community that existed prior to immigration by introducing Jewish immigrants to American institutions and ultimately creating a distinctly American Judaism.[30]

The Alliance's civics courses explained the structure of American government, the importance of voting, and the evils of machine politics. Civic training was intended to instruct the immigrants on the most appropriate means of expressing their desires, developing "spontaneity in matters social and political; to start with demanding a right ... and to finish with acknowledging and assuring a duty."[31] This task was especially onerous, however, because the immigrants were highly suspicious of government. In an article entitled "The Making of Americans" Blaustein asserted that the pervasiveness of political corruption in Eastern Europe imbued immigrants with the belief that government was "the [minor] official with whom he comes into contact." Experiences in his homeland taught the newcomer "the value of bribery [and] the absolute necessity of corruption in all Europe." In America the scars of the old world philosophy were still visible. The immigrants believed the enforcers of the law were its inventors, while "the court that applies the statute, the judge who interprets it, is to him the despot who willed it."[32]

Corrupt politicians preyed on Jewish immigrants' ignorance, engendering apprehension about American institutions. As a consequence newcomers were likely to become apathetic or, worse, pursue action outside of the political mainstream. Expanding on the sentiments expressed above, Blaustein argued in 1909 that civic training was designed to teach the newcomers their rights and to thereby serve as a bulwark against radicalism. "The people on Fifth Ave. who know their rights can always get what is due them as citizens," he asserted, "but the people on the lower East Side do not know their rights and cannot get them." The poor wretched immigrant was besieged by "people who pretend to be his friend and advisers ... everybody exploiting him until he becomes disgusted and curses the day Columbus discovered America." Arguing that civic training was the best means of inoculating immigrants against despair and ensuring that they would become "loyal law-aiding citizen[s]," he asserted that it is only when the immigrant "learns to know America as it is, that he drops his 'isms,' which to those who do not understand the immigrant appear to be anarchism."[33]

Alliance members believed that anarchism, like socialism, and other forms of "antisocial" behavior hampered the assimilation of Jewish newcomers. As Lee Kohns asserted, the Alliance had to impress upon the immigrant "the folly of a point of view which leads some to feel that they must be against the established agencies for maintaining the perpetuity and integrity of our government.... We want the newcomer, his wife, as well as his sons and his daughters, to realize how his every act reacts not alone upon himself but upon all his people."[34] By 1916 the Alliance, under the leadership of Judge Samuel Greenbaum, published its Doctrine of Citizenship, which declared that becoming an American citizen meant pledging one's "loyal, unwavering fealty to the United States of America and that if he yields one bit of his loyalty thereto he deserves to be stripped of his American citizenship."[35] Such sentiments were, of course, especially common around World War I, reflecting the rise of American nationalism as well as the growing influence of eugenics. The Alliance had, however, expressed views of this nature from its inception. Given that anarchists were linked to the Haymarket riot, the assassination of President William

McKinley, the Industrial Workers of the World, and a host of other so-called un-American activities, Alliance members feared that radicalism would only retard East European Jews' progress.

The Committee on Education's efforts to insulate the newcomers from moral degradation, and the subsequent decline of the Jewish race, were also reflected in the group's efforts to enhance newcomers' human capital. In 1893 the Alliance created the Preparatory Vocational Committee to provide occupational training to Lower East Side residents. Reasoning that immigrants could receive comparable training from existing institutions, the Alliance resolved to discontinue this work except for its classes in domestic arts and science in 1903.[36] In December 1906, Judge Greenbaum led an in-depth discussion regarding the difficulty with which immigrant children acquired manual training. Although the Hebrew Technical Institute (HTI) specialized in providing vocational training to young people, too many immigrant children were ill prepared to meet the challenges posed by the HTI's advanced course work. The few manual training courses the Alliance offered were neither funded nor organized sufficiently to adequately prepare immigrant children for the HTI. Working with immigrant parents and the HTI, the Committee on Education intensified its vocational activities, establishing its own classes within HTI by spring 1907.[37]

By late 1910 the Alliance's interest in manual training blossomed into the Preparatory Vocational School. The Preparatory Vocational School was to provide training for children who had been ignored by existing institutions. Julia Richman argued that because existing technical schools operated on the premise that the most effective work could be done only among children above the age of fourteen

> a vast army of boys and girls after being graduated from Public Schools at the age of fourteen, are thrust upon a glutted labor market for the sake of a comparatively negligible weekly wage with no standard of efficiency, and with no experience, training or original talent, or do a definite piece of work well, or to engage in a minor capacity in an industry where if they had had preliminary training, their rise might be gradual and steady.

Richman believed that this inefficiency contributed to the degradation of the working class, for it was these children who grew up to become the "inefficient errand boy and cash girl; the stray wreckage of the mill and factory"; and finally those workers who were "worn out at middle age." The Preparatory Vocational School, therefore, targeted children at the crucial ages of twelve to fourteen.[38]

By assisting immigrants in acquiring skills, vocational training, like the civics courses, set out to channel the newcomers' energies into socially acceptable outlets. While Richman's interest in Jewish youth was undeniably driven in part by an honest concern about their future, embedded in her solicitude was the threat that unfocused children and "indifferent" workers posed to Jews in America.

In her first few years with the Alliance, Richman, echoing concerns voiced earlier by Blaustein, criticized the Alliance for failing to confront the needs of the residents of the Lower East Side directly. She asserted that the schools on the Lower

East Side swarmed with gangs, lawbreakers, and criminals because the Alliance's courses on Shakespeare and Plato failed to capture the imaginations of the children. The young people of the Lower East Side—described by at least one Alliance worker as "virile animals"—wanted excitement and action rather than checkers and chess.[39] Richman and the Alliance thus developed playgrounds and established supervised activities for children in order to channel their energies away from the streets.[40] The Preparatory Vocational School was part of this agenda.

In November 1912, however, the committee was forced to face the reality that it could not meet its initial aims. While vocational courses were originally designed to meet after school (4:00–6:30 P.M.), in part to reduce the teens' "idle time," insufficient funding forced it to limit its work to daytime activities by 1913. The Alliance's ability to provide vocational training for "normal" children who were simply doing poorly in school was further undermined by a lack of cooperation from both parents and the public schools. This, the committee claimed, permitted it to attract only "unruly" girls and a handful of boys. Since the program's original aim was preventive rather than curative, the committee was forced to revamp its approach.[41]

It is unclear exactly how residents of the Lower East Side felt about the Preparatory Vocational School, but the fact that it failed to draw as many students as it had hoped may provide some indication. Furthermore, the Lower East Side residents' hostility to the Board of Education's interest in the so-called Gary Plan of 1917 indicates that some Jewish immigrants may have been offended by the Alliance's efforts to provide vocational training for their children. Inspired by educational innovations in Gary, Indiana, in 1914, Mayor John P. Mitchell, an anti-Tammany reformer, pursued an initiative to create highly specialized public education. Fearing that this was a scheme to "cut their children off from routes to professional advancement," Jews on the Lower East Side took to the streets. The Gary Plan was a central issue in the mayoral election of 1917. Mitchell's opponent, John Hylan, stumped the city asserting that "our boys and girls shall have an opportunity to become doctors, lawyers, clergymen, musicians, artists, orators, poets or men of letters, notwithstanding the views of the Rockefeller Board of Education." Hylan won the election, having received overwhelming support from the East Side.[42]

The Preparatory Vocational School's motives were laden with condescension. It had hoped that by providing training that made effective use of the teens' free time it could—along with the Alliance's club and religious activities—prevent juvenile delinquency. Mischievous, disorderly, and criminal children had one thing in common: a lack of appropriate supervision. The Alliance's Vocational Bureau was thus designed to provide them with training at the hands of responsible adults in a wholesome environment. It also provided job placement assistance, which included periodic visits with employers, in an effort to ensure that the working environment was salutary and that placements were performing well. By matching students with the right job, it tried to reduce the possibility that employees, particularly young girls, would be led astray by disreputable employers. Furthermore, it hoped to reduce friction between employers and employees by increasing the workers' efficiency, insulating them from poverty and perhaps a life of crime.[43]

The peripatetic, inefficient workers who Richman described were more likely to be swayed by radical philosophies or to pursue livings outside of industry either as criminals or lawbreakers, both of which were embarrassments to more prosperous Jews. The Jewish peddlers on the Lower East Side, Richman believed, had been just such workers. While many peddled seasonally, Richman held that a significant number of pushcart merchants did so because they lacked the skill and discipline to compete in industrial society. Furthermore, their paltry earnings, the constant harassment from natives, and the temptations of the street made them particularly susceptible to corruption. Arguing that peddlers were essentially vagabonds with capitalist delusions, Richman fought for stricter enforcement of licensing laws and eventually called for the deportation of repeat offenders.[44] Vocational training was, therefore, likely to have been one of Richman's more "gentle" means of reducing the number of pushcart merchants.

The Alliance's shock troops in the war against juvenile delinquency were the Committee on Moral and Religious Work and the Committee on Social Work.[45] Both groups attempted to combat the "disorganization" accompanying immigration by organizing the lives of immigrants. While children had always been of great concern to the Alliance, by the early 1900s the necessity of working with young people had become quite apparent. In September 1908 Police Commissioner Theodore Bingham described the area "south of Fourteenth Street" as a criminal camp "thoroughly organized financially, politically, and legally for offense and defense." He went on to state that 50 percent of the crimes committed on the Lower East Side were committed by Jews and that "among the most expert of all the street thieves are Hebrew boys under sixteen who are brought up to lives of crime."[46] Though demonstrations on the Lower East Side would lead Bingham to apologize, at least some members of the Alliance believed that Bingham was not completely wrong.

Louis Marshall of the Educational Alliance's Committee on Morality and Religion asserted that East European Jews bore much of the responsibility for Bingham's disparaging remarks. Though Jews were responsible for fewer than 50 percent of the crimes on the Lower East Side, Marshall declared that if only 10 percent of New York's criminals were Jews "that is 10 percent too many." He argued that residents of the East Side should spend less time protesting and more time working toward the eradication of the causes leading to juvenile delinquency and the creation of professional Jewish criminals. "We have cried because a corn has been trodden on, and we are entirely indifferent to the cancer which is gnawing at our vitals."[47] As Judge Greenbaum declared in 1908, combating crime in the Hebrew quarters was the responsibility of all Jews, for few gentiles bothered to make distinctions between law-abiding and criminal Jews.[48]

Statistics compiled by Isaac Hourwich revealed that in 1907 the percentage of convicted criminals among Jews in New York was half that among gentiles. But to Hourwich's dismay, juveniles and young men between the ages of fifteen and twenty accounted for the largest number of Jewish lawbreakers.[49] The Alliance believed that the single greatest contributing factor to the rise of juvenile delinquency was the cultural gap between parents and children that resulted from immigration. The problem as David Blaustein described it was that immigrant children were likely to assimilate more quickly than their parents. "The old customs, dear to [parents] ... are likely to be dropped more or less contemptuously by the children." The children believe that "all that is not American is something to be ashamed of." Compounding the problem was the fact that only the "superficial qualities" were easily assimilated; because the immigrant parents were ignorant of American ways, they frequently failed to provide the appropriate direction.[50]

Since religion grounded the immigrants' sense of morality, the Alliance believed that its preservation among the young would help to maintain order.[51] Parents' reluctance to adopt American values and customs, however, threatened order as well. The creation of an insular Jewish community would impede the development of an American identity and perhaps threatened the status of the Jewish people in the United States. In 1916, Jacob Schiff, who was the Alliance's first president, argued that if discriminatory laws had not segregated Jews in Russia and Poland "the prejudice and persecution to which they have been subject would not have reached the stage to which we all regret it has." The same would be true in the United Sates if hundreds of thousands of American Jews insisted that Yiddish "be retained to the exclusion of English." Schiff concluded that if the immigrants continued to treat Yiddish as their "language of intercourse, it would be a misfortune to our people."[52]

Many believed that proselytizing crusades by Christian settlement house workers on the Lower East Side widened the gap between Jewish parents and children. Thus the Alliance hoped that its religious work would reconcile "the heart of the parent to the heart of the child." "The old should not be assailed with ideas and customs so alien to them as to repel them from everything American," Blaustein argued. Instead "they should be inspired with the idea that Americanism does not demand the sacrifice of one's racial character and religious faith." Religious classes were therefore designed to teach the child to respect the traditions of the parents, while parents were taught "through lectures and other means ... to be in sympathy with the progressive ideas of America."[53] Thus the Alliance called for creating a distinctly American Judaism.

The desire to create a distinctly Jewish American identity fueled the Alliance's efforts to draw the immigrants into the mainstream of American Society. This not only entailed training their beneficiaries; it occasionally called for relocation or containment of those who might pose a threat to order. Richman's calls for the deportation of peddlers, and the Alliance's assertion that disloyal immigrants should be stripped of their citizenship, were part of a broader tendency. During the Panic of 1893 the Alliance supported a moratorium on immigration, reasoning that the continued influx of poor Jews would burden existing charitable institutions. More important, the Alliance, with the assistance of the Industrial Removal Association, attempted to relocate some immigrants outside of New York in an effort to reduce tensions on the Lower East Side.

In 1903 Blaustein published a Yiddish pamphlet titled "Hello Immigrant" to be distributed at Ellis Island. Among the many topics discussed were the opportunities existing outside of New York City. He described Gotham as an expensive den of iniquities whose only redeeming quality was its public school system. The pamphlet celebrated rural life and recommended that the newcomers take up farming out west, where people were honest and life was simple and clean.[54]

In an attempt to assist East European Jews find employment in other parts of the country, the Alliance established the Information Bureau in 1907. Like the Alliance's other subgroups, the Information Bureau operated on the premise that unrest was the result of the disparity between the immigrants' experiences in the homeland versus the realities of life in America. Believing that urban conditions undermined the integrity of Jewish communal life, the Alliance held that a return to rural settings would allow for a smoother transition from the *shtetl* to America. Thus while the Information Bureau served as a clearinghouse for information on employment opportunities across the nation, dispersal of America's Jewish population was also intended to alleviate urban tensions.[55]

Like the civics and vocational courses, the Information Bureau hoped to impress upon the newcomers that, when faced with adversity, their first impulse should be to try to improve their own situation rather than to blame "the system." By broadening the East European Jews' geographic horizons beyond New York City, the Information Bureau attempted to introduce them to opportunities frontier. If New York's labor market was glutted, don't damn America—move to Cincinnati or Galveston! Combating ghettoization in this fashion would reduce unemployment and juvenile delinquency and prevent pauperization among Jews.[56] It would also reduce the possibility that Jewish immigrants would come to develop their own separate interests.

THE URBAN LEAGUE IN NEW YORK

Like the Alliance, the Urban League assumed that proper behavior was essential to improving Afro-Americans' economic and living conditions. The League's programs were thus similarly concerned with protecting middle-class blacks from the pernicious influence of their poor cousins. The Urban League's class interests were ultimately expressed in two policy approaches. The first comprised efforts to either acculturate or contain those who failed to meet the challenges of the industrial city. The second consisted of initiatives intended to directly buttress the status of black elites. As I shall discuss below, such efforts profoundly shaped the League's attempts to improve the lives of black tenants and workers. Far from representing an integrationist vision that was free of class bias, the League's uplift programs reflected its preoccupation with the so-called better classes of Negroes.

The history of the Urban League in New York begins with the Great Migration. Responding to the increased demand for black labor brought about by World War I, about 1.5 million black southerners poured into the nation's cities between 1915 and the onset of the Great Depression. New York City was an especially attractive destination for black migrants. In 1910 only about 91,000 blacks claimed New York as their home. By 1930 Gotham's black population had grown to 327,706. Its black population growing nearly fourfold over just twenty years, New York City had become the largest Negro metropolis in America.[57]

Northern demand for black labor allowed thousands of Afro-Americans to finally escape the Jim Crow regimes and the economic malaise that characterized life below the Mason-Dixon Line. Blacks in New York and other northern cities possessed political, social, and economic freedoms that were unimaginable in the South. Still, in departing Dixie, migrants had not escaped race discrimination. Residential segregation confined black New Yorkers largely to Manhattan's Harlem district. The victims of intense overcrowding, blacks residing in the once-tony Harlem were forced to pay exorbitant rents for rapidly decaying units.[58] Moreover, while blacks made their first significant gains in industry in this period, more than two-thirds of the city's gainfully employed Afro-Americans worked as manual laborers. Concentrated in unskilled positions with little or no room to move up, black workers commanded low wages and were highly vulnerable to layoffs.

Although race prejudice was largely to blame for the problems confronting black migrants, many longtime residents of New York argued that migrants themselves bore part of the responsibility for their travails. Afro-American and white Progressives never lost sight of the impact of the pernicious effects of racism; however, both feared that the migrants possessed qualities that undermined their assimilation into the socioeconomic mainstream. Black migrants and immigrants (from the Caribbean) were disproportionately young, single, unskilled, uneducated, and female, all of which reformers believed were impediments to their advancement. Thus both friends and foes of the Negro attributed racial animosity, ranging from the 1905 San Juan Hill riot to labor market segmentation, to the "maladjustment" of black newcomers.[59]

The growing presence of unacculturated Afro-American migrants, unaccustomed to industrial employment and urban living, galvanized reformers to take action to uplift the benighted migrants. The creation of the National Urban League represented one of the most significant responses to the problems posed by migration. Like the Educational Alliance, the League was the product of a merger of three New York self-help organizations: the National League for the Protection of Colored Women, the Committee for Improving the Industrial Conditions of Negroes in New York, and the Committee on Urban Conditions Among Negroes. Although the three groups focused on different aspects of the migrant experience, they shared an integrationist philosophy that identified the acculturation of blacks as essential to the task of mitigating debilitating effects of prejudice—the biggest obstacle to black uplift. Each hoped to eradicate race prejudice by preparing blacks for urban industrial life through vocational and/or moral guidance. Possessing a common goal and similar strategies, the three groups combined in 1910 to form the National League for Urban Conditions Among Negroes, later renamed the National Urban League.[60]

Unlike the National Association for the Advancement of Colored People (the well-known NAACP), the National Urban League eschewed political or legal challenges to institutional racism. Conceived as a social-work organization, the

Urban League focused primarily on the immediate needs of urban blacks, namely housing and employment. Like its parent organizations' the Urban League's uplift vision proceeded from the view that prejudice was the chief impediment to blacks' advancement. The Urban League ultimately attempted to bridge the gulf between the races via a two-point strategy. First, the Urban League worked directly with employers and landlords in order to expand the employment and housing available to blacks. Second, it attempted to prepare blacks for life in an industrial city. The League thus provided assistance to both Afro-American newcomers and longtime residents in locating housing, finding employment, using city services, and comporting themselves in the big city.[61]

In many respects the League's approach represented an important counterpoint to the eugenics movement. A number of leading Urban Leaguers were influenced by the theories of social disorganization and reorganization advanced by University of Chicago sociologists W. I. Thomas and Robert Park. The League's philosophy was, therefore, predicated in part on the assumption that the problems confronting black migrants paralleled those experienced by immigrants.[62] While Leaguers identified racism as the chief obstacle confronting blacks, they generally believed that migrants' maladjustment to urban life played an important role in explaining such issues as unemployment and neighborhood decay. Reasoning that migrants' adherence to cultural norms that were out of place in the industrial North had much to do with criminality, delinquency, and poor job performance among Afro-Americans, the Urban League set out to establish "standards" for blacks at work and at home.

Ultimately the League's efforts to reorganize blacks' lives were intended to dispel race prejudice. By equipping blacks with the skills and values necessary to succeed in the industrial city, Leaguers hoped to demonstrate that Afro-American renters and workers were every bit as capable and conscientious as were whites. But while the League's attempts to show the triumphs of nurture over nature represented an important effort in the struggle against scientific racism, its emphasis on shaping the behavior of black newcomers reveals its class biases. As I shall discuss below, the League's decision to hinge its integrationist philosophy, at least in part, on blacks' ability to demonstrate their acceptance of mainstream values led it to devote particular attention to the more "advanced" strata of the black community. This tendency is most apparent in the League's housing and employment work.

Housing

From the beginning, Leaguers made elevating the moral and physical character of Harlem a significant component of their work. In the Urban League's first year of operation, segregation had already begun to create severe overcrowding. While New York City contained a number of black enclaves, by 1910 Harlem accounted for more than 60,000 of the city's 91,709 blacks—roughly two-thirds of the total. Worse yet, Afro-Americans within Harlem faced a paucity of housing options. A 1913 League house-to-house survey of Harlem, for example, revealed that 49,555 blacks lived in just 1,100 houses contained within only 23 blocks. Galvanized by its findings, the

Urban League came to identify the dearth of decent housing as one of the major problems facing black New Yorkers.[63] By the next year, the League would create a separate department dedicated to elevating the character of ghetto communities.

In 1914 the Urban League established the Housing Bureau of New York. Led by John T. Clark, the Housing Bureau focused on three major tasks. It furnished prospective tenants lists of respectable homes. It also attempted to improve existing housing by petitioning real estate agents, property owners, and city officials to comply with or enforce "Tenement House, Board of Health [and] Police regulations." Finally, it encouraged Afro-Americans to take an active role in the upkeep of their own neighborhoods.[64]

The League's efforts to elevate the conscience of tenants were among its most important activities. Leaguers believed that black tenants were, in many respects, best equipped to maintain ghetto communities. Spending more time in these neighborhoods than anyone else, residents could police their communities for housing infractions with comparative ease. The Urban League therefore educated black tenants as to their rights and responsibilities, both to ensure proper sanitation and to safeguard against disreputable landlords. But while assisting tenants in creating as well as maintaining safe and attractive communities was certainly an important endeavor, Urban Leaguers were explicit that the elevation of neighborhood standards required the insulation of the better classes of blacks from their unacculturated brethren.[65]

Residential segregation ultimately denied middle-class Afro-Americans the opportunity to escape ghetto communities. Many Leaguers feared that the moral integrity of the better classes of Negroes was thus threatened by their proximity to less advanced blacks. As George E. Haynes, the National Urban League's first executive secretary, asserted: "Municipal protection and freedom from the pressure of less moral elements of the environing group go a long way toward elevating the standards of morality."[66] John T. Clark linked such sentiments to League policy when he stated that the Housing Bureau's creation was "the result of just indignation of the residents at the indiscriminate mixing of reputable and disreputable persons in tenement houses."[67]

Motivated, at least in part, by a desire to ensure the probity of the black middle class, the League's attempts to improve living conditions in Harlem frequently centered on programs designed to either contain or retrain tenants of questionable character. While containment was less frequent than the reorganization of black renters' lives, it was nonetheless an important part of the League's uplift vision. In fact, the Housing Bureau claimed that one of its greatest accomplishments in its first six months was "having a number of 'undesirables' dispossessed," the majority of whom were alleged prostitutes. Specifics regarding such efforts are not clear, but National Urban League and New York Urban League records indicate that the League continued to assist landlords in identifying disreputable tenants for eviction through the 1920s.[68]

Certainly the removal of alleged sex workers from black neighborhoods does not necessarily indicate that the League was more concerned with the black middle class than with less prosperous Afro-Americans who derived their income through legitimate channels. However, the Housing Bureau's stated objectives make evident that this was part and parcel of the League's desire to maintain the integrity of the better classes. When viewed in the broader context of the League's work, such activities reflect the League's preoccupation with the needs of the middle class.

Containment was an important part of the League's neighborhood activities; however, the reorganization of the lives of Afro-Americans took up the greater share of its efforts in this regard. To combat landlord indifference and urban isolation, the League urged the tenants themselves to take collective action against disreputable landlords. The overarching objective of such endeavors was to encourage black renters "to refuse absolutely to tolerate carelessness and indifference to management and control of houses advertised for rental to respectable tenants" in order to elevate living conditions within Harlem.[69] Leaguers enlisted the services of black tenants and children to compile lists of decent apartments and to improve the quality of life in black neighborhoods. The League also called for "the establishment of Neighborhood Unions" in order to instill in tenants a "sentiment against unsanitary conditions, immoral practices and other improper conditions."[70]

Though the Urban League's records yield nothing about neighborhood unions in Gotham, the League did use its preventive work with juveniles to create an organization that was designed both to equip black children with the tools of good citizenship and to assist it in improving the living conditions in Harlem. In 1914 the Urban League organized the Juvenile Park Protective League (JPPL) of Harlem. As part of the League's broader effort "to make the city better and cleaner," the JPPL organized "626 school boys" into a neighborhood watchdog association. JPPL members reported violations such as "obstructed fire escapes, unlighted hallways, illegal sale of liquor and cigarettes to minors," and littering to the Urban League. After reviewing the data, the League referred quality-of-life and housing infractions to the appropriate agencies. To maintain interest, Leaguers rewarded young men who had been particularly adept at spotting such infractions with "badges of meritorious service."[71]

While the JPPL was a civic organization, its overarching objective was to combat juvenile delinquency, which the Urban League believed was on the rise in Harlem. Leaguers had long been concerned about the social consequences arising from black households' dependence on the wages of both husband and wife. Delinquency, Urban Leaguers feared, was attributable to a lack of sufficient parental guidance resulting from the prevalence of working mothers in black households. Though the overarching issue was the dearth of economic opportunities, the Urban League addressed both the symptom and the cause.

Like the Educational Alliance, the Urban League used programs such as the JPPL to channel the raw energy of urban youth into socially constructive avenues. Trained as social scientists, many Leaguers believed that ghetto decay stemmed partly from the dissolution of institutional life brought about by the Great Migration. Charles S. Johnson, sociologist and director of research for both the Chicago Urban League and the National Urban League, argued that while institutions such as "the church" were able to maintain social norms in the South, the atomizing effects of urban life undermined the ability of southern institutions to do so in the North. The collapse of these mechanisms of social control, according to Johnson, had much to do with increases in black criminality, delinquency, and vice taking place in cities across the north. Ira de Augustine Reid of the New York Urban League and George E. Haynes echoed these sentiments in separate publications on the impact of migration on communal norms. To redress the rise in social disorganization, both Johnson and Reid called for the creation of secular organizations that instilled in migrants the importance of collective action.[72]

The League's housing work did not merely focus on efforts to improve the character of ghetto neighborhoods and their residents. The Urban League actively courted assistance from landlords and developers to improve the supply of decent affordable housing in Harlem. These efforts likewise reflected a desire to insulate the better classes from their unacculturated brethren. Moreover, due at least in part to the extremely disadvantaged position blacks maintained in New York's housing market, the League's attempts to entice respectable real estate development in Harlem appear to have benefited only a tiny elite.

Between 1914 and 1915 the Housing Bureau performed a study of "1,002 families in 726 apartments and 443 houses in Harlem between 131st and 142nd streets." It found that blacks paid substantially higher rents than German Jews in a comparable neighborhood. Furthermore, rent accounted for a much larger portion of their earnings (36 percent). The League found that blacks supplemented their incomes by taking in boarders, as more than 60 percent of those surveyed had lodgers. In the League's view, lodgers posed a threat to the black community's moral integrity, particularly for young people, because the loose pull of social controls on itinerant roomers might bring decent tenants into contact with people of questionable character. The League thus set out to combat "the lodger evil" by promoting the use of respectable black superintendents, rent collectors, and real estate agents who would serve as race-relations managers. Furthermore, the Housing Bureau tried to induce "responsible real estate companies" to remodel existing units and to construct new ones.[73]

In his effort to attract responsible real estate companies to Harlem, Eugene K. Jones, who became the League's executive secretary after George E. Haynes resigned, urged social workers to try to entice potential investors by calling attention to the profitability of such an endeavor. Jones argued that since residential segregation limited the number of units available to blacks, property owners in predominantly black neighborhoods could charge rents above market rates. By 1916 the League claimed that Jones's arguments caught the eye of a number of new investors, providing some relief.[74]

While Jones's declaration was clearly indicative of the desperate housing conditions confronting black New Yorkers, his tactic ultimately encouraged price-gouging in Harlem's housing markets. It seems unlikely, however, that encouraging investment in this fashion could have significantly benefited most Harlemites who already paid higher rents than whites. Though the League's records do not divulge specifics about the aforementioned housing developments, the New York Urban

League's involvement with Harlem's Dunbar Apartments a decade later provides some insights into the League's inability to meet the needs of working-class blacks in Harlem.

The New York Urban League continued its efforts to court responsible real estate investors through the 1920s. When John D. Rockefeller Jr. announced plans to build the Dunbar Apartments in Harlem in 1926, the New York Urban League's housing division appeared to have achieved its greatest success. Leaguers asserted that the Dunbar complex, which opened its doors in February 1928, would provide Harlemites with attractive affordable housing that would engender in residents a sense of both self-worth and community.[75] To bolster residents' interest in the maintenance of the property's physical plant and its social environment, Rockefeller conceived the apartments as cooperatives. This would, of course, have the added benefit of giving many blacks their first taste of homeownership. The New York Urban League assisted in creating a salubrious environment within the complex by screening more than 5,000 applicants vying for Dunbar's 511 units. Applicants were screened to determine ability to pay, as well as family stability and moral integrity.[76] On-site management further ensured that respectable blacks would not be forced to live, as the apartment's manager Roscoe Conkling Bruce put it, "cheek by jowl lives the deacon with the dope fiend."[77]

The New York Urban League believed that the presence of the modern and attractive Dunbar complex would elevate Harlem's housing by injecting competition into the housing market that would encourage other landlords to improve their properties. Likewise, Leaguers hoped that the apartments would demonstrate the profitability of decent affordable housing. To be sure, Dunbar represented a vast improvement over existing housing in Harlem. Nevertheless, two obstacles prevented Dunbar Apartments from meeting the League's expectations. First, possessing a scant 511 units, Dunbar could not possibly spur sufficient market competition to prompt Harlem's landlords to improve existing units.

Second, Dunbar was unable to meet its most basic objective: providing affordable housing. Units in the Dunbar apartments were more expensive than in Harlem generally. The monthly rents for three-, four-, and five-room apartments in Dunbar—the most popular size units—averaged $43.50, $58, and $72.50, compared with just $36.28, $41.79, and $51.12 in Harlem at large. The most expensive units in Dunbar were as much as 70 percent higher than black New York's average. Worse yet, because Dunbar was a cooperative, residents had to pay between $150 and $350 for a down payment, on top of rent, just to buy into the complex. Though financing was available, a minimum down payment of $100 was required.[78] Due to the high rents, Dunbar's renters tended to be fairly well-to-do. Roscoe C. Bruce estimated in 1931 that half of Dunbar's residents earned between $1,776 and $2,124 per year.[79] Considering that four years earlier (two years before the Great Depression) the New York Urban League estimated that the average Harlemite earned only about $1,032 per year, Dunbar's residents were comparatively prosperous.[80] The League's efforts to improve housing in Harlem by attracting responsible real estate investment seemed to have benefited only a privileged few.

Employment and Vocational Guidance

The Urban League's interest in housing and community development was equaled only by its commitment to improving Afro-Americans' economic conditions. The problems confronting black workers paralleled those encountered by black renters. The demand for labor sparked by World War I opened new fields of work to Afro-Americans. Prior to World War I, the majority of New York's gainfully employed black men and women were domestic and personal service workers. The war in Europe would precipitate a decline in the importance of this work for black men, whose participation in these fields would drop from 50 percent to 35 percent between 1910 and 1920. At the same time, the percentage of black men employed in industry more than doubled, with 21 percent of black men working in manufacturing and mechanical trades.[81] Despite such gains, however, the opportunities available to black workers were far from boundless. Blacks continued to work the least desirable positions. Black women continued to rely chiefly on domestic and personal service work. Moreover, more than two-thirds of the city's gainfully employed Afro-Americans worked as manual laborers. Concentrated in unskilled positions with little or no room to move up, black workers had little income and were highly vulnerable to layoffs.

Shifting with changes in the opportunities available to blacks, the League's employment programs were nothing if not dynamic. World War I, for example, profoundly altered the League's approach. Sharing the Educational Alliance's circumspection about the consequences of surplus labor, the Urban League discouraged northward migration in the years preceding World War I. By 1917, however, the National Urban League began to direct black migrants to jobs in the urban North. While flexible, the Urban League's economic programs ultimately rested on a simple foundation. Even before the outbreak of war in Europe, the League's efforts to improve blacks' employment opportunities focused on three areas. First, Urban Leaguers worked with employers and employment agencies to create openings in fields in which blacks had generally been denied access. Second, they called for the creation of vocational training opportunities, so that black workers could improve their standards of work and be provided with the skills necessary to advance in industry. Finally, the League promoted blacks' participation in trade unions.[82]

Vocational guidance was perhaps the central component of the League's economic program in this period. While the Urban League worked directly with both industry and unions to encourage the use of black workers, ultimately the League assumed that workplace efficiency was the key to opening employment opportunities. Leaguers believed that competent job performance would demonstrate black labor's productive potential, dispelling stereotypes that had heretofore discouraged employers from hiring blacks. The Urban League did have some evidence to support this view. George E. Haynes argued that the overrepresentation of West Indians among the city's skilled black workers and businessmen evinced training's potential to overcome racism.[83] The gains blacks made in industry during World War I likewise demonstrated the ability of market forces to mitigate prejudice, since demand for labor during the war had led employers to use black workers in industries in which they had previously been excluded. In identifying efficiency as the key to eliminating workplace racism, vocational guidance—aiding black workers' productivity—would necessarily play a crucial role in the League's uplift agenda.

In the 1910s and 1920s, the National Urban League's vocational activities consisted primarily of directing blacks to occupations in which they might reasonably hope to advance. Like the Educational Alliance's Bureau of Information, the League assisted black job-seekers by providing lists of available openings in various cities, urging only those who were qualified to apply or migrate. Utilizing secondary schools, as well as social-work and vocational courses at black colleges, Leaguers tried to impress upon black students the value of an industrial arts education. These policies were intended to facilitate the adjustment of black migrants and to develop within them the understanding that any lasting change must first begin with them. But while the Urban League's emphasis on black workplace competence was not unreasonable, its decision to hinge blacks' economic advancement on the respectable behavior and job performance of Afro-American labor occasionally led it to take punitive action against those who did not measure up.[84]

The League's efforts to shore up the employment of black police officers as well as its own vocational training work during World War I, for example, reveal the limits of its politics of respectability in addition to the class leanings of the organization's vocational work. In September 1917, the National Urban League utilized the services of the New York Police Department to assist its vocational training programs. Anticipating the War Department's "work or fight" order, the League requested "the Police Department to assign two colored policemen to [its] Harlem office to corral idle young men who were hanging around poolrooms and clubs and to send them to positions found for them through the League's employment services." The National Urban League continued this campaign for a period of ten weeks. As a result, the League claimed that it had "helped to clear the streets of Harlem of ruffians and dissolute women."[85]

The National Urban League's attempts to clean up Harlem in this fashion highlight the extent to which its vocational endeavors were infused with a desire to maintain social order. The Urban League had long called for expanding the ranks of black police officers in Negro districts, both to broaden Afro-American employment opportunities and to reduce racial tensions engendered by the seemingly colonial relationship between the lily-white police force and ghetto residents. These were, of course, laudable goals; however, the League's attempt to establish black police officers' worth by using them to identify Afro-American "idlers" for arrest and retraining is indicative of the organization's fear that idle and unproductive workers posed a threat to the race's advancement. Although vocational guidance was intended to provide blacks with marketable skills, such endeavors were likewise perceived as hedges against moral decay and even radical political activism. The League's belief in the acculturating properties of industrial arts training was made most plain during the Great Depression.

Throughout the 1920s, the job placement and vocational components of the New York Urban League's Department of Industrial Relations went through a number of changes. Since the League's employment endeavors were chiefly concerned with expanding the fields of work available to Afro-Americans, it devoted little attention to occupations in which blacks had already secured a footing. Leaguers therefore tended to look past fields such as domestic and personal service work. By 1926, the League would no longer assist black job-seekers in finding work as domestic and personal service workers, choosing instead to focus on the better types of employment that blacks had been denied.[86] The Great Depression, however, would ensure that this policy would be short-lived.

The stock market crash of 1929 brought with it a reversal of most of the economic gains blacks had made earlier in the decade. That year, the Urban League estimated that some 300,000 Afro-American industrial workers were laid off nationwide. Throughout the Depression, the unemployment rate among Harlem's blacks was estimated to have ranged between 1.5 and three times that of whites.[87] The high levels of unemployment rekindled the New York Urban League's interest in domestic and personal service work. By 1931 the New York Urban League reinstituted its training and job placement programs for domestic and personal service work. Using the Dunbar Apartments complex as a domestic arts training academy, Leaguers hoped to offset competition from white workers who, in desperation, were making inroads in Negro work. The New York Urban League thus established occupational classes "where employed workers may improve their efficiency and the unemployed may use their *enforced leisure* in making themselves more efficient for future jobs" (emphasis added).[88]

While training sessions were obviously intended to enhance blacks' human capital, these courses were also designed to shape Afro-Americans' use of leisure time. Like the Alliance, the League operated under the assumption that an idle mind was the devil's workshop. As Ira de Augustine Reid, former director of the New York Urban League's Department of Industrial Relations, asserted, unemployment left "the individual in idleness with time to contact chronic idlers, to seek any amusement and excitement to avoid ennui or thought of future consequence, if he does not find work."[89] The New York Urban League's 1931 report echoed these sentiments, asserting that the failure to acquire meaningful employment was chiefly responsible for illicit and immoral behavior. Interestingly, the only remedies the New York Urban League proposed to combat the "lowliness, hardship, and suffering" that gripped black New York were the vocational guidance and the domestic training sessions held at the Dunbar Apartments. Vocational training courses of this sort were therefore intended to ensure the civic virtue of idle blacks by channeling the energies of the unemployed into constructive outlets.[90]

Vocational courses likewise served as a bulwark against militant and radical political activism. Like the Educational Alliance, the Urban League perceived participation in alternative politics as an outgrowth of social disorganization. Both Ira Reid and Charles S. Johnson, for example, described the appeal of Marcus Garvey's Universal Negro Improvement Association as the product of the unstable state of America's ghettos and the "partial assimilation" of their residents. Many blacks, they argued, were made susceptible to the sway of fringe political movements due to the combination of America's failure to treat them as equals and the diminishing effectiveness of social controls in the North. Though the sun had set on Garvey's movement by the early 1920s, his departure from the political landscape only begged the question raised in an article by Charles S. Johnson: "After Garvey—What?"[91]

As Leaguers feared, the economic and social instability that blacks experienced during the Great Depression precipitated a new wave of political activism. Black communists, nationalists, and racial liberals would lead countless protest campaigns in the North against discrimination in employment and housing throughout the Depression. Though the League actually offered assistance to campaigns such as "Don't Buy Where You Can't Work," it remained circumspect about such activities. Fearing that protest movements could easily fall prey to racial opportunists, Leaguers came to view vocational guidance as a means of preventing the racial polarization and anchoring blacks to America's dominant political and economic ideology.

The National Urban League's director of industrial relations, T. Arnold Hill, declared in a generally positive assessment of the "Don't Buy Where You Can't Work" campaigns in 1930 that picketing for better jobs was not a panacea. He asserted that before any meaningful change in occupational status were to occur, Afro-Americans needed to adjust their own attitudes since the success of protest efforts ultimately hinged on blacks' willingness to first take greater care in their work.[92] In a February 1932 article ("After the Depression—What?"), Hill observed that while agitation for collectivization was becoming commonplace, capitalism was nevertheless the economic and political system to which Afro-Americans had to accommodate. Though Hill did believe that some degree of economic planning would be necessary to counteract cyclical and seasonal unemployment, he held at present that "the Negro youth must plan his career more wisely" to combat constantly increasing job competition. Hill thus recommended that "more study is required to select a suitable vocation and more application to master it than heretofore." He concluded that regardless of the economic system under which one labored, proficient performance was essential. "Even in Russia," he said, "efficiency pays more."[93]

The League's concerns about the social consequences of idleness during the Great Depression were not limited to unemployment's impact on the unemployed. Many Leaguers feared that the psychology accompanying idleness would vitiate the integrity of middle-class Afro-Americans. Likening idleness to a contagious disease, T. Arnold Hill worried that Depression-era unemployment threatened the probity of the poor as well as that of "the better classes of Negroes." Hill asserted that the middle class's proximity to unemployed, dissolute blacks might eventually lead the better classes to tolerate illicit activities. The middle class's capitulation to the ghetto's most unsavory characters, Hill feared, would ultimately reduce blacks to mere "purveyors of illegal goods."[94]

Such concerns about the economic and social health of the black middle class profoundly shaped the New York Urban League's Depression-era jobs programs. To a large extent, the organization's interest in domestic employment during this period was attributable to the fact that the better classes of blacks were forced to seek such work. As mentioned above, the New York Urban League ceased making job placements in domestic and personal service work in March 1926 in order to devote full attention "to securing the better types of positions which have been denied to Negro Workers." Though the League dropped this area of work in part to make the best use of its resources, the New York Urban League's explanation for this decision reveals a bias against domestic workers themselves. In accounting for its lack of interest in these fields, the organization asserted that since the trend was moving "away from domestic service of any sort" it would be "difficult to keep an intelligent and industrious type of Negro interested in domestic service" without reorganizing it "on some systematic basis."[95]

The Great Depression would ultimately force the New York Urban League to reevaluate domestic and personal service work's place in its economic program. By 1931, it finally decided to reorganize domestic service work. In fact, the domestic training courses that the New York Urban League operated at the Dunbar Apartments were part of this agenda.[96] But while this was certainly a reasonable endeavor, the timing of the League's decision to reorganize the field is indicative of the Urban League's overarching preoccupation with the health and integrity of the black middle class.

The New York Urban League did not reinstate its domestic and personal service work until a large number of the better classes were forced to seek such employment. Between 1930 and 1931, the Urban League estimated that the percentage of black New Yorkers employed in domestic and personal service work increased from 55 percent to 80 percent.[97] The latter year is, of course, when the New York League reintroduced domestic and personal service placements. While the New York Urban League's records do not fully explain this decision, the position laid out by the National Urban League during the same time makes clear that Leaguers' interest in such activities reflected a heightened concern with middle-class blacks.

In response to blacks' growing reliance on domestic work and personal service work, the National Urban League created the National Committee on Employer-Employee Relationships in the Home. The committee's first report, in 1931, stated that its interest in these areas of employment stemmed directly from the fact that even Afro-Americans with "specialized training" were now forced to seek employment in these occupations. Troubled by the failure of a large number of workers experiencing what it called "technological unemployment" to seek jobs as domestics, the committee called for "reorganization of many households on a more impersonal and businesslike basis." The committee thus set out to reeducate individual workers "who through specializing in too narrow skills . . . have become blocked in their development and are unable to adapt themselves to their present situation."[98] In this context, the New York Urban League's efforts to reorganize domestic work are emblematic of the Urban League's tendency to devote a disproportionate share of its energy to ensuring the success of the talented tenth.

Though racial uplift scholarship has generally presumed that black and white Progressive reformers were motivated by somewhat different class concerns, strong parallels in orientation between the Educational Alliance and the Urban League may hint at a more complicated story. Without question, Alliance members and Leaguers perceived their self-help endeavors as beneficial to each of their groups as a whole. How the Educational Alliance and the Urban League chose to define collective advancement, however, reflected the class apprehensions common to these ethnic elites. In identifying proper conduct as the key to overcoming the impediments to Jewish and Afro-American progress, the Alliance and the League came to view their poor cousins as potential threats to assimilation. Both Jewish and black leaders ultimately feared that the failure of their brethren to adopt mainstream values would undermine group advancement, believing that evidence of maladjustment—such as poor job performance, juvenile delinquency, and radical political activism—validated race prejudice. The Alliance and the Urban League were thus motivated by a common fear that the progress of their entire racial group might be thwarted by the misconduct of a visible minority.

This assessment is not altogether different from David Lewis's "Parallels and Divergences," which likewise notes a shared anxiety between black and Jewish Progressives. Lewis ultimately contends, however, that black and Jewish elites pursued different assimilationist strategies. In fact, he argues that, prior to the New Deal, Afro-American reformers tended to eschew the self-help programs and protest politics adopted by Jewish activists in favor of an arts movement, the Harlem Renaissance, intended to demonstrate the gift of black folk.[99] Yet the histories of the Educational Alliance and the Urban League indicate that, in at least some significant cases, white ethnic and black reformers not only voiced similar assimilationist concerns but also adopted related strategies for group advancement.

While the Educational Alliance and the Urban League worked for the betterment of different racial groups, similarities in the obstacles confronting Jews and blacks led the two organizations to develop parallel approaches. Afro-American and Jewish newcomers faced discrimination, an alien urban environment, and high rates of unemployment and poverty. Fearing that such difficulties might impede their respective group's assimilation by fueling racial animus and by retarding the acculturation of Jewish immigrants and Afro-American migrants, the Alliance and the League embarked on a two-front campaign to adjust or contain those who did not measure up. Their efforts to adjust poor Jews and blacks to their new urban industrial settings were intended to not only improve their clients' employment options and living conditions but also to bolster race relations in general.

Such concerns would lead both Jewish and black leaders to try to adjust the attitudes of immigrants and migrants, as well as to attempt to contain those who threatened group progress. The Alliance and its members declared that "un-American" Jews, be they radicals or Julia Richman's peddlers, should be stripped of their citizenship and deported. Leaguers likewise worked to assist tenants, landlords, and employers in eliminating "disorganized" blacks from decent housing and good jobs. In the end both adjustment and containment were intended to insulate the better classes from the pernicious influence of unacculturated masses.

Though the Alliance and the League share points of common concern and work, differences are nonetheless apparent. Notably, the Urban League appears to have placed greater emphasis on programs directly benefiting the better classes of

Afro-Americans, as evidenced by the trajectory of its job placements and its role in the Dunbar Apartments. This is likely due to the fact that blacks confronted stiffer barriers to integration compared to Jewish immigrants. By the end of the first decade of the twentieth century, the Lower East Side was no longer the center of Jewish cultural life; thriving Jewish communities existed in Harlem, Brooklyn, and the Bronx. Jewish immigrants, moreover, experienced greater economic mobility, as evinced by the fact that by 1914 the majority of Jewish employers were of East European origin.[100] Blacks, however, would not be so fortunate. By 1930, residential segregation confined the majority of New York City's Afro-American population to the worst parts of Harlem, preventing middle-class blacks from escaping maladjusted newcomers. Furthermore, Afro-Americans possessing even specialized training were unable to acquire employment equal to their talents. Educated blacks were, therefore, forced to continue to seek employment as either manual laborers or as personal service and domestic workers. In its efforts to assist those best suited to challenge racial stereotypes, the League tended to devote a larger share of its resources to support the so-called better classes. Thus, rather than muting black elites' apprehensions about their poor brothers and sisters, the intense racism experienced by Afro-Americans may have actually intensified Leaguers' class concerns.

NOTES

1. David L. Lewis, "Parallels and Divergences: Assimilationist Strategies of Afro-American and Jewish Elites from 1910 to the Early 1930s," *Journal of American History* 71, no. 3 (December 1984): 547–550.

2. Ultimately, Lewis contends that Afro-American elites' relative economic disadvantage led them to focus more heavily on the arts as an engine of assimilation rather than either protest politics or self-help endeavors. This contention, however, looks past strong parallels in the employment, housing, and acculturation projects created by Jewish and black leaders.

3. This is not to suggest that historians have ignored the study of black-Jewish relations. Historian Cheryl Greenberg's recently published *Troubling the Waters,* for example, offers a richly detailed account of the historic relationship between Afro-Americans and Jews. Like Lewis, however, Greenberg is principally concerned with tracing the political and social interchange between these groups rather than comparing black and Jewish reformers' visions for racial-ethnic progress. See Cheryl L. Greenberg, *Troubling the Waters: Black-Jewish Relations in the American Century* (Princeton, NJ: Princeton University Press, 2006).

4. In her study of the National Baptist Convention, Evelyn Brooks Higginbotham argues that Afro-American women's uplift endeavors were characterized by the privileging of collective progress over personal gain. Denied access to traditional political avenues, black churchwomen set out to uplift the race through the "politics of respectability." Afro-American churchwomen, according to Higginbotham, encouraged blacks to embrace middle-class values such as thrift, industry, and temperance in order to challenge the perception of the race as inherently debauched. Though Higginbotham acknowledges that this approach was not altogether free of class tension, she ultimately contends that black reformers' racial "nationalism" muted the class anxieties of even middle-class black churchwomen. The combination of Evangelical communalism and whites' failure to acknowledge class and cultural differences among Afro-Americans, Higginbotham argues, prevented middle-class black Baptist women from making sharp distinctions between

themselves and their poor sisters. Their uplift strategies were therefore characterized by a greater egalitarianism than Progressive era reform generally. Evelyn Brooks Higginbotham, *Righteous Discontent: The Women's Movement in the Black Baptist Church, 1880–1920* (Cambridge, MA: Harvard University Press, 1993), 56–58, 58–65, 67–72, 190–193, 195–97, and 213–215.

5. Though Stephanie Shaw's multigenerational study of black professional women differs significantly in focus from Higginbotham's, Shaw's *What a Woman Ought to Be and to Do* echoes many of Higginbotham's conclusions regarding the interplay between racial and class identification on the uplift vision of middle-class black women. According to Shaw, Afro-Americans' attempts to counter the debilitating affects of racism during the Jim Crow era required the use of far-flung social networks—neighbors, distant friends and family, and even loose acquaintances—to nurture the talents and aspirations of black girls and boys. Shaw claims that the importance of communal ties in fulfilling professional goals ultimately led middle-class black women to develop what she calls a "socially responsible individualism" in which Afro-American professional women linked their personal advancement to the race's generally. While Shaw does acknowledge the existence of parallels between black and white reformers, she nonetheless contends that middle-class black women developed a vision of racial progress that generally overrode the class biases that shaped the reform endeavors of their white counterparts. Stephanie Shaw, *What a Woman Ought to Be and to Do: Black Professional Women Workers During the Jim Crow Era* (Chicago: University of Chicago Press, 1996), 4, 6, 54–56, 60–61, 66, 74, and 170.

6. This is to suggest neither that European Jews are not considered "white" today nor that blacks and Jews experienced equal degrees of discrimination in the United States. Recent scholarship has demonstrated, however, that the meaning and conception of "whiteness" as a racial category has evolved over the course of the nation's history. Therefore, my point is simply that Jewish "whiteness" was in question in the early twentieth century. Thus, as historians have long noted, the perception of East European Jews and other so-called New Immigrants as racially impure, hybrid white races manifested in myriad forms of racialized discrimination including: discriminatory housing and labor markets, state-sanctioned violence, and, of course, the Immigrant Restriction Acts of the 1920s. Matthew Frye Jacobson, *Whiteness of a Different Color: European Immigrants and the Alchemy of Race* (Cambridge, MA: Harvard University Press, 1998), 64–68, 78–90.

7. Ethnic cycle theory, a facet of interaction cycle theory, characterized assimilation as a four-stage process consisting of competition, conflict, accommodation, and assimilation. This model presumed that conflict between immigrants and natives would necessarily arise as the two competed for work and space. Internal conflicts within immigrant groups likewise arose from the decline in institutional life that accompanied a foreign-born group's transition from rural communities to urban societies. Conflict, according to sociologist Robert Park, would eventually subside once immigrants adjusted, or accommodated themselves, to their new environments. Ultimately, Chicago school sociologists such as W. I. Thomas and Robert Park believed that assimilation was to be a shared experience between natives and strangers. Immigrants were to maintain certain aspects of their cultural heritage both to facilitate their transition to industrial society and to inject new vitality into American culture and society. Though I will argue that the Urban League was directly influenced by Chicago school sociology, I advance no such claim for the Educational Alliance. Nevertheless, the Chicago school model had much in common with melting-pot theories articulated by white ethnic leaders such as Isaac Berkson and Judah L. Magnes.

8. John Higham, *Strangers in the Land: Patterns of American Nativism, 1860–1825* (New Brunswick, NJ: Rutgers University Press, 1967), 88.

9. Moses Rischen, *The Promised City: New York's Jews, 1870–1914* (Cambridge, MA: Harvard University Press, 1977), 20. In 1870–1880, an estimated 40,000 arrived; 1880–1890, 200,000; 1890–1900, 300,000; 1900–1914, 1.5 million.

10. Rischen, *The Promised City,* 94.

11. Ronald Sanders, *The Downtown Jews: Portraits of an Immigrant Generation* (New York: Harper and Row, 1969), 47.

12. The Baron De Hirsch Fund's survey of 111,690 Jews (of some 200,000 Jews in New York City in 1890) revealed that children accounted for more than half of the city's Jewish population. The study also found that 67 percent of the 22,393 individuals who claimed to be gainfully employed identified as shop workers, the majority of whom being employed in the needle trades. Another 10 percent of respondents were peddlers.

13. Irving Howe, *World of Our Fathers* (New York: Harcourt Brace Jovanovich, 1976), 69, 80, and 86.

14. Higham, *Strangers in the Land,* 96–103.

15. The term *meshumed* refers to a convert from Judaism.

16. Howe, *World of Our Fathers,* 73–75. The first Christian mission school on the Lower East Side was opened in 1864; it was soon followed by several others.

17. Joseph Dorinson, "The Educational Alliance: An Institutional Study in Americanization and Acculturation," in *Immigration and Ethnicity: American Society—"Melting Pot" or "Salad Bowl"?* ed. Michael D'Innocenzo and Josef P. Sirefman (Westport, CT: Greenwood, 1992), 93–95. The HFSA attempted to Americanize East European Jews by offering religious instruction, vocational training, and courses in history, etiquette, and hygiene.

18. "Physical culture" refers to athletic and exercise programs. The Educational Alliance would eventually follow the YMHA's lead in stressing the social value of such activities.

19. Dorinson, "The Educational Alliance," 93–95. Founded originally in Baltimore in 1854, it opened its doors in New York City in 1883.

20. Ibid., 94–96; Rischen, *The Promised City,* 101

21. Ande Manners, *Poor Cousins* (New York: Coward, McCann and Geoghegan, 1972), 87–89.

22. Ibid., 111–112.

23. Dorinson, "The Educational Alliance," 94; *Official Souvenir Book of the Fair: In Aid of the Educational Alliance and the Hebrew Technical Institute,* 1895, 19–23, Educational Alliance Papers, YIVO; By-Laws of the Educational Alliance, 1907, Educational Alliance Board Minutes, Educational Alliance Papers, YIVO.

24. Minutes of the Board Meeting, April 10, 1905, Educational Alliance Board Minutes, Educational Alliance Papers, YIVO.

25. Dorinson, "The Educational Alliance," 95; Minutes of the Committee on Education, March 13, 1905, Educational Alliance Board Minutes, Educational Alliance Papers, YIVO.

26. Minutes of the Committee on Education, March 13, 1905, Educational Alliance Board Minutes, Educational Alliance Papers, YIVO.

27. Ibid., February 12, 1905.

28. Born in Russia in 1866, Blaustein immigrated to the United States at the age of twenty. Choosing to avoid the cramped ghetto in New York, he settled initially in Boston, where he would soon establish a modern German and Hebrew school. While attending Harvard, earning a bachelor's degree from the prestigious university in 1893, he befriended the son of Isidor Straus. This meeting would eventually lead Blaustein to the Educational Alliance. Alliance leaders believed Blaustein, a Harvard-educated rabbi of Russian descent, was both an ideal spokesman for the Educational Alliance and liaison to Lower East Side residents.

29. David Blaustein, "The Making of Americans" (paper read before the New York State Conference of Charities, November 19, 1903), in the *Memoirs of David Blaustein: Educator and Communal Worker,* ed. Mirium Blaustein (New York: Arno Press, 1975), 128–129.

30. Blaustein, *Memoirs of David Blaustein,* 194–195.

31. Ibid., 46–49.

32. David Blaustein, "The Making of Americans," *American Hebrew* (November 28, 1903): 48.

33. Blaustein, *Memoirs of David Blaustein,* 174.

34. Lee Kohns, "Americanizing the Immigrant," *American Hebrew* (May 14, 1915): 1, 28.

35. "The Educational Alliance," *Federation Review* (March 10, 1916), address given by Henry Morgenthau and Jacob Schiff.

36. Minutes of the Committee on Education, December 5, 1913, Educational Alliance Board Minutes, Educational Alliance Papers, YIVO.

37. Ibid., December 12, 1906; Regular Executive Committee, May 6, 1907, Educational Alliance Board Minutes, Educational Alliance Papers, YIVO.

38. Special Committee Preparatory Vocational School, March 13, 1911, Educational Alliance Board Minutes, Educational Alliance Papers, YIVO.

39. Howe, *World of Our Fathers,* 276. As a member of the Board of Education, Richman would make similar claims about New York's public schools.

40. "Report of the Henry Street Boys' Club," 1913, Lillian Wald Papers, New York Public Library.

41. Report of the Committee on Education, January 6, 1913, Educational Alliance Board Minutes, Educational Alliance Papers, YIVO; Report of the Committee on Education, November 10, 1912, Educational Alliance Board Minutes, Educational Alliance Papers, YIVO. The Alliance attributed its difficulty in attracting boys to the fact that girls were more likely than boys to obtain jobs that did not require much physical strength; therefore, they were able to compete with women more effectively than their male counterparts could with men. Girls thus realized the advantages of possessing skills at a younger age than boys.

42. Howe, *World of Our Fathers,* 279–280.

43. Julius Mayer, "The Children and the Children's Court" *American Hebrew* (August 1903): 367–369; Report of the Committee on Education, January 6, 1913; Maurice Lewisohn argued that "manual training and mental exercises" were perhaps the best means of occupying children's time, for vocational guidance provided young people with valuable skills that they would carry with them through life. "The Jewish Social Center," *American Hebrew* (September 3, 1915): 431, 446.

44. Rischen, *The Promised City,* 55, 287.

45. The Committee on Social Work was ultimately designed to provide "wholesome recreational activities" for children of the poor and thus shared the overarching objective of the Prep Vocational School.

46. Arthur Goren, *New York Jews and the Quest for Community: The Kehillah Experiment, 1908–1922* (New York: Columbia University Press, 1970), 25, 138.

47. Louis Marshall, "Letter to the Tageblatt," reprinted in *American Hebrew* (September 24, 1908): 502.

48. Samuel Greenbaum, "Address to Federation of Jewish Organizations," *Federation Review* (April 1908): 7, 17.

49. Isaac Hourwich, "Jewish Criminality in New York in 1907," *Federation Review* (June 1908): 1.

50. Blaustein, *Memoirs of David Blaustein,* 60–62. When describing the work of the Educational Alliance in 1915, Lee Kohns made a similar argument in "Americanizing the Immigrant."

51. Just a few years prior to Bingham's assertion, at a meeting of the Committee on Moral Work, Louis Marshall expressed concern at the fact that some of the correctional institutions for juvenile offenders were planning to limit admission of Jewish children. At the same time, the resources of comparable Jewish institutions were insufficient to meet the demand. He also noted that non-Jewish institutions failed to meet the cultural needs of Jewish youth. "Report of

the Committee on Moral and Religious Work," October 10, 1904, Educational Alliance Papers, YIVO.

52. Jacob Schiff, "Americanism and Judaism," *American Hebrew* (1916): 79.

53. Ibid., 41–43.

54. Dorinson, "The Educational Alliance," 96.

55. Regular Meeting of the Board of Directors, December 10, 1906, Educational Alliance Board Minutes; Special Meeting of the Board of Directors, April 23, 1907.

56. "The Jewish Chautauqua Assembly," *American Hebrew* (1908): 343.

57. Seth Scheiner, *Negro Mecca: A History of the Negro in New York City, 1865–1920* (New York: New York University Press, 1965), 6; Gilbert Osofsky, *Harlem: the Making of a Ghetto, Negro New York, 1890–1930* (New York: Harper and Row, 1971), 127.

58. Guichard Parris and Lester Brooks, *Blacks in the City: A History of the National Urban League* (Boston: Little, Brown, 1971), 41.

59. Mary White Ovington, for example, attributed the 1905 San Juan Hill riots to the behavior of the community's black residents, who, she claimed, were "known for their rough behavior and readiness to fight"; Mary White Ovington, *Half a Man: The Status of the Negro in New York* (New York: Schocken Books, 1911), 39–41, 199–200; Scheiner, *Negro Mecca,* 26–27.

60. In 1918 the National League for Urban Conditions Among Negroes (NLUCAN) was reorganized and changed its name in to the National Urban League (NUL).

61. A social-work organization first and foremost, the NUL's first annual report stated that its primary objective was "to promote and to do constructive and preventive social work for improving the social and economic conditions of Negroes in urban centers." *NLUCAN Bulletin,* 1911–1912, NUL Papers, Series 13, Box 1, Library of Congress.

62. The ideological origins of the Urban League have been a source of some scholarly debate. Historian Nancy Weiss has traced the Urban League's ideological lineage to Booker T. Washington. Historian Jesse T. Moore, by contrast, places the National Urban League in a tradition of black militant organizations such as the NAACP. Though each author's view holds merit, their attempts to pour the League into one of two antipodal molds leads each to conclusions that are not fully satisfying. Weiss's claim ultimately rests on the author's equation of self-help with the Wizard of Tuskegee. Moore, in contrast, errs antithetically. While he correctly identifies the League as a social-work group, his effort to cast the National Urban League as a militant organization ultimately leads him to overlook the League's predilection for self-help nostrums. It is my contention that the League's work and ideology lay somewhere between the two. The League was, indeed, shaped by sociological theories, as Moore suggests, but it is this very influence that led the organization to treat *self-help* as an engine of uplift.

63. Guichard Parris and Lester Brooks, *Blacks in the City: A History of the National Urban League* (Boston: Little Brown, 1971), 41.

64. Ibid., 46.

65. NLUCAN Registration Bureau of Tenants, *NLUCAN Bulletin,* 1912–1913, NUL Papers, Series 13, Box 1, Library of Congress; Parris and Brooks, *Blacks in the City,* 46.

66. George E. Haynes, *The Negro at Work in New York City* (New York: Longmans, Green, 1912), 34.

67. *NLUCAN Bulletin,* 1912–1913, NUL Papers, Series 13, Box 1, Library of Congress; Parris and Brooks, *Black in the City,* 46–47.

68. *NLUCAN Bulletin,* 1912–1913, NUL Papers, Series 13, Box 1, Library of Congress.

69. Ibid.

70. *NLUCAN Bulletin,* 1910–1911, NUL Papers, Series 13, Box 1, Library of Congress.

71. *NLUCAN Bulletin,* November 1915, NUL Papers, Series 13, Box 1, Library of Congress.

72. Charles S. Johnson, "Black Workers and the City," *Survey Graphic* 53 (1924–1925): 642–643, 719; George E. Haynes, "The Church and the Negro Spirit," *Survey Graphic* 53 (1924–1925): 697; Ira de Augustine Reid, "The Negro Goes to Sing Sing," *Opportunity* (July 1932): 215.

73. Parris and Brooks, *Blacks in the City*, 46–47: *NLUCAN Bulletin*, November 1915, NUL Papers, Series 13, Box 1, Library of Congress.

74. Parris and Brooks, *Blacks in the City*, 48.

75. "Steps in Social Progress: Memorandum on the NYUL, 1926," NUL Papers, Series 5, Box 10, Library of Congress; "Report of the Executive Secretary of the NUL," February 2, 1927, 9, NUL Papers, Series 11, Box 1; "Progress in Racial Adjustment," *Opportunity* (March 1927): 79.

76. "The Cooperative a Very Present Help in Time of Trouble," *Dunbar News* (March 9, 1932); "Rockefeller's Resident Manager in Address to Interracial Conference Tells How Apartments Helped Harlem," *New York Age* (January 26, 1929); "Executive Board Members of NYUL," Newsletter, September, 1926, NUL Papers, Series 13, Box 19, Library of Congress.

77. Roscoe C. Bruce, "The Dunbar Apartment House: An Adventure in Community Building," *Southern Workman* 60 (October 1931): 420, 423.

78. Alfred Alexander, "The Housing of Harlem," *Crisis* 35: 335, 351.

79. Bruce, "The Dunbar Apartment House," 424–425.

80. James H. Hubert, "Harlem—Its Social Problem," NUL Papers, Series 5, Box 10, 44, Library of Congress.

81. Blacks' share of skilled and white-collar workers also increased in this period. A small number of Afro-Americans, roughly 16 percent, managed to gain employment as clerks, foremen, and skilled workers.

82. NUL Department of Industrial Relations, "Activity and Field Reports," NUL Papers, Series 4, Box 1, Library of Congress.

83. Haynes, *The Negro at Work*, 47.

84. NUL Department of Industrial Relations, "Activity and Field Reports," NUL Papers, Series 4, Box 1, Library of Congress.

85. NYUL Report, 1917–1918, NUL Papers, Series 13, Box 1, Library of Congress.

86. NYUL Report, 1927, NUL Papers, Series 5, Box 10, Library of Congress.

87. "Unemployment Among Negroes Activities of the National Urban League: Data on Twenty-Five Industrial Centers," NUL Papers, Series 4, Box 1, Library of Congress.

88. NYUL Report, 1931, NUL Papers, Series 13, Box 19, Library of Congress.

89. Ira de Augustine Reid, *In a Minor Key: Negro Youth in Story and Fact* (New York: Glenwood, 1940), 76.

90. NYUL Report, 1931, NUL Papers, Series 13, Box 19, Library of Congress.

91. Charles S. Johnson, "After Garvey—What?" *Opportunity* (December 1923): 231–233; Ira de Augustine Reid, "Some Aspects of the Negro Community," *Opportunity* (January 1932): 19; Ira de Augustine Reid, *The Negro Immigrant: His Background, Characteristics, and Social Adjustment, 1899–1937* (New York: Columbia University Press, 1939), 119–122.

92. T. Arnold Hill, "Picketing for Jobs," *Opportunity* (July 1930): 216.

93. T. Arnold Hill, "After the Depression—What?" Opportunity (February 1932): 53.

94. T. Arnold Hill, "Labor—Comrades in Crime," *Opportunity* (October 1929): 316.

95. NYUL Report, 1927, NUL Papers, Series 5, Box 10, Library of Congress; Ira de Augustine Reid, NYUL Department of Industrial Relations Report, June 1925, NUL Papers, Series 5, Box 10, Library of Congress.

96. NYUL Report, 1931, NUL Papers, Series 13, Box 19, Library of Congress.

97. "Unemployment Among Negroes Activities of the National Urban League: Data on Twenty-Five Industrial Centers," NUL Papers, Series 4, Box 1, Library of Congress.

98. NUL Department of Industrial Relations Report, 1932, "The Program of the National Committee on Employer-Employee Relations in the Home," NUL Papers, Series 1, Box 6, Library of Congress.

99. Lewis, "Parallels and Divergences," 560–562.

100. Howe, *World of Our Fathers,* 131–133, 164–165; Rischen, *The Promised City,* 67.

6
The Chicago School of Human Ecology and the Ideology of Black Civic Elites

Preston H. Smith II

The purpose of this chapter is to trace the influence of the University of Chicago's human ecology school of thought on ideas about urban growth, race relations, and social disorganization on the ideology of black civic elites in Chicago in the 1940s and 1950s. I am particularly interested in how these ideas influenced black elites' conceptions and positions on relevant issues such as public housing, fair housing, and urban renewal affecting black citizens in Chicago. These black civic elites included intellectuals and race relations professionals who shared a discourse[1] on housing issues both locally and nationally. This group included individuals such as Horace R. Cayton, executive director of Parkway Community House (located in Chicago's so-called Black Belt) and coauthor of the classic *Black Metropolis*; Robert C. Weaver, economist, former New Deal federal housing and labor official, and, in 1944, chairman of the mayor of Chicago's Committee on Race Relations; Earl B. Dickerson, former city alderman, president of the Chicago Urban League, and legal counsel for Supreme Liberty Life, a black-owned insurance company; Archibald Carey, alderman, lawyer, and minister; Sidney R. Williams, executive director of the Chicago Urban League (1947–1955); and Robert Taylor, chairman of the Chicago Housing Authority board and manager of Julius Rosenwald Michigan Boulevard Apartments. These men are tied together by a practical and policy interest in housing; in addition, all of them worked in Chicago at some point and were active in debates and actions that shaped the representation of black housing interests and attempted to influence housing policymaking.

The postwar period in Chicago represented a crucial time when the city's physical and social landscapes were reconfigured by redevelopment, highway construction, migration, and capital and human flight. Chicago led and reflected national trends in federal housing and transportation policies that fostered the growth of suburbs through subsidized mortgages and highway construction. The availability of affordable, single-family dwellings attracted a large number of young middle-class whites leaving behind the poor, elderly, and minorities who were barred from the new subdivisions on the periphery of the city. The flight of middle-income taxpayers and consumers caused fretting among downtown retail interests who strategized ways to stop the decline of downtown property values. Downtown business officials, in alliance with big-city mayors and real estate interests, crafted an urban renewal policy to build up the downtown and eliminate the surrounding slums to attract middle-income whites to shop and live downtown. This public-private coalition took as its first order of business the clearance of the deteriorated housing that typified many of the areas targeted for redevelopment. Upper-income and middle-income housing for employees who worked downtown and for nearby universities and hospitals was built in formerly black-occupied slums. The first urban renewal project completed in Chicago was the Lake Meadows Apartment Complex, housing mainly black professionals in the early 1950s. Other redevelopment projects in the city facilitated the expansion of universities, hospitals, and housing for the affluent. The former residents of redeveloped areas, who were mostly black, were displaced into nearby, similarly overcrowded slums. Because location was more important to city officials and their business and professional allies than the actual conditions of the neighborhood and its housing stock, the single-family dwellings of middle-income blacks and black businesses were considered expendable in this process. Although the ghetto (referred to as the "Black Belt") expanded by converting contiguous "white" neighborhoods to nearly all-black areas, blacks suffered a net loss of housing units. The city fathers' commitment to racial segregation meant that blacks would be confined to a slowly expanding Black Belt. Eventually, blacks gained more housing not by horizontal expansion but by the vertical extension of public housing buildings.[2] It was in this political and economic context of housing scarcity and residential restrictions in Chicago that black civic elites found themselves formulating policy and plotting actions in order to defend and extend black housing interests. How black housing interests were defined, and what positions on housing policy were developed to address those interests, had to do with a set of assumptions and values shared by black professionals who headed black social institutions during this period.

THE CHICAGO SCHOOL OF HUMAN ECOLOGY

The changes in the spatial and social composition of postwar Chicago provide a context in which to understand the ideological commitments and policy goals of black civic professionals. In this chapter I explore the ideas that animated the ideological framework[3] of a group of black civic elites who wrote, spoke, and acted during the gestation of urban renewal, public housing, and fair housing policies and actions. Black civic intellectuals and professionals, I argue, adopted some of the prevailing ideas regarding the structure and growth of cities, the relations between blacks and whites, and the role that behavior plays in the incidence of social problems. The Chicago school of sociology was a dominant source of ideas pertaining to urbanization, race relations, and social development.[4] In addition to its national presence, sociologists such as Robert E. Park, Ernest W. Burgess, and Louis Wirth at the University of Chicago attempted to use the city as a "social laboratory." This orientation toward empirical research helped to fill out the theoretical skeleton of human ecology and brought these sociologists to the black community as an object of study. In particular, African American sociologists who were trained at the University of Chicago produced the most substantive and sophisticated studies of black social life in Chicago. These studies include *The Negro in Chicago,* a commissioned study after the 1919 race riot and directed by Charles S. Johnson; E. Franklin Frazier's *The Negro Family in Chicago* (1932); and St. Clair Drake and Horace Cayton's *Black Metropolis* (1945).[5] These seminal works reflected and influenced the thinking of black civic elites. Frazier, a former student of Robert Park, was research director of the Chicago Urban League while also conducting research on the black family in the 1920s. Probably the most influential black sociologist of his generation, Frazier was the chief conduit of ideas, though not unmodified, from the Chicago school to black civic professionals.[6] Horace Cayton, also a former Park student, can be identified as a major source of the ideas of human ecology in the community of civic activists until he left the city at the end of the 1940s.[7] I will draw the intellectual connections between Frazier and Cayton and the Chicago school of human ecology. Through the work of E. Franklin Frazier and Horace Cayton, the postwar cohort of black civic professionals was introduced to the influential ideas of human ecology.

The human ecology school of thought dominated thinking about cities, race, and spatial relations in the 1920s and 1930s. I will explore the contributions of this school on three topics: (1) the structure and growth of cities and what drives that growth; (2) the nature of spatial relations between the races; and (3) the notion that the lower classes suffered from a behaviorally induced social disorganization. Following an examination of these ideas I will spend a greater amount of time analyzing their impact on the writings of Frazier, Cayton, and other black civic intellectuals and professionals.

Human ecology[8] is the study of the relationships between people and institutions that are both spatial and temporal. It also includes the environmental factors that sort and structure people's relationships with each other and with social institutions. These environmental processes are often described in biological metaphors to show that, similar to plants, people fit within an orderly, predictable system. In fact, Roderick McKenzie, one of the founders of human ecology, thought that the amount of purposive action that went into the design of human communities was overstated. He argued that human communities' "processes of association and adjustment" are closer to "natural unmodificable reactions."[9] The ecological approach tends to treat conventional patterns of social behavior and action as "natural."

University of Chicago sociologists used human ecology to explain the growth and structure of cities. In this schema the determining factor in the structure of the city was its spatial relationships. (The specific issue of residential segregation is addressed below.) Different groups of people were selected and sorted into different locations through ecological processes[10] based on an unstated logic. The logic rested on market assumptions that fair and free competition determined "the best and highest use of land."[11] Robert Park said that "the city cannot fix land values, and we leave to private enterprise, for the most part, the task of determining the city's limits and the location of its residential and industrial districts."[12] The market governed the spatial locations of people and institutions. Since proponents accepted the assumptions of a self-regulating market determining the value and use of land as normal, the actions of speculators, bankers, developers, and city officials, whose actions affected the value and influenced the uses, were obscured in their schema. The selection and distribution of spatial niches according to a predictable pattern of economic value became naturalized and thus devoid of human agency. Spatial locations began to take on specific "natural" ethnic and economic characteristics. The naturalness of communities and neighborhood was expressed as their "organicity"—seamless spatial-social units of common values and practices. The ecological approach to cities and the relationships within them exhibited a spatial determinism.[13] Chicago sociology's theory of urban growth incorporated assumptions that the market governed spatial distribution of land uses and that the spatial and physical characteristics of place determined its social makeup.

Urban Growth

The location of residences and institutions within cities is determined by economic functions, property values, and proximity to a central business district. Ernest W. Burgess argued that cities largely grow in concentric circles emanating radially from a downtown area that is the financial, political, and cultural center of the city.[14] Burgess identified zones of varied land use that make up the spatial structure of American cities. He used Chicago as the prototype city while arguing that there are physical obstacles, such as rivers and railroads, to the normal patterns of growth and residence. He called the zone next to the downtown area—Chicago's famous Loop district—the "transition zone." He used that label for two reasons. One concerns the changes in land use as industrial and commercial enterprises encroach on the residential structures in the zone; the other concerns the residents themselves. Burgess saw this area as the port of entry for newcomers to the city—European immigrants in the nineteenth and early twentieth centuries and black migrants from the American South during and between the two world wars. The newcomers were attracted to this area for the cheap housing and the fact that there was little resistance to their residence because of the deteriorated conditions. It constituted a transitional area because Burgess expected that as newcomers became settled and found employment, they would eventually move out to areas of better housing.

Another zone was the "workingmen residence" zone, desirable for its close proximity to places of employment. For example, this zone included the neighborhoods near the stockyards, which were located southwest of the Loop. The next zone moving outward from the downtown area, or the "residential zone," contained a mixture of exclusive single-family homes and apartment buildings that housed the affluent. The last zone that was identified existed beyond the city limits in the suburbs and was called the "commuter zone"; it provided the residences for middle-class white-collar professional men who commuted to work downtown.

According to human ecology the factors that govern the physical growth of cities emanate from the pursuit of profits. The downtown area concentrates business transactions, political decisionmaking, and cultural events and thus attracts a lot of people. The concentration of activity generates high property values and subsequent rents that only corporate and affluent tenants can afford. "The influence of land values at the business center radiates from that point to every part of the city."[15] The commercial and industrial uses of the downtown spill over into the transition zone. The new land uses begin to negatively affect the residential uses in the area. In addition, land and buildings are allowed to deteriorate as they become the objects of real estate speculation and eventually redevelopment.[16] Although the economic factors that shape land values and in turn influence residential distribution predominate, other factors influence the location of population subgroups.

Residential Segregation

The Chicago scholars identified "segregation" as a normal characteristic in the selection and distribution of population groups. For the most part, the sociologists presented segregation as a relatively benign process. Class segregation was spatially expressed and appeared natural, as hierarchical relations were accepted in the name of market efficiency and occupational specialization. McKenzie pointed out that as a community grows "a process of differentiation and segregation takes place as well" as multiplication. Specifically, "residence sections become established, segregated into two or more types, depending upon the economic and racial composition of the population." Park said segregation, or the geographical distribution of the population, stemmed from "personal tastes and convenience [and] vocational and economic interests."[17] Human ecology assumed that segregation was voluntary, as it was based on individual tastes and interests or dictated by occupational specialization in an increasingly complex division of labor. Given this framework, racial segregation was not "normal" unless considered voluntary or explained by an economic rationale. Ethnic immigrants and racial migrants came to the city with minimal occupational skills and thus could acquire only unskilled and semiskilled jobs with lower pay. Ecological theory tended to explain the segregation of blacks as due to their poverty rather than their race. But how did they explain the segregation between black poor residents and white poor residents? There does not appear to be an answer to that question in the ecological framework. The theory mainly assumed that once settled in the transition zone the "talented and ambitious," through natural selection, would eventually become upwardly mobile and move into subsequent zones with better housing accommodations. Of course, "natural selection" normalized economic segregation, which was explained as the market recognition of unequal abilities, but it also discounted racial reasons for restricted residence.

Ernest Burgess provided a more in-depth discussion of segregation in the context of human ecology than did his colleagues. He still treated segregation as a relatively benign process. Like his colleagues he saw segregation as a process of differentiating

> into natural economic and cultural groupings [that give] form and character to the city. For segregation offers the group, and thereby the individuals who compose the group, a place and a role in the total organization of city life. Segregation limits development in certain directions, but releases it in others. These areas tend to accentuate certain traits, to attract and develop their kind of individuals, and so to become further differentiated.

The sorting process determined spatial niches by what talents and resources a resident had to contribute to the city's economic organization and/or by an affinity with others who shared the resident's cultural traits. Burgess assumed the overlap of economic and cultural segregation. "Interrelated with this economic division of labor is a corresponding division into social classes and into cultural and recreational groups."[18]

Following up on his limited discussion of segregation in "The Growth of a City," Burgess directly addressed the issue of racial segregation in another essay a few years later. He wanted to determine whether blacks represented an exceptional case or whether they would follow the European immigrants that preceded them and who became less segregated over time. He thought he could answer this question by gaining "a clearer understanding of the interplay of the factors and forces which determine the location and the movement of Negro neighborhoods within the larger community."[19] Burgess begins by locating blacks in the transition zone where other newcomers to the city had started. He pointed out: "For all new groups with one or more of the following characteristics—an alien culture, a low economic status and a different race—this point of arrival naturally tends to be in or near the central business district."[20] Burgess did acknowledge that a "different race" or nonwhite status constituted an independent reason for being restricted to the transition zone.

Relying heavily on the empirical studies of Thomas J. Woofter's *Negro Problem in the Cities* and Frazier's unpublished "The Study of the Negro Family in Chicago," Burgess found blacks more residentially concentrated compared to other ethnic groups. Nonetheless, he believed at that time that "while [blacks] possess their own institutions and unique modes of behavior [they] are less like Chinatowns and Medieval ghettos and much more of an integral part of American life than are Polish and Italian communities."[21] Here Burgess observed that blacks were more culturally American, and thus less socially isolated, than were Southern and Eastern

Europeans. Ironically, Burgess did not take into account this factor in his observation of their more severe residential segregation. He does not address the question whether blacks, if they were in fact closer to native whites culturally, should be *less* segregated than Poles and Italians, not more. Unperturbed, Burgess suggested blacks' residential mobility was not significantly different from immigrant groups, and thus "from the standpoint of human ecology, it appears to vary little, if at all, from those of other groups."[22]

Burgess acknowledged that African Americans' inordinate segregation had to do with the resistance of whites to blacks residing in "their" neighborhoods. He then outlined the ecological process of residential succession. The process involves three stages: invasion, reaction, and equilibrium. After blacks "invaded" a neighborhood, whites usually deserted the areas, but "a new equilibrium of communal stability" would eventually occur, according to Burgess. But this process was nothing new. "Every residential community offers resistance to the intrusion of a new group of imputed inferior status whether on the basis of race, economic standing, or cultural difference."[23] Again Burgess treated race as a separate but equivalent cause of segregation, which he assumed could be overcome by the individual. He concluded that "the residential segregation of the Negro in northern cities in this country is in the main not the product of race prejudice alone but the result of the interplay of factors in urban growth which determine the location and movement of all groups, institutions, and individuals."[24] Burgess did not spell out how "race prejudice" interacted with apparent race-neutral factors to create racial segregation. Racial discrimination was a factor but not the sole or perhaps even predominant one. He argued that other factors such as economic status and length of residence in a city also contributed to blacks' residential concentration.[25] Burgess seemed to not have considered how blacks' economic status was racially influenced. On the contrary, he found occupational selection less determined by the impersonal market and guided more by racial characteristics. He thought that occupational specialization was "explainable more by racial temperament or circumstance than by old world economic background, as Irish policemen, Greek ice cream parlors, Chinese laundries, Negro porters, Belgian janitors, etc."[26] According to Burgess, race influences occupational selection, but less from racial discrimination than from blacks' predisposition to make some job choices and not others. He considered race one of many factors to create segregation and, when applied to economic status, defined it as a cultural trait rather than a restriction of opportunity.

Burgess's Lamarckian view of racial temperaments was shared by Robert Park's work.[27] Park was considered to be one of the major scholars on race relations during the interwar period. James McKee argues that Park was part of a new group of sociologists on race relations who did not believe that blacks were biologically inferior, such inferiority being the prevalent notion in academic and popular circles during the 1920s and 1930s.[28] While Park eschewed biological theories of black inferiority, he did embrace a quasibiological notion of racial temperaments. According to Park, blacks did exhibit "special traits and tendencies," which he claimed depended more on "biological rather than cultural differences." Neither cultural nor historical traditions could explain the fact "that Teuton and Latin, the Negro and the Jew—to compare the most primitive with the most sophisticated of peoples—have certain racial aptitudes, certain innate and characteristic differences of temperament which manifest themselves especially in the objects of attention, in tastes, and in talents."[29] Park continued to show the specific racial temperaments of African Americans in this well-known and controversial viewpoint:

> Everywhere and always the Negro has been interested rather in expression than in action; interested in life itself rather than in its reconstruction or reformation. The Negro is, by natural disposition, neither an intellectual nor an idealist, like the Jew; nor a brooding introspective, like the East Indian; nor a pioneer and frontiersman, like the Anglo-Saxon. He is primarily an artist, loving life for its own sake. His métier is expression rather than action. He is, so to speak, the lady among the races.[30]

It was this position that Ralph Ellison found akin to the social Darwinism of William Graham Sumner. Ellison attributed Park's racial conservatism to the time he spent with Booker T. Washington and was "responsible for inflating Tuskegee into a national symbol."[31] Park's embrace of racial temperament meant that although he rejected the notion of intellectual inferiority, he nonetheless argued that blacks show a biologically based *inclination* toward not being intellectuals or entrepreneurs. Moreover, his feminization of blacks reinforced invidious stereotypes of blacks as passive, expressive, childlike, impatient with worldly matters, too shallow for introspection, and generally not suited for the public world of business and politics. Of course, these broadly shared ideas helped to affirm and subtly support African Americans' disenfranchisement during the Jim Crow era.

Park's and Burgess's racial essentialism dovetailed with their ecological theory of residential succession. Their racial essentialism made it difficult to view blacks as suitable for modern citizenship, which after World War II included homeownership in the affluent outlying neighborhoods of the metropolis. Given these ideas, whites' negative "reaction" to blacks' "invasion" seemed natural. Whites' aversion to blacks' residing in their neighborhoods set into motion the phenomenon that became known as "white flight." The cycle of invasion, reaction, and equilibrium became rigid and took on the status of "social law." In this context, "equilibrium" meant resegregation. No wonder that the Chicago sociologists' racial essentialism and the cycle of residential succession became codified in the real estate guidelines to evaluate property based on its racial homogeneity.[32]

Social Disorganization

Another important idea from human ecology that became significant to black civic intellectuals was social disorganization. This idea generally referred to the situation of low-income people who experienced social problems such as juvenile delinquency, illegitimacy, poverty, and desertion. Consistent with their model's feature of biotic equilibrium, Burgess saw social disorganization and organization as part of the process of urban growth that is "analogous to the anabolic and katabolic processes of metabolism in the body."[33] Given the penchant for seeing social phenomena as part of an evolving social organism, he did not consider social disorganization to be a static or permanent condition but a continuous process. Burgess explained:

> Normally the processes of disorganization and organization may be thought of as in reciprocal relationship to each other, and as cooperating in a moving equilibrium of social order toward an end vaguely or definitely regarded as progressive. So far as disorganization points to reorganization and makes for more efficient adjustment, disorganization must be conceived not as pathological, but as normal.[34]

For Burgess and his colleagues, disorganization presented the opportunity for reorganization in the evolutionary trek from premodern ways of life to modern urban civilization. Of course, he leaves the door open, pointing out that disorganization can lead to reorganization and readjustment, but it does not *necessarily* lead to this state. In the case of a disorganized family, or a neighborhood's failure to reorganize on its own, an external force would be necessary to regain equilibrium. McKenzie described slum neighborhoods as "areas where there are no standards of decency or social conduct except those imposed by outside authority."[35]

William F. Whyte, in his critique of the idea of social disorganization, pointed out a contradiction within the Chicago school of thought. Some scholars such as McKenzie and Harry Zorbaugh described the slums as socially disorganized or unorganized, whereas others like Robert Park, H. A. Miller, and Louis Wirth signaled the "existence of indigenous organizations in the slums."[36] Perhaps Whyte drew too fine a distinction in suggesting that disorganization meant *no* organized community exists at all and disorder reigns. Human ecology theorists acknowledged that indigenous organizations existed only to argue that they were dysfunctional (e.g., juvenile gangs). Nonetheless Whyte was accurate when he said disorganization had supplanted the normative use of the nineteenth-century distinction of worthy and unworthy poor.[37] Given these different tendencies, it would be important to understand under what conditions disorganization leads to a more efficient reorganization and when it becomes a semipermanent pathological state associated with poor people's values and lifestyles.

The unit of analysis is important for Burgess's discussion of social disorganization. He has referred to both the individual and the racial or ethnic group. But consistent with human ecology's spatial determinism, geographically "natural" areas can be characterized as *environments* of social disorganization. Burgess identified the transition zone as the area most associated with disorganization. He described this zone as "deterioration encircling the central business section ... always to be found the so-called slums and badlands with their submerged regions of poverty, degradation, and disease and their underworlds of crime and vice." In Chicago, these areas have contained "immigrant colonies—the Ghetto, Little Sicily, Greektown,

Chinatown—fascinatingly combining old world heritages and American adaptations. Wedging out from here is the Black Belt, with its free and disorderly life." To be fair, Burgess did see the transition zone as both one of "decay" and "regeneration" with "the mission, the settlement, the artists' colony, radical centers—all obsessed with the vision of a new and better world."[38] In his scheme, "reorganization" was associated with racial and ethnic groups moving outward from downtown into more socially organized zones. Readjustment was evidenced by upward and spatial mobility. It was here that the social and spatial became fused.

It is unclear what causes social disorganization in the human ecology model. Does social disorganization derive from the black individual's newcomer status? From her family structure, her race, or her residence in the transition zone? The *environment* emerges as the site and cause of disorganization because other racial and ethnic groups in the same area experienced similar problems to blacks. Environments as "natural areas" have unchanging characteristics. They are either "wholesome" or "degrading" and "vicious." Neighborhood conditions as well as peoples' behavior constitute the environment and thus cause social disorganization. Proponents of human ecology are not clear whether conditions and/or behavior cause social disorganization. Since the distribution of economic resources is a given through the self-regulating market, the political-economic institutional impact on neighborhood conditions is minimized in ecological theory. The indicators of social disorganization such as crime, desertion, illegitimacy, and juvenile delinquency highlight proximate human behaviors but obscure the social terrain of constrained choices that underlie those behaviors. According to their tautological schema, these social indicators both *indicate* and *cause* social disorganization.

It is clear, however, that disorganization refers to a circumstance that occurs as the newcomer to the city is making the transition from traditional to modern society. Burgess posited that disorganization was experienced by the new resident until he could shed the "habitual . . . and often of what has been to him the moral" in the process of reorganization and adopt "attitudes" that were more appropriate to the urban environment.[39] Burgess thought that some of the migrants, or more likely their children, were caught in some transition from a premodern way of life to a more complex, and thus conflicting, way of life. "Personal disorganization may be but the failure to harmonize the canons of conduct of two divergent groups."[40] In other words, the individual could also become disorganized by attempting to live simultaneously in two different realms governed by, respectively, mainstream and marginalized cultural practices. This conflict represented the particular circumstance of newcomers readjusting to new rules of conduct. Burgess said that "expansion and metabolism [could] indicate that a moderate degree of disorganization" existed but still may lead to social organization. However, he also warned that "rapid urban expansion is accompanied by excessive increases in disease, crime, disorder, vice, insanity, and suicide, [as] rough indexes of social disorganization."[41] It appeared that the extent and rate of population increase, residential density, spatial mobility, and social change were important indicators of whether social disorganization led to reorganization or demoralization. Pathological social disorganization will more likely occur during periods of rapid expansion such as mass immigration and migration and not lend itself easily to readjustment.[42]

While Burgess's discussion spoke in more general and abstract terms, Robert Park's depiction was particular to African American migrants. He stressed that black migrants' difficult adjustment from a premodern, traditional, and primitive existence to modern urban civilization suggested that their behavioral response to urban conditions caused their social disorganization. Park argued that migration, even though it felt liberating, was "disorganizing" for both the sending and receiving communities.[43] This is where Park's time with Booker T. Washington becomes important for his social theory. Park utilized a prevalent conceptual dualism of community and society to analyze his observations of black rural life.[44] "Community" represented primary, spontaneous social relations, whereas the "society" represented formal, impersonal, and secondary ties between people. Park regarded blacks as "the American peasant still living, in the rural South, in a world of primary personal relations which imposed the local morality on the individual through face to face contacts with family and friends."[45] In a community, social control is informal, embedded in the relationships of authority in families, churches, and tight-knit neighborhoods. Informal social control breaks down when confronted with the mobility, density, and size of a complex urbanized society.[46] Young people were tempted to eschew the informal norms of traditional life in favor of manifold leisure activities and the vices of modernity. Park argued that rural young folk, uninfluenced by urban vice and crime, are "strong, vigorous, kindly and industrious people; simple-minded, wholesome and good as God made them ... earnest and ambitious. The young folk from the cities on other hand are very likely to be indifferent and frivolous, and disposed to live by their wits."[47]

Park contended that "the race problem will eventually solve itself" if the majority of blacks are allowed to "grow up slowly and naturally" in the rural South rather than become "superficial and trifling" by moving to the city.[48] Park's skepticism about migrants' ability to adjust to city life increased the likelihood that social disorganization would be attributed to their maladjustment. This assumption—that migrants could not "reorganize" or adjust their lives without outside intervention and thus were the cause of social disorganization—became a core assumption of black civic ideology in postwar Chicago.

HUMAN ECOLOGY AND BLACK CIVIC IDEOLOGY

In this section I want to explore the ways in which black civic intellectuals engaged the ideas of the ecological framework on urban growth, segregation, and social disorganization. By reconstructing the positions that these intellectuals took on these issues, we can construct part of the ideological frame that shaped their peers' thinking about housing interests. In this section I examine primarily the work of E. Franklin Frazier, which arguably had the most significant influence on African American professionals who conducted race-relations work in Chicago during and after World War II. I will also treat the work of Horace R. Cayton and Robert C. Weaver.

Urban Growth

Frazier adapted Burgess's theory of urban growth to the residential patterns of Chicago's black South Side. He adopted Burgess's growth patterns of concentric circles emanating from the downtown area. Frazier argued that the movement of blacks "was similar to the movements of other racial and immigrant groups in the city of Chicago" and that because of their poverty they "acquired a foothold in and near the center of the city where less resistance is offered to the invasion of alien elements."[49] Frazier divided the black community into seven residential zones that fitted within Burgess's citywide structure of five zones. Black residential zones began in the transition zone (Burgess's second zone) and ended just inside the residential zone (zone IV) near the "bright light area" and short of the "restricted residential district."[50] These zones corresponded with the Black Belt of the 1930s, which stretched south from Roosevelt Road or 12th Street to 71st Street. The eastern border was Lake Michigan and Cottage Grove Avenue after 39th street. The western border was Wentworth Avenue and, farther south, State Street. According to Frazier, these zones were approximately ten blocks long (or about 1.25 miles). In addition, blacks in Chicago also lived in smaller "racial colonies" on the near west side and near north side and, farther south, on the outskirts of the city.[51]

He proceeded to show how each zone could be distinguished by a variety of physical and social characteristics. These characteristics included the condition of housing and infrastructure, rates of homeownership, male head of household, literacy, education, length of residence in the city, and rates of desertion, illegitimacy, and juvenile delinquency. In Frazier's rich and detailed case study, the social characteristics indicated the class and family organization of the African American residents in the city. He attempted to counteract the prevailing popular and academic opinion that blacks were immoral, something insinuated by their "deviant" family patterns and social disorganization. He wanted to challenge, in particular, the notion that *all* black families were pathological. According to Frazier, blacks were "slowly acquiring Western civilization" as a group, though some "sections" were able to acquire "civilization" faster than others. It was this differential rate that explained why some black families were conventional whereas others were dysfunctional.[52] Frazier admitted that black families that had recently migrated to the city often exhibited high rates of desertion, illegitimacy, and juvenile delinquency, suggesting they had not had enough time or instruction to adopt the normative standards of middle-class urban-industrial civilization.[53]

Frazier's schema showed different black family and social characteristics sorted geographically. He adopted the spatial relations of human ecology to exhibit the social differences among black classes. He depicted a spatial arrangement that linked social characteristics to specific localities. Thus, like his teachers Park and Burgess, Frazier embraced the fusion of spatial and social characteristics.[54] Given the racial climate that assumed black inferiority, one can see the attraction to black intellectuals of attributing aberrant social traits to a spatial environment rather than to racial biology or culture.[55] In a climate where whites saw blacks as incapable of having moral standards, Frazier felt it important to point out class distinctions and varied moral behavior among the African Americans he studied. Equally important, Frazier found that all ethnic groups that had resided in citywide zones known for social disorganization experienced similar high rates of delinquency, illegitimacy, crime, and desertion. Frazier followed Burgess in an attempt to characterize a zone as socially disorganized based on a quantitative scale of rates of social indicators. The statistical correlation of social indicators and population does not explain causality and acts as a poor substitute for the lived social and economic experiences of a zone's residents.[56]

Although Frazier provided the most thorough adaptation of human ecology's urban growth theory to a black community, the theory's influence was prevalent among black civic intellectuals and elites in Chicago. Horace Cayton studied with Robert Park and, later, directed Parkway Community House. In a seminal essay on black housing published in 1940, Cayton started his discussion by describing Chicago along the lines of the concentric theory of urban growth. Cayton relied heavily on the research gathered by the Chicago city council's Subcommittee on Negro Housing, headed by Alderman Earl B. Dickerson. Cayton's description of the residential zones mirrored Burgess's observations from fifteen years earlier.[57] Cayton described the process of residential mobility implicit in the model. A new group of migrants "settles in the 'area of transition' and takes low skill work—steel mills or meat packing for men and garment or lamp shade industry for women." Next, this group (or at least its ambitious members) moves to the working-class district of modest but respectable housing. Eventually, the sons and daughters of this group move up the economic and social ladder into managerial and professional occupations and residentially either to the luxury apartments of the residential zone or to the new bungalow section of the "commuter zone." Cayton thus embraced the model's implicit linkage between social and spatial mobility. With this outward and upward mobility comes assimilation. On the eve of World War II, he observed that "the new American has dropped his racial or national characteristics and has taken on the class characteristics of the group with which he is identified."[58] Whereas European immigrants took this assimilation trek, blacks were not allowed to follow.

Cayton asserted that the growth pattern that he witnessed worked against the housing interests of black citizens. He saw the Black Belt being squeezed from the north by the "the invasion of Business." Commercial enterprises had taken over many contiguous residential areas as the Loop district expanded. But because he adopted the model of urban growth (and its assumptions) as normative, Cayton found this land use "transformation" to be natural and commensurate with "the process of city growth and is typical of the entire circle surrounding the central business district." The problem was that blacks, unlike other groups, did not have an outlet to move to in response to this "natural" incursion.[59] He also concurred with Park's assessment that the areas around downtown were allowed to deteriorate in order to drive down property values for speculative purposes. Cayton argued that the northern section of the Black Belt from downtown to 39th Street was held for "speculation." He lamented that no "capital has gone into the creation of new living units since 1928."[60] Cayton, like Park, accepted what both viewed as the normal geographic expansion of business enterprise through economic growth, but both were critical of the manipulation of land values by real estate interests.[61]

Residential Segregation

Although Cayton and other black civic intellectuals adopted the human ecology model of urban growth as natural, and thus inevitable, not surprisingly they disagreed with the founders over the issue of segregation. Economic (or class) segregation was seen as a natural feature of a city's organization and growth. People were sorted into and selected for specific geographical areas by their position within the occupational hierarchy. It is unclear just how "natural" racial segregation was considered by the Chicago school of thought. It was normal in the sense that all newcomers started at the bottom both economically and residentially (in the deteriorated areas of the transition zone). It was also the case that blacks, because they had a low economic status as a group, would be more segregated compared to their European immigrant counterparts, who began the trek to middle-class respectability after World War II. The Chicago sociologists did acknowledge that color was an extra burden that blacks carried.[62] The question is whether racial segregation would be temporary—assuming that African Americans would overcome racial obstacles over time—or whether racial segregation was so entrenched that it would take more intervention by public and private authorities.

Frazier concurred with his teachers that blacks were similar to all other ethnic groups and thus subject to the normal factors of urban growth and distribution.[63] Furthermore, "within the Negro community there are processes of selection which bring about segregation on the basis of occupation, intelligence, and ambition."[64] As a result of this selection process, the more driven and ambitious members of the immigrant and racial groups move into more stable neighborhoods. For Frazier, blacks experience the normal sorting of groups because of economic or individual reasons, but he contended that this normal process could be skewed because of race.[65]

Frazier clearly was aware of residential segregation of blacks as the key factor impeding conventional patterns of residential distribution, but his focus was on black families, not the institutionalization of segregation. Cayton and Robert Weaver were more concerned with that institutionalization. Cayton thought that a black ghetto had formed in Chicago around 1910. Before this time blacks, although usually in small homogeneous enclaves, were distributed more evenly among the white population areas. It is significant that the formation of the first ghetto occurred *before* World War I, when the Great Migration commenced. In other words, racial boundaries were hardening even before the influx of "unadjusted" southern migrants. Later, Cayton (with St. Clair Drake) drew attention to a "color line which marks Negroes off as a segregated group deemed undesirable for free association with white people in many types of relationships."[66] The residential color line was maintained by acts of terror and violence by white neighborhood "improvement" associations. Restrictive covenants started by the real estate industry replaced white violence as a means to maintain racial boundaries.[67] These covenants—written into the deeds or agreed upon by the neighborhood association—restricted the selling or renting of land and housing to nonwhites and nongentiles.[68]

Cayton believed that restrictive covenants were the main vehicle for creating and maintaining segregation. He blamed "real estate interests" for the development and perpetuation of residential segregation. He quoted Robert R. Taylor, vice chair of the Chicago Housing Authority at the time, as saying that 80 percent of the city's land was covered by restrictive covenants.[69] In 1938, Alderman Earl B. Dickerson concurred that "segregation has spread until now it covers the entire Metropolitan area. The restrictive covenants prevail in every section of the city."[70] Drake and Cayton found that restrictive covenants were pernicious because white residents used them to subordinate and segregate blacks. "They confine Negroes to the Black Belt, and they limit the Black Belt to the most rundown areas of the city."[71] Furthermore, Cayton articulated what has become a long-standing fear: that these interests wanted to displace blacks from the desirable midsouth section of Chicago. "There are indications that real estate interests hope to force all Negroes from the lake front and from the district west of South Parkway to make room for a South Side real estate development which would house white people only."[72]

Robert Weaver was also very explicit about who crafted restrictive covenants. In addition to the real estate interests (which included property managers, developers, and financial institutions), Weaver added national housing agencies. Weaver, a New Deal liberal,[73] criticized the Federal Housing Administration (FHA) and the National Housing Agency for failing to provide "nonsegregated privately financed housing for war workers [that] not only reduced [the] scope of Negro participation in the war housing program but also further institutionalized residential segregation." He mentioned the *Underwriting Manual* used by these agencies as supporting racial covenants at a time "when the housing program was conceived as a part of the all-out effort to preserve the democratic way of life." He criticized these agencies' acquiescence to prejudice within the private housing industry, especially at a time of FHA-insured financing, when all risks were socialized but profits remained in private hands.[74] Weaver blamed private interests with public authorities' compliance as the facilitators of residential segregation. But this collaboration was not surprising, because former real estate industry professionals moved easily into federal housing bureaucracies and wrote the guidelines for mortgage financing.

Many of the black civic intellectuals recognized that while restrictive covenants were an affront to racial democracy, residential segregation had its benefits for some sectors of the black middle class. Many observers have remarked on the "vested interests" that the ghetto's black elite had in residential concentration. The benefits became more evident with the development of an institutional structure in Chicago's Black Belt after the Great Migration.[75] For politicians it meant a solid racial voting bloc and the ability to gain some leverage for patronage from the political machine.

For businessmen and women it meant "captive" consumers to keep their businesses afloat and earn profits. For real estate professionals it provided a geographic area (albeit restricted) to buy and sell properties to black clients. Drake and Cayton suggested, however, that an acceptance of racial concentration was widespread among black citizens: "Although Negroes know that residential segregation has implications of inequality and inferiority—that it implies subordination—they do not oppose residential segregation with the same vigor that they display in attacking the Job Ceiling." Essentially, blacks wanted more room to expand and desired access to better quality living spaces commensurate with their incomes—but not necessarily away from the Black Belt.[76] They argued that the "Black Metropolis, too, is an object of pride to Negroes of all social strata. It is their city within a city. It is something 'of our own.'" Largely, blacks were "ambivalent about residential segregation: they see a gain in political strength and group solidarity, but they resent being compelled to live in the Black Belt."[77] Weaver found such thinking shortsighted, arguing that blacks developed a vested interest in segregation "largely as a means of protection from rejection."[78] Black civic elites were also ambivalent. They fought for the principle of free access to housing and living spaces, but they also recognized the value of maintaining an intact black community. In this case, racial democracy is achieved by racial parity, the mirroring of white class structure in an intact black world.

Social Disorganization

Black civic intellectuals adopted the notion of social disorganization when describing conditions within segregated black communities. They defined *social disorganization* as the failure to adopt conventional social patterns, evidenced by social problems such as delinquency, crime, illegitimacy, poverty, and female-headed households. According to urban ecologists, social disorganization is normal when it is temporary and eventually leads to reorganization, but if it becomes permanent it is defined as pathological. They assumed, like the Chicago sociologists, that social disorganization results from rapid urban expansion and accompanying social change such as wartime migration. Social disorganization can result from a faulty adjustment to urban expansion, or it can result from externally imposed conditions such as residential segregation.[79] Again, a look at Frazier's work can help us see how black intellectuals appropriated this idea from the Chicago school of thought.

For Frazier there is a contrast between his characterizations of the family patterns of poor blacks and the process of readjustment to urban life. In his book *The Negro Family in Chicago,* Frazier discusses the prevalence of characteristics of family disorganization—juvenile delinquency, desertion, illegitimacy—in the different geographical zones that he outlines. He finds that the closer to the transition zone, the higher the rates; alternatively, farther south and closer to the city's periphery, the rates of family disorganization were lower. Frazier pointed out that these varying rates reflect the class composition of the Black Belt. Thus he found that family disorganization was more prevalent among poorer blacks who lived near downtown than the black bourgeoisie who were "segregated in the southern half of the Negro community."[80] There is not a progressive correlation between a residential area's class composition and rates of family disorganization. For instance, Frazier considers the third zone within the Black Belt, because of its proximity to a red light district, encompassing "the greatest social disorganization."[81] Nonetheless, the general pattern is clear in Frazier's depiction: Poorer blacks who live near downtown experience more disorganization compared to more affluent blacks who have "stable," male-headed nuclear families and live on the southern periphery.

Because Frazier conducted his research in the 1920s during the continuous massive migration of blacks from the rural South, he signifies their migrant status[82] (rather than their poverty) as the larger reason for some blacks' susceptibility to pathology. He writes: "But among the migrants there were thousands of ignorant and impoverished peasant families released from the customary controls of rural southern communities, and solitary men and women who have become demoralized in wandering from city to city."[83] Frazier emphasizes that the Great Migration, similar to Emancipation, represented social upheaval for southern blacks. Particularly, traditional social controls such as family, church, and small communities were left behind during black southerners' trek northward.[84] It is not surprising that newcomers would be at the bottom of the occupational hierarchy, engaging in unskilled labor and personal service. However, during this period blacks gained a foothold in industry, indicating that migrants were adjusting to city life and adequately meeting the demands of modern industry.[85]

Even though black migrants who were poor experienced the most family disorganization, their newcomer status allowed Frazier to be hopeful about their adjustment to modern urban life. Thus Frazier's discussion of disorganization as *process* rather than *condition* makes sense given the context from which he wrote about black family life. In an important passage, Frazier indicates that from the point of view of the "most optimistic social workers ... the disorganization of Negro life in the city seems at times to be a disease, whose painful manifestations can only be alleviated until the disease reaches its fatal consummation"; for policemen it is "something to be kept in check in order that it will not overwhelm the rest of the city." For the city's fathers racial segregation becomes a necessary device to contain blacks' social pathology. Despite these official and white perspectives, Frazier, in borrowing his notion of social disorganization from Burgess, is hopeful that through the migrant's readjustment process disorganization does not become "pathological" but leads to reorganization and normality. He argues that "within the disorder and confusion in this world, there is a slow process of renewal of life. If, in the struggle to survive in a strange and hostile environment, many succumb to disease, poverty, and vice, there are others who prove that the travail of urban life is a forerunner of new birth."[86] Similar to the process of normal residential distribution, those blacks who are more ambitious, talented, and hardy will adjust to modern capitalist conditions.

Sociologist James B. McKee fits Frazier within the Chicago school of thought that viewed social disorganization as a process rather than a condition.[87] "Frazier's use of the concept of social disorganization was clearly that of process, not social condition. His use of the concept made evident his training as a Chicago sociologist and as a student of Park. He was not in the melioristic tradition of the social pathologists, nor did he share that tradition's moral judgments."[88] A more careful reading of *The Negro Family in Chicago* would suggest that Frazier did make moral judgments. More precisely, he linked superior moral status to middle- and upper-income groups of blacks (a linkage that continues today in role model ideology). At one point in his study he refers to the old middle class prior to the Great Migration losing out to the new middle class of the newly formed ghetto as "the small group of Negroes who, because of superior culture, emerged from the mass of the population and constituted the upper class." Or, when referring to the location of affluent black groups: "The *better-class* families have been seeking *better* neighborhoods in the seventh zone beyond Sixty-Third Street."[89] The evaluative language that Frazier uses to characterize different black classes indicates his position that more affluent blacks are "culturally superior" to poorer blacks. Frazier fits within the Chicago school's evolutionist view of civilization—for instance, that premodern rural black migrants were located at a lower scale culturally and needed to adjust or evolve to higher cultural standards of a modern urban environment modeled by black middle- and upper-income citizens.[90]

Black civic elites embraced Frazier's cultural developmental schema regarding class differences within the black community. There was broad agreement among them that new migrants to the city were unprepared for the rigors of urban industrial living.[91] Weaver adopted Frazier's distinction between pre– and post–World War I migrants. According to Weaver, pre–World War I migrants came from the border states and expressed a familiarity with town life that rendered them more prepared than later migrants who came from the rural Deep South.[92] This distinction by black civic elites continues to look upon World War I–era migrants more favorably than those who migrated during World War II. The idea that black rural migrants were unprepared for the city was based theoretically on an assumption that rural areas represented a more simple way of life based on personal and informal social relationships compared to an urban mode of living that was more complex and based on impersonal and formal relationships. Sociologist Louis Wirth, one of the Chicago theorists and a white contemporary of Frazier, wrote a definitive essay in 1938[93] outlining a rural-urban dichotomy. This dichotomy was a feature of the Chicago founders' beliefs. For instance Robert Park, following his erstwhile employer, Booker T. Washington, favored the wholesome living of rural blacks compared to the frivolous living of urban blacks. And this formalizes what Frazier had discussed in his studies of black family structure in the 1920s and 1930s. Wirth defines "urbanism" by its distinction from rural social organization. He theorizes: "The distinctive features of the urban mode of life have often been described sociologically as consisting of the substitution of secondary for primary contacts, the weakening of bonds of kinship, and the declining social significance of the family, the disappearance of the neighborhood, and the undermining of the traditional basis of social solidarity."[94]

The significance of the weakening or disappearance of primary, direct, face-to-face relationships in the migration from rural to urban areas was due to its impact on lessening social control. In other words, the family, church, and tight-knit community were able to control the deviant behavior of youths and adults alike. In cities, the absence of these institutions because of the larger population, increased competition, and accelerated rate of social change left black newcomers detached from familiar moorings, susceptible to corrupt influences. These influences contributed to antisocial behavior that fueled "social problems" such as desertion, illegitimacy, alcohol and drug abuse, crime, juvenile delinquency, and poverty. In short, migration led to a breakdown of informal social control that led to social disorganization.

One of the main persons dramatizing this rural-urban dichotomy and its relationship to deviant black behavior was the writer Richard Wright. Wright, although not an active participant in housing policy debates and actions, was an important part of the intellectual milieu of black civic elites in postwar Chicago. Wright is explicit about the influence that the University of Chicago Department of Sociology had on his fiction and nonfiction writing.[95] While researching his *Twelve Million Black Voices*[96] on periodic trips to Chicago, Wright stayed at the Parkway Community House, which was a social services agency directed by Horace Cayton at the time.[97] He talked about using, for his book, material that Cayton had gathered for future research projects, located in the basement of the community center.

Wright discusses how migration shifted the national black population northward and to cities. He characterizes rural life not as idyllic, as Park had described, but (using Wirth's framework) less complicated. I quote Wright at length because he dramatizes the rural-urban dichotomy adopted by black civic intellectuals.

> Perhaps never in history has a more utterly unprepared folk wanted to go to the city; we were barely born as a folk when we headed for the tall and sprawling centers of steel and stone. We, who were landless upon the land; we, who had barely managed to live in family groups; we, who needed the ritual and guidance of institutions to hold our atomized lives together in lines of purpose; we, who had known only relationships to people and not relationships to things; we who had never belonged to any organizations except the church and burial societies; we, who had had our personalities blasted with two hundred years of slavery and had been turned loose to shift for ourselves—we were such a folk as this when we moved into a world that was destined to test all we were, that threw us into the scales of competition to weigh our mettle. And how were we to know that, the moment we landless millions of the land—we men who were struggling to be born—set our awkward feet upon the pavements of the city, life would begin to exact of us a heavy toll in death?[98]

Wright identifies the industrial city with modernity and the rural land with feudalism. He talks about the experience that black migrants had in the city and what happened to their rural-based culture. Industrial work, for Wright, would play the key role in assimilating former black southerners to modern urban civilization. "But it is in industry that we encounter experiences that tend to break down the structure of our folk characters and project us toward the vortex of modern urban life."[99] Later he argues that some residue of rural culture survives in the migrants' leisure life. Wright says that segregation has not allowed blacks the full benefits of

Western civilization: "Its incentives and perspectives, which form the core of meaning for so many millions, have yet to lift our personalities to levels of purpose. Instead, after working all day in one civilization, we go home to our Black Belts and live, within the orbit of the surviving remnants of the culture of the South, our naive, casual, verbal, fluid folk life."[100] The idea that racial segregation artificially preserved folk cultural remnants and blunted full assimilation to industrial civilization linked segregation to creating conditions ripe for social disorganization.

Black civic elites appropriated the Chicago school's rural-urban dichotomy and its relationship to social disorganization in order to explain what they observed in poor blacks' lives through their middle-class lens. Again they overstated the lack of preparation for black migrants moving to the city. Sidney Williams wrote in the 1950 annual report of the Chicago Urban League:

> We in the League movement know that for the American Negro or any other peasantry or *folk* people to make a workable adjustment to and survive in our complex *urban* communities they will have to be helped. Helped in accommodating themselves to a new social setting. Helped in modifying their folk habits to fit into new expectations and ways of life. This is not a painless process even under the most favorable conditions.[101]

Williams wrote a few years later that the black or white family "that leaves the rural South and overnight finds itself in Chicago suffers the same traumatic experiences that the Polish peasant family of old knew so well."[102] Williams, like his colleagues, was careful to point to blacks' difficulty not as racial but due to the circumstance of being rural newcomers.

Williams recognized that some of the folk habits that migrants brought to Chicago should be maintained. In the process of urban adjustment, according to him, "the Urban League must not seek to mutilate the finer folk qualities of these our domestic colonials." He argued that the league should preserve them because not only were these "folk traits" important to the migrants themselves but could "wind their way into the mainstream of American life." Williams felt the league should "speedily" teach these migrants how to organize and work together for controlling their environment.[103]

But there appeared to be a shift in the 1940s. World War II and the rhetoric of fighting for democracy called into question evaluative terms such as "the better classes."[104] Also, the growing residential concentration of blacks meant less explicit discussion about the impact of migration on the incidence of social disorganization. Drake and Cayton do point out that "desertion and illegitimacy, juvenile delinquency, and fighting and roistering are common in lower-class circles."[105] But they are clear that the source of social pathology was external: "Maintaining any sort of home life at the lower-class level in Bronzeville has always been a problem because of low and fluctuating annual incomes and inadequate housing."[106]

Moreover, they point out the hypocrisy of using "illegitimacy" as an indication of low moral standards: "The high illegitimacy rate in Bronzeville is sometimes cited as evidence of the 'immorality' of Negroes, and the particularly high rate within the lower class as evidence of the special 'immorality' of that class. Lower-class Negroes are quick to counter with the assertion that white people and higher-status Negroes 'do everything they're big enough to do, but they don't have the babies.'" Here is a recognition that the middle classes are able, through abortion or adoption, to dispose of the supposed evidence of lower morals. However, Cayton and Drake were not able to totally escape the normative standard of nuclear family in analyzing sex and family among the "lower class." They write: "The Second World War, while it resulted in larger family incomes, even further disorganized these homes, owing to the absence of men in the armed forces and the increased use of women in industry."[107] For these authors, "disorganization" refers to the deviance from the norm of male breadwinners' and females' place in the household. Also, the following passage clearly expresses a moral evaluation of the poor blacks: "Middle-class neighborhoods in Bronzeville thus became the beach upon which broke the human flotsam which was tossed into the city streets by successive waves of migration from the South. There it mixed with the jetsam thrown off by lower-class families as they expanded within their restricted living quarters or disintegrated under the impact of economic crises or the explosion of family discord."[108] Nonetheless, Cayton and Drake are usually careful to depict social forces that contribute to family disorganization.

Cayton and Drake also gave more emphasis to the effects of residential segregation on social disorganization. The linkage was overcrowding. Restricting blacks to a circumscribed area increased its density. Blacks averaged more people per room and dwelling, causing wear and tear on the physical structure that led to housing deterioration. More central to social disorganization was the lack of privacy due to adults and children of both genders sharing bedrooms and toilets with other kitchenette apartments. "The dominant household pattern of older, established families was the flat of three to six rooms in which family, boarders, lodgers, and impecunious relatives lived double up, overcrowded, and without privacy."[109] The practice of adding roomers who were not family members to meet the exploitative rents charged by slum landlords contributed to the lack of privacy.[110] Black civic reformers believed that this lack of privacy led to moral failings that started or perpetuated the spiral of family and social disorganization.

Despite the expectation that social disorganization among the poor was not permanent, there was little evidence of the reorganization or readjustment presented by Ernest Burgess. Frazier characterized different residential zones by the levels of social organization and disorganization. He identified, like Burgess, a transition zone in the black community that was populated by poor blacks and had a high incidence of the social problems associated with disorganization. Frazier's whole premise of showing differential incidence of immorality within the black community in order to defend the "race" assigns moral status to different black classes. He clearly views affluent blacks as having attained a superior culture by which they are able to avoid the social problems that plague the poor. Cayton and Drake mainly see social causes to the problems experienced by the black "lower classes."

They cite, in particular, racial discrimination that led to inadequate incomes and housing. They rely less on the sense that bourgeois culture is a solution rather than antidiscrimination policies.

I have argued that black civic elites in Chicago adopted and adapted some of the ideas about cities, segregation, and social pathology from University of Chicago sociologists and its school of thought on human ecology. The ideas of the founders, in particular Robert E. Park and Ernest W. Burgess, in turn influenced E. Franklin Frazier, Horace R. Cayton, and Robert C. Weaver. The latter three were black intellectuals who conveyed similar ideas in their writings, which contributed to the discourse on race relations and influenced black civic professionals.

Burgess's theory of urban growth was accepted and utilized by all these intellectuals. Necessarily, the fusion of social and spatial characteristics migrated into the work of Frazier, Cayton, and Weaver. They endorsed the spatial determination of assigning relatively fixed social characteristics to geographical location, giving them an alternative explanation of black social problems without apparently resorting to a biological or cultural one. Actually, black civic intellectuals did utilize a cultural explanation arguing that regardless of race, specific geographic zones take on a class culture. If the transition zone normally features social problems such as crime, delinquency, illegitimacy, desertion, and poverty, over time this pathology becomes part of the fixed cultural characteristics of the location. Thus in the case of Frazier, social problems in this zone resulted from losing the social controls of a traditional, premodern culture that has yet to attain a middle-class culture suitable to urban and industrial living.

Black civic intellectuals accepted Burgess's sense that segregation along economic or cultural lines was normal and acceptable given the market assumptions of human ecology. Burgess recognized that blacks did not easily assimilate into white neighborhoods because of white racial prejudice. He still felt that blacks' status was not unlike European immigrants except for the added burden of a stigmatized skin color. Black intellectuals were in agreement, though they believed that segregation was more institutionalized and thus needed governmental intervention. Despite the naturalistic cast given to urban growth patterns, these intellectuals had no difficulty in seeing human agency behind the coercive devices of racial discrimination and segregation.

Finally, black civic intellectuals did adopt human ecology's assumptions about social disorganization. There is theoretical agreement about the temporary nature of social disorganization amid social change and the possibility for reorganization. This possibility is tied to spatial mobility to upgraded housing in a zone closer to the city's periphery. Most of the black commentators cite statistics of social problems as evidence of social disorganization by geographical location. The statistical correlation of social problems and spatial location lends itself to a class cultural explanation for social disorganization. Some black intellectuals argue that racial discrimination, which translates to inadequate earnings and housing, is behind the social disorganization of the black poor. The belief in human agency supports seeing both racial discrimination and, alternatively, class cultural inferiority as causes of social disorganization. Black civic intellectuals' adoption of human ecology's naturalization of class inequality meant that they could only interpret social disorganization as resulting from either racism or from the black poor's inferior class culture.

Black civic ideology adopted conventional academic thinking about urban growth and social disorganization. These ideas would inform the positions that black civic elites took when it came to postwar housing policies. This ideology is sensitive to the role that human agency plays through its view of racial segregation and the ability of race to pervert conventional urban growth patterns and social reorganization. In other words, for this group of influential black intellectuals, human agency in shaping housing policy was manifest only when it was race-based. This combination of an acceptance of market factors and recognition of human agency only when it is race-based leaves racism or the lack of bourgeois culture as the only legitimate explanations for the pathology of poor blacks and their neighborhoods. These explanations would go a long way to justify a class-stratified housing market and a public housing policy of which the rationale was to promote better citizenship among poor blacks. The only two avenues for black housing reformers influenced by human ecology theory were antidiscrimination policy or the promotion of middle-class culture as a vehicle for upward mobility and racial progress.

NOTES

1. I employ David A. Hollinger's notion of discourse when discussing black civic elites. "Discourse is a social as well as an intellectual activity; it entails interaction between minds, and it revolves around something possessed in common. Participants in any given discourse are bound to share certain values, beliefs, perceptions, and concepts—"ideas," as these potentially distinctive mental phenomena are called for short—but the most concrete and functional elements shared, surely, are questions." David A. Hollinger, "Historians and the Discourse of Intellectuals," in *New Directions in American Intellectual History,* ed. John Higham and Paul Conkin (Baltimore: Johns Hopkins University Press, 1980), 42–43. I also agree with Beauregard's characterization of the "meaning of discourse" about urban decline. "The meaning of the discourse, I argue, can be found in the ways that it conveys practical advice about how we should respond to urban decline and mediates among the choices made available to us, the values we collectively espouse, and our ability to act. The discourse is about how we should live and invest, where, and with whom, and woven throughout it are reasons for making choices." Robert A. Beauregard, *Voices of Decline: The Postwar Fate of U.S. Cities* (Cambridge: Blackwell, 1993), 5–6.

2. See Arnold R. Hirsch, *Making the Second Ghetto: Race and Housing, 1940–1960* (Cambridge: Cambridge University Press, 1985). David A. Wallace, "Residential Concentration of Negroes in Chicago" (Ph.D. diss., Harvard University, 1953).

3. I borrow Beauregard's definition of ideology. Ideology "is first and foremost a world-view that integrates cultural dispositions, current material conditions, and aspirations within a historical frame of reference. It can be self-serving, deceive, provide practical advice and make sense of the world." *Voices of Decline,* 32.

4. See James B. McKee, *Sociology and the Race Problem: The Failure of a Perspective* (Urbana: University of Illinois Press, 1993).

5. Charles S. Johnson and Associates, *The Negro in Chicago* (Chicago: University of Chicago Press, 1922). E. Franklin Frazier, *The Negro Family in Chicago* (Chicago: University of Chicago

Press, 1932). St. Clair Drake and Horace R. Cayton, *Black Metropolis: A Study of Negro Life in a Northern City* (New York: Harcourt, Brace, 1945).

6. McKee, *Sociology and the Race Problem,* 200. Frazier was arguably the most keen observer of black social life at midcentury. First of all, unlike subsequent scholarship he took the structure of black social life seriously and sought to explain its contours and dynamism.

7. St. Clair Drake, an anthropologist trained at the University of Chicago, did have ties to the Department of Sociology in that there was quite a bit of collaboration between the two fields. See McKee, *Sociology and the Race Problem,* 153. Parkway Community Center on the city's South Side attracted many intellectuals, artists, and activists including Richard Wright, who lived there while researching his book *Twelve Million Black Voices* (New York: Thunder Mouth Press, 1941). See also Richard S. Hobbs, *The Cayton Legacy: An African American Family* (Pullman: Washington State University Press, 2002), 122–123.

8. Chicago sociologist Roderick McKenzie defines "human ecology as a study of the spatial and temporal relations of human beings as affected by the selective, distributive, and accommodative forces of the environment. Human ecology is fundamentally interested in the effect of *position,* in both time and space, upon human institutions and human behavior." Throughout the article he attempts to show how similar human ecology is to plant ecology. He says that "the same processes of competition and accommodation are at work determining the size and ecological organization of the human community." R. D. McKenzie, "The Ecological Approach to the Study of the Human Community," in *The City,* ed. Robert E. Park, Ernest W. Burgess, and Roderick D. McKenzie (Chicago: University of Chicago Press, 1925), 63–64.

9. McKenzie, "The Ecological Approach," 64–65.

10. "By ecological process is meant the tendency in time toward special forms of spatial and sustenance groupings of the units comprising an ecological distribution. There are five major ecological processes: concentration, centralization, segregation, invasion, succession." R. D. McKenzie, "The Scope of Human Ecology," in *The Urban Community: Selected Papers from the Proceedings of the American Sociological Society,* ed. Ernest W. Burgess (Chicago: University of Chicago Press, 1926), 172.

11. The assumption is that the market determines the best use of land by assigning it high property values. See John R. Logan and Harvey L. Molotch, *Urban Fortunes: The Political Economy of Place* (Berkeley: University of California Press, 1987), 4, 6.

12. Moreover, he says "The modern city ... is primarily a convenience of commerce, and owes its existence to the market place around which it sprang up." Robert E. Park, "The City: Suggestions for the Investigation of Human Behavior in the Urban Environment," in Park, Burgess, and McKenzie, eds., *The City,* 5, 12. See also Robert E. Park, "The Urban Community as a Spacial Pattern and a Moral Order," in Burgess, ed., *The Urban Community,* 9. Park's assumption of the market determination of "city limits," meaning a city's location and distribution of land uses, creates a legacy more recently carried on by Paul Peterson's argument for the transparent and uncontested unitary interests of urban politics in his study *City Limits* (Chicago: University of Chicago Press, 1981).

13. Park writes, "It is not impossible that all we ordinarily conceive as social may eventually be construed and described in terms of space and the changes of position of the individuals within the limits of a natural area; that is to say, within the limits of an area of competitive co-operation." "A Spacial Pattern and a Moral Order," 12. "Each formation or ecological organization within a community serves as a selective or magnetic force attracting to itself appropriate population elements and repelling incongruous units, thus making for biological and cultural subdivisions of a city's population." McKenzie, "The Ecological Approach," 78. Also see Park, "The City," 6.

14. Ernest W. Burgess, "The Growth of the City: An Introduction to a Research Project," in Park, Burgess, and McKenzie, eds., *The City,* 47–62.

15. Park, "A Spacial Pattern and a Moral Order," 6.

16. "If the growth at the center is rapid it increases the diameter of the area held for speculative purposes just outside the center. Property held for speculation is usually allowed to deteriorate. It easily assumes the character of a slum; that is to say, an area of casual and transient population, an area of dirt and disorder, 'of missions and of lost souls.'" Park, "A Spacial Pattern and a Moral Order," 6.

17. McKenzie, "A Ecological Approach," 73, 74. Park, "The City," 5. Park rarely focused on *segregation* in his writings on race. McKee says he was more concerned with *isolation* rather than segregation when discussing the consequences of racial residential concentration. This approach looks more at the impact of segregation rather than the institutional forces that produce it. *Sociology and the Race Problem,* 132, 133. Wallace says the early urban ecologists "regarded the concentration of population groups as a function mainly of deterministic and competitive market processes of selection; they used the term segregation to summarize these processes." He argues that later ecologists, especially black sociologists, viewed segregation as exclusion. They emphasized the "coercive and manipulative elements in the processes by which residential concentrations are created and maintained." "Residential Concentration of Negroes," 15, 16.

18. Burgess, "The Growth of the City," 56, 57.

19. Ernest W. Burgess, "Residential Segregation in American Cities," *Annals of the American Academy of Social and Political Science* (1928): 115.

20. Ibid., 109.

21. Ibid., 105.

22. Ibid., 110.

23. Ibid., 112.

24. Ibid., 115.

25. Ibid. Mainstream sociology by the time of World War II began to see segregation less benignly. See Gunnar Myrdal, *An American Dilemma: The Negro Problem and Modern Democracy,* vol. 2 (New York: Pantheon Books, 1972 [orig. 1944]), 618–622.

26. Burgess, "The Growth of the City," 57.

27. Burgess and Park's notion of racial temperaments fits George Stocking's definition of Lamarckianism in American social science from 1890 to 1915. Stocking argued, "The central concept of the Lamarckian view of race formation was 'adaptation': changes in organic behavior or structure which were caused either by direct environmental influences or were the product of the organism's responses to such influences were transmitted by heredity from parent to child." George W. Stocking Jr., "Lamarckianism in American Social Science, 1890–1915," in *Race, Culture, and Evolution: Essays in the History of Anthropology* (New York: Free Press, 1968), 243. Park, in a controversial essay, wrote: "I have sought in this brief sketch to indicate the modifications, changes and fortune which a distinctive racial temperament has undergone as a result of encounters with an alien life and culture. This temperament, as I conceive it, consists in a few elementary but distinctive characteristics, determined by physical organization and transmitted biologically. These characteristics manifest themselves in a genial, sunny and social disposition, in an interest and attachment to external, physical things rather than to subjective states and objects of introspection; in a predisposition for expression rather than enterprise and action." Robert E. Park, "The Conflict and Fusion of Cultures With Special Reference to the Negro," *Journal of Negro History* 4, no. 2 (April 1919): 129. Burgess and Park's notion of racial temperaments embodied attitudes and preferences for jobs and lifestyles that originated during slavery that were inherited by future generations of former slaves. Thus, they argued that blacks were "temperamentally" predisposed in their day to remain servants! Also see R. Fred Wacker, *Ethnicity, Pluralism, and Race: Race Relations Theory in America Before Myrdal* (Westport, CT: Greenwood, 1983), 46.

28. "The new sociologists of race relations . . . retained the idea of the race problem, though modifying it to eliminate the biological assumptions on which it had rested for so long. They replaced biological inferiority with cultural inferiority, and in doing so they sustained the older,

denigrating image of black people they had inherited from the social-problems sociologists." McKee, *Sociology and the Race Problem,* 133.

29. Park, "The Conflict and Fusion of Cultures," 112.

30. Ibid., 129.

31. Ellison traced this "racial conservatism" from Robert Park to Gunnar Myrdal's assertion that all of black social thought was a poor imitation of theories held by whites. Ralph Ellison, "An American Dilemma: A Review," in *The Shadow and the Act* (New York: Quality Paperback Book Club, 1994), 307–308. McKee says "that Park came to regret the 'lady-among-the-races' phrase because of the criticism it was to evoke, particularly from educated blacks, in fact it was an appropriate expression of Park's belief in racial temperament." He says Park still held onto the idea until 1931. It was during the 1930s when the concept of a racial temperament as "the last vestige of the argument for the racial determination of human attributes" disappeared and was replaced by a cultural interpretation. McKee, *Sociology and the Race Problem,* 93, 95. Park's biographer, Fred Matthews, attempts to defend Park's idea of racial temperament by asserting that W. E. B. Du Bois "stressed the emotional, expressive nature of 'the Negro.'" Fred H. Matthews, *Quest for an American Sociology: Robert E. Park and the Chicago School* (Montreal: McGill-Queen University Press, 1977). Matthews tries so hard to absolve Park of racism that he misses the significance of his "hierarchical essentialism." What Park and Du Bois shared was a view of evolution that placed different races at varying levels of civilization that reflected the Lamarckianism of their day. See Adolph L. Reed Jr., *W. E. B. Du Bois and American Political Thought: Fabianism and the Color Line* (New York: Oxford University Press, 1997), 118–121.

32. Robert Park and, in particular, Homer Hoyt, also of the University of Chicago, "codified and legitimized" the notion that certain racial and ethnic groups' residence affected the desirability of neighborhoods and influenced their residential market value. These racial ratings and scales were collected in the Home Owners Loan Corporation's appraisal manuals and used extensively by real estate agents throughout the country in the 1930s. Kenneth T. Jackson, *Crabgrass Frontier: The Suburbanization of the United States* (New York: Oxford University Press, 1985), 198.

33. Burgess, "The Growth of the City," 54.

34. Ibid. McKee thinks that the Chicago School's characterizing of social disorganization as a *process* rather than a *condition* is a significant distinction that again separates the Chicago School from other sociologists. He also thinks Frazier employs this definition, which vindicates him from scholars who have identified him as characterizing low-income families as pathological. *Sociology and the Race Problem,* 206–207.

35. R. D. McKenzie, "The Neighborhood: A Study of Social Life in the City of Columbus, Ohio," *American Journal of Sociology* 27 (1922): 506, quoted in William Foote Whyte, "Social Organization in the Slums," *American Sociological Review* 8 (1943): 35.

36. Whyte, "Social Organization in the Slums," 35.

37. "Terms such as 'good' and 'evil' have been supplanted by terms like 'interstitial' and 'disorganization,' but the underlying ideas have been the same. I do not deny that there is a legitimate place for the terms, 'interstitial' and 'disorganization'; I am only objecting to their use as a means of avoiding consideration of evidences of organization in the slums." Ibid., 39. See also C. Wright Mills, "The Professional Ideology of Social Pathologists," *American Journal of Sociology* 9 (1943): 165–180. Richard Fuller and Richard Myers, "The Natural History of a Social Problem," *American Sociological Review* 6 (1941): 320–328.

38. Burgess, "The Growth of the City," 54–55, 56. "The zone in transition in Chicago, as in other cities, holds in their most intense and concentrated form the social problems of the city: bad housing, poverty, vice, and crime." Ernest W. Burgess, "The Determination of Gradients in the Growth of the City," *Publication of the American Sociological Society* 26 (1927): 178.

39. Burgess, "The Growth of the City," 54.

40. Ibid., 57.

41. Ibid.

42. Ibid.

43. "It is as the same time demoralizing to the migrating people themselves, and particularly, I might add, to the younger generation." Robert E. Park, "Community Organization and Juvenile Delinquency," in *The Collected Papers of Robert Ezra Park,* ed. Everett C. Hughes (Glencoe, IL: Free Press, 1952), 60.

44. Matthews, *Quest for an American Sociology,* 73, 40, 206. Stow Persons, *Ethnic Studies at Chicago* (Urbana: University of Illinois Press, 1987), 88. Wacker, *Ethnicity, Pluralism, and Race,* 67.

45. Mozell C. Hill, "Some Early Notes of Robert E. Park," *Phylon: The Atlanta University Review of Race and Culture* 14, no. 1 (1953): 88. In the "black belt there was 'a great deal of immorality, or unmorality, but these people are in no way vicious or degenerate; they are merely primitive.'" Matthews explains that Park believed "not yet having eaten the apple of moral self-consciousness, [these peasants] retained primal innocence." But Park did not see primitivism as a value in itself. Although an individual plantation sharecropper may be "natural man," his life was still incomplete. Park complained that "these people need guidance—need inspiration—they are merely *primitive.*" Of course, Park believed Tuskegee should have a central role in "civilizing" and inculcating "self-discipline" in this natural man. Quoted from "Land of Darkness" notes from Park's papers, *Quest for an American Sociology,* 75.

46. Wacker, *Ethnicity, Pluralism, and Race,* 5.

47. Park quoted in Matthews, *Quest for an American Sociology,* 76.

48. Ibid.

49. Frazier cites Burgess's article on "Residential Segregation in American Cities." Frazier, *The Negro Family in Chicago,* 91.

50. Frazier footnotes a long passage and reproduces the "urban areas" chart from Burgess's "The Growth of the City" describing the process of urban expansion. Frazier, *The Negro Family in Chicago,* 91–93. Weaver cites this work (1932, chap. 6), asserting that Black Belts duplicate the overall "city pattern of residential zones" though on a smaller scale. Weaver, *The Negro Ghetto,* 42. Drake and Cayton argue that "out of this moving about, this twenty-five year old search for 'a better neighborhood,' has arisen a spatial pattern within the Black Belt similar to that found in the city as a whole." They claim that Frazier's study "was the first to demonstrate clearly this progressive differentiation statistically." His study "graphically portrayed the existence of 'zones' based on socio-economic status within Black Metropolis." *Black Metropolis,* 382–383.

51. Frazier, *The Negro Family in Chicago,* 98–99. Eight years later, in 1940, Cayton found the same boundaries for the Black Belt. In addition he points out that over 80 percent of all blacks citywide lived in the South Side ghetto. Horace R. Cayton, "Negro Housing in Chicago," *Social Action* (1940): 10.

52. E. Franklin Frazier, "The Negro Family," *Annals of the American Academy of Social and Political Science* (1928): 51.

53. Frazier found that the middle class was not interested in playing the tutorial role. "The small group of Negroes, mostly mulattoes, who represented the vanguard of the race in thrift and attempts to acquire some degree of culture, had continually attempted to escape from the less energetic and the lower elements in the Negro population." *The Negro Family in Chicago,* 104. Frazier study's depiction of residentially stratified black social life flies in the face of accounts of an organic and cohesive black community. Clearly, residential segregation has truncated the living space of blacks, but within this space were clearly demarcated areas of lower-, middle-, and upper-income residents.

54. "The spatial pattern, which the seven zones in the South Side Negro community presented, was a reflection of the occupational and cultural organization of the community. . . . There has

been a selection and segregation of economic and cultural groups which has determined the social structure of the community. The social structure has been defined more or less by the relative position of certain elements in the Negro population in the community. Within this social structure the Negro's status as a member of a moral order was determined largely by his position in the community." Frazier, *The Negro Family in Chicago,* 105, 116. Drake and Cayton retrofitted Frazier's schema to fit 1930 census conditions under a map titled "Ecological Areas Within Negro Community." They superimposed on Frazier's map a determination of which areas were "best," "mixed," and "worst." "Neighborhood areas were classified on the basis of median rentals, median education, and juvenile delinquency, illegitimacy and insanity rates." *Black Metropolis,* 384.

55. Wacker, *Ethnicity, Pluralism, and Race,* 55.

56. Frazier goes as far as to adopt Burgess's attempt to measure urban growth by the rates of poverty, homeownership, and so on. "A similar method has been used to measure the differences in the character of the Negro population in the South Side community. Statistics on the Negro population were secured from census tract data, which were used as units for the federal enumeration of 1920." Frazier, *The Negro Family in Chicago,* 98 (see note 1). See Ernest W. Burgess, "The Determination of Gradients in the Growth of the City," *Publication of the American Sociological Society* 26 (1927): 178–184. For a critique of a similar method of deriving a social picture of a neighborhood by highlighting the statistical correlation of social problems used in modern ecological treatments of the "underclass," see Adolph Reed Jr., "The Poverty of the Discourse on Poverty," *Radical America* (Summer 1991): 21–39.

57. Cayton described the area surrounding the central business district as "an area in transition—formerly residential in character—which has suffered from its proximity to the business center." Just outside of this area of vice and "the slum dwellings of the newest comers to the city" is where "working men have their homes in sometimes poor but respectable neighborhoods." Next there is the "apartment house district" in large cities, and "on the periphery are the suburban settlements of the middle and upper classes who earn their living in the city but return to their 'dormitory communities' each evening." "Negro Housing in Chicago," 5, 6. Not surprisingly, Cayton and Drake use Burgess's theory in their *Black Metropolis,* written in 1945: "The two basic facts about the spatial growth of Midwest Metropolis (and of most American cities) are, first, the tendency for people to move steadily outward from the center of the city as they grow more prosperous, leaving the center to business and industry, to the poor and the vicious; and second, the tendency of the foreign-born to settle originally in colonies near the center of the city, with individual families joining the outward stream as soon as they become Americanized in thought and relatively well-to-do." *Black Metropolis,* 13. The black metropolis "has followed the same general pattern of city growth. Those Negroes who through the years have become prosperous tend to gravitate to stable neighborhoods far from the center of the city." Ibid., 382. Robert C. Weaver concurred in *The Negro Ghetto* that Burgess's model was applicable to most ghettos. Robert C. Weaver, *The Negro Ghetto* (New York: Harcourt, Brace, 1948). Given Burgess's apt description of Chicago it is not surprising that his conception informed the black civic elites' discourse on urban growth. The question is did they regard this process as natural and therefore unalterable.

58. Cayton, "Negro Housing in Chicago," 6.

59. Ibid., 13.

60. Ibid.

61. Also: "For some years, as the growth of the city had caused business and light manufacture to encroach more and more on the surrounding area of deterioration, Negroes had been steadily driven out of the Black Belt in search of homes.... It is in those zones just outside of the Loop where decaying residences and tottering frame dwellings presage the inroads of industry and business that the southern migrant is able to pay the cheap rents that landlords are willing to

accept until their property is demanded by the expanding business area. In these areas of deterioration the poorer migrant families are often forced into association with the vicious elements of the city." Frazier, *The Negro Family in Chicago,* 95, 98, 100.

62. Weaver points out the difference between European immigrants and blacks. While the former's residential concentration lessens over time, blacks "display a directly opposite tendency." He cites the causes as the "American color line" and the end of European immigration. He intimates that African Americans' color and the stigma attached to it made mobility difficult. Weaver, *The Negro Ghetto,* 41.

63. "The expansion of the Negro community was not a unique phenomenon, but was similar to the movements of other racial and immigrant groups in the city of Chicago." Frazier, citing Burgess ("Residential Segregation in American Cities," 110). Frazier, *The Negro Family in Chicago,* 91.

64. Frazier cites Park's "The Urban Community as a Spacial Pattern and a Moral Order," 9. Frazier, *The Negro Family in Chicago,* 97.

65. He cites Park and Burgess. "But as these processes take place in the Negro community, there is greater resistance offered to the movement of the Negro chiefly because of his color." Frazier, *The Negro Family in Chicago,* 97.

66. Drake and Cayton, *The Black Metropolis,* 101.

67. Cayton, "Negro Housing in Chicago," 10–12. Weaver thought the shift took place around 1925. Weaver, *The Negro Ghetto,* 39. Drake and Cayton pin down the origins of the covenants in the work of the Chicago Real Estate Board in Hyde Park, Woodlawn, Park Manor, and other upscale neighborhoods. *The Black Metropolis,* 79–80. See also Frazier, *The Negro Family in Chicago,* 97. "But neither violence nor property owners' associations have been able to prevent the expansion of the Negro community, which has been bound up, on the whole, with the processes of urban growth." Cayton said, "The 1910 migration has never stopped, nor has organized resistance to invasion by the Race of new residential areas diminished. Restrictive covenants have replaced bombings and riots." Cayton, "Our Deplorable Housing Situation," *Chicago Defender* (July 15, 1939).

68. Weaver defined these "race restrictive housing covenants" as "a mutual agreement among property owners in a given area not to sell, lease or otherwise convey their property to certain groups for a specified period." Weaver said these covenants were used more extensively in new and suburban housing and were more effective than "in-lying areas which lay in the path of the expansion of the Black Belt." Weaver, *The Negro Ghetto,* 39.

69. Cayton, "Negro Housing in Chicago," 13. Weaver disputed this number. He said that the restrictive covenants were near black areas and in the new suburban areas. He claimed that they were "an additional and, for the short run, an effective impediment.... Their real, long run importance, however, is the psychological and quasi-legal support they give to residential segregation." Weaver, *The Negro Ghetto,* 213, 214.

70. Earl B. Dickerson, "End Discrimination Dickerson Urges," *Daily Record,* n.d., 1938. Dickerson was one of the attorneys in the 1940 *Hansberry v. Lee* Supreme Court case against restrictive covenants in Chicago. Restrictive covenants were what black civic elites focused on as the principal tool of residential segregation. As a quasi-legal document, it was easier to see and attack in the juridical style of the NAACP. Although universally decried nevertheless, it did not stop the expansion of the Black Belt. There was a consensus among black civic elites that race-restrictive covenants were not effective in stopping black expansion. Cayton is quoted as saying that restrictive covenants cannot stop but can delay black expansion. "Our Deplorable Housing Situation," *Chicago Defender* (July 15, 1939). Weaver concurs that these covenants did not offer a "permanent barrier to Negro entrance, although they always delayed the normal expansion of space available to colored people." He concludes emphatically that *"race restrictive housing covenants have not and cannot prevent the expansion of living space for mounting Negro populations."*

Weaver, *The Negro Ghetto,* 212, 234–235. Historian Arnold R. Hirsch saw the covenants as a "cause célèbre" among the black elite and felt they had grown increasingly anachronistic after 1940. He claimed that housing shortage was more important for "sustaining old racial barriers" rather than restrictive covenants whose "weakness in the face of countervailing economic forces was revealed as early as 1940 in the Hansberry case, which resulted in the black occupation of the Washington Park subdivision." In fact, "the Supreme Court's ruling on restrictive covenants in 1948 simply delivered the final blow to a device that was already growing unequal to the task of preserving the racial homogeneity of white neighborhoods beleaguered by mounting economic and social pressures." Hirsch, *Making the Second Ghetto,* 30, 16.

71. Drake and Cayton, *The Black Metropolis,* 113.

72. Cayton, "Negro Housing in Chicago," 31. Though Cayton anticipated the Lake Meadows development that displaced low- and moderate-income blacks for affluent residents, he did not anticipate that those new residents would also be black. It was the city's first urban renewal project.

73. Weaver in *The Negro Ghetto* believed in an activist state. He felt that the federal government should intervene against racial discrimination and should certainly set an example of nondiscriminatory policy and practices. Also see John R. Kirby, *Black Americans in the Roosevelt Era: Liberalism and Race* (Knoxville: University of Tennessee Press, 1980), 126.

74. Weaver, *The Negro Ghetto,* 148.

75. Allan H. Spear, *Black Chicago: The Making of a Negro Ghetto, 1890–1920* (Chicago: University of Chicago Press, 1967).

76. Drake and Cayton, *The Black Metropolis,* 113–114.

77. Ibid., 114–115.

78. Weaver, *The Negro Ghetto,* 44–48, 156. Of course, E. Franklin Frazier wrote a classic essay on vested interests. See E. Franklin Frazier, "Human, All Too Human: The Negro's Vested Interest in Segregation," in *E. Franklin Frazier on Race Relations,* ed. G. Franklin Edwards (Chicago: University of Chicago Press, 1968), 283–291.

79. Residential segregation creates racial "concentration [which] prevents any permanent improvement in Negro housing quality since it carries with it doubling up, bad housing conditions, family disorganization, delinquency, and other indications of social pathology." Wallace, "Residential Concentration of Negroes," 9. See also Myrdal, *An American Dilemma,* 626.

80. Frazier, *The Negro Family in Chicago,* 90.

81. Despite the high proportion of divorced people (an indicator of family disorganization) in the fourth zone, "family life in this area, even in respect to disorganization, was a more orderly affair than in the poorer areas inhabited by the migrant families or in the third zone where family life tended to disappear." Frazier, *The Negro Family in Chicago,* 119, 121.

82. "Although nearly four-fifths of all the Negroes in Chicago were born in the South, the proportion of southern-born inhabitants in the population diminishes as one leaves those sections of the Negro community nearest the heart of the city." Frazier, *The Negro Family in Chicago,* 98. Weaver cites Frazier (90) in his study on the differences between pre– and post–World War I migrants. Pre–World War I migrants to Chicago came from the border states, "where they were much better prepared, by training, previous exposure to city and town life, and cultural advancement, to adjust quickly to the environment of a large urban community than were the later migrants from the deep South." Weaver, *The Negro Ghetto,* 16.

83. Frazier again emphasizes the differences between these migrants and longtime residents and the implications for studying the family. He argues, "All of these different elements in Negro life have struggled to survive in the stern competition of city life. But these fundamental differences in the Negro population are obscured beneath statistics which give only a picture of average conditions in Negro life." Frazier, *The Negro Family in Chicago,* 73.

84. "In the urban environment the migrant is liberated from the control that the church and

other forms of association exercised in the rural South . . . the Negro in his aimless wandering from city to city loses the conceptions of life which he acquired in the church, the most important institution in the life of the Negro in the South. He loses his old aims and ambitions, and freed from every form of group control he is the prey of vagrant impulses and lawless desires." Frazier, *The Negro Family in Chicago,* 75, 76; see also 79–80.

85. See Drake and Cayton, *Black Metropolis.* See also James R. Grossman, *Land of Hope: Chicago, Black Southerners, and the Great Migration* (Chicago: University of Chicago Press, 1989).

86. Frazier, *The Negro Family in Chicago,* 84. Frazier cites the Burgess passage from "The Growth of the City." He argues that "more important still is the fact that within the more or less defined area occupied by the Negro population the distribution of individuals and institutions is in response to the social processes going on in the community. Therefore, in order to get a measure of these processes of disorganization and reorganization, it is necessary to relate the statistics on the different aspects of Negro life to the Negro community." Frazier argues that the citywide average statistics cannot tell you about the social difference in the black community. Similarly, the average rates and prevalence of social problems in residential zones cannot tell how an individual black family struggles to overcome external obstacles to carve out a decent life. *The Negro Family in Chicago,* 85.

87. McKee criticizes William F. Whyte for not making explicit the distinction between process and condition when criticizing the Chicago School. But the distinction is implicit as Whyte finds evidence of both definitions of social disorganization in Chicago School studies. McKee, *Sociology and the Race Problem,* 206. Whyte, "Social Organization of the Slum," 35.

88. McKee cites Frazier's acceptance of "the existence of common-law marriage as the basis of family life." *Sociology and the Race Problem,* 207. I do not think this is decisive evidence of a lack of moral judgments. Frazier's acceptance of common-law marriages should be seen in the larger context of his concern for desertion and female heads of household.

89. *The Negro Family in Chicago,* 105, 135 (emphasis added).

90. McKee points out the prevalent notion that there were different levels of culture and civilization attained by different classes and races. He argues that cultural inferiority eventually replaces biological inferiority. McKee, *Sociology and the Race Problem,* 6. Unfortunately, for his discussion of social disorganization he does not bring in his insights on cultural distinctions to indicate perhaps hidden moral evaluation. There is an important distinction between the notion that the poor are and always will be culturally backward—social disorganization as condition—and the notion that the poor, although deficient, now will become normal as they develop more. But the standards by which the poor are being judged in *either* case are middle-class.

91. "The prevalence of illegitimacy among the lower class is also a reflection of the incomplete urbanization of the rural southern migrants; for, as E. Franklin Frazier has suggested, illegitimacy in the rural South is not the social disaster it is considered in the cities, but 'where the rural folkways concerning unmarried motherhood are in conflict with the legal requirements of the city, the persistence of these folkways in the urban environment will create social problems.'" Drake and Cayton, *Black Metropolis,* 593–594.

92. Weaver, *The Negro Ghetto,* 16.

93. Louis Wirth, "Urbanism as a Way of Life," 60–83, reprinted in *On Cities and Social Life: Selected Papers,* ed. Albert J. Reiss (Chicago: University of Chicago Press, 1964).

94. Wirth, "Urbanism as a Way of Life," 79–80.

95. Wright says, "But I did not know what my story was, and it was not until I stumbled upon science that I discovered some of the meanings of the environment that battered and taunted me. I encountered the work of men who were studying the Negro community, amassing facts about urban Negro life, and I found that sincere art and honest science were not far apart, that each could enrich the other. The huge mountains of fact piled up by the Department

of Sociology at the University of Chicago gave me my first concrete vision of the forces that molded the urban Negro's body and soul." He credits "the scientific findings of men like the late Robert E. Park, Robert Redfield, and Louis Wirth" for his interpretations in *12 Million Black Voices* and his fiction and autobiography. Richard Wright, "Introduction," in St. Clair Drake and Horace R. Cayton, *Black Metropolis: A Study of Negro Life in a Northern City,* 2 vols. (New York: Harper Torchbooks, 1962), xvii–xviii. In *12 Million Black Voices* (New York: Thunder Mouth Press, 1941), xx, he credits Frazier's *The Negro Family in the United States,* Cayton's study with George Mitchell on *Black Workers and the New Unions,* and Wirth's "Urbanism as a Way of Life" essay.

96. Wright, *12 Million Black Voices.*

97. Wright refers to the earlier incarnation of Parkway Community House, the Good Shepherd Community Center directed by Cayton. David Bradley credits Cayton suggesting to Wright that "property ownership" affected black life in "brainstorming discussions." Odd that Cayton would have to point this out since Wright spent time in the Communist Party. See Bradley, "Introduction," in Wright, *12 Million Black Voices,* xv. Wright credits use of Cayton's files in his foreword, *Twelve Million Black Voices,* xx. Hobbs, *The Cayton Legacy,* 122–123.

98. Wright, *Twelve Million Black Voices,* 93.

99. Ibid., 117.

100. Ibid., 127.

101. Sidney Williams, *The 34th Annual Report of the Chicago Urban League* (Chicago: Chicago Urban League, 1950), February 7, 1951, Chicago Urban League Records, Special Collections, University of Illinois, Chicago.

102. Sidney Williams, *Chicago Urban League 1954 Annual Report* (Chicago: Chicago Urban League, 1955), Chicago Urban League Records, Special Collections, University of Illinois, Chicago.

103. Williams, *34th Annual Report of Chicago Urban League.*

104. For instance, Drake and Cayton put evaluative terms in quotations. For example, they write about the findings of Cayton-Warner Research on "what happens in a ghetto when the successful and ambitious can't get out and when the city does not provide the poor and the vicious with enough living space, or enough incentive and opportunity to modify their style of life. The 'worst' areas begin to encroach upon the 'more desirable areas,' and large 'mixed' areas result. These, in turn, become gradually 'worst,' and the 'more desirable' areas begin to suffer from 'blight' and become 'mixed.'" *Black Metropolis,* 383.

105. Ibid., 523.

106. Ibid., 581. "Not alone by choice, but tossed by the deep economic tides of the modern world, pressed and molded by a usually indifferent and occasionally unkind white world, and hounded by an often unsympathetic Law, the lower social classes in Bronzeville [Chicago] have their being in a world apart from both white people and other Negroes." Ibid., 523.

107. Ibid., 581

108. Ibid., 577. Other examples: "The pursuit of 'pleasure'—direct and exciting—is a dominating feature of lower-class life." Ibid., 608.

109. Ibid., 576.

110. "The housing shortage in Bronzeville, and the intense competition for roomers and boarders, make it very hard for the 'respectable' segment of the lower class to sort out the sheep from the goats." Ibid., 598.

7

"What a Pure, Healthy, Unified Race Can Accomplish"

Collective Reproduction and the Sexual Politics of Black Nationalism

Michele Mitchell

> *Slavery brought upon us the curse of many colors within the Negro race, but that is no reason why we ... should perpetuate the evil; hence instead of encouraging a wholesale bastardy in the race, we feel that we should now set out to create a race type and standard of our own which ... in the future could be recognized and respected as the true race type.*
>
> —*Philosophy and Opinions of Marcus Garvey* (1923)

A provocative and somewhat disturbing piece of news graced the pages of the official propaganda organ of Marcus Garvey's Universal Negro Improvement Association (UNIA) during the spring of 1922. In early April, the *Negro World* reported that a contingent of African American men in Sylvester, Georgia, had come across a black woman and white man who were "maintaining improper relations." This chance meeting did more than raise a few eyebrows: it raised the black men's collective dander, and they quickly assumed intimidating postures; the overwhelmed white paramour managed to escape the wrath of the small posse as overt threats flared into active pursuit. The *Negro World* failed to divulge just how involved the couple actually was when their privacy came to an abrupt end, but the turn of events that followed the chase suggest that coitus had indeed been interrupted.[1]

With one attempt to mete out physical punishment foiled, the race men remained sufficiently riled to seek out their wayward sister next. They subsequently lectured her on the "sanctity of Negro womanhood," white men's sexual excesses during slavery, and the lynchings of black men accused of "look[ing] hard" at white women. Verbal assault then became bluntly physical as the mob gave the woman "a severe whipping" in order to "impress her ... with their 'determination to preserve race purity.'" Of course we cannot know whether she eventually rejected her lover as the result of being brutalized by angry vigilantes, but from the pages of the *Negro World* we do know that the involved parties allegedly appeared in court the next day. The presiding judge fined the white man $20, the woman was ordered to pay $15, and each assailant had to come up with $5. One witness, according to reports, wryly mused, "Guess it was worth $5 to teach her a lesson," as the judge either adjourned court or turned to the next case on the docket.[2]

Why would a black nationalist newspaper consider this story newsworthy? For one, black men terrorizing a white man in a small southern town during the 1920s challenged racialized patterns of daily life endured by many people of African descent; what transpired in Sylvester could ostensibly embolden one segment of the *Negro World*'s readership to guard their communities with manly resolve. But why was the article drafted so as to suggest that intraracial violence—between a group of men and a lone woman at that—could amount to collective uplift?[3] If we think about the UNIA as a back-to-Africa scheme, or if we analyze the movement solely in terms of Garvey as man and myth, this scandal-tinged human interest story appears to be little more than tantalizing filler. However, if we embed what happened that night in Georgia within the fundamental principles of Garveyism, a potentially trivial news item takes on emblematic proportions.

Although the *Negro World* covered a variety of international, national, and local issues, column space was primarily reserved for the tenets of the Universal Negro Improvement Association. Marcus Garvey established the UNIA as a nonpolitical benevolent society in his native Jamaica during the summer of 1914, but the movement failed to garner much attention or gather sufficient momentum.[4] The itinerant printer with a knack for elocution subsequently emigrated to Harlem in 1916, and by 1919 his movement called for racial consolidation, "founding a great nation," and African redemption.[5] Over the next six years the association peaked in membership, influence, and notoriety, for once the movement became explicitly political, Garveyism touched the raw nerves of aspiring-class, working-class, and working-poor blacks across the United States, the Caribbean, and Africa. The regional variety of UNIA branch divisions within the United States alone reflected both the magnitude of African American migration and the rapid spread of Garveyism: locals existed in southwestern, Rocky Mountain, and southern states as well as in New England, the Middle Atlantic, the Pacific Northwest, and the Midwest. Although most African American divisions were concentrated in urban centers, several locals sprang up in small towns and rural hamlets as well.[6]

The UNIA's motto of "One God! One Aim! One Destiny!" simultaneously captured the movement's spirit and spoke to a long-standing tradition of

Afro-American discourse on racial destiny. The sentiment endowed within the movement slogan "race first" provocatively indicated critical motivations behind Garveyism: "Reasonably interpreted it means that in the situation of racial strife ... Negroes should give preference to members of their own ... so as to conserve their resources ... to combat those forces that oppose them."[7] The dictum of "race first" was, moreover, inclusive in that it was intended to apply to manifold aspects of black life. From the eradication of socioeconomic oppression to the acquisition of political power, from the promotion of collective endeavor to the inculcation of self-love, racial chauvinism shaped the UNIA's economic, industrial, cultural, and social programs for group preservation. The emphasis on staying within the group had still more personal ramifications. To begin, Garveyites could not realize any of their goals without the actual biological perpetuation of the race. If the UNIA was to be successful in promoting—and ultimately creating—a strong, healthy nation, sexuality had to be monitored and controlled so that it benefited the race; if that nation were to be "black," Garveyites would need to enforce racial purity as well. As both ideology and practice, then, "race first" applied to the sex lives of Garveyites and, by extension, all people of African descent—including the unfortunate woman in Sylvester.

Given that "race first" was an organizing principle of the UNIA and because it had a sexual cast, it is not surprising that there were other occasions when either Marcus Garvey or his followers dealt with intimate matters. A few months after it reported the events in Georgia, the *Negro World* reprinted a speech that Garvey gave in Harlem during which he justified his infamous summit meeting with Edward Young Clarke, Imperial Wizard of the Ku Klux Klan. Garvey's speech maintained that in the course of his meeting with Clarke, the two men had agreed that their respective members needed to safeguard racial purity through actively policing the sexual conduct of others. Boasted Garvey:

> The Universal Negro Improvement Association is carrying out that doctrine splendidly. When I arrived at Baton Rouge ... I was visited by the president and some officers of the nearby division. They brought me this report: ... seven white men came into a colored neighborhood ... [and were found] at midnight sleeping in homes where they had no business.... [Men of the UNIA] flogged them and drove them out of the neighborhood.

Afterward, these ardent race men went before a white judge who not only belonged to the Klan but also released them with the blessing to "do some more of that."[8] Doing "more of that" likely involved subsequent surveillance of girls and women in those homes, since well-timed nocturnal interventions had the potential to disrupt continued interracial couplings. Sustained harassment and ostracism could compel a woman to abandon certain sexual practices—at least momentarily. Regardless of whether the men in Baton Rouge actually continued to take matters into their own hands, Garvey highlighted the initial incident in order to drive home a pointed argument: black men needed to flex their muscles and "strike back on white men trying to get too close to black women."[9] While Garvey desired that all black people seize control over "the social question of race," he wanted the UNIA to assume the vanguard of safeguarding "the purity of the black race not only down South, but all through the world."[10]

The staff of the *Negro World* could have omitted the portion about Louisiana without altering Garvey's overall message. Yet it was purposefully included for—like the dispatch from Georgia—the lesson of Baton Rouge was that if sustained, quotidian maintenance of racial purity entailed physical intervention on occasion, then black men should take it upon themselves to prevent interracial sex through force or, if need be, outright violence. Women's role in preserving racial purity was broached somewhat differently in UNIA rhetoric: Garveyite women were urged to influence their sisters through example; they could sway men through reason or perhaps denunciation. A few women sought notably more proactive ways of discouraging white men. The *Negro World* relayed a report about black women who, during the late months of 1925, had allegedly lynched a lone white "libertine" in order to prevent coerced sexual congress. Over a year earlier, one reader from Philadelphia sent a letter to the *Negro World* in order to solicit aid in her quest to hunt down a white man who tried to molest her daughter. The girl's mother, Nellie Edwards, sought a confrontation with the assailant, and she pointedly expressed her wish to be the one who "riddle[d] him with bullets."[11] Such reports aside, the *Negro World* never so much as intimated that livid race matrons could, or should, horsewhip a black man for enjoying an illicit rendezvous with a white woman.

Such an overarching emphasis on race purity was neither incidental nor fleeting, for speeches, editorials, and letters vetted the subject, while almost half of the UNIA's nine basic doctrines opposed miscegenation. Published in 1924, the eight-point "What We Believe" also opened with a call for "the uniting and blending of all Negroes into one strong, healthy race" and swiftly warned of racial suicide. Notably, "What We Believe" made sure to distinguish between types of interracial liaisons by labeling both "rich blacks marrying poor whites" along with "rich or poor whites taking advantage of Negro women" as inimical to the enterprise of race-building. An explicit desire for total racial purity was yet another tenet, while an allied point called for self-determination and nationhood via "social and political physical separation."[12] Moreover, Garvey's pamphlet "Aims and Objects" decried "mongrelization" as it called upon "off-Colored people" to "re-establish the purity of their own race."[13] Rather than being tertiary or even secondary to Garveyism, homogenizing the race was part and parcel of core movement ideology.

The particular brand of antimiscegenationist thought that permeated Garveyite ideology translated into action and shaped a broad range of relationships. Yet the UNIA's maintenance of racial purity primarily resulted in prescriptive—if not proscriptive—gender roles. Gender not only shaped the contours of any given member's responsibility to the race; sexual accountability was parsed inequitably and experienced differently among female and male members of the collective. Movement discourse encouraged women to monitor sexuality, yet as women, they were usually the targets of protection, coercion, and control. Men, by contrast, were chided for having carnal appetites that led them to stray beyond the race, but they were more typically exhorted to stand tall, "be men," and guard the sexual integrity of black women.

This is not to say that husbands, brothers, and sons were not held accountable for their actions: female delegates at one major convention spoke out against men who looked beyond the race for social companionship and spent an entire afternoon chastising those who "had very little regard for their wom[en]."[14] And relationships involving black men and white women were certainly considered taboo. One member, Richard Tate, urged women to "keep tab[s] on your Negro men." Male sexual impulses needed to remain within the confines of blackness as a matter of fundamental practice, for if too many men chose women without African heritage as partners, the Atlanta resident reasoned, "large numbers of [our women will] die old maids." Tate's remarkably pithy March 1925 letter to the *Negro World* clearly labeled the erotic proclivities of some of his brothers as detrimental to the enterprise of race-building, but the letter also spoke to black female sexuality in that Tate implied suitable husbands could be found if women would only "rally to Garveyism ... where the Negro [man] can see more attraction within his race than any other." Richard Tate's comment about "old maids" reflected an anxiety that any intraracial benefit to be derived from black female sexuality might go unfulfilled. Viewed another way, his quick comment on how women should make themselves available for display suggested that it was up to women to do whatever was necessary to catch, hold, and wed a man.[15]

Although Tate remained silent about couplings between black women and white men, that silence nonetheless spoke to black women's sexuality because it ironically underscored that female indulgence in forbidden love was all but out of the question. This particular opprobrium existed for at least two reasons: liaisons between black women and white men conjured up slavery with its sexualized hierarchy, a hierarchy that undoubtedly left a number of black men feeling somewhat impotent well into the twentieth century. Deeply gendered notions about racial reproduction additionally implicated women as primary conduits for both pollution and dilution. Tate, then, likely harbored fears about black women's role in perpetuating miscegenation and their potential to thwart the realization of the UNIA's goals.

Women could—and did—harbor similar apprehensions to those expressed by Richard Tate. Less than two months after Tate aired his views, Eva Aldred Brooks penned an article about comparative birthrate statistics, ethnic distinctiveness, evolutionary law, and racial extermination. "The world today is thinking in terms of self-determination," Brooks observed, "[and we] see ... other races within the Caucasian group ... doing their utmost to perpetuate themselves." Brooks was deeply chagrined that black people were not doing the same and was especially irked over women who lacked race pride. Then she cut to the quick:

> Is it not true ... that many of our women and girls deem it an honor to be the mistress of some white man rather than to be the wife of one of her own race? It is the duty of every Negro woman to put an end to this abomination.... If we allow

> these conditions to exist, a weak-kneed progeny shall arise.... If we correct the abuses of the race we shall see within a short while what a pure, healthy, unified race can accomplish.

The very deed of interracial sex was, for Brooks, highly problematic, but she did not consider the actual deed more damaging than its potential outcome: Being a white man's mistress was an "abomination" largely because it compromised optimal race reproduction by limiting the numbers of robust "black" babies born. Both sexuality and motherhood were thus central to realizing the movement's nationalist project for Brooks, but as she claimed an active role for women in realizing a grand collective destiny, she also blamed women for hindering racial health and unity. Eva Brooks's views were anything but aberrant. Rather, Brooks's strategic gendered and sexualized interpretation of "race first" was shared by many other members of the UNIA.[16]

For all the anxieties that it produced, interracial sex was but one means through which matters pertaining to gender, copulation, and reproduction seeped into Garveyism. The columns in the *Negro World* and the UNIA's political program systematically dealt with gender issues along with a range of sexual topics as Garveyites—rank-and-file members as well as movement leaders—assessed sex in terms of nationhood, gradual racial purification, popular eugenic theory, and the possibility of extinction. But since racial reproduction was, to a large degree, contingent upon the issue of heterosexual intercourse, the sexuality of women faced extensive scrutiny. Thus, it is through the sexualized, gendered implications of the UNIA program for race betterment that the incidents in Georgia and Louisiana must be viewed and Garveyites' rhetoric of progress and degeneration must be analyzed. Understanding the sexual politics of racial reproduction within the black nationalist UNIA program also entails highlighting intraracial dynamics, and it particularly requires close consideration of the places accorded women by the movement.

Modeled after late nineteenth- and early twentieth-century fraternal orders,[17] the Universal Negro Improvement Association operated under the basic assumption that males and females had separate arenas and different functions.[18] Within the movement, "women had an important economic function" as fund-raisers, workers, and stockholders; some women were even able to "ac[t] ... in autonomous 'male' ways."[19] Still, the movement institutionalized the reinforcement of gender roles. The movement's constitution established juvenile programs that served the dual purpose of being primers in Garveyism and gender-specific activity: young girls prepared for homemaking while little boys engaged in industrial education; teenaged girls received instruction in hygiene and "domestic science" as adolescent boys were ushered into the political infrastructure of the association through military training.[20] Sex-segregated activity continued into adulthood, with most UNIA women—whether they channeled their energies into auxiliary work or participated in general forums—finding themselves in situations that mirrored places in the home.[21] As men formulated movement policy in meetings and practiced military maneuvers in the streets, women served as support staff, provided food at UNIA functions, and discussed their role during special "ladies' days." Even the militaristic women's Motor Corps, whose members received basic training in automobile repair, was formed primarily to "assist the [male] Universal African Legions in the performance of their duties."[22] Garveyism inspired girls and women to contribute their energies toward collective uplift, but the form of their contribution assumed a different design than it did for boys and men.[23]

All the same, girls and women were engaged participants who joined the UNIA in numbers equal to males as Garveyism altered their perceptions of self and surroundings.[24] Gertrude Hawkins of Maryland sold the *Negro World* and felt compelled to write the paper about the impact the movement was having on her young life: "My parents are . . . trying to get an organization of the Universal Negro Improvement Association at a church out here by us, and everyone my parents meet they tell them about this organization. . . . I am only ten years old . . . and I see where we need a state and a home for ourselves." Violet McCracken was another youthful convert. At sixteen, McCracken stood before her local in Muskogee, Oklahoma, and beseeched those present to "work with all the zeal and interest that behooves us to better the condition of the Negro race." Women in their twenties and beyond felt similarly committed: Rosetta Stenson believed the movement was uniquely capable of elevating the race; Mary Carter prayed that she would not die until Garveyites delivered Africa; members in New Orleans avowed the UNIA "is our church, our clubhouse, our theatre, our fraternal order, and our school" and that none would "forsake it while we live [and] neither will our men."[25]

When it came to being active in terms of political discourse, however, women faced resistance sufficient enough to prompt open frustration with their assigned functions. For example, when Garveyism was at its crest in the United States, the association held annual conventions in Harlem where members had major opportunities to discuss pertinent issues, exchange ideas, and influence each other's thought. At the raucous 1922 International Convention, during which internecine struggles and street brawls erupted, a contingent of women literally seized the floor on the last day to protest their status in the movement. Victoria Turner, a delegate from St. Louis, presented a lengthy list of women's grievances ranging from the paucity of women in "important offices . . . [and] initiative positions" to the existing leadership structure of women's auxiliaries. When Turner stepped down, other women took the floor and testified that they were "being curbed to a great extent" by men of the UNIA. Significantly, some of these women served in atypical capacities—such as field organizer—and they apparently faced questions about their "competence" and "conduct"; even among these dissenters, at least one still believed that if women performed certain organizational tasks, men would fail to take them seriously and even question their claims on respectable femininity.[26]

There were, then, exceptional movement women who stood apart from rank-and-file women with families, husbands, or children, but by and large, women who served in atypical capacities were single, otherwise unattached, or past childbearing age. International Organizer and Assistant President-General Henrietta Vinton Davis was an older woman without children; the manager of UNIA's printing plant, Lyllian Galloway, was young and unmarried.[27] Amy Jacques Garvey was in yet another category still: a prolific, talented, and politically astute writer who all but led the UNIA while Garvey was imprisoned for mail fraud, Amy Jacques gained her prominence, to some degree, from being Marcus's second wife. Maymie De Mena—one of few married women with a high profile in the movement—understood that her own relative power was somewhat of an anomaly. De Mena's rueful assessment of gender roles in the UNIA was that "women were given to understand that they were to remain in their places, which meant nothing more than [being] a Black Cross Nurse or a general secretary of [a] division."[28]

De Mena's comments—along with those made by protesters in 1922—underscore how even women with unusual visibility could feel constrained by the province allowed women within organizational structure. Prominent UNIA women were skilled and often charismatic. Yet "the success of Davis, De Mena, and Jacques as UNIA leaders was seemingly owing not only to their own merit as strong intellects and forceful organizers but to their perceived status as Garvey's representatives—a status that prevented them from being seen as 'real' leaders in their own right."[29] Not surprisingly, then, female participation in ostensibly nonpolitical activity was a different matter. Many women in the UNIA therefore chose to underscore their centrality to the movement by invoking social roles, by naming motherhood a key site of nation-building.

This strategy is not surprising given that the movement lauded black parenthood in general but glorified race motherhood specifically: the UNIA's chaplain provided print sermons regaling selfless madonnas, the *Negro World* offered constant commentary on maternal contributions to race-building, festive Mother's Day programs became gala events.[30] At one Mother's Day observance, women were encouraged to view motherhood as "the noblest career in which a woman can succeed," and even men were prodded to "pay greater respect to women and more attention to production of offspring." Predictably, it would be women who received more than their share of prodding to procreate that May afternoon as Chaplain General George Carter flatly told his audience that real women—true women—longed to reproduce. Although he assured listeners that women played a quintessential role in "put[ting] over [our] program," the chaplain general more than implied that motherhood should be their primary contribution.[31] Carter's particular approach to extolling black mothers might not have appealed to every woman who heard him speak, yet his views nevertheless echoed those held by a number of women. At the same time that men such as Carter could derive benefits from encouraging women to embrace childbearing along with domesticity, women could also have a special stake—both rhetorically and literally—in representing motherhood as a political locus of racial reproduction.

Philadelphia's Lady President Estelle Matthews was one such woman who politicized mother work. When she begged her sisters to heed the call of motherhood and determine the destiny of future race women and men, for instance, she decided to couch her plea in "the redemption of Africa." Matthews chose not to pressure women to have more children but instead stressed that girls and boys forever bore the imprint of racial instruction received at mother's knee. Women could therefore act as critical agents in realizing the movement's aims by turning the home into a place that reinforced race pride on a daily basis. More specifically, she urged women to be highly selective in choosing images to adorn their walls; Matthews even more emphatically urged women to give their children toys that celebrated blackness.[32]

Estelle Matthews's expansive view of mothering was certainly in sync with movement ideologies that expressly politicized attainment of a "pure" racial integrity. Upholding motherhood in such a fashion was ultimately problematic, however: Matthews's promotion of race motherhood augmented the importance of a familiar, familial role, but it also detracted from other political or creative aspirations a woman might harbor. And, if the primary function of a UNIA woman was to bear fruit and nurture the collective, then reproductive capacity arguably set women apart as objects of special concern. Since the political realm of the movement was cordoned off as the domain of men, the movement spent considerably less time promoting men's familial roles or responsibilities beyond encouraging them to provide adequate financial support, "respect women," and, in the words of member Hannah Nichols, "practice self-control."[33] Both women and men of the UNIA would find ways to locate motherhood in new arenas, however. And they would do so, in part, by invoking scientific motherhood, racial reproduction, and popular eugenics.

Garveyite concepts about racial reproduction were in many regards distinct, although they mirrored contemporary currents of thought. For instance, when members of the UNIA chose to apply scientific principles to the production of future redeemers of Africa, they certainly drew from modern notions about hygiene, but they also turned to popular eugenic theories. Eugenics, a voice for progress throughout the early twentieth century, sprang from social Darwinism, which argued that "natural selection" irreversibly rendered certain racial groups less "fit" to compete in the struggle of life. Unlike its progenitor, however, eugenic theory held that through regulation of heredity, environment, and sexuality, racial stock could actually be improved. Such improvement could, theoretically, be realized in at least three ways: the "unfit" could bear a limited number of offspring or be sterilized altogether; the "best elements" could be induced to reproduce at a prolific rate in order to combat racial degeneration; all prospective parenthood could be encouraged to create the best babies possible.[34] In the United States, the eugenics movement was based on classist, nativist, and racist assumptions and had obvious ideological limitations for people of African descent. Eugenicist theory influenced a diverse range of black intellectuals nevertheless: the NAACP's W. E. B. Du Bois and Howard University's

Kelly Miller were concerned that the "masses" were more fecund than the "classes"; socialist activist Chandler Owen and educator Mary Burrill both felt birth control could improve the quality of children born to the race.[35] Not only did a range of black writers invoke "metaphorical eugenics" during the 1920, but "uplift ideology adapt[ed] quite readily to the period's characteristic eugenic thinking."[36]

Garveyites and Garveyism were no exception. Whereas most Garveyites were downright leery of sterilization—not to mention birth control—men and women of the movement appropriated popular eugenic vernaculars concerning heredity and physical improvement that, in turn, reinforced the UNIA's concept on the relationship between sexuality and race first.[37] During the 1924 convention, the relevance of eugenics for black people was tackled in at least one session when physician—and loyal Garveyite—J. J. Peters offered his observation that "in the interest of the next generation ... [we must] banish prudery and mock modesty ... and give procreation more eugenic attention." Two men who offered allied opinions followed Peters: One speaker was a doctor who described how venereal disease compromised reproductive health; the other commentator claimed that the problems sexually transmitted ailments presented to the race were largely due to black men who slept with "women of other races."[38]

The *Negro World* was also instrumental in filtering popular eugenics into routine movement discourse. On its women's page, "Our Women and What They Think," Amy Jacques Garvey regularly deployed eugenic arguments in editorials on motherhood and "childlife." In one of her more subtle offerings, Jacques Garvey wrote that

> much needs to be done as yet before motherhood and childhood will be placed upon the scientific basis where the very best results can reasonably be expected in the production of best and brightest type of manhood and womanhood.... We shall hardly be able to meet the growing need for a properly trained childhood ... for many years to come.... [But I am] proud of the splendid work our women have done in the home and school and church ... and [I] have faith to hope that they will do better work in the coming days.[39]

Eugenicist concepts appeared in a number of general articles as well.[40] Lester Taylor contributed an especially lengthy discourse on racial reproduction in which he pointedly suggested that the race needed to give the breeding of children serious consideration:

> Show me a race that sets a high premium on childbearing and that strives ever to improve the quality of children it produces, and I will show you a race destined to outnumber, overcome, and survive all other races ... in the game of life. Show me, on the other hand, a race ... careless of the quality of the children it produces ... [and I] will show you a race doomed ... [to produce] an ever increasing percentage of abortions and deformities, of cowards and weaklings ... a race doomed to disappear.

Tropical climates enabled people of African descent to double their numbers within the relatively short span of forty years, Taylor claimed, and the reproduction of the race suffered in North America due to economic pressures as well as racist sterilization practices. Ample replenishment of North American blacks therefore required "clean, orderly sexual relations" and the production of "high physical and mental types" who would secure black people's place at "the vanguard of human progress."[41]

Taylor was hardly alone in his conviction that life entailed racial competition, that when it came to reproducing the race, quality counted as much—if not more—than quantity. Carrie Mero Leadett, a secretary for the Black Star Line who joined the movement in 1919, used her discourse on maternal responsibility to assert that the race could ill afford "children who [were] physically, mentally, and morally unfit for life's struggle." Leadett then urged all women devoted to the cause to produce "100 percent" babies capable of winning full-fledged racial competitions. If the black nationalist program of the UNIA was to succeed, she concluded, the production of "high physical and mental types" was nothing less than vital.[42]

If Leadett's convictions were slightly trenchant, Marcus Garvey's views could veer toward the alarmist. "The Negro is dying out, and he is going to die faster ... in the next fifty years," Garvey warned. "[And] if we do not seriously reorganize ourselves as a people ... our days in civilization are numbered."[43] Garvey also told a 1921 New York audience that if black people failed to preserve themselves and pay attention to declining birthrates, nothing short of "doom" awaited.[44] It is not completely clear whether Garvey actually believed the race was dying out, but he manipulated the concept of extermination to push sex, the black birthrate, and collective health as critical items on the "race first" agenda. He was successful: UNIA members debated whether blacks were on the verge of extinction as they discussed the significance of census figures, venereal disease, and sex reform.[45]

Such reform and "reorganization" entailed active redirection of sexual activities so that they resulted in prolific, eugenic childbearing within the confines of an endogamous marriage. Along with Garvey, many adherents of the movement were often preoccupied with the possibility of extinction because they held widespread, contemporary assumptions about how birth control, venereal disease, promiscuity, and premarital sex ultimately led to race suicide. Their interest in comparative birthrate statistics was, furthermore, shared by a range of intellectuals and politicians in the United States, where the majority of UNIA locals existed during the 1920s. While some American pundits worried that white, native-born women were lagging dangerously behind in their rate of childbirth, many had a perverse fixation with the birthrates of European immigrants, and more still with those of women of African descent. Ironically, while census figures from the U.S. government did not necessarily support claims that African Americans faced extinction, census data fueled racial and ethnic comparisons nonetheless.

According to the U.S. Census Bureau, the number of African Americans nearly doubled between 1870 and 1920. Between 1900 and 1910 alone, the decennial increase in black population was around 11 percent; the aggregate figure of approximately 10 million people of African descent translated into about 10 percent of the total population in 1910. In contrast, whites—both native and immigrant—comprised over 80 percent of the total population. Whereas these percentages did not deviate all that much from those reported in previous decennial counts, the black birthrate continued to be in sharp decline in comparison to native-born white or immigrant women. Not only were more and more black women limiting their pregnancies, but between 1910 and 1920, the influenza epidemic was especially harsh on black communities, which—again, in comparison to other ethnic groups—had higher overall mortality rates. Whether due to birth control, morbidity, war, migration, or careless census enumerators, the 1920 census announced that African Americans entered the third decade of the century as less than 10 percent of the national total. Black people in the United States might not have been moribund, but to many observers, it certainly appeared that the race was stagnant and in decline.[46]

To exacerbate matters, economic immiseration vitiated urban communities such as Washington, D.C., Baltimore, New York, New Orleans, Philadelphia, Detroit, and Chicago.[47] These cities had particularly large black populations and housed some of the largest UNIA branches. Not surprisingly, locals in large cities frequently responded to the demands of urban life through providing a variety of business enterprises that created jobs and offered services: some divisions offered soup kitchens for the unemployed or provided sleeping quarters for homeless black men and women; the "Liberty Halls" of other locals gave out information about affordable lodging.[48] Movement programs therefore addressed the consumer demands in black communities and provided pragmatic solutions to material needs. Such pragmatism hardly meant that facilities and programs were not aimed at realizing the movement's ideology, however.

The response of Garveyites to disease and morbidity was at once pronounced and pragmatic. In an attempt to bridge ideology and reality, the Universal Negro Improvement Association stood prepared to combat needless deaths in black communities through public education; *Negro World* health columns offered plain talk about disease, hygiene, and prevention; while women in Black Cross auxiliaries lectured and demonstrated the latest sanitary methods. Black Cross nurses provided a range of grassroots services in their communities, many oriented toward alleviating symptoms of poverty. Despite the grittiness of some of the work the Black Cross performed within communities, nurses were idealized in the iconography of the movement, which presented them as angels of mercy draped in white, as intraracial missionaries bearing the light of knowledge.[49] Whether their routine duties actually veered toward the messianic or the mundane, women of the auxiliary prioritized outreach work—especially among mothers of the race. In addition to the Black Cross maintaining "baby health stations" that were staffed by women ready to dole out advice, the auxiliary promoted eugenic concepts of scientific motherhood and counseled women to patronize black health workers rather than risk being "tampered with by prejudiced white doctors."[50] Even further, a Black Cross nurse from Chicago, Clara Morgan, contributed a regular column directed at mothers in the *Negro World*; there she circulated the U.S. Child Welfare Department's "ABCs of Child Welfare," regularly advised women on how to improve their household habits, and promoted the idea that creating a "more intelligent and better Negro motherhood" should top the UNIA's agenda.[51]

But prioritizing the reproductive development and destiny of the race was a complex matter. For one, improving racial stock could well involve increasing and purifying that stock as much as it could involve upgrading the living conditions of black people to a respectable if not bourgeois standard—whether such a standard was actually attainable is another matter. For another, it was one thing to issue rhetorical calls for increased racial reproduction but quite another to influence actual reproductive choices. UNIA members might not have demanded that their sisters bear children, but they certainly tried to inspire, if not shame, childless women into action.

As a result, typical UNIA rhetoric about collective perpetuation was littered with blunt pronouncements as well as veiled phrases signifying the evils of delayed childbearing and birth control. Amy Jacques simply proclaimed that birth control suited whites rather than blacks.[52] Hubert Cox, a *Negro World* staffer, condemned birth control as inherently contrary to "correct" sexual impulses that resulted in children. Whereas Cox maintained that both men and women possessed an "[innate] desire for children," he declared that women who practiced birth control as a means of accessing contemporary liberties were doing far more than harming themselves. His words of warning were at once foreboding and fantastic: "[Currently women] desire the freedom from motherhood and in consequence, we are on the brink of active racial suicide. The penalty that nature exacts is very severe. The suppression of restriction of innate desire for children by women result[s] in hysteria, melancholy, nervousness, unhappiness ... disease and an early grave." Cox, for his part, actively associated contraception with women's independence and their eschewing of reproduction as the primary means of serving both family and race. Men who shunned fatherhood were not much better off in his mind: a childless man was at risk of degenerating into a murderer or facing "self-debasement, masturbation, deadening of conscience, corruption of heart ... suicide or untimely death."[53]

Like Jacques Garvey and Cox, Black Cross nurse Kate Fenner disapproved of contraception, and she accepted the notion that mothers were rightfully assigned the difficult task of "build[ing] up a pure black generation." However, Fenner also believed that black men had all but prostituted women of the race. She wryly concluded that once they started acting manly, ceased hiding "behind [women's] skirts," and did their "duty as men ... there [would] be no cause for the other side to preach birth control among black women."[54] But whether it was Fenner chastising men for irresponsible behavior or Cox conjuring up future torments for women who used contraception, prevailing movement ideology considered birth control inimical to a progressive black nation.[55] Unlike Margaret Sanger and other proponents of birth control who viewed contraception as having a positive eugenic effect,[56] movement rhetoric consistently suggested that birth control was a dysgenic, or negative, drain on racial reproduction. For the purposes of the UNIA, racial degeneration could be minimized through proper sexual conduct, not birth control. Some of its members would even hint that birth control led to debilitating perversions.

If Hubert Cox argued that the "restriction of innate desire for children" led to "self-debasement," a few Garveyites ventured further and dealt with homosexuality.[57] Direct references to lesbians and gay men were rare if not absent from the pages of the *Negro World,* but veiled messages that could ostensibly be interpreted as applying to homosexuality relied upon the language of perversion and degeneration. One contributor, however, was clearly homophobic and was not afraid to condemn people who were not heterosexual. As he bemoaned social forces he believed to be warping black youth, John Houghton harshly critiqued interracial sex. But another sexual interaction vexed him more: "Some of the older women of the race ... have a way of discouraging young girls, and endeavor to fill the places of men—for most of them prefer that they die maidens.... If this condition continues and this immoral practice of some of our women and men keeps up ... race extinction within a given period of time [is inevitable]." Houghton's focus upon lesbianism echoed Richard Tate's fears about "old maids," and he further intimated that lesbians played a role in leading black people down the road to race suicide. Granted, Houghton implicated gay men as well, but by the gendered tone of his self-labeled expose, he clearly considered lesbianism the greater danger.[58]

When Garveyites inveighed that the race had to produce better children and more children, their arguments were gendered in such a way that women's sexuality was the focal point of discussion. Furthermore, appropriations of eugenic theories, anxieties over racial purity, worries about black women's fecundity, and fears about homosexuality fortified the existing gendered structure of the UNIA: in toto, these concerns reinforced a notion that men and women had distinct and separate racial responsibilities. Members of the organization outlined varied characteristics of race manhood and race womanhood in striking detail, but perhaps the most important and sustained manipulation of gendered concepts in the UNIA was the reification of racial motherhood. Members did discuss the duties and responsibilities of fathers and men, yet the concept of racial fatherhood was not as clearly or extensively articulated.[59] Both the *Negro World* and the movement behind it simply paid more attention to issues surrounding black women's sexuality. Black men who strayed from the race were derided, but women might be forced to endure assault for their transgressions. Again, men might sire mixed-race children, but women, the literal bearers of the race, were expected to view race motherhood as their primary duty in the struggle for self-determination.

If it was indeed the case that "no race could rise higher than its motherhood," it was just as true that the UNIA's ideal of race motherhood entailed a degree of struggle, if not sacrifice.[60] Maida Springer Kemp's mother, for example, was an immigrant from Panama who ran a New York City beauty shop; a single parent, she was an active Garveyite throughout the 1920s as well. In describing her own childhood, Kemp recalled that when her "mother marched as a Black Cross Nurse ... she had [me] by the hand and I went to meetings because there were no babysitters.... Wherever [my mother] went, I went."[61] Kemp's mother might have been unusually energetic and enterprising, but in one critical regard, her life was typical—multiple demands commanded the lives of most black women. It is unlikely, therefore, that the majority of women in the UNIA could single-mindedly focus on motherhood or avoid work outside of the home.

Given that many black men were chronically underemployed and not all black households were structured around nuclear families, certain UNIA beliefs were moored as much in assumptions of class as of gender. Furthermore, not all black people chose to be sexually active within the confines of a heterosexual, intraracial marriage or relationship. Irrespective of the realities and choices facing Garveyites—female and male, working poor and middling, U.S.-born and immigrant—movement ideology viewed sexuality as a means to foster racially "pure" black families, encourage a bold and potent manhood, create a progressive childhood, and enforce a maternally virtuous womanhood. And as much as these ideological lenses created a holistic vision where both men and women were integral to African redemption, women were considered particularly responsible for reproducing the race.

Whereas Garveyism might have been radical in some respects, it contained an abiding conservatism in that the movement and its attendant ideology sought to conserve people of African descent as a distinct "race."[62] Furthermore, members of the Universal Negro Improvement Association resorted to fairly rigid, conservative gender conventions in pursuit of this aim. If the UNIA's "retreat from radicalism" occurred as soon as Garvey "resorted to the ideology of racial purity" in the early 1920s, such a contention implies that Garveyites' embrace of antimiscegenationist beliefs was somehow incongruous with the movement's initial aim of sustained race-building.[63] Linking the pursuit of racial purity to political retreat without interrogating the politics implicit within a racial purist vision obscures how Garveyism is similar to other nationalisms as it elides the ways in which gender and sexuality are crucial informants to nationalist projects such as the UNIA.

Similarly, if we go back to the incidents in Georgia and Louisiana, consider them as the ideology of racial purity in action, and leave it at that, then our ability to understand the significance of those incidents is severely compromised. In and of itself, merely noting the existence of racial purist ideology neither explains why the UNIA institutionalized gender-specific functions and activity nor fully contextualizes the race purist cast of Garveyite pronatalism. It also, frankly, does not account for *whose* sexuality was affected most and why sexuality was part and parcel of the politics of racial destiny.

In order to understand why racial purist thought emerged as a critical component of the Garvey movement's vision of racial destiny it is therefore essential to assess how assumptions about gender within the UNIA—or, for that matter, the gendered warp and woof of nationalist politics generally—encouraged Garveyites to zero in on sexuality. Nationalisms tend to prioritize the preservation and perpetuation of ethnic, religious, or national groups.[64] On some level, then, nationalisms are also concerned with biological, social, and "racial" processes of reproduction.[65] The politics of Garveyism must therefore be scrutinized in ways that fully engage theories of sexuality within other nationalisms; scholars of black nationalism must continue to interrogate the gendered, sexualized politics of racial reproduction.[66]

Garveyites assessed black people's sexuality in light of contemporary exigencies as well as historical discourses on black sexuality. Throughout much of the history of the United States, a value-laden dialogue about black sexuality has existed. Not all Garveyites that lived in the United States or contributed to the *Negro World* during the UNIA's peak—including Amy Jacques Garvey, Maymie De Mena, Marcus Garvey, and countless others—were native born, but many were deeply influenced by U.S. racial discourses. Most significantly, late nineteenth- and early twentieth-century stereotypes about black sexuality worked in conjunction with assertions that slavery tainted gender roles among people of African descent and compounded the already complex ways in which Garveyites viewed their own sexuality. The mere possibility that blacks could not achieve the "sexual purity . . . [needed] to survive and develop" therefore led Garveyites to search for their own solutions. Some of those very solutions, however, were somewhat reactionary when it came to gender and sexuality in that they drew upon popular eugenics and looked toward pronatalist solutions for race-building.[67] Garveyites embraced eugenics as a sexual corrective for the race at large, then, due to perceived needs, problematic stereotypes, and material realities.

If the eugenic and pronatalist strains in movement rhetoric reveal that Garveyites' expectations for sexual behavior carried additional implications for women, then a major question bears revisiting: why were women singled out? The divergent ways in which women and men experienced the racial purist impetus behind Garveyism emerged from the social, biological, and gendered division of labor involved in having children. Women do more than have babies, they "reproduc[e] the race"; their sexual activities are a source of greater anxiety as a result.[68] And if "those who are preoccupied with the 'purity' of the race [are also] preoccupied with the sexual relationships between members of different collectivities,"[69] the ideology of Garveyism contained such a preoccupation. The movement, in other words, placed the blame for miscegenation at the feet of black women, if not in their beds.

If we simply consider that the movement's constitution institutionalized sex-specific responsibilities and functions, then gender might seem merely a consideration that shaped how Garveyites organized meetings and activities. Once we also consider that members of the UNIA were concerned with both racial purity and black women's reproductive function, that prolific and eugenic childbearing was considered a primary duty for race women, it becomes all but impossible to assert that male and female Garveyites truly shared the same purpose in the movement's overarching vision of "One God! One Aim! One Destiny!"[70] By examining the programs and precepts of Garveyites with gender and sexuality in mind, it is abundantly clear that in the quest for racial redemption and black nationhood, the UNIA might have had one God and one aim, but men and women in the movement had somewhat separate destinies.

NOTES

1. "Georgia Negroes Whip Woman to Impress Race Purity," *Negro World* (hereafter *NW*), April 1, 1922, 2.

2. Ibid. Sylvester might not have had a UNIA division when this incident occurred, but a local did exist by 1926. See Mary Gambrell Rolinson, "The Universal Negro Improvement Association in Georgia: Southern Stronghold of Garveyism," in *Georgia in Black and White: Explorations in the Race Relations of a Southern State, 1865–1950,* ed. John C. Inscoe (Athens: University of Georgia Press, 1994), 202–224, esp. 204.

3. This *Negro World* article—in my reading, at least—does not contain the slightest hint that this assault was unwarranted or excessive, and the inclusion of the speech allegedly given on the occasion is rather revealing: "The angry mob read a certain lecture to the woman on 'race purity.' . . . 'A new day has dawned and there will be no toleration of any liaison between colored women and white men. The times are changing; these are not days when Negro women could not protect themselves and were at the mercy of the white man's lust. There is no excuse at this day and time for Negro women to maintain clandestine relationships with white men.'" "Georgia Negroes Whip Woman." Hazel V. Carby's work on sexual policing provides a provocative analytical prism through which to view this incident. See Carby, "Policing the Black Woman's Body in an Urban Context," *Critical Inquiry* 18, no. 4 (Summer 1992): 738–755.

4. Monographs on Garvey and Garveyism include Edmund Cronon, *Black Moses: Marcus Garvey and the Universal Negro Improvement Association* (Madison: University of Wisconsin Press, 1953); Theodore Vincent, *Black Power and the Garvey Movement* (San Francisco: Ramparts Press, 1971); Tony Martin, *Race First: The Ideological and Organizational Struggles of Marcus Garvey and the Universal Negro Improvement Association* (Westport, CT: Greenwood Press, 1976); Judith Stein, *The World of Marcus Garvey: Race and Class in Modern Society* (Baton Rouge: Louisiana State University Press, 1986); and Ula Yvette Taylor, *The Veiled Garvey: The Life and Times of Amy Jacques Garvey* (Chapel Hill: University of North Carolina Press, 2002).

5. See volume 1 of Robert A. Hill, ed., *The Marcus Garvey and Universal Negro Improvement Association Papers,* 7 vols. (Berkeley: University of California Press, 1983–1986, 1989–1990) (hereafter Hill, *Garvey Papers*), esp. 384. For a detailed elaboration of early political aims of the UNIA, see "Declaration of Rights of the Negro Peoples of the World" (ca. 1920) in Hill, *Garvey Papers,* 2:571–580; for an articulation of the UNIA's racial nationalism, see "Universal Negro Catechism" (ca. 1921), in Hill, *Garvey Papers,* 3:302–320. Robert Hill outlines the political shifts of the UNIA in his "General Introduction," in *Garvey Papers,* 1:xxxv–xc. Here, it is important to note that when Marcus Garvey decided to relocate to the United States he was part of a steady stream of black immigrants from South America, Central America, and the Caribbean. David Hellwig notes that this stream crested in the mid-1920s; his work further chronicles tensions between African Americans and recent black arrivals. See David J. Hellwig, "Black Meets Black: Afro-American Reactions to West Indian Immigrants in the 1920s," *South Atlantic Quarterly* 77, no. 2 (Spring 1978): 206–224. For critical analysis of radicalism and Caribbean migration to the United States, see Winston James, *Holding Aloft the Banner of Ethiopia: Caribbean Radicalism in Early Twentieth-Century America* (London: Verso, 1998). Relevant analysis may also be found in Charles V. Carnegie, "A Politics of Transterritorial Solidarity: The Garvey Movement and Imperialism," in Carnegie, *Postnationalism Prefigured: Caribbean Borderlands* (New Brunswick, NJ: Rutgers University Press, 2002), 145–175.

6. The movement's constitution established that seven or more people could form a chapter. "Constitution and Book of Laws" (article I, section IV), in Hill, *Garvey Papers,* 1:257. Tony Martin provides a comprehensive roster of UNIA branches in North, Central, and South America, as well as the Caribbean, Africa, and Great Britain in an appendix (*Race First,* 361–373). Mary Rolinson's work contains critical insight into smaller divisions located in the American South;

she asserts that "Garvey gave inspiration to latent black consciousness in isolated rural communities." Rolinson, "The Universal Negro Improvement Association in Georgia," 203.

7. "RACE FIRST!" *NW,* July 26, 1919, reprinted in Hill, *Garvey Papers,* 1:468–470, esp. 469.

8. "Hon. Marcus Garvey Tells of Interview with Ku Klux Klan," *NW,* July 15, 1922, reprinted in Hill, *Garvey Papers,* 4:707–715, esp. 709, 713, and 714. Along these lines, Nancy MacLean's *Behind the Mask of Chivalry: The Making of the Second Ku Klux Klan* (New York: Oxford University Press, 1994) provides highly relevant analysis of the Klan's intraracial policing of sexuality and morality. Garvey also forged unlikely relationships with at least two other white supremacists in addition to Clarke over the question of racial purity: John Powell, founder of the Anglo-Saxon Clubs of America, and Earnest Sevier Cox, author of *White America.* Refer to J. David Smith, "John Powell and Marcus Garvey: The Peculiar Alliance," in *The Eugenic Assault on America: Scenes in Red, White, and Black* (Fairfax, VA: George Mason University Press, 1993), 23–35; William A. Edwards, "Racial Purity in Black and White: The Case of Marcus Garvey and Earnest Cox," *Journal of Ethnic Studies* 15, no. 1 (Spring 1987): 117–142.

9. Speech by Marcus Garvey (original title unknown), *NW,* July 15, 1922, reprinted in Hill, *Garvey Papers,* 4:707–715. Even with its publication of Garvey's desideratum that black men must "strike back on white men," the *Negro World* would also acknowledge that doing so often resulted in a less than desirable outcome. In the spring of 1921, for example, the paper publicized the case of W. T. Bowman, a Mississippi teacher who had been attacked by a mob upon expelling a seventeen-year-old schoolgirl whose lover was a local white man. See "Southern Mob Whips Negro Teacher," *NW,* April 23, 1921, 1.

10. Garvey made this argument about the "social question of race" while discussing President Warren Harding's aversion to "social equality." Speech by Marcus Garvey (original headline unknown), *NW,* November 5, 1921, reprinted in Hill, *Garvey Papers,* 4:141–151, esp. 145. For remainder of text quoted here, see *Garvey Papers,* 4:714.

11. "The Women Lynched the White Libertine," *NW,* December 29, 1923, 4. Interestingly, the writer observed that "if the Negro women of Fayette County did lynch the white libertine for insulting one of their number, they have done more ... than any Negro man has done in Fayette County." Given that the *Negro World* article opens with the disclosure that they knew about this event because of a reader, however, it is possible that the women themselves did not belong to the UNIA. For the item on Nellie Edwards, see "Moral Leper Attempts to Assault Negro Child," *NW,* July 19, 1924, 2. The *Negro World* followed the unsuccessful campaign to pass the Dyer Anti-Lynching Bill during the early 1920s and featured brief items about lynching. One such item, "An Eye for An Eye" (May 27, 1922, 4), decried lynching as it implored "black men [to] rise en masse and wage war on the licentious violators of black womanhood!" For a statement suggesting that combating lynching entailed maintenance of race purity, see "Negro Race Purity" (July 12, 1930, 4).

12. Marcus Garvey, "What We Believe," in *The Philosophy and Opinions of Marcus Garvey or, Africa for the Africans,* 2 vols., comp. Amy Jacques Garvey (rpt., Dover, MA: Majority Press, 1986), 2:81. The remaining three points refer to universal rights, black pride, and "the spiritual Fatherhood of God and the Brotherhood of Man."

13. Marcus Garvey, *Aims and Objects of Movement for Solution of Negro Problem Outlined* (New York: Press of the Universal Negro Improvement Association, 1924), 3, 6.

14. "Convention Report," *NW,* September 2, 1922, reprinted in Hill, *Garvey Papers,* 4:934–942, esp. 936 and 939.

15. Richard Tate, "Negro Men Should Marry Negro Women," *NW,* March 7, 1925.

16. Eva Aldred Brooks, "A Pure, Healthy, Unified Race, Plea of Women," *NW,* May 23, 1925, 7. A similar call for race "standardization" may be found in "Black Peoples Must Dignify Own Homogeneity" (September 28, 1929, 2).

17. Fraternal orders were familiar institutions in late nineteenth-century and early twentieth-century America, and their popularity reflected, in part, an attempt to reestablish "traditional" order during an era when gender constructions and sexual relationships were in a state of flux. According to Mary Ann Clawson's provocative work on fraternalism, one of the foremost reasons behind brotherhoods as social institutions was to "make [men] aware of their separation from women, and thus to enforce the exercise of masculine power." Mary Ann Clawson, *Constructing Brotherhood: Class, Gender, and Fraternalism* (Princeton, NJ: Princeton University Press, 1989), esp. 131–135 and 178. Since most brotherhoods routinely excluded blacks, African American men typically participated in segregated offshoots of mainstream orders. The link between fraternal orders and Garveyism is explored in Robert Hill's introduction to the first volume of the *Garvey Papers,* lx–lxiii.

18. Arguably, these same notions could be considered "bourgeois" and/or "conservative." One of the first works to assert that black nationalist politics are inclined toward "bourgeois conservatism" rather than being inherently working-class, militant, or radical is Wilson Jeremiah Moses's *The Golden Age of Black Nationalism: 1850–1925* (New York: Oxford University Press, 1988), esp. 5–31.

19. Barbara Bair, "'Ethiopia Shall Stretch Forth Her Hands unto God': Laura Kofey and the Gendered Vision of Redemption in the Garvey Movement," in *A Mighty Baptism: Race, Gender, and the Creation of American Protestantism,* ed. Susan Juster and Lisa MacFarlane (Ithaca: Cornell University Press, 1996), 38–61, esp. 46.

20. The only juvenile group for both girls and boys was the "Infant Class" for ages 1 to 7; it provided "Bible Class and Prayer" along with schooling on UNIA doctrine, the Black Star Line, Negro Factories Corporation, and African history "in story book fashion." Older juveniles also studied race history and were indoctrinated in "race pride and love." See "Rules and Regulations for Juveniles," articles I-IV, in Hill, *Garvey Papers,* 3:770–772.

21. Men could participate in women's groups to a limited degree, but women were prohibited, according to the constitution, from engaging in any activities designated specifically for men. See "Rules and Regulations for Universal African Legions of the U.N.I.A. and A.C.L.," articles I, III, VI, IX, XI, and XVIII, in Hill, *Garvey Papers,* 3:755–759; "Rules and Regulations Governing the Universal African Black Cross Nurses," articles I–V, in Hill, *Garvey Papers,* 3:766–768; "Rules and Regulations Governing the Universal African Motor Corps," Articles I–IV, in Hill, *Garvey Papers,* 3:769. Although other interpretations of the UNIA differ from my own in several regards, critical discussions of women and gender in the UNIA include Mark Matthews, "Our Women and What They Think: Amy Jacques Garvey and the *Negro World,*" in *Black Women in United States History,* ed. Darlene Clark Hine (New York: Carlson, 1990), 7:866–878; William Seraile, "Henrietta Vinton Davis and the Garvey Movement," in Hine, *Black Women in United States History,* 8:1073–1091; Tony Martin, "Women in the Garvey Movement," in *Garvey: His Work and Impact,* ed. Rupert Lewis and Patrick Bryan (Trenton, NJ: Africa World Press, 1991), 67–72; Honor Ford-Smith, "Women and the Garvey Movement in Jamaica," in Lewis and Bryan, *Garvey: His Work and Impact,* 73–86; Barbara Bair, "True Women, Real Men: Gender, Ideology, and Social Roles in the Garvey Movement," in *Gendered Domains: Rethinking Public and Private in Women's History,* essays from the Seventh Berkshire Conference on the History of Women, ed. Dorothy O. Helly and Susan M. Reverby (Ithaca: Cornell University Press, 1992), 154–166; Ula Yvette Taylor, "The Veiled Garvey: The Life and Times of Amy Jacques Garvey" (Ph.D. diss., University of California, Santa Barbara, 1992); Karen S. Adler, "'Always Leading Our Men in Service and Sacrifice': Amy Jacques Garvey, Feminist Black Nationalist," *Gender and Society* 6, no. 3 (September 1992): 346–375; Martin Anthony Summers, "Nationalism, Race Consciousness, and the Construction of Black Middle Class Masculinity during the New Negro Era, 1915–1930" (Ph.D. diss., Rutgers University, 1997); Ula Y. Taylor, "'Negro Women Are Great Thinkers as Well as Doers': Amy Jacques-Garvey and Community Feminism in the

United States," *Journal of Women's History* 12, no. 2 (Summer 2002): 104–126; and Taylor, *The Veiled Garvey*.

22. In addition to yearly conventions that formally allotted time for "Women's Industrial Exhibits" where culinary feats, handicrafts, and fashions were proudly displayed, sex-specific activities occurred on the local level as well. The bulk of *Negro World* reports on women's activities in local UNIA divisions mentioned conversations on women's loyalty and duty to the cause; the *Negro World* frequently gave reviews of local "Ladies' Days" on its "News and Views of U.N.I.A. Divisions" page. The following citations provide but a *few* examples: "Boston Div. Celebrates Ladies' Day," *NW*, April 1, 1922, 9; "Wonderful Program Rendered by Ladies of Oakland, Cal., Division," *NW*, March 3, 1923,4; "Ladies' Day Observed at Denver, Col., Division," *NW*, April 8, 1922, 8; and "Wonderful Pageant Given By Women's Department of New Haven Division of U.N.I.A.," *NW*, July 16, 1921, 9. Also see "U.N.I.A. in New Orleans on the Upward March," *NW*, February 19, 1921, 8; "Ladies Stage Great Program at U.N.I.A. Mass Meeting in Oakland, Cal.," *NW*, January 20, 1923, 7; and "The Baltimore, Md., U.N.I.A.," *NW*, October 1, 1921, 11. For a quote on the function of the Motor Corps, see "Rules and Regulations Governing the Universal African Motor Corps," in Hill, *Garvey Papers*, 3:769.

23. Revealing analysis of how Garveyite women viewed their position in the movement—including an argument about women of African descent and "community feminism"—may be found in Taylor, "'Negro Women Are Great Thinkers.'"

24. Hill maintains that the earliest years of the UNIA witnessed virtual parity in male and female membership. Such parity would soon change: in early 1922, at the apex of Garveyism's popularity and influence, Marcus Garvey was indicted for mail fraud. FBI agents had monitored Garvey and UNIA activities for well over two years; the federal government alleged, among many things, that Garvey's flagship project, the Black Star Line, was an illegitimate business enterprise and that Garvey abused the mail for purposes of extortion. After serving a three-month portion of his five-year sentence in 1923, Garvey was finally imprisoned at Atlanta's Tombs Prison in 1925. In 1927, he was released only to be expeditiously deported to Jamaica. It was not until the movement was in decline that its membership came to be overwhelmingly dominated by women. Phone interview with Robert Hill, November 1990. In contrast, Beryl Satter maintains that the UNIA was always predominantly male; see Satter, "Marcus Garvey, Father Divine and the Gender Politics of Race Difference and Race Neutrality," *American Quarterly* 48, no. 1 (March 1996): 43–76.

25. Gertrude Hawkins letter, *NW*, January 12, 1924, 10; "Sixteen-Year-Old Colored Girl Addresses Oklahoma Division," *NW*, August 27, 1921, 11; "African Redemption Fund," *NW*, October 1, 1921, 3; Editorial letter, *NW*, October 1, 1921, 6; and "New Orleans Division in Letter to Mayor Defends the U.N.I.A.," *NW*, March 24, 1923, 8. In an interview conducted in 1978, Audley Moore recalled that when she lived in New Orleans during the early 1920s she heard Garvey speak in person; that very first encounter inspired Moore to become a fast and ready adherent to the principles of Garveyism. See Cheryl Townsend Gilkes, "Interview with Audley (Queen Mother) Moore," *The Black Women Oral History Project* (Cambridge, MA: Schlesinger Library, Radcliffe College, 1978), 9–10.

26. Hill, *Garvey Papers*, 4:1037–1038. Robert Hill and Theodore Vincent offer further comment on these women; see Hill, *Garvey Papers*, 4:xxxv; and Vincent, *Black Power and the Garvey Movement*, 124–125. Barbara Bair's analysis of this conflict is particularly useful; Bair, "True Women, Real Men," 160–161. Mark Matthews, Beryl Satter, and Karen Adler (who focuses mostly on the rift between Amy Jacques and Marcus) also explore more general tensions between women and men in the movement: Matthews, "'Our Women and What They Think,'" 11–12; Satter, "Marcus Garvey, Father Divine," 51; and Adler, "'Always Leading Our Men,'" 354–366. Further details of the crises that marred the 1922 convention may be found in Hill, *Garvey Papers*, 4:xxxi–xxxv.

27. Davis had been married during the 1880s. Whereas it is not altogether clear whether Galloway was a practicing Garveyite, she did, at the very least, refer to the UNIA's minister of industries and labor, Ulysses S. Poston, as her "'boss.'" Presumably, then, the two worked together; thus Galloway was familiar with some of the movement's basic tenets and was also willing to work for the UNIA. "Thriving Business Enterprises of the Universal Negro Improvement Association," *NW,* July 8, 1922, 3.

28. M. L. T. De Mena, "Part Women Must Play in the Organization," *NW,* January 23, 1926, 7. A woman who served the UNIA in a variety of capacities, De Mena was from Nicaragua and had a daughter (who also was a Garveyite). De Mena apparently was affiliated with Father Divine during the 1930s. Robert A. Hill, ed., *Marcus Garvey: Life and Lessons, a Centennial Companion to the Marcus Garvey and Universal Negro Improvement Association Papers* (Berkeley: University of California Press, 1987), 376–377; Satter, "Marcus Garvey, Father Divine," 51.

29. In her account of the assassination of Laura Adorkor Kofey, Barbara Bair provides a chilling example of what happened to one woman who seized unusual power for herself within the movement. For quote cited in text and for information on Kofey, see Bair, "True Women, Real Men," 163.

30. Examples of typical paeans to race motherhood may be found in George Carter, "Weekly Sermon," *NW,* May 13, 1922, 6; and Carrie Mero Leadett, "The Obligations of Motherhood," *NW,* March 29, 1924, 10.

31. "The Women of the Race Are Lauded in Liberty Hall on Observance of Mother's Day," *NW,* May 17, 1924, 3.

32. Estelle Matthews, "Message for the Negro Women of the World," *NW,* February 4, 1922, 11. For an extended argument along these lines, see J. H. A. Brazelton, *Self-Determination: The Salvation of the Race* (Oklahoma City, OK: Educator, 1918). Useful examination of how a range of women politicized motherhood during the late nineteenth and early twentieth centuries appears in Eileen Boris's "The Power of Motherhood: Black and White Activist Women Redefine the Political," in *Mothers of a New World: Maternalist Politics and the Origins of Welfare States,* ed. Seth Koven and Sonya Michel (New York: Routledge, 1993), 213–245.

33. Examples include "The Hand that Rocks the Cradle," *NW,* July 5, 1924, 12; Hannah Nichols, "Lady Delegate . . . Demands Single Standard for All," *NW,* August 23, 1924, 16; Kate Fenner, "Negro Men Must Beard the Lion," *NW,* March 25, 1922, 3. One article, "The Glory of Fatherhood," somewhat stands out in that it claims that a man who is not a father is merely "half a man." However, this piece contains no specific reference to people of African descent and might not have been written by a member of the movement; it could also have been pulled from another periodical. See Mrs. Walter Ferguson, "The Glory of Fatherhood," *NW,* December 25, 1926, 8.

34. Although Charles Darwin was never involved in the movement that adopted his name, social Darwinism evolved into a broadly influential movement following publication of *Origin of Species* (1859). In turn, it begat eugenics, which advocated active engagement in eradicating "degenerate" elements from society. Social Darwinists and eugenicists alike favored a host of legislation, from immigration quotas to antimiscegenation laws to enforced sterilization. Historical analyses of race, ethnicity, social Darwinism, and/or eugenics include Richard Hofstadter, *Social Darwinism in American Thought: 1860–1915* (New York: G. Braziller, 1959); Thomas Gossett, *Race: The History of an Idea in America* (New York: Schocken Books, 1963); Mark Haller, *Eugenics: Hereditarian Attitudes in American Thought* (New Brunswick, NJ: Rutgers University Press, 1963); Daniel J. Kevles, *In the Name of Eugenics: Genetics and the Uses of Human Heredity* (New York: Alfred A. Knopf, 1985); Edward J. Larson, *Sex, Race, and Science: Eugenics in the Deep South* (Baltimore: Johns Hopkins University Press, 1995); Martin S. Pernick, *The Black Stork: Eugenics and the Death of "Defective" Babies in American Medicine and Motion Pictures since 1915* (New York: Oxford University Press, 1996); Lisa Lindquist Dorr, "Arm in Arm: Gender, Eugenics, and Virginia's Racial Integrity Acts of the 1920s,"

Journal of Women's History 11, no. 1 (Spring 1999): 143–166; Gregory Michael Dorr, "Assuring America's Place in the Sun: Ivey Foreman Lewis and the Teaching of Eugenics at the University of Virginia," *Journal of Southern History* 66, no. 2 (May 2000): 257–296; and Wendy Kline, *Building a Better Race: Gender, Sexuality, and Eugenics from the Turn of the Century to the Baby Boom* (Berkeley: University of California Press, 2002). For the connection between race, gender, eugenics, nationalism, and empire, see Nancy Leys Stepan, *"The Hour of Eugenics": Race, Gender, and Nation in Latin America* (Ithaca: Cornell University Press, 1991); Alexandra Minna Stern, "Buildings, Boundaries, and Blood: Medicalization and Nation-Building on the U.S.-Mexico Border, 1910–1930," *Hispanic American Historical Review* 79, no. 1 (February 1999): 41–81; Alexandra Minna Stern, "Responsible Mothers and Normal Children: Eugenics, Welfare, and Nationalism in Post-Revolutionary Mexico, 1900–1940," *Journal of Historical Sociology* 12, no. 4 (Fall 1999): 369–397; and Laura Briggs, *Reproducing Empire: Race, Sex, Science, and U.S. Imperialism* (Berkeley: University of California Press, 2002).

35. W. E. B. Du Bois, "Opinion," Annual Children's Number, *Crisis* 24, no. 6 (October 1922): 247–253; Kelly Miller, "The Eugenics of the Negro Race," *Scientific Monthly* 5, no. 1 (July 1917): 57–59; Chandler Owen, "Women and Children of the South," *Birth Control Review* 3, no. 9 (September 1919): 9 and 20; and Mary Burrill, "They That Sit in Darkness: A One-Act Play of Negro Life," *Birth Control Review* 3, no. 9 (September 1919): 5–8. See also W. E. B. Du Bois, "The Damnation of Women," in *Writings,* ed. Nathan Huggins (New York: Literary Classics, 1986), 952–968; and Chandler Owen, "Marriage and Divorce," *Messenger* 5, no. 3 (March 1923): 629–631. Other black intellectuals who wrote on eugenics include Theodore Burrell, "Negro Womanhood—An Appeal," *Crusader* 2, no. 11 (July 1920): 18; J. A. Rogers, "The Critic," *Messenger,* April 1925, 165–166; and E. Franklin Frazier, "Eugenics and the Race Problem," *Crisis* 31, no. 2 (December 1925): 91–92.

36. Daylanne English, "W. E. B. Du Bois's Family Crisis," *American Literature* 72, no. 2 (June 2000): 291–319, esp. 298 and 311.

37. Tony Martin observes that "Garvey's belief in the necessity for self-reliance led him occasionally to speak in the language of Social Darwinism" *(Race First,* 32), while Wilson Moses assesses how social Darwinism influenced black nationalist ideology during the late nineteenth and early twentieth centuries (*Golden Age of Black Nationalism,* 27). The following sources illuminate how Garvey appropriated social Darwinist concepts: "Report of UNIA Meeting" (original headline unknown), *NW,* November 1, 1919, reprinted in Hill, *Garvey Papers,* 2:138–142, esp. 139–140; editorial letter by Marcus Garvey, *NW,* May 8, 1920, reprinted in Hill, *Garvey Papers,* 2:330–331; Marcus Garvey, "Shall the Negro Be Exterminated?" in *Philosophy and Opinions,* 1:63–67; and Marcus Garvey, "Blazing the Trail of African Redemption," *NW,* May 5, 1923, 1. Also see "Women Who Refuse Responsibility of Parenthood Traitors to Race," *NW,* July 12, 1924, 12. This particular editorial—which was reprinted from the *New York Times*—in "Our Women and What They Think" contains classist, eugenic injunctions to "women of intelligence and culture" to bear children. Several Garveyites mouthed the language of social purity as well. Although the Progressive era was effectively over by the time the UNIA took off in the United States, the redress of social "impurities" remained on the agenda of American reformers, educators, writers, and politicians. Examples of social purist language in the UNIA include "We Must Maintain A High Standard of Morality," *NW,* August 2, 1924, 4; Hannah Nichols, "Lady Delegate:. Demands Single Standard for All," *NW,* August 23, 1924, 16; Florence Bruce, "The Great Work of the Negro Woman Today," *NW,* December 18, 1924, 8; and "Convention Report," August 12, 1924, in Hill, *Garvey Papers,* 5:717–722. Relevant commentary on social purity may be found in Christina Simmons, "African Americans and Sexual Victorianism in the Social Hygiene Movement, 1910–1940," *Journal of the History of Sexuality* 4, no. 1 (1993): 51–75, esp. 53; and Linda Gordon, *Woman's Body, Woman's Right: A Social History of Birth Control in America* (New York: Grossman, 1976), 116–158.

38. "Convention Report," August 12, 1924, in Hill, *Garvey Papers,* 5:717–722.

39. "The Hand That Rocks the Cradle." Also see "More Attention Given to Our Child Life," *NW,* May 31, 1924, 10.

40. In one article written exclusively for the *Negro World,* black bibliophile Arthur Schomburg went as far as to assert that European and American scientists poached the concept from ancient African cultures; "Arthur A. Schomburg Pays a Tribute to [the] African Woman," *NW,* April 2, 1921, 7. For other examples, see "The Question of Race Superiority," *NW,* October 8, 1921, 4; and "The World Suffers from Shortage of Big Minds," *NW,* October 22, 1921, 6.

41. Lester Taylor, "Children and the Race," *NW,* October 29, 1921.

42. Carrie Mero Leadett, "The Obligations of Motherhood," *NW,* March 29, 1924, 10. Also see Mrs. W. Waldron Pitt, "A Woman's Appeal to Ethiopian Women," *NW,* January 6, 1923, 6.

43. Marcus Garvey, "Speech Delivered at Carnegie Hall," in *Philosophy and Opinions,* 2:101–102. Refer to the following as well: Garvey, "Shall the Negro Be Exterminated?" 1:64; Marcus Garvey, "Garvey Quotes Hearst and Other White Writers Who Believe Negro is Slowly, Inevitably Diminishing in Numbers ... ," *NW,* December 3, 1921, reprinted in Hill, *Garvey Papers,* 4:221–228; '"Race Extinction," *NW,* May 20, 1922, 4; and Kelly Miller, "Educated Negroes Said Not to Marry and Raise Large Families," *NW,* February 7, 1925. Some Garveyites invoked Native Americans when they discussed the possibility of genocide; one such example is Ida Jacques, "Fate of Red Indians Should Be a Warning to Negroes," *NW,* January 24, 1925. A group of Garveyites in Kansas went in a different direction: They associated the threat of extinction with a need to leave the United States for Africa. See [Alfred D. House?] et al. to Earnest Sevier Cox; Earnest Sevier Cox Papers, Special Collections, Perkins Library, Duke University, Durham, NC, box 3, folder 1929–1930.

44. Speech by Marcus Garvey (original title unknown), *NW,* September 10, 1921; reprinted in Hill, *Garvey Papers,* 4:26.

45. See, e.g., "Report of Committee on 'The Future of the Negro in America,'" *NW,* September 9, 1922; reprinted in Hill, *Garvey Papers,* 4:1017–1021. An especially compelling counterargument to Garvey's appears in A[rnold] H[amilton] Maloney, "Maloney Says Negro Race Is Not Doomed to Extinction," *NW,* September 16, 1922, 3. Maloney, a professor at Wilberforce University who would later publish *Race Leadership* (Xenia, OH: Aldine Publishing House, 1924), also provided one of the only articles in the *Negro World* to advocate miscegenation. See "Miscegenation Only Local Alternative to Social and Economic Serfdom-Maloney," *NW,* June 7, 1922, 2.

46. For detailed, comparative statistics, refer to U.S. Department of Commerce, Bureau of the Census, *Negro Population,* 1790–1915 (Washington, DC: Government Printing Office, 1918. Rpt. 1969), 22–24, 283–287; also refer to U.S. Department of Commerce, Bureau of the Census, *Negroes in the United States,* 1920–1932 (Washington, DC: Government Printing Office, 1935), 1–2. Mainstream epidemiology during the late nineteenth and early twentieth centuries consistently supported the view that black children, women, and men were anything but vital. Examples of arguments that venereal disease and tuberculosis were especially prevalent among blacks may be found in Frederick L. Hoffman, *Race Traits and Tendencies of the American Negro* (New York: Macmillan, 1896); Mary White Ovington, *Half a Man: The Status of the Negro in New York* (New York: Longmans, Green, 1911); and Mark J. White, "Report of the Committee on Venereal Diseases of the State and Provincial Health Authorities," *American Journal of Public Health* 13 (1923): 723–737.

47. Health-related coverage in the *Negro World* appeared on a fairly regular basis: Dr. B. S. Herben, "Are You Strong for the Race?" (April 7, 1923, 3); "Negro Race Needs More Medical Men among the People" (July 28, 1923, 9); "Saving Our Children" (November 10, 1923, 8); "Negro City Death Rate" (December 8, 1923, 7); "Life Expectation of Negroes Is Much Greater" (July 5,

1924, 7); "Communicable Diseases and Health and Wealth" (April 18, 1925, 10); "Birth Rate Is Lowest Recorded in America" (December 19, 1925, 5); "Eugenics and Civilization" (September 11, 1926, 7); and "Alarming Rise in Negro Death Rate Reported" (July 16, 1927, 2).

48. In *Garvey and Garveyism* (Kingston: United Printers, 1963), Amy Jacques Garvey recorded that the UNIA's "Liberty Halls, wherever located, served the needs of the people.... Public meetings ... concerts and dances were held.... Notice boards were put up where one could look for a room, a job." *Garvey and Garveyism,* 91. John Charles Zampty, a Trinidadian who belonged to the UNIA local in Detroit, remembered that his division ran "'laundries, restaurants, shoe shine parlors, drugstores, and ... even ... theaters.'" See Jeannette Smith-Irvin, comp. and ed., *Footsoldiers of the Universal Negro Improvement Association (Their Own Words)* (Trenton, NJ: Africa World Press, 1989), 11.

49. In particular, the *Negro World* periodically ran an idealized image of a nurse with the following caption: "carrying the torch of knowledge about health and rightful living for the enlightenment of our people ... and eradicating the fatalistic theory that disease is God-sent." *NW,* March 31, 1923.

50. Josephine Spence, "Black Cross Nurses Trained to Care for Mothers and Babies," *NW,* November 1, 1924, 10. See also Isabella Lawrence's "Conservation of Child Life a Race Duty," *NW,* August 2, 1924, 12.

51. Morgan's column was entitled "Universal African Black Cross Nurses Child Welfare Department." For examples cited in text, please see "ABCs of Child Welfare," *NW,* February 4, 1922, 8; and *NW,* July 15, 1922, 6.

52. Amy Jacques Garvey, "Listen Women!" *NW,* April 9, 1927, 7.

53. Hubert Cox, "Birth Control Condemned as Heinous, Corrupted, Inhuman," *NW,* January 14, 1922, 7.

54. Katie Fenner, "Negro Men Must Beard the Lion in Its Den," *NW,* March 25, 1922, 3; Fenner, "Woman, Lovely Woman," *NW,* September 9, 1922, 10. Lucius Lenan-Lehman of California was sufficiently incensed by Fenner's opinions that he wrote a pointed rebuttal to her "Negro Men." See Lucius Lenan-Lehman, "Mrs. Katie Fenner," *NW,* September 30, 1922, 8.

55. Also refer to Benito Thomas, "Advocates of Birth Control Flayed," *NW,* April 4, 1925, 10; as well as "Birth Control Called Crime," in "Our Women and What They Think," *NW,* November 7, 1925, 7. In 1934, at the Seventh International Convention of the UNIA in Kingston, Jamaica, Garveyites unanimously approved a moratorium on the practice of birth control for all women of African descent. *The Black Man* 1, no. 6 (November 1934): 34. See also Jessie M. Rodrique, "The Black Community and the Birth-Control Movement," in *Unequal Sisters: A Multi-Cultural Reader in U.S. Women's History,* ed. Ellen Carol Du Bois and Vicki L. Ruiz (New York: Routledge, 1990), 333–344, esp. 336.

56. Margaret Sanger, *Woman and the New Race* (New York: Blue Ribbon Books, 1920). For arguments about the relationship between contraception and eugenics, see Gordon, *Woman's Body, Woman's Right,* 116–135.

57. For insight on African Americans' attitudes about homosexuality during the Harlem Renaissance, see Daphne Duval Harrison, *Black Pearls: Blues Queens of the 1920s* (New Brunswick, NJ: Rutgers University Press, 1988), 14, 53, 103–104; and Eric Garber, "A Spectacle in Color: The Lesbian and Gay Subculture of Jazz Age Harlem," in *Hidden From History: Reclaiming the Gay and Lesbian Past,* ed. Martin Bauml Duberman, Martha Vicinus, and George Chauncey Jr. (New York: New American Library, 1989), 318–331. Refer also to Siobhan B. Somerville, *Queering the Color Line: Race and the Invention of Homosexuality in American Culture* (Durham, NC: Duke University Press, 2000). An overview of interracial sexuality—one that explores same-sex desire—during this period may be found in Kevin J. Mumford, *Interzones: Black/White Sex Districts in Chicago and New York in the Early Twentieth Century* (New York: Columbia University Press, 1997).

58. John Houghton [also Haughton], "The Plight of Our Race in Harlem, Brooklyn, and New Jersey," *NW,* April 21, 1923, 8. Also see J. C. Cake, "Sex Truths," *NW,* May 19, 1923, 8. In addition, Benito Thomas's and Hubert J. Cox's language of social evil may be interpreted as references to homosexuality; Thomas, "Advocates of Birth Control Flayed"; and Cox, "Birth Control Condemned."

59. For examples of how black manhood was discussed by male and female Garveyites, see R. T. Brown, "A Call to Negro Manhood," *NW,* September 23, 1922, 9; Amelia Sayers Alexander, "A Brave Man Betrayed," *NW,* March 14, 1925, 7; and P. L. Burrows, "Black Man's Duty to His Women," *NW,* August 16, 1924, 16. Works that explore reifications of motherhood in nationalist ideologies include Deborah Gaitskell and Elaine Unterhalter, "Mothers of the Nation: A Comparative Analysis of Nation, Race, and Motherhood in Afrikaner Nationalism and the African National Congress," in *Woman-Nation-State,* ed. Nira Yuval-Davis and Floya Anthias (New York: St. Martin's Press, 1989), 58–78; Leila J. Rupp, "Mother of the *Volk:* The Image of Women in Nazi Ideology," *Signs* 3, no. 2 (Winter 1977): 362–379; Leslie Lynn King, "Gender, Nation, Pronatalism: Encouraging Births in France, Romania, and Israel" (Ph.D. diss., University of Illinois, Urbana-Champaign, 1998); and Taylor, "'Negro Women are Great Thinkers.'"

60. It is critical to note that using the word "sacrifice" in this context is not a presentist, feminist rendering of the past given that articles in the *Negro World* by both women and men frequently coupled that very word to motherhood. See Laura Thomas, "Living for Others," *NW,* June 14, 1924, 12; and Hubert Cox, "The Women of the Race," *NW,* January 21, 1922, 8. For an elaboration of the "double-edged" nature of motherhood as used in the context of political struggle, see Patricia Stamp, "Burying Otieno: The Politics of Gender and Ethnicity in Kenya," *Signs* 16, no. 4 (Summer 1991): 843–844; also refer to Patricia Hill-Collins's discussion of black women and motherhood in *Black Feminist Thought: Knowledge, Consciousness and the Politics of Empowerment* (New York: Routledge, 1991), 115–137, esp. 132.

61. Elizabeth Balanoff, "The 20th Century Trade Union Woman: Vehicle for Social Change. Oral History Interview with Maida Springer Kemp, International Ladies Garment Workers Union," in *The Black Women Oral History Project* (Cambridge, MA: Schlesinger Library, Radcliffe College, 1978), 6.

62. Moses, *Golden Age of Black Nationalism*; Stein, *The World of Marcus Garvey.* Additional commentary on racial conservatism may be found in Kevin K. Gaines, *Uplifting the Race: Black Leadership, Politics, and Culture in the Twentieth Century* (Chapel Hill: University of North Carolina Press, 1996), 120–127.

63. Robert Hill, "Introduction," in *Philosophy and Opinions of Marcus Garvey,* ed. Amy Jacques Garvey (New York: Atheneum, 1992), lxxxiv.

64. George L. Mosse, *Nationalism and Sexuality: Middle-Class Morality and Sexual Norms in Modern Europe* (Madison: University of Wisconsin Press, 1985). Refer also to Andrew Parker et al., eds., *Nationalisms and Sexualities* (New York: Routledge, 1992); Margaret Jolly, "Motherlands? Some Notes on Women and Nationalism in India and Africa," *Australian Journal of Anthropology* 5, nos. 1–2 (Winter–Spring 1994): 41–59; Nilanjana Chatterjee and Nancy E. Riley, "Planning an Indian Modernity: The Gendered Politics of Fertility Control," *Signs* 26, no. 3 (Spring 2001): 811–845; and Jennifer A. Nelson, "'Abortions under Community Control': Feminism, Nationalism, and the Politics of Reproduction among New York City's Young Lords," *Journal of Women's History* 13, no. 1 (Spring 2001): 157–180. A complex statement on the complex relationship between feminisms, ethnicities, and nationalisms is Daiva K. Stasiulis, "Relational Positionalities of Nationalisms, Racisms, and Feminisms," in *Between Woman and Nation: Nationalisms, Transnational Feminisms, and the State,* ed. Caren Kaplan, Norma Alarcon, and Minoo Moallem (Durham, NC: Duke University Press, 1999), 182–218.

65. Floya Anthias and Nira Yuval-Davis, "Introduction," in *Woman-Nation-State,* 1–15,

esp. 7–8. In addition to acknowledging that "reproduction" refers to a range of processes (childbearing, material production, maintenance of citizenry, replication of "national" groups), Yuval-Davis and Anthias offer a theoretical etymology of "reproduction" as an analytical term that is worth quoting at length: "A word of caution is necessary in relation to the use of the term 'reproduction.' We consider this concept as problematic on more than one ground. First of all, its use in the literature includes many and indeed inconsistent meanings, from a definition of women's biological role to explanations of the existence of social systems over time.... Even more importantly, the term 'reproduction' has been criticised as being tautological on the one hand, often implicitly assuming that 'reproduction' takes place, and static on the other hand, therefore unable to explain growth, decline, and transformation processes" (ibid., 7–8). I view reproduction as dynamic, as a means through which people, households, identities, and "race" are both created and maintained. See Michele Mitchell, "Commentary," *Cuban Studies* 33 (2002): 124–128.

66. Such work has been under way for some time and includes E. Frances White, "Africa on My Mind: Gender, Counterdiscourse, and African American Nationalism," *Journal of Women's History* 2, no. 1 (Spring 1990): 73–97; Wahneema Lubiano, "Black Nationalism and Black Common Sense: Policing Ourselves and Others," in *The House That Race Built: Black Americans, U.S. Terrain*, ed. Wahneema Lubiano (New York: Pantheon, 1997), 232–252; Summers, "Nationalism, Race Consciousness, and the Constructions of Black Middle Class Masculinity"; and Tracye Ann Matthews, "'No One Ever Asks What a Man's Place in the Revolution Is': Gender and Sexual Politics in the Black Panther Party, 1966–1971" (Ph.D. diss., University of Michigan, Ann Arbor, 1998).

67. George M. Fredrickson, *The Black Image in the White Mind: The Debate on Afro-American Character and Destiny, 1817–1914* (New York: Harper and Row, 1971), 251. Refer to John D'Emilio and Estelle B. Freedman's *Intimate Matters: A History of Sexuality in America* (New York: Harper and Row, 1988) for further analysis of race and sexuality.

68. Mariana Valverde, "'When the Mother of the Race Is Free': Race, Reproduction, and Sexuality in First-Wave Feminism," in *Gender Conflicts: New Essays in Women's History*, ed. Franca Iacovetta and Mariana Valverde (Toronto: University of Toronto Press, 1992), 3–26, esp. 4.

69. Nira Yuval-Davis, "Gender and Nation," *Ethnic and Racial Studies* 16 (1993): 621–632, esp. 628.

70. This central movement proclamation was frequently printed in the pages of the *Negro World* and also appeared on parade banners.

8
Black Power Nationalism as Ethnic Pluralism

Postwar Liberalism's Ethnic Paradigm in Black Radicalism

Dean E. Robinson

The most consequential feature of black nationalism in the United States has been not its radical critique of American politics and thought but its *inadvertent reproduction of them.* As I argue in *Black Nationalism in American Politics and Thought,* in its modal form black nationalism is a more conservative than revolutionary force—more the Universal Negro Improvement Association and the Nation of Islam than the African Blood Brotherhood or the Black Panther Party. Drawing on Wilson Moses I argue that "classical" and "modern" black nationalism[1] has tended to take on the shape of its historical container, and that one of its fundamental characteristics is its "apparent inability to diverge from what could be considered the 'normal politics' of its day."[2] For a host of reasons, including government suppression, the forms of black nationalism that have stood on a critique of racial and class inequality have not drawn the greatest numbers, have not enjoyed the longest tenure, and have not had the impact on black politics in the United States that more conservative forms have. Garvey's embrace of racial purity, which Michele Mitchell examines in Chapter 7, and entente with the Ku Klux Klan is an easy example, as is the Nation of Islam's embrace of "black capitalism." This pattern is evident as well even in the mid-1960s to early 1970s period marked by a renewed, insurgent, black nationalist politics, the Black Power era.

Adapted from my book, the two parts of this chapter provide an account of the main expressions of Black Power–era political and economic radicalism that highlights their critical and programmatic subordination to the frameworks of cultural and political pluralism that defined the common sense of postwar American liberalism. I argue as well that this largely unrecognized characteristic has had a significant impact on black politics since the Black Power era. It also continues to shape scholarly reflection on black radicalism in the 1960s and beyond.

Taken as a body of social and political thought, the forms of black nationalism[3] that became prominent in the 1960s offered conceptual innovations that proponents advanced through publications like *The Liberator* and the *Black World* as well as numerous underground publications. Chief among these was the attempt (1) to identify a black nationalist tradition against an integrationist one; (2) to identify the struggle for black equality as akin to anticolonial struggles around the world; and (3) to fashion an epistemology and ontology that broke from American and, more broadly, Western conventions on culture, politics, and economics.[4] Still, excluding the ideas and strategy that understood racial inequality in relation to broader, more fundamental issues of economic inequality, much of what was associated with Black Power ideology rested on an older conceptual scaffolding that Stephen Steinberg calls "the ethnic paradigm."[5]

Where Christianity and civilization once represented the central concepts on which nineteenth- and early-twentieth-century black nationalism rested, modern black nationalism rested on a new set of assumptions: (1) that American culture is purely, or largely, Anglo-Saxon; and (2) that "culture" determines a group's social, political, and economic status in U.S. society. These ideas emerged over the course of the twentieth century to form a residual set of assumptions—a sort of social epistemology—that appeared to explain cultural identity and the processes of acculturation and economic mobility in the United States. Like all ideologies, the ethnic paradigm grew out of the need for people to make sense of social hierarchy in the United States, particularly in a land of immigrants and relatively great economic mobility. Like the civilizationist paradigm of earlier times, the ethnic paradigm rested on a view of social hierarchy according to which the "lower" groups rise and prosper to the extent that they become like those at the "higher" end. The assumptions about higher and lower cultures served as proxies for class and also depended on Victorian, patriarchal (and heterosexual) conceptions of gender and social mores, again not unlike the civilizationist paradigm. Where Christianity and civilization once represented the central concepts on which Anglo-Saxon and Anglo-African nationalism rested, modern black nationalism rested on the ethnic paradigm.

Ethnic paradigmatic assumptions informed the enormous twentieth-century body of thought concerning the culture, assimilation, and upward mobility of the poor, of immigrant groups, and of blacks and other minority populations. There have been a number of theoretical strands—"Anglo-conformity," the "melting pot," and "cultural pluralism."[6] Each strand took shape in the context of high immigration, chiefly from Europe, in the late nineteenth and early twentieth centuries. "Anglo-conformity" was associated with the attempts, draconian in some instances, to get immigrants to conform to an Anglo-Saxon, individualistic, Protestant ethos; and it underlay important studies of assimilation in American life, beginning with the "Chicago school" of sociology. This tradition of scholarship informed policy and thinking about assimilation for much of the past century. As we will consider later, the Chicago school also influenced the "culture of poverty" perspective that became central to public policy debates during the 1960s. This theory held that "cultural traits" of the poor themselves—evident in family structure—reproduced poverty independent of, or largely independent of, political and economic factors.

Melting pot and cultural pluralist theories had a more democratic core: Melting pot theorists focused on cultural exchange between immigrants and the mainstream; cultural pluralists highlighted and defended the preservation of tradition, language, and customs of the Old World. Cultural pluralists have therefore historically opposed both the Anglo-conformist and melting pot perspectives. Nevertheless, these terms—*Anglo-conformity, melting pot,* and *cultural pluralism*—are not mutually exclusive. Scholars and commentators often wove analyses beholden to more than one of these perspectives. All were subsumed by the ethnic paradigm.

ANGLO-CONFORMITY

When black nationalists challenged integration they rejected the tradition of thought and practice known as "Anglo-conformity." The basic assumption that has united Anglo-conformist views and policy is that Americans should maintain English institutions, speak the English language, and follow "English-oriented patterns as dominant in American life."[7] In some senses, Anglo-conformity predated American independence; however, although the idea that American political institutions and values reflect inherent Anglo-Saxon traits is an old one, the notion that people could adopt Anglo-Saxon cultural patterns had its origins in the early part of the twentieth century.

Since that time, Anglo-conformity has ranged from biological notions about Aryan supremacy to arguments that immigrant populations should adopt "standard Anglo-Saxon cultural patterns."[8] Anglo-conformity arguably reached its most fevered pitch during the Americanization movement of the World War I period, and it was organizationally and politically represented in the Ku Klux Klan of that period. Federal agencies like the Bureau of Education, the Bureau of Naturalization, and the Committee on Public Information, state and city governments, and numerous private organizations encouraged immigrants to learn English, pursue citizenship and join the war effort.[9] Private groups like the Daughters of the American Revolution, the Society of Colonial Dames, and the Sons of the American Revolution worked to design educational programs that would teach immigrants about American political institutions and about the naturalization process. The business and industrial community also attempted to educate and indoctrinate immigrants along Anglo-conformist lines. A typical statement of Anglo-conformist sentiment went as follows: "Broadly speaking, we mean ... an appreciation of the institutions of this country, absolute forgetfulness of all obligations or connections with other countries because of descent or birth."[10]

THE CHICAGO SCHOOL OF SOCIOLOGY

Anglo-conformity subsumed a tradition of sociological scholarship unrivaled in its impact on popular and academic thinking about ethnic group assimilation—the process through which immigrants adopt the customs, values, and social institutions of a particular society. Beginning in the second decade of the twentieth century, sociologists affiliated with the University of Chicago offered perspectives on urban ecology (see Smith, chapter 6) and assimilation that rejected the racism and xenophobia that marked the era in which they operated. By so doing, they contributed to an intellectual climate that was more open to the incorporation of immigrants into American life.

Nevertheless, the sociologists at the University of Chicago understood assimilation in Anglo-conformist ways, and they advanced a general method that influenced academic thinking about assimilation for the better part of the twentieth century. The Chicago school's methodological innovations included the following: First, in contrast to earlier "biologically" oriented approaches to racial differences, the Chicago approach emphasized the significance of culture and descent.[11] "'Culture' in this formulation included such diverse factors as religion, language, 'customs,' nationality, and political identification."[12] Second, they emphasized conflict and interaction among human groups. Beginning with W. I. Thomas, Robert E. Park, and Ernest Burgess, the Chicago school's fundamental framework emphasized social interactions as a dynamic process—a cycle of assimilation. The cycle involved a number of stages, including contact, competition, accommodation, and ultimately assimilation and amalgamation. Park and his student Louis Wirth identified ethnic enclaves as representative of one of the phases of the assimilation cycle. Assimilation and amalgamation occurred for immigrant groups of European stock; however, the phenotypical differences of blacks, "Orientals," and other racial minority groups thwarted their assimilation. Finally, this school of thought deemphasized the significance of politics and class as it affected the culture, assimilation, and socioeconomic mobility of immigrant groups.[13] And rather than understanding "culture," "race," and class as social and political constructions, they took these categories to be fairly fixed, if not natural.

A number of key concepts grew out of their general methodological approach. Imperfect assimilation created the "marginal man"; such an individual straddled more than one set of cultural traditions. Jews and mulattos were the prototypes, but the term also applied to plantation blacks, Eurasians, mestizos, and the Cajuns of Louisiana. Park's student Everett V. Stonequist provided the most elaborate theory of the marginal man in his book *The Marginal Man: A Study in Personality and Culture Contact* (1937).

Another Chicago theme has special relevance to discourse about ethnicity and culture during this century—that of "disorganization" and the related notion of "demoralization." W. I. Thomas and Florian Znanieki characterized disorganization as the process whereby "the influence of existing social rules of behavior upon individual members of the group" decreases.[14] Disorganization could lead to "demoralization," which in turn seemed to take the form of a lack of discipline, criminality, and disrespectful attitudes, especially evident among second generation immigrants. Thomas and Znanieki identified this apparent phenomenon by comparing Old World and immigrant Poles in *The Polish Peasant* (1918). The notion of disorganization pivoted "on a premise that a hierarchy of norms of social behavior exists and is discernable." Deviance from those norms impeded assimilation and allegedly promoted dysfunction.

Another legacy of the Chicago school method was the tendency to draw analogies between European peasants and rural blacks. Classifying rural black Americans as peasants carried a number of implications. One was that it allowed the sociologists to apply the same concepts to blacks as they did to European immigrants. Another was that comparisons between migrant blacks and European immigrants minimized the particular forms of discrimination that blacks confronted.

Of the black sociologists connected to the Chicago school, E. Franklin Frazier was of special significance.[15] His studies of the "Negro family" focused heavily on the themes of assimilation and "disorganization." He argued, for instance, that the rampant "disorganization" of black families in northern cities—evident in rates of illegitimacy, family desertion, juvenile delinquency, and so forth—resulted from the erosion of the folk culture of the rural community during the process of urban migration.[16]

No scholars associated with this school made assimilation their primary focus of study; and scholars even not directly connected to the Chicago school would reproduce this analytical weakness. Park and Burgess, for instance, characterized assimilation as an exchange of culture between majority and minority populations.[17] They "also defined assimilation as the process by which the culture of a country was transmitted to its adopted citizens." Without acknowledging any sense of inconsistency, Park and Burgess offered both Anglo-conformist and melting pot–type definitions of assimilation.[18] Another product of Chicago's Department of Sociology, Edward Bryrn Reuter, characterized assimilation as "the incorporation and conversion into the substance of the assimilating body."[19]

"Assimilation" remained broadly defined through the 1940s, 1950s, and 1960s. Brewton Berry, for instance, suggests that "by assimilation we mean the *process whereby groups with different cultures come to have a common culture.*"[20] In his 1956 text *Sociology: The Study of Human Relations,* Arnold Rose defined assimilation as "the adoption by a person or group of the culture of another social group to such a complete extent that the person or group no longer has any characteristics identifying him with his former culture."[21]

Perhaps the most important study of acculturation in the 1960s, Milton Gordon's *Assimilation in American Life* (1964), noted that "if there is anything in American life which can be described as an over-all American culture which serves as a reference point for immigrants and their children, it can best be described, it seems to us, as the middle-class cultural patterns of, largely, white Protestant, Anglo-Saxon origins."[22] For Gordon, assimilation has occurred when an ethnic group (1) has changed its cultural patterns to match those of the majority; (2) has taken on primary group relationships with the majority; (3) has intermarried and interbred fully with the majority; (4) has developed a sense of peoplehood, or nationality, or ethnicity that matches that of the majority population; (5) has "reached a point where they encounter no prejudiced attitudes"; and (6) does not raise demands relating to matters of "value and power conflict with the original group."[23]

Despite the ambiguity around the concept of "assimilation," scholars typically defined blacks as cultural outsiders. In his introduction to Johnson's *In the Shadow of the Plantation,* Robert E. Park offered commentary indicative of this tendency:

> It is very curious that anyone in America should still think of the Negro, even the Negro peasant of the "black belts," as in any sense an alien or stranger, since he has lived here longer than most of us, has interbred to a greater extent than the white man with the native Indian, and is more completely a product than anyone of European origin is likely to be of the local conditions under which he was born and bred ... There is, nevertheless, a sense in which the Negro, even culturally be he a purely native product, is not assimilated, though in just what sense this is true it is difficult to say.[24]

Edward Byron Reuter casually remarked that "the assimilation of the Negroes by the European culture went on with remarkable ease and unusual rapidity. The individual Negroes were highly plastic and the external conditions were highly favorable."[25] Reuter also noted that "the participation of the Negroes in the group life was always limited and their assimilation of the culture values correspondingly retarded and imperfect. *Even today there are many Negroes who are not in the European culture.*"[26]

Frazier's insistence that blacks had lost all ties to African culture and traditions suggests that he viewed black Americans as assimilated.[27] Although "distinguished from other racial or cultural minorities the Negro is not distinguished by culture from the dominant group." Slowly, he wrote, "the Negro, like the European immigrant has acquired the manners and customs of America."[28] Frazier also found that middle-class blacks had "no cultural roots in either the Negro or white world."[29]

Gordon argued that cultural assimilation differed within the black population according to class standing. In a footnote Gordon asserts,

> Although few, if any, African cultural survivals are to be found among American Negroes, lower-class Negro life with its derivations from slavery, post–Civil War discrimination, both rural and urban poverty, and enforced isolation from the middle-class white world, is still at considerable distance from the American cultural norm. Middle- and upper-class Negroes, on the other hand, are acculturated to American core culture.[30]

MODERN BLACK NATIONALIST THEORY ON ASSIMILATION

Many black nationalists, like Maulana Ron Karenga and, for a time, Amiri Baraka, and others rejected assimilation both as an analytic concept and as a goal of social policy and argued for cultural and political pluralism. As an analytic tool, the model was defective, wholly inapplicable to black people and other "racial" minorities. White Americans were not interested in assimilating blacks into American life, and hence the analogy between blacks and European immigrants was fundamentally flawed. In fact, such an analogy belittled the intensity and duration of discrimination, racial bigotry, and disenfranchisement that black Americans had faced. Plus, the idea that groups became increasingly Anglo-American did not seem to explain black cultural uniqueness.

Moreover, during the 1960s and 1970s black nationalists argued that blacks should resist assimilation. As history demonstrated, Anglo-conformity, embodied in Protestant Christianity and U.S. political institutions, was linked to materialism, racism, and exploitation. Why should blacks care to embrace these values? Certainly the most voluminous articulations of the antiassimilationist perspective flowed from the pens of those associated with the Black Arts movement and appeared in publications like *Umbra, Black World, Journal of Black Poetry, Soulbook, Nommo, Dialogue, Black Collegian, Black Expressions,* and *Black Books Bulletin.*[31]

Nevertheless, modern black nationalist theory was no less loose in its formulations of black culture and assimilation than were other theoretical perspectives. Elijah Muhammad, neo-Garveyite Carlos Cooks (of the African Nationalist Pioneer Movement),[32] Maulana (Ron) Karenga, Amiri Baraka, and others were undecided on the question of black assimilation. For most nationalists, blacks were assimilated enough to engage in acts of self-hatred: modifying their looks to conform to a white standard, and desiring to "integrate" into a racist society. Because slavery had stripped black people of their heritage and culture, they had no "knowledge of self." With no knowledge of self, black people did misguided things—used drugs, engaged in crime, and so on. While the specific "knowledge" differed between the Nation of Islam and other nationalist groups, the message was the same. Karenga's cultural nationalistic framework rested on a view of the harmful effects of assimilation, and so his *Kawaida* doctrine—a secular version of Elijah Muhammad's religious teachings—offered a corrective to a population whose ideas and values reflected its Western socialization. His pseudo-African principles included *Umoja* (unity), *Kujichagulia* (self-determination), *Ujima* (collective work and responsibility), *Ujamaa* (cooperative economics), *Nia* (purpose), *Kuumba* (creativity), and *Imani* (faith). These values aided the goal of nation-building by allowing black people to recapture a lost "African" identity.[33]

In contrast, many nationalistic theorists suggested that black culture was already distinct, or somewhat distinct. In the *New York Times Magazine* ("The Case for Two Americas—One Black, One White"), economics professor Robert S. Browne justified his call for racial separatism in response to "a growing ambivalence" among blacks that "arose from the question of whether American Negroes are a cultural group significantly distinct from the majority on an ethnic rather than a socio-economic basis."[34] Carmichael and Hamilton suggested, like Frazier and Gordon, that only a certain stratum of blacks had adopted "mainstream" white culture. Blacks who experienced any social mobility in the United States did so by assimilating into "mainstream" white culture, not unlike the *assimilado* of Mozambique and Angola, who adopted "Portuguese custom, dress, language, and has achieved at least high school education." American society provided "avenues of escape from the ghetto for those individuals who adapt to the 'mainstream.'"[35]

CULTURAL PLURALISM

In its rejection of Anglo-conformity, modern black nationalist theory most closely resembled cultural pluralism, particularly in its later, 1960s manifestations. Jewish scholar Horace Kallen first articulated the classic cultural pluralist position in 1915 in a series of articles published in the *Nation*. In these articles, Kallen rejected the idea of Anglo-conformity both as a prescription for European immigrant assimilation and as a description of what actually happened to immigrant culture. Instead, Kallen highlighted the ways in which ethnic groups preserved their languages, religions, and customs over time. Kallen based his idea on kinship and lineage: "Men may change their clothes, their politics, their wives ... they cannot change their grandfathers."[36]

The cultural pluralist perspective lay dormant until the 1960s, when Nathan Glazer and Daniel Patrick Moynihan offered a new account of ethnic group politics and acculturation. In *Beyond the Melting Pot* (1963), Glazer and Moynihan noticed that ethnic groups both maintained cultural distinctiveness and assimilated American cultural patterns, especially political ones. Yet unlike Kallen, Glazer and Moynihan's concept of "pluralism" was taken from political science. "Pluralism" described the workings of the American political system as one of vying and contending interest groups. "Ethnic group pluralism" wedded political pluralism to cultural pluralism. Glazer and Moynihan argued, somewhat like Kallen, that ethnic identity did not melt. Rather, modified ethnic identities were tied to political behavior. As they explained, "Someone who is Irish or Jewish or Italian generally has other traits than the mere existence of the name that associated him with other people attached to the group. A man is connected to his group by ties of family and friendship. But he is also connected by ties of interest. The ethnic groups of New York are also 'interest groups.'"[37] Still, according to Glazer and Moynihan, some assimilation had occurred:

> The assimilating power of American society and culture operated on immigrant groups in different ways, to make them, it is true, something they had not been, but still something distinct and identifiable ... In the third generation, the descendants of the immigrants confronted each other, and knew they were both Americans, in the same dress, with the same language, using the same artifacts,

troubled by the same things, *but they voted differently, had different ideas about education and sex, and were still, in many essential ways, as different from one another as their grandfathers had been.*[38]

But Glazer and Moynihan's study didn't explain only how and why ethnic identities failed to melt. These authors also attempted to explain social mobility and political power as a function of cultural traits and familial patterns. The Irish had not prospered as much as, say, the Jews, because of their propensity toward alcoholism. Catholicism explained both Irish success in the political process and Irish failure to achieve the same sort of socioeconomic mobility that Jewish Americans had acquired.[39] Moreover, the form of "individuality and ambition" characteristic of Protestant and Anglo-Saxon culture was absent among Italian Americans. Jews prospered partly because of their thirst for education. Marital breakup was less common among Jews, and the Jewish parents' control of their children resulted in significant "neurosis" but "less psychosis."[40]

Blacks, by contrast, had been crippled by slavery. The peculiar institution weakened black family structure, and that weakness had important effects. One was that blacks lacked the clannishness that other ethnic groups had used to create and sustain separate economic markets and clientele. The relatively large number of female-headed households also increased the chance of psychological difficulties among black boys. Despite the many social problems that afflicted Afro-Americans, "the middle-class Negro contributes little, in money, organization, or involvement, to the solution" of these problems.[41]

Moynihan expanded the thesis of black familial pathology in his controversial *The Negro Family: The Case for National Action* (1965). Drawing on Frazier's studies of social disorganization among black families, Moynihan suggested that slavery, Jim Crow, continuing disparities in employment opportunities (especially for males) and income, as well as grinding poverty forced "the Negro community" into a matriarchal family structure. This structure, Moynihan contended, "seriously retards the progress of the groups as a whole, and imposes a crushing burden on the Negro male and, in consequence, on a great many Negro women as well."[42] Thus assigning a range of statistical patterns—work and educational achievement, crime and delinquency—to one source, matriarchy, Moynihan could declare, "The present tangle of pathology is capable of perpetuating itself without assistance from the white world."[43]

While focused on the urban rebellions of the period, *The Kerner Report* (1968) also linked the lack of black mobility partly to family structure among blacks. "Cultural factors ... made it easier for the immigrants to escape from poverty." Their "families were large, and ... patriarchal ... so men found satisfactions in family life that helped compensate for the bad jobs they had to take and the hard work they had to endure." Blacks, by contrast, "came to the city under quite different circumstances." Because of slavery and unemployment, "the Negro family structure had become matriarchal," thus providing fewer "cultural and psychological rewards" to the black man.[44]

In light of the reigning theories about culture, family structure, dysfunction, and mobility, it should not be entirely surprising that nationalist calls for "manhood" were linked to demands for female subordination and patriarchal family structures. The Nation of Islam was the best example of this tendency, with extreme gender segregation in school and mosque, and with middle-class, nuclear (and strictly heterosexual) standards of family life; but cultural and revolutionary organizations operated on similar assumptions of patriarchy, sexuality, and gender subordination. That most black nationalist organizations saw a rehabilitated "manhood" as essential to black progress and esteem shows the extent to which their ideas fit within a broader constellation of American social and political thought.[45]

Like Glazer and Moynihan, black nationalists of the 1960s and 1970s linked disparities in wealth, income, and social stability to weak efforts on the part of black people themselves. Neo-Garveyite Carlos Cooks and onetime Nation of Islam minister Malcolm X, for instance, offer similar versions of this perspective. Cooks complained that blacks failed to prosper in a predominantly black Harlem, while Jews, Chinese, Italian, Irish, and "other minorities" had utilized all the advantages of the system and simultaneously retained "an affinity with the old sod."[46]

Malcolm X offered a similar analysis in an October 1963 speech at Berkeley. Still representing the Nation of Islam, Malcolm X took this occasion to explain the causes and meaning of rising racial tensions. He also spoke about the conditions that led to the problems poor blacks faced in the United States. For my purposes, the most interesting aspect of this talk was a response he gave during the question-and-answer period. A member of the audience asked how descendants of immigrants had come to develop prejudicial attitudes, even though their parents and grandparents had faced virulent xenophobia. Malcolm X responded by suggesting that "modern slavery"—by which he meant patterns of white exploitation of blacks—perpetuated racial prejudice. Because black people occupied the bottom tier of the socioeconomic ladder—again, as a result of white supremacy—white people could easily "blame the victim" and develop a set of ideas to justify their attitudes. Yet Malcolm X also took the opportunity to expound on the failure of black leadership to do what other ethnic leadership had done: "*The mistake that we made differs from the mistake you didn't make. Your parents solved your problems economically, of their own volition, with their own ingenuity. Our leaders have done nothing to teach us how to go in business. They have done nothing to teach us how to elevate the levels of our schools.*"[47]

Rather than responding in the way one might expect—"numerous discriminatory practices frustrated efforts of black entrepreneurs to create viable businesses," for example, or "white ethnic groups deliberately kept Afro-Americans out of their unions"—Malcolm X, like Glazer and Moynihan, identified black leaders as a large part of the problem. Since black American leadership had not encouraged the development of black businesses and had not adequately stressed the importance of education, blacks had been unable to achieve the gains of other groups. Hence, from Malcolm X's perspective, black Americans had failed to do what other "ethnic" groups had done.

BLACKS AS CULTURAL OUTSIDERS

Through his entire public career, novelist and essayist Ralph Ellison repeatedly insisted that the view of blacks as alien to American culture was inaccurate. In an essay published in *Time* magazine in 1971, Ellison argued that those who would rid America of its black inhabitants never stop to "imagine what the United States would have been, or not been, had there been no blacks to give it—if I may be so bold as to say—color."[48] The short answer is "nothing recognizably American." The long answer takes us through a complex and certainly underappreciated story of political, economic, and cultural history in the United States, which bears a decidedly Afro-American stamp. From the patterns and style of American colloquial speech to jazz, rock 'n' roll, and hip-hop in the contemporary period, blacks have influenced American popular culture (the latter point is thoroughly developed in William Jones, chapter 3). Without blacks, U.S. economic and political history would have been different. "No slave economy, no Civil War; no violent destruction of the Reconstruction; no K.K.K. and no Jim Crow system." Without the disenfranchisement of black Americans and the "manipulation of racial fears," southern politicians would not have enjoyed the disproportionate power they have enjoyed over domestic policy. "Indeed," Ellison wrote, "it is almost impossible to conceive of what our political system would have become without the snarl of forces—cultural, racial, religious—that make our nation what it is today."[49]

Ellison's observations contrast sharply with Anglo-conformist theory in general and the Chicago school version in particular. Anglo-conformist theory assumes that "out-groups" assimilate into a fundamentally Anglo cultural milieu. While it is true that an Anglo tradition has profoundly influenced American culture, that same Anglo tradition evolved in response to uniquely American demographic, economic, and intellectual trends. Further, from any angle one approaches the matter of American culture, one must conclude that it is part Afro-American.

Ellison's theory contrasts in the same way with black nationalist theory of the 1960s and early 1970s. Through the black nationalist lens of this period, American culture was Anglo, Protestant, and white. By definition, blacks were cultural outsiders, and their culture was defective. But again, the ambiguous and even arbitrary constructions of black culture, consciousness, and aesthetics—from the US organization to the Black Arts movement—suggest that cultural identity sprang not from organic sources but was self-consciously constituted. After all, "racial," "ethnic," and "cultural" categories ultimately result from social and political practice. Further, while we can easily speak of, say, different linguistic patterns or dietary patterns among immigrant populations of specific times in specific places, "culture" is under constant transformation, shaped again by dynamics of modern capitalism.

Aside from its interpretive error—that of conceiving U.S. culture in wholly inadequate "black" and "white" terms—the idea that black people are cultural outsiders has been offered as an explanation for their unequal status and relative lack of socioeconomic mobility. The style of thought that Stephen Steinberg calls "New Darwinism" holds that different cultural attributes resulted in different rates of success for white ethnic groups. The required values, according to Steinberg, "are familiar to anyone who has heard Benjamin Franklin's homilies or read Horatio Alger novels—frugality, industry, foresight, perseverance, ingenuity, and the like."[50]

But culture did not and does not explain mobility and its opposite. As Steinberg persuasively argues, pre-immigration factors—skills, literacy, or lack thereof—more effectively explain different rates of upward mobility among, say, Irish, Italians, and Jews than does culture. For instance, at the height of European immigration, the vast majority of Jewish immigrants were classified as skilled laborers. Conversely, Irish and Italian immigrants were overwhelmingly unskilled laborers. This fact alone would give Jewish immigrants some advantage in the U.S. labor market. Concerning blacks, Steinberg points to patterns of housing discrimination, job discrimination, and poor education to explain why blacks have not kept pace with other "ethnic" groups.[51] Glazer and Moynihan completely ignored such factors and focused instead on alleged group behaviors that were thought to separate European immigrant populations.

Thus, when nationalists like Maulana (Ron) Karenga, and others argued about the cultural distinctiveness of black people, they followed an old script, modified by a new political and intellectual landscape. For example, a proponent of the Black Arts movement, Barbara Ann Teer, identified black culture in "the way we talk (the rhythms of our speech which naturally fit our impulses), the way we walk, sing, dance, pray, laugh, eat, make love, and finally ... the way we look, make up our cultural heritage."[52] More sophisticated arguments suggested that "a unique and particular way of being" was born out of "the conditioning of black people leasing time on a planet controlled by white men."[53] But in suggesting that the "black way" was opposed to the "white way," nationalists buttressed essentialist claims about black identity, ones that ultimately simplified a more complex political and economic story.

For Black Power–era nationalists, it appeared that a template for ethnic politics existed in urban America. After all, the history of city politics was the history of ethnic politics. Robert Dahl's important *Who Governs?* (1961) identified ethnic politics as a sort of phase of urban political development. According to Dahl, ethnic politics provided the means by which immigrants and children of immigrants were assimilated into U.S. society, politically and economically. For much of the twentieth century, Dahl noted, "ethnic" politicians—by which he meant those descendants of European immigration—had sought to win votes "by conferring divisible benefits on individuals ... according to ethnic criteria."[54] More important, "ethnicity" had deep and lasting significance in politics, because it had deep and lasting significance in American society. Unlike other advanced industrial democracies, where class represented the fault line, "ethnic characteristics" seemed to supersede class in the United States. This "ethnic awareness of identification" was created not by politicians but "by the whole social system." Ethnic similarities," Dahl wrote, "are palpable reality, built into the everyday awareness of the ethnic from early childhood to old age. Nor are they always subordinate to socioeconomic ones."[55] Dahl wrote at a time when the story of urban politics *appeared* to match his description.

For the range of activists during the middle to late 1960s and the 1970s that might be described as "black nationalist," the Irish case was especially noteworthy. As Steven Erie notes in his study *Rainbow's End: Irish-Americans and the Dilemmas of Urban Machine Politics, 1840–1985* (1988), the Irish enjoyed great success as ethnic machine bosses, and used control of governmental to provide access to public sector jobs.

Not surprisingly, then, "Irish power" served as a blueprint for Black Power, as by the late 1960s black people were poised to assume a more significant role in city politics across the country. The conditions were especially ripe in northern cities. By virtue of black migration to northern cities and white flight, black people could rightly expect greater influence in electoral politics.

The protest and unrest of the late 1960s and early 1970S had the effect of increasing black representation in institutions of all sorts—from mayoral offices and city councils to social welfare agencies run by federal, state, and local governments. From 1970 to 1974, the number of black-led municipal regimes increased, as did the number of blacks working in housing authorities, redevelopment agencies, and welfare departments. Much of the increase in black employment "can be traced to the Great Society, either in terms of legislative initiatives (Medicare, Medicaid, public housing, manpower training) or in terms of such as the massive expansion of preexisting programs, such as AFDC, due to the political climate created by the declaration of the national anti-poverty objective."[56] This significance of War on Poverty programs to black politics of the 1960s and 1970s cannot be understated. When Congress created the Office of Economic Opportunity (OEO) in 1964, it transformed city politics across the country by establishing thousands of community action agencies "designed to give low-income Americans an opportunity to identify, design, plan, and initiate their own priorities and emphases in more than a thousand communities across the nation."[57] These agencies were created to provide services to low-income and minority groups; some of the OEO's noteworthy programs included Head Start, Upward Bound, VISTA, Legal Services, the Job Corps, and the Neighborhood Youth Corps.[58]

At base, the federal government's War on Poverty started with conservative assumptions about the sources of, and solutions to, poverty in the United States. One was the view that, in large part, poverty resulted from attributes of individuals or groups. A common view of the time held that poor people (and groups) suffered from a "culture of poverty"—an allegedly debilitating set of behaviors and attitudes thought to constrain the actions of the poor, independent of, say, business cycles or structural shifts in the economy. "Citizen participation" was thought to be the cure, as War on Poverty soldiers hoped to increase poor people's participation in projects that would counter their sense of helplessness and hopelessness. This view was explicit. Consider, for instance, text of the *Community Action Program Guide:* "The long-range objective of every community action program is to effect a permanent increase in the capacity of individuals, groups, and communities afflicted by poverty to deal effectively with their own problems so that they need no further assistance. Poverty is a condition of need, helplessness and hopelessness."[59]

This focus on alleged individual attributes conformed to a second notion about poverty and economic matters that united Republicans and Democrats during the postwar period. Godfrey Hodgson and Alan Wolfe discuss these ideas in their *America in Our Time* (1976) and *America's Impasse: The Rise and Fall of the Politics of Growth* (1981), respectively. The "liberal consensus" (for Hodgson) and "pro-growth ideology" (for Wolfe) held, in part, that the solution to social problems like poverty lay in an expanding economy, a perspective that offered a smoother and more harmonious solution than struggles over issues of redistribution. As Wolfe argues, speedy economic growth would "expand the pie sufficiently, so it would not have to be cut in a different way."[60]

In the 1960s and 1970s, federal government plans for economic development of poor neighborhoods conformed to this vision. As a first step, the Economic Development Administration (EDA) was established in 1965 to "encourage economic development in certain 'lagging communities' throughout the country." EDA, a federal agency under the Department of Commerce, offered public works grants and loans, business loans, and grants for technical assistance. The average loan in fiscal 1969 was $1,004,000. For smaller amounts, EDA referred borrowers to the Small Business Administration—the first agency that would "attempt to promote minority economic development."[61]

Notions of citizen participation and economic development dovetailed. Across the political spectrum, politicians reasoned that economic development would ultimately lift individuals out of poverty.[62] Robert Kennedy's remarks in 1966 demonstrate how citizen participation meshed with ideas about economic development:

> The measure of the success of this or any program will be the extent to which it helps the ghetto become a community—a functional unit, its people acting together on matters of mutual concern, with the power and the resources to affect the conditions of their own lives. Therefore, the heart of the program, I believe, should be the creation of community development corporations [CDCs] which would carry out the work of construction, the hiring and training of workers, the provision of service.[63]

President Richard Nixon's Executive Order No. 11458, which created the Office of Minority Business Enterprise, expressed a related perspective: "I have often made the point," Nixon declared, "that to foster the economic status and pride of members of our minority groups, we must seek to involve them more fully in our private enterprise system." "Involvement in business," he reasoned, "has always been a major route toward participation in the mainstream of American life."[64]

Many commentators of that time noted the limitations of War on Poverty efforts, including insufficient funding and its failure to facilitate meaningful participation by the nation's poor. More fundamentally, critics also challenged the idea of economic development, or growth, as a solution to enduring economic inequality, noting that questions about the distribution of vital resources, principally income and wealth, were fundamental to the problem of poverty and that, further, macroeconomic policies, not insufficient social services, were what drove the production and reproduction of poverty.

CITIZEN PARTICIPATION AS COMMUNITY CONTROL

In this period of fertile, if failed, political and economic effort, black nationalism/ Black Power had its comparable agenda. In the language of Black Power ideology "citizen participation" submerged and came up as "community control." In his *Model Cities* (1970), Alan A. Altshuler characterizes community control in the following manner:

> (1) devolution of as much authority as possible to neighborhood communities; (2) direct representation of such communities on the city council, the board of education, the police commission, and other significant policy bodies; (3) black representation at all levels of the public service in far more than token numbers; (4) similar representation on the labor forces of government contractors; and (5) the vigorous application of public resources to facilitate the development of black-controlled businesses.[65]

Stokely Carmichael and Charles Hamilton's *Black Power* (1967) can almost be read as a blueprint for community control. Carmichael and Hamilton started with the notion that the political arena in the United States was one of competing ethnic groups, and they also offered suggestions for how black Americans could ensure self-determination despite their "colonial subject" status. Before a group could "enter the open society, it must first close ranks.... By this we mean that group solidarity is necessary before a group can operate effectively from a bargaining position of strength in a pluralistic society."[66] As a necessary component of this "closed ranks" strategy, the authors pointed to the need for black people to "lead and run their own organizations. Only black people can convey the revolutionary idea—and it is a revolutionary idea—that black people are able to do things themselves." Black people, put simply, needed more control over institutions that affected their lives. Black police officers would end police brutality. A black board of revenue could "channel tax monies for the building of better road and schools serving black people." Indeed, black people had to do what other ethnic groups had done: Traditionally, each new ethnic group had "found the route to social and political viability through the organization of its own institutions with which to represent its needs within the larger society."[67]

Black-Power-as-community-control informed the efforts of black people in cities across the country. Yet their demand for community control derived not from Carmichael and Hamilton's treatise but rather from observing the failures of school systems, social service agencies, and "urban renewal" plans, as well as the limitations of War on Poverty projects. In cities across the country, Black Power advocates thus worked to reorient the institutions most central to the daily lives of black people—schools, hospitals, government agencies, and city councils—in a way that would bring the goals of these crucial institutions in line with the needs of the black population.

The battles over school control provide a good example. City governments had not equalized resources between wealthier and poorer city schools. Further, from the standpoint of many Black Power advocates, schools taught black children how to be "white." That is, they failed to offer a curriculum that reflected the emerging sense of black consciousness. Commenting on the dramatic, bitter, and tumultuous battle raging in Harlem in the late 1960s, Albert Vann, principal of P.S. 271 in New York, explained that "'The Man' is not going to give these values to us," but rather that "they have to be earned by a new kind of black man that we don't have yet. His values are going to have to be different."[68] Schools like the African Free School of Newark, Uhuru Sasa in Brooklyn, and Boston's Roxbury Community School were schools that tried to instill a certain type of black consciousness into their pupils.

BLACK CAPITALISM

Community control had an economic component, and that was generally known as "black capitalism" or "black economic development." Despite the fact that black capitalism could be tied to non-nationalistic agendas, black-run businesses were central to the strategies of numerous nationalist groups. Even before the idea of creating black-run businesses gained national attention under Nixon, groups like the Nation of Islam had achieved relative success in establishing a number of businesses in cities across the country.[69] Indeed, by the early 1960s the Nation of Islam was the most successful black business of that period, with restaurants, hair salons, and other enterprises.

By the mid-1960s, the Congress of Racial Equality (CORE)—an organization that for years supported the more modest goal of civil rights—was supporting black nationalism as a strategic orientation. Black capitalism was not, according to then head of the organization, Roy Innis, a matter of the government creating or opening jobs for black people. Nor did black capitalism mean inviting white corporations into ghettos in order to create jobs. Rather, capitalism was tied to the project of nation-building, in the sense of greater political sovereignty for blacks as a collective. "A modern nation," Innis explained, "becomes viable through the creation of capital instruments. We can't make money through jobs. You make money through owning capital instruments: land and other properties."[70]

The first step in securing capital instruments involved controlling various institutions in inner cities—community control. Innis was part of the failed effort to pass the Community Development Act. The key institution set up by the act, the Community Development Corporation, "was to be a private profit-making corporation operating in a poor urban or rural area. Any resident of the area sixteen or over could buy a share in the corporation at par value of five dollars."[71]

Economist Robert S. Browne had another plan for capitalist development. With a gift of $1 million from a benefactor, Browne launched three associated institutions: the Black Economic Research Center, the Emergency Land Fund, and the Twenty-first Century Foundation. According to Browne, these organizations shared the goal of "encouraging and supporting those efforts which will extend the area of black economic independence in the hope that some far off day there will have developed an array of financially independent black institutions which can fund the needs of the black community without reliance on sympathetic whites or on special government programs."[72]

The idea of black economic development was the main goal of an organization called NEGRO (National Economic Growth and Reconstruction Organization). NEGRO was originally established in "the early sixties as the Interfaith Health Association, a nonprofit corporation which owned and operated a 140-bed hospital in Queens." Its aim was to promote "the self-help concept among the Negro people." The president of the organization, Thomas W. Matthew, offered the group's definition of black power. He considered black power to be the "marshaling of all the resources of a particular group." Matthew reasoned that through proper training black people could gain the skills and respect necessary to enter the industrial workforce as other ethnic groups had done. Blacks who had been chronically unemployed lacked the proper attitude and work ethic. Black Power, then, took the form of self-help capitalism. NEGRO's projects included a chemical plant, a paint factory, a metal-fabricating plant, bus companies in Watts and Harlem, a textile firm, and more than six hundred housing units, "many of which had been refurbished by its own Spartacus Construction Company." By the summer of 1968, NEGRO had more than seven hundred employees.[73]

Other leaders and groups across the country turned to economic development schemes. Jesse Jackson, as one example, created Operation Breadbasket to "feed the poor and to create black business." The Rochester-based militant organization FIGHT built an electronics plant. And in Los Angeles, "a group of unemployed blacks was running a toy factory making dolls." Xerox helped the FIGHT organization, while General Electric invested $250,000 in the toy factory.[74]

POLITICS

Community control had political implications. Amiri Baraka's efforts were most notable in this regard. By the mid-1960s, Amiri Baraka was a well-established poet and community activist in Newark, New Jersey. Baraka and his Committee for a United Newark (CFUN) were instrumental in electing Newark's first black mayor, Kenneth Gibson. And to the extent that Baraka did have a grassroots constituency during the early 1970s, he was able to exert some pressure on Mayor Gibson.[75] Baraka's vision of the politician's role was clearly informed by the idea that black-run governments could do for blacks what, for instance, Irish-run governments had once done for Irish Americans. Black mayors had to use their power to dispense patronage to benefit blacks. They should hire Afro-Americans to direct the police and fire departments. Blacks should head medical, educational, and social welfare services. For Baraka, success in Newark could serve as a model for cities across the country. During the early 1970s many black nationalists like Baraka had real grassroots political bases, and it was this support that caught the attention of mainline black political officials.[76]

CORE was another black nationalist organization that would have a large impact on electoral politics during the late 1960s. Especially active in Harlem and Cleveland, CORE registered voters in the hope of influencing city elections. CORE's efforts helped Carl Stokes win his mayoral bid in Cleveland in 1968, becoming that city's first black mayor.

NATIONAL CONVENTIONS

Community development, economic development, and electoral strategy were themes addressed in a number of national black nationalist/Black Power conventions during the late 1960s and early 1970s.[77] These conventions all represented efforts by a broad range of nationalists and mainstream politicians to formulate broad social, political, and economic agendas. For my purposes, the conferences are also important because they demonstrate the extent to which notions of ethnic pluralism and progrowth capitalism formed the parameters within which nationalistic agendas were generated.

The first Black Power conference was held in Washington, D.C., in 1966 with the sponsorship of Congressman Adam Clayton Powell; the second was held in 1967 in Newark.[78] The Newark conference was held under the chairmanship of the Reverend Nathan Wright Jr., who was then urban affairs director for the Newark Episcopal Diocese.[79] This conference attracted some two thousand delegates from a variety of political persuasions and came one week after a major riot in Newark had left twenty-six dead.

The delegation was quite diverse, including members of the Nation of Islam and the socialistic Revolutionary Action Movement, "cultural nationalists" of various sorts, younger activists from the Student Nonviolent Coordinating Committee (SNCC) and CORE, black Greek-letter organizations, black student organizations, the Southern Christian Leadership Council (SCLC), the National Association for the Advancement of Colored People (NAACP), Pepsi-Cola, the National Medical Association, and the National Council of Negro Women. The familiar themes of Black Power were evident at the conference. Placards urged black people to "buy black," to support neighborhood credit unions, to pursue cultural autonomy, and to exercise community control of key institutions like school boards. A number of resolutions grew out of this conference. The economic resolutions included such ideas as promoting "buy black" campaigns, establishing neighborhood black credit unions, and establishing a general fund for the creation of nonprofit and cooperative ventures. The political resolutions included plans to generate a Black Power lobby in Washington, D.C.; to work toward tripling the black congressional representation; and to hold a "national grass roots political convention following the conventions of the two major political parties in the same city." Resolutions also proclaimed the right of self-defense and the desire to consider partitioning the United States into separate black and white nations. From Wright's perspective, Black Power as addressed at this conference was informed by the knowledge that "no rising ethnic group in this nation ... has ever asked for integration." The Black Power conference dealt with the two most "pervasive problems of our society—identity and empowerment for fulfillment." According to Wright:

> We had 14 parallel workshops dealing with such subjects as "the City and the Black People, Black Power and American Religion, New Roles for Black Youth, the Black Home, Black Power Through Economic Development," etc.... The conference issued a "Black Power Manifesto" which spoke to the need of setting up regional black-power conferences, and a year hence to hold another national conference. And after that, within 18 months, an international congress of black power.[80]

Like the Black Power Conference, the Congress of African Peoples attracted activists and groups committed to some idea of nationalism and/or pan-Africanism. We should note, in both cases, that more mainstream politicians and activists were attracted to nationalist rhetoric partly because "militants" appeared to wield increasing power over informal constituencies. Not surprisingly, then, even at the Congress of African Peoples, individuals like Whitney Young Jr. of the Urban League and Ralph Abernathy of SCLC were in attendance. Amiri Baraka presided at this meeting in Atlanta, in September 1970. The conference drew organizations like the socialist Republic of New Africa, proponents of black art like Haki Madhubuti (Don L. Lee), and intellectuals committed to nationalism like Robert S. Browne and John Henrik Clarke. The conference included workshops on political liberation, social organization, creativity, black technology, religion, education, community organization, law and justice, history, communications, and economics. The primary focus of the gathering was the formation of the Congress of African Peoples (CAP), which "was conceived as a party as well as a united front."[81]

Drawing on U.S. leader Maulana Karenga's *Kawaida* concept, Baraka discussed four areas of political power based on (1) public office (elected or appointed), (2) community organizations, (3) alliances and coalitions, and (4) and disruption (actual or threatened).[82] An independent black political party, according to Baraka, needed to pursue all four strategies. Baraka proposed a number of measures directed toward the final goal of an independent black party, including voter registration, mobilizing black citizens to face racist policy, running candidates who supported the interests of black communities, and establishing alliances with third world governments and movements.[83]

In statements that foreshadowed those proposed at the Gary Convention of 1972, the delegates concluded that the main objective of blacks in the political arena was the formation of a political party. This was clearly spelled out in a statement by the Philadelphia Congress of African Peoples: "A PARTY IS THE FIRST STEP TOWARD BUILDING A NATION. HISTORICAL CIRCUMSTANCES

DICTATE THE NEED FOR FORMING A NATIONAL BLACK POLITICAL PARTY AT HOME."[84]

The proposed black political party would invite a new type of black politician to participate. Further, the black political party would be "involved in community control of institutions such as health, welfare, housing, land, or any struggle deemed important by Black people."[85] Among the Philadelphia CAP's proposals were registering all black people to vote, electing black men and women to every public office, and the freeing of political prisoners, to name a few. Following this convention, CAP grew. Activists eventually established chapters in Chicago, Boston, Albany, San Diego, and many other cities.

Because of its sheer numbers, perhaps no event highlighted the black nationalist and non-nationalist attempts to formulate a common political agenda better than the Gary Convention held in Gary, Indiana, in March 1972. This convention invited some four thousand delegates from forty-five states, though according to participants as many as eight thousand people made the trip.[86] The convention's theme was Unity without Uniformity, and the goal of the delegates was to formulate a national black agenda. The city of Gary, Indiana, was draped in red, black, and green for the occasion.

As at other conferences of this period, black nationalists represented a substantial proportion of the total body of delegates. Amiri Baraka chaired much of the convention and did so in part to mediate any conflicts that developed. A general if inchoate sense of nationalism was expressed in a chant that erupted on many occasions during the convention—"Nation Time!" The hope that the body of delegates would formulate a national black agenda reflected the idea that black people shared a common political destiny.

The *National Black Political Agenda* came out of the Gary Convention and declared that no basic change for the benefit of black people could occur "unless [black people] organize to initiate that change."[87] This document represented the delegates' attempt to formulate some basic agreement on general goals, and it was quite sweeping in its demands: "*The American system does not work for the masses of our people, and it cannot be made to work without radical fundamental change.*"[88] This fundamental change was necessary given the fact that, historically, both political parties had betrayed the interests of black people whenever they had found it necessary. The failure of white liberalism, "unbridled monopoly capitalism," and "ruthless military imperialism" set the stage for the crises affecting black people. Some of the numerous agenda items included reparations for slavery, opposition to busing, proportional representation of blacks in Congress, and national health insurance.[89]

Despite the seeming convergence of nationalist and non-nationalist sentiment,[90] the Gary Convention did reveal important tensions within the general body of delegates. Unity without Uniformity, from our historical vantage point, blurred important conflicts of interest that existed among blacks. Delegates were divided on substantive issues like busing and the Israeli-Arab conflict in the Middle East, as well as strategic matters concerning tactics and leadership.[91]

These cleavages were even more apparent by the time of the second National Black Political Convention, held in Little Rock in 1974. This convention had the same theme, Black Unity without Uniformity, and attracted some two thousand delegates. Unlike the convention at Gary, however, notable politicians and civil rights leaders were absent; many of them had become increasingly uneasy about the nationalists' posture. Even among the members of the steering committee, there was some dissension about the agenda of the convention and the extent to which the nationalist cadre dominated the event. Indeed, Congressman Charles Diggs vacated the presidency of the National Black Political Assembly following the Little Rock convention. Ron Daniels, an avowed nationalist, replaced Diggs.[92]

Out of the Gary meeting, a cultural nationalist group headed by Baraka established the National Black Political Assembly. This organization formed around the same Unity without Uniformity theme, and activists involved hoped to steer elected officials toward a more nationalist agenda and consciousness. There was also great overlap in terms of membership with another organization, the African Liberation Support Committee (ALSC). Both organizations attempted to mark a place for black radicalism in the postsegregation context. ALSC hoped to organize political actions in support of African liberation movements. It arguably had a greater focus on popular mobilization and was less "oriented to building formal relationships with mainstream politicians."[93]

Before we consider the reasons why black nationalism/Black Power of the 1960s looked like the politics of its day, it is worth reiterating a few points. First, the various strategies associated with black nationalism that called for black control of social, political, and economic institutions were not "nationalist" in the strict sense of the term. Second, my generalizations exclude the far-reaching goals of black revolutionary organizations, like, say, the Black Panther Party and the Revolutionary Action Movement, for reasons that will be explored shortly. Minus the revolutionary forms, modern black nationalism looked like ethnic politics both for structural and ideological reasons. Without demands for separate territory, Black Power ideology was close in form to ethnic pluralism. After all, "community control" ultimately meant that blacks ought to have greater representation in various public and private institutions.

BLACK POWER IN THREE CITIES

Brief consideration of the characteristics and development of Black Power politics in New Haven, Cleveland, and St. Louis during the period of roughly the mid-1960s through the early 1970s may illustrate how the practical imperatives of conventional liberal politics operated within and shaped this strain of "nationalist" assertiveness. Black nationalist agendas were advanced and achieved different rates of success in these three cities. Nevertheless, the range of political and economic strategies shows some interesting parallels. In both New Haven and Cleveland far-left nationalist groups were not significant players—mostly because of coercive efforts by law enforcement officials, but also because of the failure of these groups to fashion broad popular support. All three cities had Black Power organizations demanding community control. New Haven had the Hill Parents Association (HPA) led by Robert Harris; and Cleveland and St. Louis had CORE.

Each city had an umbrella organization, informed by a Black Power orientation and generally directed toward community control. New Haven had the Black Coalition; Cleveland had the Operation Black Unity; and St. Louis had the Black United Front. These generalizations do not, of course, tease out the subtle distinctions in strategy and orientation among these various organizations or address differences in local political context. Nevertheless, looking at the three cities together is useful.

In these cities and elsewhere, the threat of urban unrest provided the catalyst for federal action.[94] For much of the 1960s the federal government directed money toward inner cities in the hope of quelling discontent. In the cases we've considered, some black nationalist/Black Power advocates received resources and "status" following these outbreaks. CORE arguably benefited most. Under a $150,000 grant from the Ford Foundation, Cleveland's chapter of CORE started the Target City Project, specifically designed to help end racial tensions on Cleveland's East Side. The Target City Project, which got under way in November 1967, included a "four point program which was to include leadership training, voter education and registration, research in economic development and conferences to focus attention on the problems of the black community."[95] CORE received a second grant from Ford in the amount of $300,000. Indeed, as early as 1961 the Ford Foundation had donated money to projects aimed at quelling urban unrest. As Robert Allen explains:

> From the Foundation's point of view, old-style moderate leaders no longer exercised any real control, while genuine black radicals were too dangerous. CORE fit the bill because its talk about black revolution was believed to appeal to discontented blacks, while its program of achieving black power through massive injections of governmental, business, and Foundation aid seemingly opened the way for continued corporate domination of black communities by means of a new black elite.[96]

Roy Innis's business schemes coincided with the Ford Foundation's funding initiatives. Interestingly, it was also "the Ford Foundation's underwriting of a CORE voter registration project that enabled Stokes to win the Cleveland mayoral election on his second attempt."[97]

Similar events unfolded in other cities. Following a relatively small riot in New Haven in 1967, Yale gave money to the Black Coalition ($100,000) and offered summer jobs to local youth.[98] Local firms started the Urban Alliance of Greater New Haven, a development organization.

The St. Louis–based Danforth Foundation directed funds in "response to the distress and turmoil of the city."[99] Jolly notes that the Danforth Foundation administered in excess of $500,000 between 1968 and 1971. The Ford Foundation provided more than $400,000 over the same period.[100]

The result of these developments, combined with state repression of far-left groups like the Black Panther Party, was that black nationalist/Black Power radicalism was contained, and thus did the nationalistic agenda take its concrete shape. First, public and private institutions directed money toward conventional community control projects. Second, the federal government gave professionals control of most of the antipoverty and development agencies, which in turn employed neighborhood leaders to the exclusion of the more militant, and more radical, groups and individuals. Partly out of their concern to avoid blame for urban unrest, and sometimes because of public outcry, OEO bureaucrats forbade the use of community action funds in connection with militant nationalist activity. Thus, for example, Baraka's short-lived Black Arts Theater was cut off from Harlem's antipoverty agency in 1965. The OEO suspended a summer training program that had employed Ron Karenga in 1967. Nashville's Metropolitan Action Committee in 1967 eliminated the "liberation school" that was staffed by a number of SNCC members.[101] These patterns suggest that the type of black "nationalists" who could take most advantage of the new policies and funding tended to be those already more inclined toward conventional politics, like those working with the HPA and CORE.[102] As the Federal Bureau of Investigation neutralized nationalists on the far left, the structure of urban policy, and the project of electoral strategies, tended to mold Black Power radicalism into ethnic pluralist patterns.

Over time, a cohort of mainstream black functionaries emerged, partly from the ranks of Black Power activists, in federally funded programs like OEO and Model Cites as well as Ford and other foundation-based initiatives.[103] Mainly from this cohort came the stratum of conventional politicians and public officials who, during the 1970s, defined the boundaries and horizons of black American politics.

CONCLUSION

Assessments of the Black Power era are difficult for many reasons, one of which is the ambiguity of the terms "black nationalism" and "Black Power" as they were employed in the 1960s, as well as the multiple ways researchers have understood the concept and its significance for black politics since then. Given these challenges, my work starts with the view that black American politics and thought is a subset of American politics and thought. Although black nationalist activists were inspired by anticolonial struggles around the globe, activists drew on theories, and confronted challenges, born on American soil. Nationalists/Black Power proponents ultimately faced uniquely American—not Algerian, Kenyan, or Ghanaian—conditions, shaped again by *local* political terrain.

My analysis also starts with the premise that we must evaluate the success of black nationalism/Black Power with the criteria we typically use to determine the success of social movements: We should look for changes in law and public policy; and we should determine who, precisely, benefited from these changes. Leaving aside revolutionary groups that sought to topple capitalism, most of what passed as black nationalism/Black Power during the 1960s (especially by the mid-1960s) looked much like black efforts to do what other "ethnic" groups had done: to pursue "black" interests in a pluralist political system, subsumed by a capitalistic economic one. A decade after the enunciation of Black Power in 1966, none of the more elaborate nationalistic schemes succeeded. No group established political sovereignty in the United States or elsewhere. Few groups created lasting, alternative "African" lifestyles. Black radicalism of the more Marxian bent failed as an effective organizing tool. Even the more conservative plans for black capitalism had little success and impact. Thus, in cities across the country black nationalism/Black Power yielded important, but limited, gains: *professional* blacks enjoyed greater access to jobs and political power.

In retrospect, a number of contemporary critics sympathetic to the black freedom struggle had identified the shortcomings of Black Power and predicted the outcome. In the pages of *Commentary,* Bayard Rustin expressed major doubts about what Black Power advocates could hope to achieve. His thoughts were prescient. Rustin noted that Black Power was born out of "psychological and political frustrations of the Negro" and therefore "must be seem as part of the ... rejection of white supremacy, part of the rebellion against the stereotypes which have been ascribed to Negroes for three hundred years." But nevertheless Black Power lacked real value. "It [Black Power] diverts the movement from a meaningful debate over strategy and tactics, it isolates the Negro community, and it encourages the growth of anti-Negro forces."[104] Black Power also rested on fallacies about group empowerment. The pluralistic, "close ranks" strategy accepted "a historical myth ... that the Irish and the Jews and the Italians, by sticking together and demanding their share, finally won enough power to overcome their initial disabilities." He reminded readers that these groups did not "'pull themselves up by their own bootstraps'" but depended on alliances with other groups.[105] Harold Cruse expressed profound doubts about Black Power in the epilogue of his massive and influential *The Crisis of the Negro Intellectual* (1967). His complaint started with the fact that Black Power was a conceptual muddle, that it represented "nothing more than a strategic retreat for a purpose." Black Power proponents wanted to change "the black world" and not the "white world," and this impulse was, at best, "reformist" and not "revolutionary." Robert Allen's *Black Awakening in Capitalist America* (1967) reviewed black nationalism of the period and argued that groups like CORE and proponents of "cultural" nationalism sought not an "end to oppression, but the transfer of the oppressive apparatus into their own hands."[106]

These analyses contrast sharply with a number of major studies of the period that have been published in the last two decades, of which I will focus on three. Van DeBurg's *New Day In Babylon* (1992) examines Black Power from 1965–1975. Although Van DeBurg agrees that the movement was short-lived—the author mentions external (governmental) pressure and internal schisms among proponents—he argues that Black Power benefited the cause of black liberation in at least two respects: Drawing on Herbert H. Haines's *Black Radicals and the Civil Rights Mainstream, 1954–1970* (1988), Van DeBurg argues that "Black Power generated a crisis in American institutions which made the legislative agenda of ... mainstream organizations more attractive to societal decision-makers."[107] Further: "by decolonizing their minds, cultivating feelings of racial solidarity, and contrasting their world with that of their oppressor ... sixties activists discovered a deep well of untapped energy which enabled ordinary people to do extraordinary things."[108] Thus, to evaluate Black Power on "quantifiable 'political' gains" is to overlook "the realm of the psyche."(294)

Jeffrey O. G. Ogbar's *Black Power: Radical Politics and African American History* (2004) covers the same historical ground and adopts a similar interpretive stance. Ogbar argues that "to explain Black Power" we must examine the efforts of the Nation of Islam and the Black Panther Party, "organizations that did the most to foment the cultural shifts that reconfigured politics and identity in America." Apart from the creation of black studies departments, Ogbar does not point to programmatic gains for evidence of Black Power's legacy but rather to "black conscious" hip-hop music of the late 1980s and early 1990s, new emergent groups like the New Black Panther Party, increasing preference among blacks for African and Muslim names, and the celebration of the pseudo-African Kwanzaa holiday. Like Van DeBurg, Ogbar sees the value and legacy of Black Power in "self-determination and a particular celebration of what it means to be a black person in America."[109]

Peniel E. Joseph's *Waiting for the Midnight Hour: A Narrative History of Black Power in America* (2006) retraces Black Power by looking at key actors of the period like Malcolm X, and especially Stokely Carmichael, and credits the movement for transforming "America's racial, social, and political landscape."[110] In an epilogue, Joseph points out that Black Power as a movement "pales in comparison" to the "political legislation ... and landmark court cases associated with the civil rights movement."[111] Still, Joseph argues that Black Power activists "embraced a different political radicalism" and fueled "the casually assertive identity and cultural pride that marks African American life today" and thereby accomplished "a no-less-remarkable task."[112] Though subsequent "expression of racial pride, from the late 1960s to the present, would achieve enough mainstream legitimacy to be co-opted by corporate entities and liberal politicians ... Black Power's legacy remains relevant to contemporary political organizing taking shape on street corners, in labor unions, on college campuses, and at ballot boxes."[113]

In light of the short-lived duration and limited programmatic gains of Black Power, the generally positive judgments of Van DeBurg, Ogbar, and Joseph are puzzling and stand in stark contrast to leftist critics of Black Power who wrote in the 1960s, as well as from more contemporary assessments by scholars like Adolph Reed Jr., Robert Smith, and Cedric Johnson.[114] Let me start with a fundamental question that studies of this period must confront (an issue I do not fully address): What was the connection between black nationalist/Black power advocacy and the militant insurgency of the period? Beginning with Harlem in 1964, the riots and unrest of the 1960s pushed policy debate and forced governmental response. But it was the riots that propelled black nationalist/Black Power advocacy, not the other way around. The "rebellions" of the era were far more spontaneous than planned, and this comes from the judgment of the Federal Bureau of Investigation, an agency that worked to stop black radicals from fomenting revolution.[115]

Lurking behind these positive assessments is the assumption of unitary black interest. Harold Cruse challenged this thinking. In response to CORE leader Floyd McKissick's assertion that "Black Power ... seeks to achieve economic and political power ... that would make changes that are vast and significant," Cruse asked: "*But economic power for whom?* For workers? Black capitalists? Black farmers? Black middleclass? Black racketeers? Welfare clients?"[116] (emphasis in original). We know the answer to Cruse's question: The benefits of Black Power activism—greater representation in public employment, access to contracts and loans tied to black economic development, and so forth—disproportionately helped black middle and professional classes. From that standpoint of policy there is little other legacy, as even a cursory examination of current indicators like school segregation, incarceration rates, unemployment, and health statistics demonstrates.

Even arguments for "cultural" or "consciousness" gains are questionable, and that is because these claims depend on a string of problematic assumptions: (1) that historically "black culture" was hermetically sealed from "white culture"; (2) that black people shared this discrete set of values and orientation; (3) that this "culture" explains some (or all) of black disadvantage; (4) that it is possible to identify or constitute an autonomous black counterculture in mass consumption society;[117] and (5) that if this could be done the benefits would be uniformly good: that the forty-year-old custodian mother of two would benefit as much as her college professor counterpart.

A final point concerns the strategic usefulness of Black Power, a point that Joseph asserts, and an interpretation that is suggested in a number of other works.[118] Yet this evaluation depends on the view that black nationalism/Black Power only failed because of factors like COINTELPRO, inter- and intragroup rivalries, and the opportunism that Allen and other contemporary observers identified. But black nationalism/Black Power had fundamental theoretical limitations that Rustin noted at the time: It was a strategic and conceptual black hole. Problems like low wages, unemployment, inferior education, and insufficient/inadequate housing stemmed from factors that originated far beyond community control, and these could not be addressed through political and economic strategies derived from ethnic pluralism, understood at that time in the language of unity and racial solidarity. That black nationalism/Black Power was blind to other sources of inequality—for example, class, gender, and sexual orientation—has only became more obvious with the passage of time.

Indeed, despite revisionist accounts by authors like Van DeBurg, Ogbar, and Joseph, there is little evidence to support the view that Black Power had the positive impact that activists claimed at the time and that some scholars have since asserted. Rather, the historical evidence and developments of the past forty years suggest that contemporary critics like Rustin, Cruse, and Allen were prescient, and these earlier observations have been supported by subsequent historical analyses by Reed, Smith, Johnson, and others.

NOTES

1. See Wilson J. Moses, ed., *Classical Black Nationalism: From the American Revolution to Marcus Garvey* (New York: New York University Press, 1996); William L. Van Deburg, ed., *Modern Black Nationalism: From Marcus Garvey to Louis Farrakhan* (New York: New York University Press, 1997).

2. Dean E. Robinson, *Black Nationalism in American Politics and Thought* (Cambridge and New York: Cambridge University Press, 2001), 1.

3. For the purposes of this discussion, I take "black nationalism" and "Black Power" as synonymous. In my book I use a strict definition of black nationalism for the "classical" (1850–1925) period—specifically the goal of territorial sovereignty—and a more relaxed definition for the mid-1960s that would include ideas and projects that did not only seek land (e.g., the Nation of Islam and the Republic of New Africa) but also discourse and programmatic activity that favored solidarity among blacks as an inviolable first principle of politics over strategies that would require broader alliances.

4. See Robinson, *Black Nationalism in American Politics and Thought,* 70–87.

5. I am using the term differently from the way Michael Omi and Howard Winant do in *Racial Formation in the United States: From the 1960s to the 1990s,* 2nd ed. (New York: Routledge, 1994). They use the term ethnic paradigm to identify the "mainstream of the modern sociology of race." Ibid., 14.

6. Milton Gordon, *Assimilation in American Life* (New York: Oxford University Press, 1964).

7. Ibid., 88.

8. Ibid., 89–90.

9. Ibid., 11.

10. Quoted in ibid., 100–101.

11. Stow Persons, *Ethnic Studies at Chicago, 1905–1945* (Chicago: University of Illinois Press, 1987), 53–54.

12. Ibid., 62.

13. Ibid., 31.

14. William I. Thomas and Florian Znaniecki, *The Polish Peasant in Europe and America,* vol. 2 (New York: Dover, 1918), 1128; emphasis in original.

15. Persons, *Ethnic Studies at Chicago,* 131–132.

16. E. Franklin Frazier, *The Negro in the United States* (New York: Macmillan, 1951), 623–639.

17. Robert E. Park and Ernest W. Burgess, *Introduction to the Science of Sociology* (Chicago: University of Chicago Press, 1921), 735.

18. Ibid.

19. E. B. Reuter and C. W. Hart, *Introduction to Sociology* (New York: McGraw-Hill, 1933), 349.

20. Gordon, *Assimilation in American Life,* 64–66; Brewton Berry, *Race and Ethnic Relations,* 2nd ed. (Boston: Houghton Mifflin, 1958), 210.

21. Arnold M. Rose, *Sociology: The Study of Human Relations* (New York: Knopf, 1956), 557.

22. Gordon, *Assimilation in American Life,* 72.

23. Ibid., 70.

24. Robert E. Park, *Race and Culture* (Glencoe, IL: Free Press, 1950), 70–71.

25. Edward Byron Reuter, *The American Race Problem* (New York: Thomas Y. Crowell, 1966), 115.

26. Ibid., 121 (emphasis added).

27. E. Franklin Frazier, "The Changing Status of the Negro Family." *Social Forces* 9 (March 1931): 386–393.

28. Frazier, *The Negro in the United States,* 680, 689.

29. E. Franklin Frazier, *Black Bourgeoisie* (New York: Free Press, 1957), 112.

30. Quoted in Gordon, *Assimilation in American Life,* 76.

31. Jennifer Jordan, "Cultural Nationalism in the 1960s: Politics and Poetry," in *Race, Politics, and Culture: Critical Essays on the Radicalism of the 1960s,* ed. Adolph Reed Jr. (Westport, CT: Greenwood, 1986), 39.

32. Cooks had served as an officer in Garvey's UNIA and organized around the theme of "African nationalism." Charles "Nwokeoji" Peaker led the African Nationalist Pioneer Movement following Cooks's death in 1966.

33. Imamu Amiri Baraka, "7 Principles of U.S. Maulana Kaenga and the Need for a Black Value System," in his *Raise Race Rays Raze* (New York: Random House, 1969), 133–159.

34. Robert S. Browne, "The Case for Two Americas—One Black, One White," *New York Times Magazine* (August 11, 1968): 48.

35. Stokely Carmichael and Charles Hamilton, *Black Power: The Politics of Liberation in America* (New York: Vintage Books, 1967), 30.

36. Gordon, *Assimilation in American Life,* 145.

37. Nathan Glazer and Daniel Patrick Moynihan, *Beyond the Melting Pot* (Cambridge, MA: MIT Press, 1963), 14–16.

38. Ibid., 13–14 (emphasis added).

39. Ibid., 230–231.

40. Ibid., 165. Like Glazer and Moynihan, Carmichael and Hamilton adopted a strategy that began with the premise of ethnic group pluralism: "Black Power recognizes . . . the ethnic basis of American politics" and seeks "an effective share in the total power of society." Echoing Glazer and Moynihan, the authors of *Black Power* pointed out that studies of voting behavior made it clear that the pot had not melted in the political arena: "Italians vote for Rubino over O'Brian; Irish for Murphy over Goldberg, etc." While this phenomenon was hardly ideal, it nevertheless remained "a central fact of the American political system." Carmichael and Hamilton, *Black Power,* 47 and 45.

41. Ibid., 53.

42. Daniel P. Moynihan, "The Negro Family," in *Slavery and Its Aftermath,* ed. Peter Rose (New York: Atherton Press, 1970), 389.

43. Ibid., 412.

44. National Advisory Commission on Civil Disorder, *The Kerner Report: The 1968 Report of the National Advisory Commission on Civil Disorders* (New York: Pantheon, 1988), 280.

45. Black women commentators and activists of the time critiqued the flawed assumption that "black manhood" needed buttressing, principally because it demanded female subordination. See, e.g., Betty Frank Lomax, "Afro-American Women: Growth Deferred," *Liberator* 6, no. 5 (May 1966): 18; Linda La Rue, "The Black Movement and Women's Liberation," *Black Scholar* 1 (May 1970): 41.

46. Robert Harris, Nyota Harris, and Grandassa Harris, eds., *Carlos Cooks and Black Nationalism: From Garvey to Malcolm* (Dover, MA: Majority Press, 1992), 38.

47. Bruce Perry, ed., *Malcolm X: The Last Speeches* (New York: Pathfinder, 1989), 78 (emphasis added).

48. Ralph Ellison, *Going to the Territory* (New York: Random House), 108.

49. Ibid., 111.

50. Stephen Steinberg, *The Ethnic Myth: Race, Ethnicity and Class Is America* (Boston: Beacon, 1989), 79.

51. Ira Katznelson shows that during the 1930s and 1940s social policy treated blacks

differently, or excluded them entirely, effectively leading to "affirmative action" for whites. See his *When Affirmative Action Was White: An Untold History of Racial Inequality in Twentieth-Century America* (New York: Norton, 2005).

52. Barbara Ann Teer, "Needed: A New Image," in *The Black Power Revolt,* ed. Floyd B. Barbour (Boston: Extending Horizons, 1968), 222.

53. Ronald Milner, "Black Theater—Go Home," in *The Black Aesthetic,* ed. Addison Gayle Jr. (New York: Anchor Books, 1971), 288. This formulation of culture is similar to the one offered by negritude proponent Leopold Sedar Senghor. See, for example, his "The Problematics of Negritude," *Black World* 20, no. 10 (1971): 6.

54. Robert Dahl, *Who Governs? Democracy and Power in an American City* (New Haven, CT: Yale University Press, 1961), 53.

55. Ibid., 54.

56. Michael K. Brown and Steven P. Erie, "Blacks and the Legacy of the Great Society: The Economic and Political Impact of Federal Social Policy," *Public Policy* 29, no. 3 (1981): 317–318.

57. Arthur I. Blaustein and Geoffrey Faux, *The Star-Spangled Hustle* (Garden City, NY: Doubleday, 1972), 114–115.

58. This was also the era of "Model cities," an aspect of Johnson's War on Poverty, that focused on improving coordination of planning and service provision.

59. In Barbara Cruikshank, "The Will to Empower: Technologies of Citizenship and the War on Poverty," *Socialist Review* 23, no. 4 (Spring 1994): 36.

60. Alan Wolfe, *America's Impasse: The Rise and Fall of the Politics of Growth* (Boston: South End, 1981), 10; Godfrey Hodgson, *America in Our Time: From World War II to Nixon—What Happened and Why* (Princeton, NJ: Princeton University Press, 2005).

61. Blaustein and Faux, *Star-Spangled Hustle,* 117–118.

62. Ibid., 34.

63. Quoted in ibid., 116.

64. Quoted in ibid., 130.

65. Alan A. Altshuler, *Community Control: The Black Demand for Participation in Large American Cities* (New York: Pegasus, 1970), 14.

66. Carmichael and Hamilton, *Black Power,* 47.

67. Ibid., 44.

68. In Alex Poinsett, "Battle over Control of Ghetto Schools," *Ebony* (May 1969): 44.

69. See Kenneth S. Jolly, *Black Liberation in the Midwest: The Struggle in St. Louis, Missouri, 1964–1970* (New York: Routledge, 2006), 133–142.

70. Quoted in Robert Allen, *Black Awakening in Capitalist America* (Trenton, NJ: Africa World Press, 1992), 186.

71. Blaustein and Faux, *Star-Spangled Hustle,* 47.

72. Quoted in Thomas L. Blair, *Retreat to the Ghetto: The End of a Dream* (New York: Hill and Wang, 1977), 167.

73. William L. Van Deburg, *New Day in Babylon: The Black Power Movement and American Culture, 1965–1975* (Chicago: University of Chicago Press, 1992), 116–117.

74. Blaustein and Faux, *Star-Spangled Hustle,* 42–43.

75. Blair, *Retreat to the Ghetto,* 207. Baraka enjoyed the most political success, but other coalitions sprouted in cities across the United States. "There was a Black United Front of Washington, D.C., the North City Congress in Philadelphia, the United Front in Boston, the Black United Conference in Denver, and the Black Congress in Los Angeles, to mention a few. All of these sought to use their influence in order to seize control of local political and economic institutions." (From Allen, *Black Awakening,* 142.) See also Komozi Woodard, *A Nation within*

a Nation: Amiri Baraka (LeRoi Jones) and Black Power Politics (Chapel Hill: University of North Carolina Press, 1999), 114–115.

76. Adolph L. Reed Jr., *Stirring in the Jug: Black Politics in the Post-Segregation Era* (Minneapolis: University of Minnesota Press, 1999), 133.

77. Komozi Woodward suggests that these conventions represented a process of "black nationality" formation. See 159–218. For a more critical appraisal see Cedric Johnson, *Revolutionaries to Race Leaders: Black Power and the Making of African American Politics* (Minneapolis: University of Minnesota Press), 85–130.

78. There were also conventions in Philadelphia, August 31–September 1, 1968, and in Bermuda in July 1969.

79. Blair, *Retreat to the Ghetto,* 202.

80. Interview with Dr. Nathan Wright Jr. in *Christian Science Monitor,* September 18, 1967.

81. Imamu Amiri Baraka, *The Autobiography of LeRoi Jones* (Chicago: Lawrence Hills, 1997), 403. See Woodward, *A Nation with a Nation,* 162–173, and Johnson, *Revolutionaries to Race Leaders,* 74–82.

82. Imamu Amiri Baraka, ed., *African Congress* (New York: Morrow, 1972), 115.

83. Ibid., 168.

84. Ibid., 139 (emphasis in original).

85. Ibid., 140.

86. Sam Pollard et al., *Eyes on the Prize II: Ain't Gonna Shuffle No More* (Alexandria, VA: PBS Video, 1989).

87. "The Gary Declaration" (unpublished document), 138.

88. Ibid., 140 (emphasis in original).

89. Ibid., 6–30.

90. Johnson described the meeting as "a shotgun wedding of the radical aspirations of Black Power and conventional modes of politics." Johnson, *Black Revolutionaries,* 129.

91. Robert Smith, *We Have No Leaders: African Americans in the Post-Civil Rights Era* (Albany: State University of New York Press, 1996), 49–56.

92. Ibid., 6–64.

93. Reed, *Stirrings in the Jug,* 137. The ALSC's concern was to support African liberation movements.

94. James Button, *Black Violence: Political Impact of the 1960s Riots* (Princeton, NJ: Princeton University Press, 1978).

95. Pranab Chatterjee, *Local Leadership in Black Communities* (Cleveland, OH: School of Applied Science, Case Western Reserve, 1975), 77.

96. Allen, *Black Awakening,* 147.

97. Adolph Reed Jr., "The Black Urban Regime: Structural Origins and Constraints," in *Power, Community and the City: Comparative and Community Research,* vol. 1, ed. Michael P. Smith (New Brunswick, NJ: Transaction, 1988), 147.

98. Fred Powledge, *Model City: A Test of American Liberalism: One Town's Efforts to Rebuild Itself* (New York: Simon and Schuster, 1970), 225.

99. Quoted in Jolly, *Black Liberation in the Midwest,* 134.

100. For more in-depth explorations of related trends in other cities see, e.g., Robert O. Self, *American Babylon: Race and the Struggle for Postwar Oakland* (Princeton, NJ: Princeton University Press, 2003), and Jolly, *Black Liberation in the Midwest.*

101. U.S. Office of Economic Opportunity Archives, RG 381.

102. Reed, "The Black Urban Regime," 145–147. See also Ralph M. Kramer, *Participation of the Poor* (Englewood Cliffs, NJ: Prentice-Hall, 1969); Allen, *Black Awakening,* 143.

103. Albert K. Karnig and Susan Welch, *Black Representation and Urban Policy* (Chicago: University of Chicago Press, 1980).

104. Bayard Rustin, "'Black Power' and Coalition Politics," *Commentary* (September 1966): 35.

105. Ibid., 36.

106. Allen, *Black Awakening,* 191. Rustin suggested that what Black Power activists "are in fact arguing for (perhaps unconsciously) is the creation of a new black establishment" (emphasis in original). Rustin, "'Black Power' and Coalition Politics," 36.

107. William L. Van Deburg, *New Day in Babylon: The Black Power Movement and American Culture, 1965–1975* (Chicago: University of Chicago Press), 306.

108. Ibid.

109. Jeffrey O. G. Ogbar, *Black Power: Radical Politics and African American Identity* (Baltimore: Johns Hopkins University Press, 2004), 204–205.

110. Peniel E. Joseph, *Waiting 'til the Midnight Hour: A Narrative History of Black Power in America* (New York: Holt, 2006), xiv.

111. Ibid., 302. Another study that adopts a similar interpretive approach is Scot Brown's *Fighting for US: Maulana Karenga, the U.S. Organization, and Black Cultural Nationalism* (New York: New York University Press, 2003). Interviews with members at the time provide new insight into US's activities and significance to black politics on the West Coast, as well as its broader influence on cultural nationalism in the middle to late 1960s. Brown details a number of issues that constrained the growth and effectiveness of the organization: its cult of personality around Karenga, its problematic gender politics, and its "vanguard self-perceptions." Nevertheless, for Brown, while US did not achieve its goal of influencing other organizations toward the goal of a "cultural revolution," it "along with others with cultural-nationalist leanings, produced aesthetic conceptions, philosophical paradigms, ritual representations, and political institutions that continue to defy the anti-African mandate of Western cultural hegemony in the post–Civil Rights/Black Power era." Ibid., 162.

112. Ibid., 303.

113. Ibid.

114. Reed, *Stirrings in the Jug;* Smith, *We Have No Leaders;* Johnson, *Revolutionaries to Race Leaders.*

115. Kenneth O'Reilly, *Racial Matters: The FBI's Secret File on Black America, 1960–1972* (New York: Free Press, 1989), 261–292.

116. Cruse, *The Crisis of the Negro Intellectual,* 556 (emphasis in original).

117. Adolph Reed Jr., "The 'Black Revolution' and the Reconstitution of Domination," in *Race, Politics, and Culture,* ed. Adolph Reed Jr. (Westport, CT: Greenwood, 1986), 78.

118. See ibid.

Part III
The Post–Jim Crow Era

Limning black political and intellectual life during the period after the fight against constitutionally sanctioned segregation had succeeded requires recognizing the extent to which scripts for black politics, black academic critique, and black imaginative literature written during the Jim Crow era have continued to exert interpretive and normative force into the present moment. As we noted in the introduction to Part II, "most of what most of us recognize, or imagine we do, about black Americans came into existence" during the long moment of Jim Crow. The persistent recurrence to these assumptions as guiding coordinates by commentators on black America, even as the terrain to which they were supposed to correspond has changed, reflects the way that the "elite-brokerage politics" developed under Booker T. Washington and the "race-relations" discourse it spawned continue to serve a black elite that derives its legitimacy from claims to speak authentically for a black community whose political representation requires mediation by self-appointed or otherwise anointed spokespersons.

The two lengthy chapters here draw out the terms of this continuity and discontinuity in conceptualizations of black intellectual life. Madhu Dubey's "The Postmodern Moment in Black Literary and Cultural Studies" analyzes how the economic, political, technological, and cultural shifts during the 1970s—shifts that collectively define the moment of postmodernism—present both aesthetic and political challenges to the regimes of representation that had long defined the imagined relations between black writers of fiction and the black communities they sought to depict. As Dubey notes, postmodern black novelists register problems within the logic of racial representation even as they find it difficult fully to shrug off the call to represent the plight of urbanized black populations.

Adolph Reed's "The 'Color Line' Then and Now: *The Souls of Black Folk* and the Changing Context of Black American Politics" rounds out this volume with a contextualist examination of the origins of, and the continual recourse to, the "color-line" formulation in W. E. B. Du Bois's *The Souls of Black Folk,* a book that has become the touchstone of black intellectual and political thinking since the late 1980s. After bringing to light the conditions that gave Du Bois's idea its pertinence, despite its limitations, as a frame for black politics at the turn of the twentieth century, Reed goes on to illustrate how the conditions at the turn of the twenty-first century make the lens of race, which the color-line formulation presumes, not only less useful but also obscurantist, in providing an understanding of the devastating inequalities that define the contemporary effects of neoliberalism. Reed's chapter, which critiques both the scholarly efforts to retool Du Bois's color-line formulation for the present moment as well as the efforts by policymakers to confront the aftermath of Hurricane Katrina in New Orleans, illustrates how intellectual history, carefully undertaken, can clarify the terms through which we understand both the past and the present.

9
The Postmodern Moment in Black Literary and Cultural Studies

Madhu Dubey

It is difficult to write about late-twentieth-century U.S. culture without taking on the term *postmodernism,* which, without clear consensus about its meaning, circulates widely as a periodizing concept. Generally dated from the 1970s, postmodernism is believed to mark a decisive break from the modern era at the cultural, epistemic, and socioeconomic levels. In most theories of postmodernism, the modern period is identified with industrial capitalism, although its successor is variably characterized as a postindustrial society or a new stage of capitalism. No account of which I am aware makes a convincing case for seeing the postmodern as a socioeconomic order radically discontinuous from the modern, although certain significant changes—such as greater global integration of capital or the spread of advanced information technologies—have undoubtedly occurred. At the cultural and epistemic levels, the novel elements associated with postmodernism, such as philosophical and aesthetic antirealism, heightened consciousness about representation, refusal of totality and closure, or fragmented and unstable subjectivity, have been persuasively shown to have modernist antecedents.[1]

Regardless of whether the term *postmodernism* has any decidable referent, it has become a cultural fact, given that artists and intellectuals across a broad spectrum in the United States believe in the reality of a decisive shift that has thrown the category of the modern into crisis. Trying to account for this sense of crisis in the field of African American literary and cultural studies is one of my main intentions in this chapter. But I also use *postmodernism* in a stronger sense—as a content-laden term—to refer to a cluster of socioeconomic developments that have occurred since the 1970s and are best described in David Harvey's study *The Condition of Postmodernity*. In contrast to the postindustrial thesis or even to claims of a new stage of capitalism, Harvey views the 1970s as "a troubled period of economic restructuring and social and political readjustment,"[2] a moment of transition from the rigidly organized and massified system of postwar Fordism to a more flexible regime of accumulation. Harvey extensively details recent changes in production, labor markets, finance, and consumption, but he regards these changes as a new wave of modernization and global industrial reorganization rather than as fundamental breaks with industrial modernity or with the capitalist mode of production. Although Harvey's discussion of the distinctions between modern and postmodern culture is often dichotomous, his seems to me the most coherent and measured account of the material force-field of postmodernism.

Following Harvey, I treat socioeconomic developments since the 1970s as novel in significant respects yet part of an intense round of modernization. For this reason, I refrain from using the term *postmodernity*, which implies an epochal shift, a supercession of the modern era. I do, however, make frequent use of phrases such as *postmodern period* or *postmodern times* as shorthand references to the ensemble of political, economic, technological, social, and cultural transformations that have occurred in the United States since the 1970s. In the realms of art, culture, and intellectual discourse, I employ the term *postmodern* to describe a moment of perceived crisis within the modern. One of the most vexed issues in debates on postmodernism is the precise relation between socioeconomic and cultural levels of change. On this count, my approach is fairly straightforward: The racial crises associated with postmodernism are so emphatically understood in cultural terms that culture not only operates as a pressure point but also begins to feed back into political and economic policy decisions. To bluntly anticipate my argument, I focus on two facets of late-twentieth-century political-economic and technological developments: their drastic alteration of U.S. urban space and community, and their severely damaging effects on the vast majority of African Americans. These facets are linked in the sense that the deteriorating conditions of African American life—hardening spatial segregation and high levels of poverty and unemployment—are taken to be the main indices of postmodern urban crisis. In addition to being decisively racialized, this crisis is explained in cultural terms, as a failure on the part of urban African Americans to sustain healthy traditions and communities. With black culture so directly implicated in popular and academic accounts of socioeconomic crisis, African American novelists and literary and cultural critics begin to play defining roles, registering as well as countering or stoking the sense of crisis. But before I enter into the specifics of this argument, some preliminary remarks seem necessary on why the category of postmodernism should even be considered relevant to African American literary and cultural studies.

PERIODIZING BLACK POSTMODERNISM?

In the most common usage of the term, derived from Jean-Francois Lyotard, the *postmodern* is understood as a posture of incredulity toward the "grand narratives" of the modern West.[3] Although Lyotard names several such narratives, he reserves his strongest fire for the meta-narrative of the "emancipation of humanity" (51), which casts the human in universal and totalized terms. Two of Lyotard's utterances, from his appendix to *The Postmodern Condition,* have become the mantras of most variants of postmodernism: "Let us wage a war on totality" and "Let us activate the differences" (82). For Lyotard, the idea of "humanity as the hero of liberty" (31) has lost credibility in the postmodern era, when this unitary subject is seen to dissolve into a plethora of differences (40). Within the national context of the United States, Lyotard's pronouncements on the demise of the modern political subject seemed to be confirmed by the eruption, during the 1960s, of micropolitics of difference organized around race, gender, sexuality, and so forth. Importantly, however, even as they attacked the idea of a modern Western subject that arrogated the power to speak for all humanity, these movements sought to extend the modern political project of liberal democracy. Most versions of the politics of difference have modeled themselves on the civil rights and Black Power movements, suggesting the enabling centrality of African American politics and culture to the emergence of postmodernism in the United States.

The politics of difference is greeted as a crisis by critics of postmodernism such as David Harvey because it splinters the putatively universal subject of modern (class-based) politics into a host of special-interest constituencies. In *The Condition of Postmodernity,* Harvey trenchantly argues that differences are reified and rendered mutually incommunicable in postmodern cultural theories, which generally neglect the political and economic systems that make differences mean in historically specific ways (116–117). Harvey's book has been rightly criticized by feminist geographers such as Doreen Massey for its often sloppy formulation of universalism and particularism.[4] In his attack on the "local" or "regional" bases of postmodern cultural politics, Harvey slides between literal and metaphorical uses of these terms, sometimes referring to place and at other times to particular political interest groups, especially women and racial minorities. When Harvey writes that "The 'othernesses' and 'regional resistances' that postmodern politics emphasizes can only flourish in particular places" (239) or when he describes political movements mobilized around race or gender as "localized struggles" (46), we have to assume that he is speaking in loosely metaphorical terms, for there is no basis for arguing (and Harvey never does actually argue this point) that feminist or racial politics are any more or less rooted in place than are class politics. Harvey's argument cannot be sustained, even if read metaphorically, to imply that the politics of difference is mired in particularity rather than that it is place-bound. The civil rights movement is but one obvious example of a politics organized around a particular racial issue that appealed to political principles of universal human rights.

A further problem with Harvey's argument, identified by scholars from feminist and African American studies, is its formulation of the cultural crises associated with postmodernism. In a multifaceted argument that I can only briefly summarize here, Harvey attributes current perceptions of cultural instability to an accelerated round of time-space compression brought about by the reorganization of global economic order during the 1970s. This capitalist restructuring has involved a new and intensified phase of modernization, rendering the meaning of time and space increasingly abstract, and sparking crises of representation across all levels of culture. In her critique of Marxist urban geography, which lumps Fredric Jameson and Edward Soja together with Harvey, Doreen Massey argues that their global theories of postmodern disorientation assume a modern, masculine, Western subject who once occupied a seemingly stable center. Invoking Toni Morrison and bell hooks as counterexamples, Massey contends that for most inhabitants of the world—those who were subjected to slavery and colonialism—the experience of place and time, home and history, has been fractured for centuries, so that what is being proclaimed as a novel feature of postmodernism has in fact been long familiar to the West's "others."[5]

If we take the discursive displacement of the modern Western subject as the sticking point of postmodernism, we would have to question the applicability of the modern/postmodern periodization to fields such as African American studies. As Wahneema Lubiano points out in a rejoinder to David Harvey, the decentering of Western cultural authority can scarcely be regarded as a crisis for African American literary and cultural studies, where skepticism about modern Western meta-narratives has a much longer history.[6] At least going as far back as the antebellum fugitive slave narratives, interrogation of the practices of modern humanism has been a driving force of African American literature. Moreover, as Phillip Brian Harper persuasively argues, the fractured subject of postmodern culture has long formed a staple element of minority literatures. Harper's point is not simply that the experience of psychological fragmentation for minority writers has predated the postmodern moment but also that it is rooted in a social history of marginalization and that this history has been a founding, albeit repressed, condition of possibility for postmodern culture.[7]

Such arguments pose important cautions for any attempt to periodize postmodernism along unitary global lines, calling attention to discrepant and asynchronous tendencies within the categories of modernism and postmodernism. Once these categories are admitted to be internally differentiated, racial and feminist politics cannot so easily be dismissed as "local" and "subordinate" to the supposedly universal politics of the modern era. The far more difficult question, however, is what exactly we do with differences once we acknowledge their importance. If Harvey fails to reckon with the divergent histories of the West's "others," many postmodern theorists lock these groups into a relation of radical alterity to the West and in this respect become vulnerable to Harvey's critique. In *Justice, Nature, and the Geography of Difference,* Harvey argues that postmodern theories of political change bank their hopes on "residual" or "surplus" areas that are placed outside the prevailing system.[8] What's more, these residual and surplus zones are generally inhabited by people who epitomize racial difference from the West.

A perfect example is Fredric Jameson's influential theory of postmodernism as the "cultural dominant" of late capitalism. Jameson's use of this phrase calls to mind Raymond Williams's discussion of residual, dominant, and emergent cultural forces, which is meant to offer a dynamic and internally contested model of periodization.[9]

But in his magisterial study of postmodernism, Jameson claims that a novel feature of the late capitalist period is the elimination of all the residual elements that were still available in the modern era: "The postmodern must be characterized as a situation in which the survival, the residue, the holdover, the archaic, has finally been swept away without a trace."[10] As a Marxist intellectual, Jameson wants to be able to theorize the possibility of critical resistance to capitalism, and here he is led to contradict himself. Advocating "third worldism" as the most promising source of social critique,[11] Jameson ends up resurrecting the very category of the residual that he had earlier banished as a viable alternative in the present. Jameson's strategy of third worldism is only one prominent instance of the logic of the residual that runs through much contemporary cultural theory, which looks to places that have been most conspicuously left behind by the processes of capitalist modernization as spaces of greatest opposition. An overly totalized notion of the "dominant" almost always entails as its corollary a romanticized notion of the "residual," with a sharply antithetical articulation of the two terms.

An instance of this romance of the residual from African American cultural studies is bell hooks's "Choosing the Margins as a Space of Radical Openness," an essay that has been widely taken up by advocates of postmodernism. The margin, or the space occupied by African Americans, operates at two levels throughout hooks's essay. First, the margin is identified with certain sites of material oppression—the racially segregated areas to which African Americans were confined in the rural South, and urban ghettoes, where African Americans are susceptible to "every postmodern mode of dying" imaginable.[12] In the course of the essay, this "site of deprivation" is rhetorically converted into "a space of resistance" (149), which hooks does not link to a particular kind of social order. hooks traces her journey from the margin, a physical place of oppression, to the center, here equivalent to mainstream U.S. society. But in this process, hooks chooses to continue inhabiting the margin, which must then refer to an epistemological standpoint rather than an actual place. Acknowledging the double inscription of the term *margin* in her essay, hooks asserts that "spaces can be real and imagined" (152). But what remains uncertain is the passage from one kind of space to the other: How exactly are the material sites of racial oppression transformed into spaces of resistance? The only clue hooks offers is that spaces "can be interrupted, appropriated, and transformed through artistic and literary practice" (152), suggesting that critical resistance is primarily conducted in the field of culture.

The elisions in this account of racial margins are even more clearly highlighted as Edward Soja appropriates hooks's essay in the service of his elusive concept of Thirdspace. Railing against the exclusive emphasis on time and history in modern social theories, Soja has long been trying to develop a postmodern theory of space. His most recent notion of Thirdspace is explicitly meant to transcend binary oppositions between margin and center, space and time, and most significant for my purposes, between real and imagined spaces. Soja claims that the category of Thirdspace opens up a new and nondualistic relation between material and discursive ideas of space.[13] The radically postmodern perspective offered by Thirdspace seems to be most accessible to racial minority intellectuals, as Soja exemplifies his concept through bell hooks's essay on the margins and through several literary passages on borderlands by Chicano/a writers. According to Soja, hooks enters Thirdspace by "deconstructing" binary modern conceptions of empirical and cognitive space (98)—in other words, through a discursive operation. Here again, as in hooks's essay, a situation of material deprivation is mysteriously transmuted into a position of cultural privilege, and notwithstanding Soja's claims about Thirdspace, it is precisely the mediation between these two realms that remains unexplained. Although Soja is ultimately interested in political change, at no point does he consider the kinds of collective political action that might be required to transform actual margins such as the urban ghetto or the segregated South into spaces of possibility. Consequently, whereas the sites of deprivation can be materially specified as actually existing places, the spaces of resistance remain strictly discursive and metaphorical realms.

Soja's and hooks's accounts are greatly revealing of the ways in which the difference of racial minorities is incorporated into theories of postmodernism. First, U.S. racial minorities are recognized to be disaffiliated from the dominant conditions of postmodern society as a result of the historical and geographical specificity of racial oppression. But somewhere along the way, the material particularity of their marginal location evaporates as they become prized carriers of epistemological or cultural difference. At this level, racial minorities become irreducibly other—not just to prevailing social conditions but even to theoretical discourse about these conditions. The condescension implicit in this move is manifest in the way Soja includes African American and Chicano/a writers in his discussion of Thirdspace. In contrast to dense theoretical expositions of Henri Lefebvre and Michel Foucault, Soja restricts himself to extended quotations from hooks's essay and from literary works by Gloria Anzaldúa, Maria Lugones, and Guillermo Gomez-Peña. These writers, it seems, cannot be subjected to critical analysis or explication but can only convey lived experience through literary, lyrical expression. In this way, certain racial minority groups become the bearers of sheer, untranslatable difference.

Theorists like Edward Soja or Fredric Jameson routinely invoke the concept of uneven development but fail to apply it consistently to their accounts of postmodernism. As used by Marxist geographers such as Neil Smith, this concept posits social and economic inequality as a constitutive rather than incidental feature of capitalism, which is understood as a geographically and historically differentiated yet systemic global phenomenon.[14] The concept of uneven development may yield a more supple and dynamic periodizing model, allowing us to grasp social differences as effects of the discontinuous spread of global capitalism and to conceive of dominant and residual trends as disparate yet systematically linked. By this logic, African American life would not be wholly subsumed within the "cultural dominant" of postmodernism. Stemming from a particular history of political and economic exclusion, developments in African American culture, such as the critique of modern Western humanism, will not always follow the same trajectory as trends in the dominant culture. At the same time, however, African American culture does not form a residual category that develops in complete autonomy from the dominant culture. I would claim that the postmodern *does* mark a moment of crisis in African American studies, although this is not a crisis occasioned by the waning authority of modern Western meta-narratives.

The postmodern moment is characterized by a widely registered crisis in the category of racial community—a crisis rooted in the specificities of African American history (notably the changed conditions of racial community after the political transformations of the civil rights movement) but also conditioned by the national and global developments (such as the shift from a Fordist to a flexible regime of accumulation, industrial restructuring, and the scaling down of the welfare state) that are said to be formative of the postmodern era. Even further specification is necessary when speaking of a postmodern crisis in racial community. Mike Featherstone and Zygmunt Bauman have correctly noted that what passes for the "cultural dominant" of postmodernism applies unevenly to certain class sectors and not others and that what is announced as a phenomenon of global proportions is essentially a crisis in the social role of elite intellectuals.[15] This also holds true for African American studies, where problems of racial representation assume special magnitude for the elite class that had previously enjoyed a position of cultural authority as spokespeople for the race and who now feel this role to be in jeopardy.

This crisis of representation is overdetermined by a constellation of political, economic, and cultural developments since the 1970s. Within the national context of the United States, processes of capitalist reorganization have clearly followed a racialized logic of uneven development, sharpening already existing inequalities and polarities. In response to heightened international competition and dwindling profits, capital relocated from its established bases in the Northeast and Midwest to less developed regions in the third world and the "Sun Belt" South, in search of higher tax incentives, lower wages, and weaker labor unions. The deindustrialization of the "Frost Belt," resulting in the loss of millions of manufacturing jobs, has severely harmed African Americans, who were concentrated in those industries that suffered the greatest job losses. The shift from manufacturing to service has resulted in a bipolar employment structure, characterized by a small proportion of well-paid, high-tech jobs, a large pool of low-skilled and poorly paid service jobs, and an evisceration of the middle levels of skill and income. African Americans are overrepresented in the lower rungs of this dual economy, holding low-waged service positions that pay much less than did the lost manufacturing jobs.[16]

These economic shifts have dramatically modified the spatial forms and social structures of deindustrializing U.S. cities. The core areas of the older industrial economy, largely inhabited by African Americans, have undergone steep economic decline as the result of the relocation of capital to suburbs and to the South. At the same time, some of these core areas are being transformed from "centers of production and distribution of material goods to centers of administration, information exchange, and higher-order service provision."[17] Due to the combined effects of a spatial and skills "mismatch," African Americans have not been able to access the new jobs opening up either in the suburbs or in revitalizing urban areas: The expanding employment sectors are either spatially remote from areas of African American residence or, when they are located in urban cores, require levels of technical skill not possessed by most central-city African Americans.[18] The conversion of cities from centers of manufacturing to hubs of finance, services, and upscale consumption has also caused the massive residential dislocation of lower-income African Americans and deepened their isolation within segregated areas of concentrated poverty.[19]

These structural changes were actively enabled by political and public policy choices. Increased mobility allowed capital to demand a "good business climate," which local and state governments vied to create through business subsidies, tax breaks, increased discipline of the labor force, and reductions of the social wage. The greater willingness of local and state governments in the South to ensure such business conditions encouraged industrial relocation out of the Frost Belt into the Sun Belt.[20] In the deindustrializing cities of the Northeast and Midwest, federal highway construction and mortgage programs smoothed the way for suburbanization, which diminished urban tax bases and hastened the economic decline of center cities.[21] Drastic cuts in federal aid to cities spurred the privatized urban redevelopment programs that are reinforcing already existing patterns of racial segregation.

In the political arena, the decisive retreat from the redistributive policies of the welfare state during the post-1960s decades was justified by recourse to an often overtly stated racial logic. Wrongly perceived to be disproportionately draining welfare resources, urban African Americans were stigmatized as the latest incarnations of the "undeserving poor."[22] The War on Poverty and community development programs of the 1960s, flawed as they were, had targeted the black urban poor as deserving recipients of public aid. These programs, enabled by the political climate established by the civil rights movement, could no longer garner public support by the end of the decade, when the short-lived national consensus on black civil rights dissolved into moral panic about African Americans as the prime threat to urban security and national community. As Margaret Weir observes, by the 1970s, the idea of black political and economic integration "no longer evoked images of passive resistance to southern racists; it now called up troubling memories of urban riots."[23] The emergence and rapidly spreading popularity of the term *underclass* in mass-media and academic debates about urban poverty clinched the racialized logic of urban crisis discourses in the postmodern era. The term *underclass* was used to refer not to the multiracial population that actually formed the ranks of the U.S. urban poor but rather to a black subset of this population seen to be actively responsible for its impoverished situation.

"Underclass" rhetoric clearly reveals the centrality of black urban culture to accounts of postmodern social crisis. The mass media as well as social-science scholarship typically portray the "underclass" as a recalcitrant mass situated utterly beyond the pale of mainstream American culture. A 1977 article in *Time* magazine described the "underclass" as "more intractable, more socially alien and more hostile than almost anyone had imagined," driven by values radically at odds with national norms.[24] In their widely publicized accounts, Nicholas Lemann and Ken Auletta concurred that it was a distinctive cultural ethos that posed the greatest obstacle to the betterment of the "underclass."[25] The most influential analysis came from sociologist William Julius Wilson, who, although he offered structural reasons and remedies for black urban poverty, gave ammunition to culturalist accounts in his extensive discussion of the "tangle of pathology in the inner city." Asserting that teenage pregnancies, out-of-wedlock births, welfare dependency, drug use, and violent crime had reached "catastrophic proportions" in black inner-city neighborhoods by the 1970s, Wilson fueled the alarmist perception that black urban America was in a state of unprecedented crisis.[26]

Wilson claimed that the grim realities of post-1970s ghetto life were a uniquely contemporary phenomenon. In earlier decades, black inner-city neighborhoods had exhibited high levels of "social organization" and intraracial class integration (3). The presence of middle-class and blue-collar residents in the ghetto had acted as a stabilizing social force, helping to acculturate the poor into mainstream (i.e., middle-class) behavioral norms such as the work ethic or the two-parent nuclear family. Following the expanded employment opportunities and the removal of formal barriers to residential integration made possible by civil rights legislation, a "black middle-class exodus" (7) from the inner cities during the 1970s removed much-needed "social buffers" and "mainstream role models," thereby hastening the cultural deterioration of ghetto life (56).

Wilson's argument continues to compel belief even though it has been vigorously refuted in social science scholarship. As Michael Katz's collection of essays, *The "Underclass" Debate: Views from History,* demonstrates, only historical myopia can sustain claims about the unprecedented cultural collapse of late-twentieth-century black urban communities.[27] Several historians have recalled the existence of class friction within black urban communities earlier in the century, such as conflicts between recent working-class migrants from the South and established black urban elites.[28] In addition, historians have tried to temper the sense of novelty that attends current discourses of urban crisis, reminding us that debates about the cultural pathology of the black urban poor go all the way back to the publication of W. E. B. Du Bois's *The Philadelphia Negro* at the beginning of the twentieth century. Drawing on Du Bois's study, Antonio McDaniel belies Wilson's idealized depiction of the black urban communities of the past. McDaniel argues that Du Bois, like Franklin Frazier and William Julius Wilson after him, overstated the beneficial role that the black middle class could serve for the black urban poor. Wilson harks back to the postwar period when the black middle class presumably played this role, yet Franklin Frazier (and, we might add, St. Clair Drake and Horace Cayton), writing in this era, scathingly depicts a black middle class indifferent to the plight of the poor. Frazier, in turn, idealizes a previous generation that Du Bois indicts for its failure to uplift the black urban masses.[29] A longer historical view reveals an infinitely regressing quest for a lost golden age of the ghetto, illustrating the "escalator" effect that Raymond Williams found endemic to pastoral critiques of the urban present.[30]

For Wilson, the ultimate responsibility for ameliorating urban poverty rests with public policy and not with the black middle class. Nevertheless, his middle-class exodus thesis places undue weight on the role played by culture in black urban poverty as well as on the role of the middle class in buffering the poor from urban crisis. Wilson's argument reverberated powerfully in the fraught debates about black middle-class accountability to the poor that raged during the 1980s and 1990s. A 1989 *Time* magazine cover story on the black middle class fanned the flames, popularizing Wilson's "persuasive theory that the worsening status of the underclass is inextricably tied to the flight from the inner city of its upwardly mobile population."[31] Various magazines geared to a general black readership, including *The Crisis, Ebony,* and *Essence,* featured stories during the 1980s debating the extent of the black middle class's responsibility to the urban poor.[32] One reason for the suddenly increased media visibility of the black middle class was that, as a consequence of the civil rights movement and the economic boom of the 1960s, this class doubled in size, forming nearly 30 percent of the black population by 1970.[33] Media focus on the expansion of this class, concurrent with its phobic attention to an allegedly growing black "underclass," further reinforced Wilson's picture of post-1970s black America as more polarized than ever before along the schisms of class.

Such discourses of communal crisis have left a sharp imprint on African-American literary and cultural studies, even as the feeling of crisis has in turn been stoked by literary and cultural critics. Writers of literary and popular fiction have also actively entered the public debate about the middle class's proper disposition toward the urban poor, with Toni Morrison cautioning against "intellectual slumming," James Alan McPherson lamenting the alienation of the middle class from the vernacular idioms of the people, Ishmael Reed lambasting black academics "posing as experts on the inner city, which for them is another planet," Toni Cade Bambara noting the linguistic gap between a "working-class sister from the projects who ... speaks in nation-time argot" and a "more privileged sister ... who speaks the lingo of postmodern theory," and Bebe Moore Campbell disputing Wilson's exodus thesis through her journalistic portraits of professional African Americans who remained or returned to help the inner-city poor.[34] Given the centrality accorded to culture in public debates on the "underclass," it is not in the least surprising that the notion of community is thrown into crisis in postmodern black literature, or that cultural critics and writers of literature have become key players shaping current debates on black urban poverty.

As Ishmael Reed bitterly remarked, the most "profitable" strategy for black intellectuals during the 1980s, one sure to bring prestigious grants, was to join the thriving "black-pathology industry."[35] Although many took strongly dissenting stances, the intellectuals who reaped the highest visibility (in middle-brow print journalism as well as television and radio) were those who complied with the terms set by dominant "underclass" discourses, polarizing the black middle class and the urban poor on cultural grounds. Orlando Patterson contrasted the "acculturated" black elite with the "hedonistic, sex-obsessed, nonfamilial, anti-intellectual, and pathetically macho" street culture of ghetto residents. Henry Louis Gates, calling attention to the existence of "two nations ... both black," declared, "It's time to concede that yes, there *is* a culture of poverty" blocking the material progress of poor urban African Americans.[36] In the most influential account, Cornel West emphasized the "structural character of culture," identifying spiritual "nihilism" rather than economic deprivation or political impotence as the "most basic issue" confronting the underclass.[37] Echoing Wilson, West found a "qualitative fissure" in African American urban history: The "trans-class character" of black urban communities disintegrated during the 1970s, directly precipitating the collapse of spiritual values and cultural traditions.[38] None of these intellectuals sought to disguise the conservative public-policy implications of their cultural portraits of the underclass. Cornel West worried that even "progressive social change" may not reverse "deeper processes of cultural decay." Henry Louis Gates exhorted the black urban poor to exercise individual responsibility. Glenn Loury, echoing Gates in his advocacy of self-help solutions, contended that the problems facing the black urban poor lie outside the scope of government remedy.[39]

Black intellectuals seeking to speak in the interests of the poor occupy a position of extreme contradiction in the postmodern era. Sharpening class divisions are highlighted by media and academic analysts as factors exacerbating the predicament of the African American urban poor. Yet these discourses enjoin black intellectuals to transcend the very class divisions that are seen as crucial components of the crisis, in order to represent the interests of the poor. Projected panaceas for urban crisis hinge on reclaiming an ideal of trans-class racial community, just as the material conditions for such community seem all but inaccessible to black intellectuals in the postmodern era. Several political scientists, including Michael Dawson and Adolph Reed, have remarked that the concept of black political "community," assuming a unified set of common interests, began to seem like a "historical anachronism" by the 1970s.[40] Although conflicting political interests obviously existed during the era of segregation, as Reed argues, the "presumption of corporate racial identity was a rational expression" of the realities of this era, when African Americans as a whole were formally excluded from participatory democratic politics.[41] But the conditions of black politics have been transformed in the post–civil rights era, as a result of legal desegregation, affirmative action legislation, increased black electoral participation, and incorporation of black elites into bureaucratic governance.

The ramifications of these developments for the notion of black political community are perhaps most clearly evident at the level of urban politics. Harold Cruse had pointed out, in his critique of Black Power militants, that they evaded the question of "which class will benefit from Black Power when it arrives and control the economic and political power that's sought." The various antipoverty and community development programs instituted by the federal government in response to the black urban insurgency of the 1960s "paid out very well in middle-class salaries," as Cruse observed.[42] These programs set in place state-sponsored mechanisms of political participation, giving rise to a new black "regime of race-relations management."[43] By virtue of the very terms of its access to political power, such a regime was structurally incapable of representing the interests of its disadvantaged constituents. As Adolph Reed argues, newly elected black mayors and public officials could only gain access to city resources by aligning themselves with progrowth economic agendas, which are invariably antithetical to redistributive goals and have been shown to reproduce class and racial inequalities.[44] The exercise of black political power since the 1970s makes undeniably clear that the political ascension of black elites will not automatically advance the interests of the lower strata of African Americans. Consequently, the racial politics forged in the era of segregation as well as the nationalist politics of the 1960s, presuming a cohesive community of racial interests, begin to appear increasingly obsolete in the post-civil rights period.

A distinguishing feature of black politics in the postmodern era is that race no longer forms the singular axial principle of all political projects affecting African Americans.[45] To argue this is not, however, to endorse William Julius Wilson's claim about "the declining significance of race" in post–civil rights America. Because racial status still significantly determines material life-chances for a vast majority of African Americans, racial politics cannot be banished as the relic of a bygone era. But racial politics can no longer be premised on models of unmediated representation or of monolithic racial community. In 1992, Toni Morrison observed that it should be "clear to the most reductionist intellect that the time for undiscriminating racial unity has passed."[46] Morrison made this statement in the wake of the nationally televised confirmation hearings for Clarence Thomas's accession to the Supreme Court, which made dramatically visible the gender and class conflicts striating black political community. Morrison's remark has been widely cited as expressive of the postmodern moment in black culture and politics, when differences within the race seem more intractable than ever before. The question of how to build an antiracist politics that gives due weight to intraracial differences forms the central challenge of the postmodern period in African American studies.

MODERN AND POSTMODERN PROJECTS OF RACIAL REPRESENTATION

A useful point of departure for a discussion of postmodern approaches to racial representation is offered by two well-publicized articles on the "new" African American intellectuals by Robert Boynton and Michael Berube, published in *Atlantic Monthly* and *Village Voice,* respectively, in 1995. Berube contends that postmodern black intellectuals are "committed to rethinking forms of African-American collectivity" while rejecting the identity politics of 1960s black cultural nationalism.[47] Both Boynton and Berube differentiate this intelligentsia not only from the preceding generation of nationalists but also from the "modern" generation of New York intellectuals commemorated in Russell Jacoby's widely read book *The Last Intellectuals.* Jacoby had argued that, with the academic institutionalization of intellectual work and the professionalization of the academy since the 1960s, "public intellectuals" (a term coined by Jacoby) who could reach an educated general readership had become extinct.[48] Boynton and Berube refute Jacoby's claim by arguing that the black intellectuals of the post-1960s generation in fact have access to a larger public than did the New York intellectuals whom Jacoby had eulogized and elegized. The wider public provenance of the new black intellectuals stems from their refusal to restrict themselves to the print-literate and high-cultural spheres privileged by the moderns. Black public intellectuals blur and cross the boundaries between high and popular culture, observes Boynton, and Berube elaborates that their "unique relationship to the vernacular of their time" affords them an "unprecedented opportunity" to speak to and from a variegated public sphere.[49]

The two key features, then, that are said to distinguish postmodern from modern black intellectual and cultural production are its quest for a politics of difference that eschews essentialist constructs of community, and a shift from print to vernacular media. But these two tendencies often work at cross-purposes in contemporary black cultural studies. The displacement of print by vernacular forms of representation is motivated by the desire to address a broad-based black community and entails claims about the authentic culture of African Americans. A lingering investment in the idea of black cultural specificity, as well as in the very problematic of racial representation, generally winds up reinstating the essentialist notions of community that postmodern cultural critics strive to surpass. This is easily evident in the writings of bell hooks and Cornel West, who have gained the highest visibility as authorities on postmodernism in the sphere of black cultural studies.

hooks and West figure centrally in Edward Soja and Barbara Hooper's essay, "The Spaces that Difference Makes," which boldly outlines the main distinctions between modern and postmodern cultural politics. Soja and Hooper describe identity politics as "modernist" and include within this category "most orthodox forms of modern Marxism and some forms of radical feminism and black nationalism."[50] Even as such politics challenge a hierarchical and dualistic ordering of differences, they remain caught within this order, seeking mainly to invert it and to centralize the subordinated term. Such movements earn the label "modernist identity politics" through their tendencies toward "master-narrative essentialism and binary totalization" (187). As an alternative, Soja and Hooper advocate a "radical postmodern politics of difference" (184) that aims to empower "a multiplicity of resistances rather than searches for that one 'great refusal,' the singular transformation to precede and guide all others" (187). For their definition of this brand of radical postmodernism, Soja and Hooper are indebted to Cornel West's essay "The New Cultural Politics of Difference," published three years earlier. By West's account, postmodern politics bases itself on the concrete and contextual rather than on the abstract and universal values of modern politics. Taking as its starting point a position of social specificity, the politics of difference aspires to new forms of affiliation, to "contingent, fragile coalition building" in place of "homogeneous unity or monolithic totality."[51]

Such accounts of the distinction between modern and postmodern politics capture important shifts in U.S. cultural studies that occurred during the 1970s. In academic fields such as feminist and African American studies, the move toward postmodernism largely involved an emphasis on the intragroup differences suppressed in radical feminism and black cultural nationalism. Indeed, the postmodern moment in African American studies is widely configured as the era of postnationalism. Greg Tate may have been the first to use the term "postnationalist" to describe currents in black culture since the 1970s.[52] In a manifesto for one such movement, Trey Ellis claims that the New Black Aesthetic (under which he encompasses recent trends in film, music, performing arts, and literature) takes a revisionist stance toward nationalist discourses of racial authenticity.[53] In the sphere of literature, Lawrence Hogue contends that postmodernism entails critical distance from the "unfragmented racial tradition" linked with nationalism.[54] However, sharp distinctions between "modernist identity politics" such as nationalism and the "new" postmodern politics of difference unravel under closer inspection. Despite claims to the contrary, it is not at all clear that most variants of postmodern cultural politics actually manage to avoid essentialist conceptions of social difference or that they succeed in balancing the claims of intragroup difference and solidarity more effectively than did earlier nationalist or radical feminist movements.

In their opposition between "modernist identity politics" and the postmodern politics of difference, Soja and Hooper draw heavily on bell hooks's formulation of these terms in her essay "Postmodern Blackness." Here, hooks labels 1960s black nationalism "modernist" on account of its "universalizing agenda" as well as its commitment to identity politics.[55] In speaking of the "universalizing agenda" of nationalism, what hooks probably has in mind is its unitary definition of racial identity and its centralizing of race as the sole axis of all emancipatory politics. This is what hooks suggests when she writes that postmodern critiques of essentialism are valuable because they compel recognition of multiple identities and divergent interests within the category of blackness. hooks further elaborates her sense of the disjunction between black nationalism and postmodernism in her essay "The Chitlin Circuit: On Black Community." Here, hooks writes that African Americans are experiencing a profound sense of loss and crisis, arising from the difficulty of constructing forms of racial community suited to the political realities of the post–civil rights era. hooks reiterates that for several reasons "neonationalist responses . . . no longer realistically address how we live as black people in a postmodern world."[56] In addition to raising the common postmodernist objection to nationalist politics—that it does not reckon with the heterogeneity of black experiences—hooks also discredits nationalism as a phenomenon linked with "black capitalism" and "patriarchy." Then, as hooks turns to the question of how African Americans can reclaim an antinationalist model of community in the postmodern era, her argument takes a curious turn. hooks draws her model of "beloved black community" from black folk life in the segregated South.

This model is more inspiring than the nationalist one because, first, its agrarian rather than capitalist basis nourished a communal ethos, and second, it epitomized "an organic unity between black women and men" that was eroded by the emergence of nationalism (36). hooks concludes with the advice that African Americans rebuild community in the post–civil rights era by renewing "rituals of belonging" associated with "traditional black folk experience" (39). hooks's proposal for recovering black community in the postmodern era hinges on an opposition between nationalism and agrarian southern life that cannot be sustained on historical grounds, as is obvious from the fact that she can offer no evidence for her contentions that southern folk life was free of "male domination" and that black nationalism introduced gender divisions into black community (36). An important reason for hooks's rejection of nationalism is that its rhetoric of racial authenticity erases the differences within black experience, yet these differences are also wished away in her own idealized image of the "organic unity" of southern black life. Although hooks assumes a postmodern perspective to condemn nationalist paradigms of community, she subsequently distances herself from postmodernism in order to defend her own version of racial authenticity. In her opinion, African Americans "cannot afford the luxury" of postmodern critiques of authenticity because they are already "coping with a sense of extreme fragmentation" (38). hooks's cure for the fragmentation of black communal life in the post–civil rights era calls for a retrieval of the very conditions that she earlier admits to be irrevocably lost—the "organic unity" and "traditional black folk experience" of the days of racial segregation. These terms exactly restore the principles of nationalist community—separatism, racial tradition, organicism, and authenticity derived from vernacular culture. The only difference is that hooks's model of beloved community is rooted in the folk culture of the segregated and rural South rather than on urban vernacular culture, and in this respect it is even more inaccessible in the present than is the nationalist model.

A similar reversion to organic forms of racial community characterizes Cornel West's pronouncements on African American life in the postmodern era. As noted earlier, West's writing adds fuel to crisis-ridden accounts of black urban community. Like hooks, West responds to this crisis by nostalgically recalling an earlier era when black cultural traditions were intact and when class differences within the race did not carry the divisive implications they do in the present. Even when explicitly addressing the state of African American life in the postmodern era, West draws his own authority to speak on behalf of the race from essentialist constructs of black community. An example of this tendency appears in West's interview with Anders Stephanson, included in Andrew Ross's collection *Universal Abandon: The Politics of Postmodernism.* Both Stephanson and West liberally make use of reductive phrases such as "the black community" or "the black political constituency."[57] In response to Stephanson's question, "What does it mean to a black American to hear that . . . we have lost the real?" West replies as follows:

> *There is a reality that one cannot not know.* The ragged edges of the Real, of *Necessity,* not being able to eat, not having shelter, not having health care, all this is something that one cannot not know. The black condition acknowledges that. It is so much more acutely felt because this is a society where a lot of people live a Teflon existence, where a lot of people have no sense of the ragged edges of necessity, of what it means to be impinged upon by structures of oppression. To be an upper-middle-class American is actually to live a life of unimaginable comfort, convenience, and luxury. Half of the black population is denied this, which is why they have a strong sense of reality. (277)

West's response is apparently materialist in its reference to class variations within American experiences of material contingency. But West goes on to elide these distinctions as he generalizes about "the black condition," which becomes synonymous with the experience of acute material deprivation. Most of the poor in the United States, who are not black, along with that "half of the black population" that is not poor, must disappear in order to permit West to speak on behalf of the race as well as the poor.

Although the postmodern cultural critic avowedly pays scrupulous attention to class differences within the race as well as to issues of intellectual/mass mediation, this is rarely borne out by practice. The claim that postmodern intellectuals more accurately represent the interests of the race as a whole than did their modern counterparts is secured through vernacular definitions of black cultural ethos. The vernacular forms the site where rifts arising from class and educational differences may be healed and an organic connection established between the intellectual and the people. The populist ambitions of postmodern projects of racial representation hinge on their critical distance from modern paradigms of the print-literate intellectual conversant in high cultural traditions. The best-known instance of this paradigm in African American studies is W. E. B. Du Bois's early-twentieth-century ideal of the Talented Tenth, those elite intellectuals who would serve as "missionaries of culture among their people." Convinced that culture filters "from the top down," Du Bois hoped that the intelligentsia, fluent in Western high culture, would deliver the black masses out of their condition of ignorance and illiteracy.[58]

Several African American intellectuals have assailed the Enlightenment inheritance of the Talented Tenth model from an explicitly postmodern perspective. In *The Future of the Race,* a book he coauthored with Henry Louis Gates, Cornel West faults Du Bois for his elitist condescension toward the black masses.[59] As "self-appointed agents of Enlightenment" (64), the Talented Tenth assume the task of civilizing the benighted masses by initiating them into high culture (64–65). West questions the assumption that highbrow culture is inherently humanizing, concluding that "we have little reason to believe that people who delight in the work of geniuses like Mozart and Beethoven or Goethe and Wordsworth are any more or less humane than those who dance in the barnyards to the banjo plucking of nameless rural folk in Tennessee" (68). Similarly, Ishmael Reed mercilessly indicts "talented tenth intellectuals" for embracing a supposedly "common culture" that is actually "Yankee or Anglo," for taking "the Enlightenment, ... which introduced scientific racism" as their "intellectual model," and for "missionizing" less privileged African Americans.[60]

Repudiating the uplift ambitions of the Talented Tenth, both Reed and West propose a countermodern model of the black intellectual authorized by vernacular rather than print or high culture. Reed's neo-hoodoo aesthetic aligns itself with the Afro-diasporic cultural traditions that have been suppressed by Enlightenment notions of a common human culture. Reed has long been singled out by literary critics as the exemplar of black postmodernism because of his incorporation of popular-cultural energies into his writing and his relentless attack on institutionalized high culture. In Reed's fiction, critique of modern Western aesthetics is indissolubly linked to celebration of a racially specific black culture. Andreas Huyssen is one of the few theorists of postmodernism to note that its challenge to the modernist cultural canon gained impetus from the self-assertion of minority cultures, which had long been relegated to the low-cultural margins.[61] In this light, 1960s black cultural nationalism emerges as a crucial constituent of postmodernism, with its stress on vernacular culture and racial particularity calculated to displace high modern ideals of universal culture.

Although this is seldom acknowledged, postmodern black intellectuals remain deeply in thrall to this nationalist legacy. Whereas Reed has been unwavering in his refusal of the Talented Tenth mission and has consistently drawn on popular culture to deflate the hubris of this mission, West advocates an incoherent amalgam of uplift and populism. Despite his scathing critique of the "service" ethic of Du Bois's talented tenth in *The Future of the Race,* West elsewhere calls for a revival of precisely this ethic of "sacrifice" and "service to the race," maintaining that it "created a moment of accountability."[62] West is equally contradictory on the issue of whether print or vernacular traditions should vouchsafe the cultural authority of postmodern African American intellectuals. Du Bois's talented tenth ideal apotheosized print culture: As Henry Louis Gates remarks, black intellectuals in the Du Bois era strove to prove that they, "too, were a people of the Book."[63] West's ambivalence about the modern print legacy derives in part from apprehensions about the impending demise of book culture that he shares with many postmodern cultural theorists. Print culture is felt to be on the brink of social irrelevance because, wedded to an exclusionary notion of humanist culture, it is less amenable to pluralist cultural demands than are the electronic media of the postmodern age. These media are apparently sweeping away not only the technology of print but also the promise of critical autonomy from the given social world proffered by modern print culture.

In the spirit of the times, West is pessimistic about the viability of print culture and, consequently, about the role of the literate intellectual in the age of electronic reproduction. Observing that there aren't that many "intellectuals of the book" anymore, West laments the fact that print literature is being sidelined by audio and video technologies.[64] West grants that the quest for print literacy is still a driving ambition among African Americans but argues that the benefits of literacy are increasingly understood in "pecuniary" terms, thus accounting for the peripheral status of intellectuals in black culture.[65] In his well-known essay on the nihilism of contemporary black urban populations, West bemoans the full penetration of commodity capitalism into black life, citing the spread of market values as a primary cause of the moral decay of black community in the postmodern era.[66] The print tradition may have delivered on its modern promise of safeguarding critical distance from commodity culture, but this hope proves futile as African Americans now seek print literacy mainly in pursuit of material gain.

When West decries the pecuniary incentives for print literacy among an unspecified black community, he probably means to refer to the middle class or to middle-class aspirants. (It seems unlikely that West would expect those who suffer material deprivation to value humanist intellectual work over the practical benefits of print literacy, such as expansion of employment opportunities.) But West's argument about the marginal status of print culture in African American life fares not much better if we assume that he is referring to the middle class. The 1980s saw a dramatic growth in specialty black bookstores and in distributors and publishers catering to a specifically African American readership, a trend that should, in one publisher's words, "lay firmly to rest the tired myth that blacks don't buy books." The highest demand, from this audience for commercially published books, was for "serious" nonfiction.[67] Even "intellectuals of the book" were poised to command a fairly good share of this new market by the beginning of the 1990s; as a university press editor remarked, "Black intellectuals who want to write for a wider audience will find one."[68] A significant proportion of this growing readership is drawn from the "new" black middle class, which saw its greatest moment of expansion during the post–civil rights decades.

The class basis of this audience discomforts many postmodern black intellectuals, as it did nationalist intellectuals such as LeRoi Jones/Amiri Baraka, who wrote of his own book, *Home: Social Essays*: "Since this book is so expensive, it will fall into the hands of more MC Negroes than people out on the block. (MC meaning middle class)."[69] Postmodern intellectuals such as Cornel West and bell hooks aspire to serve the race but cannot stomach the modern idea of acculturating the lower classes into a print-literate tradition. Because hooks and West wish to reach a black audience larger than those who can afford to buy books, print seems to them a medium of restricted social scope. Consequently, hooks cautions that given the high levels of functional illiteracy among "black folks," intellectuals cannot hope to "spread the message by books alone."[70] Similar desires for connection with a mass black audience motivate West's laments about the poverty of black print culture. Asserting that "Black America has yet to produce a single literate intellectual, with the sole exception of Toni Morrison," West claims that the two "organic intellectual traditions" of African American culture are both oral—the Christian tradition of preaching and the musical-performance tradition.[71]

In his effort to replace the literate Talented Tenth intellectual with an organic intellectual, West recapitulates all the founding moves of 1960s black cultural nationalism. His attachment to allegedly outmoded notions of racial authenticity is evident from his attempt to single out the "Ur-text of black culture," which he defines as vocative, kinetic, and nonverbal.[72] What's more, West's definition of this culture reproduces the nationalist hierarchy of (elite, inauthentic) print and (popular, authentic) vernacular culture. West exactly echoes nationalist writers such as Amiri Baraka or Larry Neal when he pits the mediocrity of black print culture against the creativity of oral traditions. In "The Myth of a Negro Literature," published in 1966, Baraka had scoffed at the "agonizing mediocrity" of black print production and identified black music as the "profound contribution" of African Americans.[73] Larry Neal concurred that black written poetry does not match the expressiveness of a "James Brown scream."[74] For both Baraka and Neal, black print literature was insufficiently expressive of racial ethos because it formed the exclusive province of the "Negro bourgeoisie," whereas black music, accessible even to "the lowest class of Negroes," more fully "represented the collective psyche."[75] In Cornel West's postmodern account, oral culture performs exactly the same function of populist legitimation as it did for the 1960s nationalists.

West's example reveals the difficulty of resisting essentialism while remaining invested in the project of authentic racial representation. This project cannot but reactivate claims of a transparent relation between the intellectual and the masses as well as reified models of black culture and community. The best reason for questioning postmodern projects of racial representation is not that they recall a supposedly passé modern era but that they fall short of their own stated goal of truly giving voice to the people. In his book *Yo Mama's Disfunktional,* Robin Kelley rightly excoriates prevailing social science scholarship on the "underclass" for its reductive view of black urban culture as an unmediated reflection of ghetto realities. One reason social scientists miss the complexity of this culture is that "they do not let the natives speak." Kelley presents his own work as an attempt to "give voice to those urban populations under siege," with his title meant to "represent what I imagine the very subjects/objects of reactionary social science and public policy might say if they could speak back to the critics and analysts."[76] Dominant discourses on the "underclass" pathologize black urban culture on the grounds of its aberration from a normative model of U.S. mainstream culture. Reacting against the uplift ideology implicit in such discourses, the postmodern intellectual assumes the vernacular voice of the cultural interpreter instead of the modern role of cultural legislator,[77] in the hope that this strategy will more accurately represent the black urban masses. But the continued silence of the "natives" is a precondition for the intellectual's attempt to speak for them. Whether deriding the nihilism of black urban culture (as do Gates, West, Loury, and others mentioned earlier) or celebrating its expressive richness, the intellectual cannot give voice to the urban masses as long as he or she claims to represent them. As Adolph Reed has eloquently argued, terms such as *masses* or the *underclass* are "homogenizing mystification[s]" in that both entities "exist only in the third person; no discernible constituency describes itself and rallies under either label." As such, these terms assume a "mute" referent that must be spoken for because it cannot be imagined as a subject of political discourse.[78]

The silence of the represented is a necessary condition of existing structures of racial representation. Claims to racial representation prove difficult to dismantle at the level of discourse because their roots lie in the structural conditions of African American access to public culture. Anders Stephanson's interview with Cornel West shows that even in the most difference-sensitive postmodern contexts, black intellectuals are still expected to speak for the entire race. As Joy James has argued, so long as institutionalized racism curtails full black access to public discourse, the part will continue to stand in for the whole, and in fact, the high visibility of a few token figures will serve to disguise a system that excludes the many. Within this kind of economy of cultural production, intellectuals engaged in racial representation will necessarily amass cultural capital at the expense of those nonelite groups that are "prohibited from a counter discourse."[79]

PRINT LITERATURE AND RACIAL REPRESENTATION

The contradictory nature of the burden of racial representation imposed on African American culture is perhaps most clearly apparent in the domain of print literature.

With its origins in the era of slavery, the African American literary tradition was launched to demonstrate the slave's membership in the human race through the agency of writing. For the earliest slave narrators, this enterprise was fraught with difficulty, as Henry Louis Gates has shown in his discussion of slave narratives published in the late eighteenth and early nineteenth centuries. Gates identifies recurrent scenes featuring a "Talking Book" in these narratives, scenes in which the narrators seek to make a Western printed text (usually the bible) speak to the slave or in the slave's voice. Gates admits that what these scenes actually exhibit is the trope of the "un-Talking Book" (165), for in most cases the book remains silent.[80] The earliest use of tropes of the book in African American literature registers the racial disqualification of slaves from print culture and, by implication, their categorical unfreedom. In the next phase of the tradition, nineteenth-century slave narrators stage scenes of reading and writing to prove their fitness for freedom. For authors such as Frederick Douglass, the act of writing itself becomes a "tacitly political gesture" (171). Gates's argument that print literacy retains its "implicitly political import" well into the twentieth century (171) is seconded and elaborated by Robert Stepto, who traces the sustained link between print literacy and political freedom for a range of African American writers from Frederick Douglass to Ralph Ellison.[81]

In Gates's narrative, this tradition comes into its own with Zora Neale Hurston, whose novel *Their Eyes Were Watching God* exemplifies the first genuinely Talking Book or "speakerly text" of African American literature (174). Hurston, along with subsequent writers such as Ishmael Reed and Alice Walker, succeeds where the eighteenth-century slave narrators failed—appropriating an alien print tradition by making it speak in a black oral voice (181). For Gates, then, the Talking Book, or the written text that achieves the condition of black vernacular speech, represents the "Ur-trope" or the culminating point of the African American literary tradition (131). Robert Stepto is careful to clarify that he does not subscribe to this sort of progressive view of the black literary tradition, but he too sees print literacy and orality as the two motors driving the tradition. Unlike Gates, Stepto does not construe print as an alien technology that best serves black interests once it is oralized. In fact, in his 1991 preface to the second edition of *From Behind the Veil,* Stepto defends his focus on print literacy as a way of liberating black culture from the "essentialist thinking" that would have it "be exclusively a vernacular construct" (xi). Nevertheless, in identifying two broad generic types that obtain in African American narrative across various historical periods, Stepto puts in place certain oppositions between print literacy and oral culture that still powerfully influence critical appreciation of this literature.

The first of these generic types is the narrative of ascent, which features heroes who become increasingly individualized and dissociated from racial community as they master print literacy. In this sort of narrative, literacy does initiate a movement toward social mobility and political freedom, but it also always fosters a stance of "solitude" or "alienation" (167). The protagonists of immersion narratives, in contrast, achieve "tribal literacy" in "oral vernacular" tradition (169), which, unlike print literacy, always works as a medium of communal fusion. In Stepto's opinion, only one African-American literary text, Ralph Ellison's *Invisible Man,* synthesizes both types of narrative, presenting a hero who ultimately acquires both print and tribal literacy, individual and group consciousness.

African American literary texts from the period covered by Stepto's study, from the mid-nineteenth century up to the 1950s, do not readily bear out his account of print literacy as a force of alienation from racial community. Only Richard Wright's autobiographical narrative, *Black Boy,* exactly corroborates Stepto's argument. Even Frederick Douglass's 1845 slave narrative, the text that has taken on archetypal status as a literacy narrative and that is often said to exemplify the individualizing effects of print literacy,[82] on closer inspection reveals a strong concern with the benefits of literacy for the race as a whole. Not only was the publication of Douglass's narrative meant to further the political cause of abolition, but the most powerful image of collectivity in the narrative is of a slave community "linked and interlinked with each other" by the activity of book reading.[83] Numerous African American authors during the decades covered by Stepto's book (including W. E. B. Du Bois, James Weldon Johnson, Frances Harper, Pauline Hopkins, Jessie Fauset, Claude McKay, Richard Wright, and Ralph Ellison) were, like Douglass before them, intensely preoccupied with the question of the collective uses of print literacy and literature. Throughout the nineteenth century, African American literature has returned to variants of the ideology of racial uplift, which affirms print literacy as a vehicle of collective racial progress.

In a later work, "Distrust of the Reader in Afro-American Narrative," Stepto draws sharper contrasts between writing and orality, especially with regard to their differential capacity to represent racial community. Here, Stepto argues that African American literature has been propelled as strongly by suspicion of literacy as by "abiding faith in it."[84] Because of their deep distrust of the racial protocols of U.S. print culture, African-American authors posture as oral storytellers rather than as writers, and they reimagine their readers as listeners, in an effort to inculcate more responsible and sympathetic habits of reading. Stepto substantiates this last claim through an opposition between the "competitive," "deconstructionist" readings encouraged by print traditions and the more "authenticating" procedures of oral traditions (201). Similar assumptions—about oral media as the most effective vehicles for representing racial community—circulate widely in criticism on African American literature. Many of the most influential studies of African American narrative have been organized around tropes derived from black oral tradition, such as specifying, signifying, conjuring, or the blues. Drawing on the oral dynamics of antiphony, or call and response, black literary texts are said not only to activate participatory and communal conditions of reception but also to figure forth a uniquely black model of democratic politics.[85]

The impetus behind such oralized critical paradigms is to establish a seamless continuity between African American literary production (including literary criticism) and a wider black cultural community. The chief limitation of such models is that they displace issues of political representation to the level of form so that, regardless of its readerships, the African American novel represents black community insofar as it incorporates black oral culture into its narrative voice and structure. Because most vernacular theories of African American fiction tend toward formalism or structuralism, they fail to capture the dynamism of black literary production, or to explain how and why recurrent tropes and generic patterns are differently modulated in response to changing historical pressures. In earlier phases of its history, African American literature was valued (and often perhaps overvalued) as a potent tool in the struggle for political freedom and equality. Since the 1970s, however, the category of print literature has been subjected to a thoroughgoing process of revaluation, under the conjoined impact of black cultural nationalism and postmodernism. Vernacular-based theories of African American literature, which blossomed during the 1980s and still exercise considerable critical sway, are profoundly indebted to the aesthetic and political legacies of 1960s black cultural nationalism.

In the mid- to late 1960s, the Black Arts movement initiated one of the most significant developments in the history of African American literature—its institutionalization as an object of academic study. Efforts to extend the literary canon since the 1960s have assumed direct links between literary and political representation whereby the inclusion of a minority writer in the canon is seen as a gain in group representation. Yet this is least likely to be the case in the sphere of print literature. As John Guillory observes, the recovery of previously excluded traditions has proceeded on the premise that "the field of writing is a kind of *plenum,* a textual repetition of social diversity," whereas in fact "the most socially consequential process of exclusion occurs primarily at the level of access to literacy."[86] Keenly conscious of the privilege attaching to print literacy, proponents of black cultural nationalism undermined literature as insufficiently reflective of black experience even as they struggled to get it recognized as worthy of academic study. Reflecting the conflict between integrationist and separatist impulses endemic to cultural nationalism, Black Arts advocates both valorized those oral vernacular traditions that were excluded from the precincts of certified American culture and sought to expand these precincts to include African American literature. In the postmodern period, African American literature bears contradictory political valences that can be directly traced back to the nationalist legacy. Thanks to the efforts of the nationalists, African American literature is now institutionalized in U.S. universities and, as such, subjected to the disciplinary methods of literary criticism. But precisely as an object of specialized academic study, print literature is also suspect for its alienation from the everyday life-world of African Americans.

The nationalist attack on literature has been reinforced by postmodern cultural theory, which has sought to unseat literature from its prestigious position as the crowning achievement of the modern print tradition. The overt rationale for this postmodern move is identical to that of 1960s cultural nationalism—to replace the modernist canon of humanist culture with a more inclusive notion of culture. Paradoxically, the combined nationalist and postmodern attacks on the literary institution seem to have been quite fertilizing for literature. Print literature by African Americans has commanded its largest commercial as well as academic audience in the post-1970s decades.

With its academic institutionalization, African American literature seems increasingly remote from generalized notions of "the black experience" yet continues to be freighted with racially representative value. Charles Banner-Haley laments that fiction by postmodern writers such as Clarence Major or Ishmael Reed has become so academicist and abstruse that it seems "emotionally out of touch ... with the reality of Afro-America."[87] But even as it is deemed to be inaccessible and superfluous to the vast majority of African Americans, literature is simultaneously charged with redemptive political hopes. Literary and cultural critics increasingly dominate African American political debates, and perhaps as a consequence, certain literary practices are upheld as forms of political activism. Illustrating this tendency, Cornel West, in his essay on the state of emergency in black urban America, suggests that only an ethic of love can arouse a sense of agency among the nihilistic poor.[88] The sole model of this love ethic that West can proffer is a scene from a literary text, Toni Morrison's *Beloved.* Yet in "Black Culture and Postmodernism," West justifies his neglect of literary artists and his focus on mass culture on the grounds that his main interest lies in "black resistance in the form of social movements." Presumably, popular cultural forms such as rap are more easily linked with social movements than is the elite medium of print literature.[89]

Political claims about African American literature have always depended on realist aesthetics, from the documentary impulse of the slave narratives to the reflectionist principles prescribed by the cultural nationalist program. Black literature could best fulfill its political purpose of bettering the collective condition of the race by telling the truth about black experience. This durable link between realism and racial representation is widely believed to have snapped, finally, in the postmodern period. In an article on black science fiction, Walter Mosley notes that black writers have just begun to gain acceptance within popular genres such as science fiction and hopes that this trend will finally free African American literature of its burden of representation, which Mosley describes as follows:

> Our writers have historically been regarded as ... best suited to address the nature of our own chains. So if black writers wanted to branch out past the realism of racism and race they were curtailed by their own desire to document the crimes of America. A further deterrent was the white literary establishment's desire for blacks to write about being black in a white world, a limitation imposed upon a limitation.[90]

Mosley draws attention to the twin facets of the demand for racial representation in literature—the obligation to always and only write as a racially particular subject, and the expectation of mimetic realism. Mosley argues that African American writers have largely been missing from popular genres such as science fiction because the logic of racial representation has trapped them within realist genres. Because black writers have finally begun to diversify into popular fictional genres, Mosley anticipates an explosion of black science fiction that will "break the chains of reality" and open up a "new world of autonomy."[91]

It seems logical to expect, as does Mosley, that representational demands would be relaxed for a popular genre that does not claim fidelity to things as they are. Surprisingly, though, this turns out not to be the case, as is clear from popular responses to Samuel Delany, one of the two well-known African American writers of science fiction. In a piece published in the *Village Voice,* Greg Tate writes that he "figured Delany for an oreo" until he read a speech given by Delany at the Studio Museum of Harlem that referred to African Americans as "our people." Although Delany informed Tate that all but one of the characters in his novel *Stars in My Pocket Like Grains of Sand* are black, this was not good enough for Tate, because the race of these characters was not at the core of their cultural identity. What Tate expected from "our one black SF writer" was fiction that imagined "the future of black culture from a more or less nationalist stance."[92] Clearly, even a popular genre known for its angular approach to social reality is still held accountable to nationalist imperatives of realism and race representation.

The links between mimetic realism and the assumption that any part can and must substitute for the whole—between the two meanings of representation as depiction and delegation—have become firmly entrenched in popular and academic responses to African American writers. As suggested by Walter Mosley's comments, the demand for verisimilitude imposes a racially particular position of enunciation on the African American writer. A writer like Delany, who thwarts both of these demands, is censured for his "racially defused" vision.[93] This tight interlock of mimetic realism, racial particularity, and delegation is perpetuated even by those literary critics who wish to surpass the problematic of racial representation. In a reading of Samuel Delany exactly contrary to Tate's, Ross Posnock argues, at two intersecting levels, that Delany manages to shed the mantle of racial representation by writing avant-garde, antirealist fiction. Posnock contends that the experimental quality of Delany's writing militates against the entailments of racial representation, "both aesthetically and politically."[94] Posnock's argument against the aesthetics of racial representation is also a brief against postmodern identity politics, which requires the African American writer to speak as a racially marked subject. In Posnock's view, African American writers can be released from the "ghetto" of group identity only by recourse to a modern ideal of "cosmopolitan universalism" (20)—a deracialized sphere of "democratic culture ... grounded in common humanity" (13).

Posnock's argument hangs on a set of dichotomies between the terms *modern* and *postmodern*: between the *politikos* of universal democratic ideals and the *ethnos* of racial particularity, and between the free-floating, cosmopolitan subject of modernism and the tribalism of postmodern identity politics (17). This opposition is based on the spurious presumptions that racial politics cannot bear universal implications and that modern political constructs have been free of race. Posnock's conception of modern and postmodern cultural politics is especially inapplicable to Samuel Delany's writing, which urges readers to reconsider precisely such dichotomies. Delany associates modern culture and politics with the "notion of a centered subject," which he describes as a "mirage" subtending the material oppression and ideological exclusion of racial and gendered "others."[95] This falsely universal subject (like Posnock's idea of the free-floating modern subject) inhabits a "dream outside of historical time," which Delany exposes as a delusion.[96] Delany advocates an alternate postmodern notion of the "subject-in-history" that can, in principle, "be denied to *no* one" (204). In Delany's clunky formulation, the postmodern subject is a "self-inseparable-from-the-material-universe-and-all-we-don't-know-about-it that is one with the notion of the self-in-history-that-is-all-we-do-know-about-our-universe" (199). Posnock is critical of identity, which he claims is reified in postmodern discourse, but extols modern subjectivity, which he believes is a more fluid category. But polarized notions of modern and postmodern subjects are easily reversible, as Delany's remarks suggest: From certain polemical perspectives, the modern subject appears as a stabilizing ideological construct, and postmodern identity is persuasively seen as more vulnerable insofar as it admits its own historical contingency.

The real problem with Posnock's binary oppositions between modern and postmodern subjects is that these are grounded in a strictly formalist approach to ideology and politics. Posnock construes the modern political subject to be dynamic because he derives his account of this subject chiefly from the formal strategies of modernist literature, which unsettle realist categories and conventions. Posnock conflates aesthetic and political representation, as when he argues that Delany eludes the problem of racial representation by refusing narrative realism. I dwell on Posnock's argument at some length here because it exemplifies the formalist bent of so much contemporary literary theory. Texts that interrupt fixed aesthetic conventions are said to challenge ideological and political constructs as well, such as essentialist notions of identity, cultural tradition, or community.

Such formalist assumptions are nowhere more clearly evident than in the critical discourse surrounding Ishmael Reed's *Mumbo Jumbo,* generally regarded as the exemplar of black literary postmodernism. Reed's novel juxtaposes a variety of texts and signifying systems (including photographs, drawings, invitations, and newspaper items), calling into question its own truth-claims as a literary text. Because of this semiotic heterogeneity and formal self-reflexivity, critics have interpreted *Mumbo Jumbo* as a postmodern novel that deflates claims to racial representation. In the most influential of such readings, Henry Louis Gates argues that Reed displaces the representational methods of the black literary tradition through the stylistic techniques of pastiche and parody. Reed's stress on the materiality of the signifier serves, in Gates's view, to dissolve the notion of a "transcendent black signified" that guarantees the truth-claims of literary texts.[97] Gates configures nationalism and postmodernism, racial essentialism and self-conscious textuality, as necessarily incongruent categories. *Mumbo Jumbo* elicits such a reading to the extent that its formal strategies are explicitly designed to thwart the realist demands of nationalist aesthetics. Reed disturbs the long-standing expectation that black literary texts should smoothly mirror racial reality by showing, as Gates argues, that truths about black culture are produced through the very process of textual signification. Reed flouts the reflectionist imperative through his parodic use of documentary devices such as photographs, newspaper reports, and footnotes. Nationalist conceptions of politicized art are overtly satirized in

Mumbo Jumbo on account of their unitary, purist, and repressive models of black culture. Abdul, a character who personifies nationalist aesthetics, squeezes black art to make it fit a particular racial ideology and burns the ancient Book of Thoth because of its uncertain political valence. As part of his reaction against cultural nationalism, Reed tries to liberate the aesthetic domain from the instrumental demands of politics, and he achieves this aim through his selective re-creation of the myth of Thoth, the Egyptian god of writing.

Reed incarnates Thoth in his ibis aspect, and the bird emblem gives rise to a series of word associations—ibis, bird, Black Birdman, Charlie "Bird" Parker, jazz, Jes Grew—that evoke the mutable, improvisatory, and resilient spirit of black culture. In a telling departure from mythical accounts of Thoth, Reed purges the god of writing of his judiciary and administrative functions, displacing these to Set, whom Reed polarizes against Osiris, god of nature, life, and fertility. As "the deity of the modern clerk,"[98] Set uses law and government to bring popular culture under official supervision. This fictional revision of the myth of Thoth is critical to Reed's project of elaborating an antinationalist conception of black art. Whereas nationalist ideologues set out to legislate the proper political uses of art, Reed celebrates a text of black culture that cannot be "herded" or "rounded up" to serve any single political ideology (140). By severing Thoth and his book from the legal and administrative spheres, Reed opens the way for an affirmative notion of black art fully freed from political co-optation. Reed also abjures the totalizing ambitions of nationalist aesthetics by suggesting that no part can stand in for the whole because black culture is multifaceted and inexhaustible.

But in disavowing nationalist aims for art, Reed does not surrender all claims to racial representation. In fact, by refusing narrative realism Reed actually strengthens his claim to capturing the essential truth of black culture. Reed spurns verisimilitude because the stabilizing representational methods of realism cannot contain the volatile energies of black culture, and in this sense, the dynamic form of his novel lays claim to a higher-order realism. *Mumbo Jumbo* suggests that the variegated reality of black art is in fact distorted when it is bent to pragmatic political uses. The formal principles of postmodern aesthetics—internal heterogeneity, polyvalence, refusal of closure—are the very core of black culture as defined by Reed and thereby help render the real essence of this culture. Patrick McGee has argued that Reed's neo-hoodoo aesthetic, affirming as it does the syncretism of black art, offers an alternative to the purist master narratives of modern Western culture and, we might add, of 1960s black nationalism.[99] Yet *Mumbo Jumbo* also contains its own grand narrative, its centuries-deep hermeneutic, about a mythical struggle between black and Western cultural forces. In this tall tale about the career of the Book of Thoth, recounted at the novel's climax by PaPa LaBas, black culture both changes and persists unchanged through the ages in that continual innovation forms the transhistorical essence of this culture. Through his contrast between a spontaneous, popular black culture and an aridly rational, codified Western culture, Reed achieves a rapprochement of sorts with 1960s cultural nationalism. Reed's playful and parodic presentation of this grand narrative is precisely what allows him to preserve a notion of black art as primitivist as any to be found in 1960s nationalist discourses.

Contrary to the formalist assumptions of postmodern literary theory, then, Reed's insistence on textual mediation is perfectly compatible with his self-avowed ambition of "trac[ing] the true Afro-American aesthetic."[100] As Reed's example demonstrates, disruptive formal strategies often leave intact claims to racial representation, and it is possible to flout narrative realism and yet purport to render authentic racial culture. The question of referentiality stubbornly persists as a vexed problem in African American fiction as well as literary criticism in the postmodern period. In sharp contrast to Henry Louis Gates's formalist approach, Cornel West has argued that Reed's fiction, like much black postmodern art, retains a political edge because it is rooted in a "reality that one cannot not know."[101] As we saw earlier, this is the reality of acute material deprivation, which West deems representative of African American experience as a whole. According to West, postmodern black art maintains its political accountability to the race by staying anchored in this bedrock reality of African American life. To be sure, most postmodern black novelists, even when they renounce narrative realism, nonetheless seek to certify the political aims of their fiction by asserting its special purchase on racial reality. Attesting to the ways in which crisis-ridden discourses on black community contour the postmodern black literary imagination, this reality is generally equated with the predicament of urban poverty. Many postmodern black novels contain explicit representations of a racialized urban "underclass," such as Octavia Butler's *Parable of the Sower,* Samuel Delany's *Stars in My Pocket,* Sapphire's *PUSH,* and John Edgar Wideman's *Philadelphia Fire* and *Reuben.* Even in those novels that do not directly engage contemporaneous discourses on urban crisis, the question of the political salience of literature hinges on its ability to advance some sort of referential claim. This is the case even for those subgenres of postmodern black fiction that shun mimetic realism, such as the marvelous realism of Toni Morrison's *Song of Solomon* and Gloria Naylor's *Mama Day* or the science fiction of Octavia Butler and Samuel Delany.

But the referential claims of postmodern African American fiction take more complex forms than is suggested by Cornel West's observation that black postmodern art is political insofar as it fingers "the ragged edges of the Real." Most contemporary African American novelists remain severely exercised by their own distance from the realities of material deprivation and are far less certain than West about what reality with a capital *R* might mean. Doubts about the political value of literature for a wider black constituency are distilled through the tropes of the book that proliferate in postmodern black fiction—tropes that always self-reflexively grapple with the question of how the literary text can vouchsafe its referential claims. Closely entwined with the problem of referentiality are doubts about the restricted social compass of print literature. Forcing attention to the print modality of literature, tropes of the book raise in heightened forms the problem of elite/popular mediation. Most contemporary African American novelists strenuously disavow or stretch modern conceptions of print literature so as to make it respond to the demands of hitherto marginalized social groups. So, for example, Toni Morrison and Gloria Naylor seek to model their writing on oral vernacular traditions that are putatively more expressive of black cultural community than is print literature. Samuel Delany strives to distance the popular genre of science fiction from the institutionalized category of "Literature with a capital L."[102] Through such populist gestures, contemporary African American novelists critically reappropriate the print legacy in an effort to extend the social and political provenance of their own representational medium.

The trope of the Book of Thoth, featured in both Ishmael Reed's *Mumbo Jumbo* and John Edgar Wideman's *Reuben,* vividly instantiates this attempted rehabilitation of the modern print tradition. Reed recasts Thoth as "the first choreographer" as well as the recorder of dance forms (164). Characterizing dance as a vital ancient ritual, Reed invokes and stretches the mythical Thoth's role as scribe of ritual formulae in order to imbue writing with performative dimensions. Accordingly, the Book of Thoth in *Mumbo Jumbo* epitomizes the dynamic text of black popular culture. Jes Grew, Reed's name for the spontaneous energies of this culture, manifests itself mainly through dance and music but is "seeking its ... text" during the 1920s era in which the novel is set (6). The Book of Thoth—a hieroglyphic anthology of dance forms and ritual formulae—is a quintessentially postmodern, that is to say, a countermodern text. Its format as an anthology militates against the modern convention of the singular author, holder of copyright and source of textual meaning. The hieroglyphic character of this text counters the abstraction of print technology, infusing it with pictorial possibilities as well as with numinous and hieratic value. Chafing against the silence and fixity of print, the contents of the Book of Thoth—ritual chants and dance movements—evoke the synesthetic, kinetic, and multimedia dimensions that are said to distinguish postmodern textuality. In the novel's present, the book circulates in "dispersed" fashion (69), in the form of a chain, in order to evade official capture.

Through the Book of Thoth, Reed profanes the fetish object of the printed book, opening it up to the volatile energies of black popular culture. Throughout the novel, Reed caricatures the administrative, political, and even military apparatus deployed to protect the exclusive and sacrosanct bastions of Western art. If the modern West mystifies art objects into fetishes that must be worshipped in special spheres removed from everyday life, black art recaptures the golden age of Osiris's reign, when "every man was an artist and every artist a priest" (164). Among postmodern African American novels, *Mumbo Jumbo* stands virtually alone in its festive and carnivalesque portrayal of black urban popular culture, and in this sense, contrary to critical consensus, it does not really exemplify black literary postmodernism. The political nuance of Reed's aesthetic project in this novel inheres in his conviction that black popular cultural energies can exceed all forms of political and official co-optation. Epitomizing a symbiosis of literary text and popular culture, the Book of Thoth projects an unusually smooth resolution to postmodern problems of literary representation. In its affirmation of the oppositional potential of urban popular culture, *Mumbo Jumbo* owes much to the black nationalist and other countercultural movements of the 1960s, during which the novel was written.

Reed's celebration of the subversive energy of black urban popular culture seems to become increasingly unavailable to subsequent African-American writers for a variety of reasons, not least the rapidly spreading popularity of discourses pathologizing black urban culture. Another crucial factor is the shrinking credibility, in the postmodern era, of the idea that print or vernacular culture can maintain autonomy from capitalist commodity culture. Andreas Huyssen has argued that postmodern art in the United States failed to muster the critical edge of earlier avant-garde movements in part because it arrived on a popular cultural scene that was thoroughly incorporated into commodity capitalism.[103] Huyssen's observation rings true for much postmodern black fiction, which either discredits a degraded mass culture or posits a folk culture displaced backward in time as the only defense against commodity capitalism. Many postmodern black novelists continue to press claims to broad-based racial representation on the strength of their links with the vernacular traditions of the people, but they find this to be a far more difficult endeavor than does Reed. The problem of mediating between print and vernacular culture is compounded by a historically specific matrix of factors, including the transformed conditions of black politics in the post–civil rights decades, the sharpening intraracial class polarities resulting from structural economic changes, the sway of crisis-ridden discourses on black urban community, and the academic institutionalization of African American literature.

The difficulties of resolving contemporary problems of racial representation through the medium of print literature form the central preoccupation of Wideman's novel *Reuben,* published in 1987. Whereas Reed's Book of Thoth symbolizes a print literary tradition regenerated by the countermodern energies of black popular culture, Wideman invokes Thoth in order to mourn the incapacity of the contemporary black writer to recapture the ritual dimensions of premodern writing or to represent the culture of his people. Wideman casts Thoth in the overlapping roles of court clerk, patron of scribes, mediator between deities, reckoner of days, officiator of sacred rituals, and guardian of the dead. In the Egyptian Books of the Dead, Thoth often appears in the judgment scenes held before the council of the gods as an advocate for the dead, overseeing their safe passage into the world beyond death. Reuben, the writer figure in Wideman's novel, aspires to this ritualistic function but in fact can only operate as a camera, freezing the dead. The writer in *Reuben* cannot reincarnate himself as a premodern figure in whom writing, law, administration, magic, and sacred ritual are all conjoined. The mythical Thoth was simultaneously a legal scribe who recorded divine decrees that he also often helped to decide, the author of the Book of Thoth, a collection of ritual formulae, and the writer of "the divine book," which recorded the details of the sun god Re's government.[104] But in Wideman's novel, these various functions are sundered into specialized domains that cannot be incorporated into any single figure.

If Wideman cannot sustain Ishmael Reed's "neo-hoodoo" conception of writing as a holistic domain of simultaneously secular and sacred dimensions, he can no more readily affirm a politically instrumental role for literature. In contrast to Reed, Wideman highlights Thoth's roles as legal mediator, court recorder, and administrative clerk in an effort to extend the pragmatic social scope of writing and to reinstate the postmodern writer as the "unacknowledged legislator" of his people. As Thoth mediated between Horus and Set, helping to settle their conflict, so the writer figure in Wideman's novel uses his knowledge of the law to mediate between the poor residents of Homewood and the powers-that-be downtown. Wideman's attempted vindication of writing in the postmodern era demands the reintegration of literary and political, symbolic and practical realms. Reuben practices legal mediation through magic: He performs rituals of empathetic identification with his clients, hoping that the force of his compassion will bring about favorable changes in their lives. Instead of actually taking his clients' cases downtown, Reuben conjures up imaginary resolutions to their legal problems. In this sense, the efficacy of Reuben's legal work depends on the saving power of fiction. His greatest service to the Homewood community is to provide its members the illusion that someone represents them and to offer them a species of justice they are unlikely to receive in real life. Its power to dodge reality and to entertain imaginary possibilities is what ultimately redeems the writing of literature in *Reuben*.

But this redemption remains tentative because Wideman can neither endorse a notion of politicized art secured by straightforwardly realist claims nor entirely banish the tricky question of literature's relation to social reality. Unlike Reed's Book of Thoth, which authentically captures the plenitudinous culture of the race, Wideman's Thoth-writer obsessively ponders the fragility of his claims to representing the black community of Homewood. The fictive terms of Reuben's legal representation of this community suggest that literary writing cannot serve immediate social uses or be wholly adequate to social reality. But for Wideman, wrestling with the question of literature's insufficiency to an extratextual real becomes the only way of keeping alive a political conception of literature. Altogether suspending this question can encourage solipsistic and masturbatory notions of self-sufficient textuality, captured in *Reuben* through a vivid image of Thoth in his baboon aspect: "a baboon, brow furrowed in deep thought, middle finger searching his asshole, was a perfect emblem for the writer."[105] In *Reuben,* unlike in *Mumbo Jumbo,* questions of textual mediation are deliberately yoked to problems of social mediation: Through heightened attention to the oblique relations between literary texts and reality, Wideman interrogates his own claims to representing the culture of the people.

Wideman's novel suggests how literature might offer a unique point of entry into postmodern debates about racial representation. Its peculiarly fictive conditions of credibility as well as its narrow social purview are a liability for literature, curbing claims of direct and mass political relevance. But this very liability can be valuable if it compels readers and writers to confront the risks and errors entailed in literary projects of racial representation. Exposing Reuben as an impostor at the end of his novel, Wideman implies that the writer's claims to representation can only proceed at a fictive level and are, therefore, necessarily caught in the meshes of mediation. An emphasis on mediation seems especially valuable in a postmodern situation where political projects either founder on dire claims about the total eclipse of the real or seek mystical fusion with pretextual realities. The value of studying postmodern African American novels in this context is that they treat the question of literature's relation to social reality as a problem that must be squarely addressed although it cannot be conclusively settled. Without surrendering political hopes for literature, these texts call for more scrupulous accounts than currently prevail of the political agency of black literature. Forcing attention to the fallible yet ineluctable nature of mediation, tropes of the book in postmodern black fiction provoke rigorously self-critical reflection about contemporary projects of racial representation. Despite widely varying uses, these tropes impart a keen awareness of the imposture always risked when writers claim to speak for those less privileged groups who are excluded from print culture.

NOTES

1. For example, see Alex Callinicos, *Against Postmodernism: A Marxist Critique* (Cambridge: Polity, 1989), chap. 1.
2. David Harvey, *The Condition of Postmodernity* (Cambridge: Blackwell, 1990), 145.
3. Jean-Francois Lyotard, *The Postmodern Condition: A Report on Knowledge,* trans. Geoff Bennington and Brian Massumi (Minneapolis: University of Minnesota Press, 1984), xxiii–xxiv.
4. Doreen Massey, *Space, Place, and Gender* (Minneapolis: University of Minnesota Press, 1994), 6–11, 136–42.
5. Ibid., 122–123.
6. Wahneema Lubiano, "Shuckin' Off the African-American Native Other: What's 'Po-Mo' Got to Do with It?" *Cultural Critique* (Spring 1991): 154, 160; Wahneema Lubiano, "The Postmodernist Rag: Political Identity and the Vernacular in *Song of Solomon,*" in *New Essays on Song of Solomon,* ed. Valerie Smith (Cambridge: Cambridge University Press, 1995), 94–95.
7. Phillip Brian Harper, *Framing the Margins: The Social Logic of Postmodern Culture* (New York: Oxford University Press, 1994), 3–4.
8. David Harvey, *Justice, Nature, and the Geography of Difference* (Oxford: Blackwell, 1996), 96–104.
9. For Raymond Williams's discussion of periodicity in terms of dominant, residual, and emergent strains, see Williams, *Marxism and Literature* (Oxford: Oxford University Press, 1977), 121–127.
10. Fredric Jameson, *Postmodernism, or, the Cultural Logic of Late Capitalism* (Durham, NC: Duke University Press, 1991), 309; also see 366.
11. Anders Stephanson, "Regarding Postmodernism: A Conversation with Fredric Jameson," in *Universal Abandon: The Politics of Postmodernism,* ed. Andrew Ross (Minneapolis: University of Minnesota Press, 1988), 16.
12. bell hooks, "Choosing the Margin as a Space of Radical Openness," in *Yearning: Race, Gender, and Cultural Politics* (Boston: South End Press, 1990), 148.
13. Edward W. Soja, *Thirdspace: Journeys to Los Angeles and Other Real-and-Imagined Places* (Oxford: Blackwell, 1996), 10.
14. Neil Smith, *Uneven Development: Nature, Capital, and the Production of Space* (New York: Blackwell, 1984).
15. Mike Featherstone, "In Pursuit of the Postmodern: An Introduction," *Theory, Culture, and Society* 5 (1988): 199–200; Zygmunt Bauman, "The Fall of the Legislator," in *Postmodernism: A Reader,* ed. Thomas Docherty (New York: Columbia University Press, 1993), 137.
16. On the racial and class polarizations produced by processes of deindustrialization, see Barry Bluestone and Bennett Harrison, *The Deindustrialization of America* (New York: Basic Books, 1982), 54, 87, 95.
17. John D. Kasarda, "Urban Change and Minority Opportunities," in *The New Urban Reality,* ed. Paul E. Peterson (Washington, DC: Brookings Institution, 1985), 33.

18. William Julius Wilson, *The Truly Disadvantaged: The Inner City, the Underclass, and Public Policy* (Chicago: University of Chicago Press, 1987), 41–42; and William Julius Wilson, *When Work Disappears: The World of the New Urban Poor* (New York: Vintage, 1996), 25–42.

19. See David Bartelt, "Housing the 'Underclass,'" in *The "Underclass" Debate: Views from History,* ed. Michael B. Katz (Princeton: Princeton University Press, 1993), 118–157.

20. Barry Bluestone and Bennett Harrison, *Deindustrialization of America,* 180–188.

21. See Michael B. Katz, "Reframing the 'Underclass' Debate," in Katz, *"Underclass" Debate,* 458–466.

22. Michael B. Katz, *The Undeserving Poor: From the War on Poverty to the War on Welfare* (New York: Pantheon, 1989), 196. On the use of underclass rhetoric to justify a political retreat from redistributive political goals, also see Stephen Steinberg, *Turning Back: The Retreat from Racial Justice in American Thought and Policy* (Boston: Beacon Press, 1995), 97–155.

23. Margaret Weir, "From Equal Opportunity to 'The New Social Contract': Race and the Politics of the American 'Underclass,'" in *Racism, the City, and the State,* ed. Malcolm Cross and Michael Keith (New York: Routledge, 1993), 98.

24. "The American Underclass," *Time,* August 29, 1977, 14.

25. Nicholas Lemann, "The Origins of the Underclass, Part 1," *Atlantic Monthly* (June 1986): 35; Ken Auletta, *The Underclass* (New York: Random House, 1982).

26. Wilson, *Truly Disadvantaged,* 21–29.

27. On the historical "myopia" of the underclass debate, see Thomas Sugrue, "The Structures of Urban Poverty," in Katz, ed., *"Underclass" Debate,* 86, 114.

28. For example, see Joe William Trotter, "Blacks in the Urban North: The 'Underclass' Question in Historical Perspective," in Katz, ed., *"Underclass" Debate,* 66–67.

29. Antonio McDaniel, "The 'Philadelphia Negro' Then and Now," in *W. E. B. Du Bois, Race, and the City,* ed. Michael B. Katz and Thomas Sugrue (Philadelphia: University of Pennsylvania Press, 1998), 187–188.

30. Raymond Williams, *The Country and the City* (London: Oxford University Press, 1973), 12.

31. Richard Lacayo, "Between Two Worlds," *Time,* March 13, 1989, 67.

32. For example, see Kenneth Maurice Jones, "The Buppies," *The Crisis* 93, no. 4 (April 1986): 17–18, 20, 22–24, 63–64; Nathan Hare and Regina Jollivette Frazier, "Is the Middle Class Blowing It?" *Ebony* (August 1987): 85–86, 89–90; Alvin F. Poussaint, "The Price of Success," *Ebony* (August 1987): 76, 78, 80; and Bebe Moore Campbell, "Staying in the Community," *Essence* (December 1989): 96–98, 100, 112.

33. Bart Landry, *The New Black Middle Class* (Berkeley and Los Angeles: University of California Press, 1987), 2–3.

34. Toni Morrison, "Home," in *The House That Race Built* (New York: Vintage, 1998), 11; James McPherson, "Junior and John Doe," in *Lure and Loathing: Essays on Race, Identity, and the Ambivalence of Assimilation,* ed. Gerald Early (New York: Penguin, 1993), 187; Ishmael Reed, *Airing Dirty Laundry* (New York and Reading, MA: Addison-Wesley, 1993), 236; Toni Cade Bambara, "Deep Sight and Rescue Missions," in Gerald Early, *Lure and Loathing,* 292; and Campbell, "Staying in the Community."

35. Reed, *Airing Dirty Laundry,* 3.

36. Orlando Patterson, "The Black Community: Is There a Future?" in *The Third Century: America as a Post-Industrial Society,* ed. Seymour Lipset (Stanford: Hoover Institution Press, 1979), 273–274; Henry Louis Gates Jr., "Two Nations . . . Both Black," *Forbes,* September 14, 1992, 138.

37. Cornel West, "Nihilism in Black America," in *Race Matters* (Boston: Beacon Press, 1993), 12–13.

38. Cornel West, "Philosophy and the Urban Underclass," in *The Underclass Question,* ed. Bill E. Lawson (Philadelphia: Temple University Press, 1992), 195–196.

39. Cornel West, "Black Strivings in a Twilight Civilization," in Henry Louis Gates Jr. and Cornel West, *The Future of the Race* (New York: Vintage, 1996), 110; Gates, "Two Nations ... Both Black," 138; Glenn Loury, "The Moral Quandary of the Black Community," *Public Interest* 79 (Spring 1985): 9–10.

40. The quoted phrase is from Michael Dawson, "A Black Counterpublic? Economic Earthquakes, Racial Agenda(s), and Black Politics," in *The Black Public Sphere,* ed. Black Public Sphere Collective (Chicago: University of Chicago Press, 1995), 199. Also see Adolph Reed Jr., *Stirrings in the Jug: Black Politics in the Post-Segregation Era* (Minneapolis: University of Minnesota Press, 1999), 15–16.

41. Reed, *Stirrings in the Jug,* 20, 36.

42. Harold Cruse, *The Crisis of the Negro Intellectual* (New York: Quill, 1984), 560.

43. Reed, *Stirrings in the Jug,* 88.

44. Ibid.

45. On this, see Howard Winant, "Postmodern Racial Politics in the United States: Difference and Inequality," *Socialist Review* 20 (1990): 124.

46. Toni Morrson, "Introduction: Friday on the Potomac," in *Race-ing Justice, Engender-ing Power: Essays on Anita Hill, Clarence Thomas, and the Construction of Social Reality,* ed. Toni Morrison (New York: Pantheon Books, 1992), xxx.

47. Michael Berube, "Public Academy," *New Yorker,* January 9, 1995, 75. Robert S. Boynton, "The New Intellectuals," *Atlantic Monthly* (March 1995): 6, similarly notes the new intellectuals' rejection of the identity politics of black nationalism.

48. Russell Jacoby, *The Last Intellectuals: American Culture in the Age of Academe* (New York: Basic Books, 1987), 5–8.

49. Boynton, "New Intellectuals," 65; Berube, "Public Academy," 75, 78.

50. Edward Soja and Barbara Hooper, "The Spaces That Difference Makes: Some Notes on the Geographical Margins of the New Cultural Politics," in *Place and the Politics of Identity,* ed. Michael Keith and Steve Pile (London: Routledge, 1993), 186.

51. Cornel West, "The New Cultural Politics of Difference," in *Out There: Marginalization and Contemporary Cultures,* ed. Russell Ferguson, Martha Gever, Trinh T. Minh-ha, and Cornel West (Cambridge: MIT Press, 1990), 35.

52. Greg Tate, "Cult-Nats Meet Freaky-Deke: The Return of the Black Aesthetic" (1986), reprinted in *Flyboy in the Buttermilk* (New York: Simon and Schuster, 1992), 206.

53. Trey Ellis, "The New Black Aesthetic," *Callaloo* 12, no. 1 (Winter 1989): 236.

54. W. Lawrence Hogue, *Race, Modernity, Postmodernity* (Albany: SUNY Press, 1996), 6.

55. bell hooks, "Postmodern Blackness," in *Yearning,* 25.

56. bell hooks, "The Chitlin Circuit: On Black Community," in *Yearning,* 36.

57. Anders Stephanson, "Interview with Cornel West," in Ross, *Universal Abandon,* 276.

58. W. E. B. Du Bois, "The Talented Tenth" (1903), reprinted in Gates and West, *The Future of the Race,* 157, 139.

59. West, "Black Strivings," 58–59, 64–65.

60. Ishmael Reed, "Introduction," in *MultiAmerica: Essays on Cultural Wars and Cultural Peace,* ed. Ishmael Reed (New York: Viking Penguin, 1997), xvi; Ishmael Reed, "Black Pleasure: An Oxymoron," in *Soul: Black Power, Politics, and Pleasure,* ed. Monique Guillory and Richard C. Green (New York: New York University Press, 1998), 170–171; and Ishmael Reed, in a roundtable titled "Ain't We Got Soul?" in Guillory and Green, *Soul,* 280.

61. Andreas Huyssen, *After the Great Divide: Modernism, Mass Culture, Postmodernism* (Bloomington: Indiana University Press, 1986), 194.

62. bell hooks and Cornel West, *Breaking Bread: Insurgent Black Intellectual Life* (Boston: South End, 1991), 14–15.

63. Gates, "Two Nations ... Both Black," 134.

64. West, "Philosophy and the Black Underclass," 194.

65. Cornel West, "The Dilemma of the Black Intellectual," in hooks and West, *Breaking Bread,* 132.

66. West, "Nihilism and Black Culture," 16–17.

67. Connie Goddard, "Blacks and the Book World: Aiming for the Mainstream," *Publishers Weekly,* January 20, 1992, 29, 32. On the expansion of a black middle-class readership during the 1980s and 1990s, also see Calvin Reid, "Blacks and the Book World: Building a Readership," *Publishers Weekly,* January 20, 1992, 36–38; and Carolyn M. Brown, "Writing a New Chapter in Book Publishing," *Black Enterprise* (February 1995): 108–118.

68. Elizabeth Maguire, "University Presses and the Black Reader," in Black Public Sphere Collective, *Black Public Sphere,* 324.

69. LeRoi Jones, "The Last Days of the American Empire," in *Home: Social Essays* (New York: William Morrow, 1966), 197.

70. hooks and West, *Breaking Bread,* 45, 162.

71. Ibid., 136.

72. West, "Black Strivings," 81.

73. LeRoi Jones, "The Myth of a Negro Literature," in *Home,* 106.

74. Larry Neal, "And Shine Swam On," in *Visions of a Liberated Future* (New York: Thunder's Mouth Press, 1989), 20–21.

75. Jones, "Myth of a Negro Literature," 106, 108–109; Neal, "And Shine Swam On," 21–22.

76. Robin D.G. Kelley, *Yo Mama's Disfunktional: Fighting the Culture Wars in Urban America* (Boston: Beacon, 1997), 16, 3.

77. I am drawing here on Zygmunt Bauman's argument ("Fall of the Legislator," 139) that, in the postmodern era, the modern notion of intellectuals as cultural legislators is replaced by the notion of intellectuals as cultural interpreters.

78. Reed, *Stirrings in the Jug,* 16–17.

79. Joy James, *Transcending the Talented Tenth* (New York: Routledge, 1997), 136.

80. Henry Louis Gates Jr., *The Signifying Monkey: A Theory of African-American Literary Criticism* (New York: Oxford University Press, 1988), 165.

81. Robert Stepto, *From Behind the Veil: A Study of Afro-American Narrative* (Urbana: University of Illinois Press, 1991 [1979]).

82. For example, see Houston A. Baker Jr., "Autobiographical Acts and the Voice of the Southern Slave," in *The Slave's Narrative,* ed. Charles T. Davis and Henry Louis Gates Jr. (New York: Oxford University Press, 1985), 253.

83. Frederick Douglass, *Narrative of the Life of Frederick Douglass, An American Slave* (New York: Penguin, 1982 [1845]), 121.

84. Robert Stepto, "Distrust of the Reader in Afro-American Narrative," (1986), reprinted in *From Behind the Veil,* 196.

85. For example, see Susan Willis, *Specifying: Black Women Writing the American Experience* (Madison: University of Wisconsin Press, 1987); and Marjorie Pryse and Hortense Spillers, eds., *Conjuring: Black Women, Fiction, and Literary Tradition* (Bloomington: Indiana University Press, 1985). On call and response in African American fiction, see Michael Awkward, *Inspiriting Influences: Tradition, Revision, and Afro-American Women's Novels* (New York: Columbia University Press, 1989); and John Callahan, *In the African-American Grain: The Pursuit of Voice in Twentieth-Century Black Fiction* (Urbana and Chicago: University of Illinois Press, 1988). Along with Callahan, others who argue that the antiphonal structure of black music yields a powerful metaphor for democracy include Paul Gilroy, *The Black Atlantic* (Cambridge: Harvard University Press, 1993), 200; and Craig Hansen Werner, *Playing the Changes: From Afro-Modernism to the Jazz Impulse* (Urbana and Chicago: University of Illinois Press, 1994), xviii.

86. John Guillory, *Cultural Capital: The Problem of Literary Canon Formation* (Chicago: University of Chicago Press, 1993), 18, 16.

87. Charles Banner-Haley, *The Fruits of Integration: Black Middle-Class Ideology and Culture, 1960–1990* (Jackson: University Press of Mississippi, 1994), 113.

88. West, "Nihilism and Black America," 19.

89. Cornel West, "Black Culture and Postmodernism," in *Remaking History,* ed. Barbara Kruger and Phil Mariani (Seattle: Bay Press, 1989), 96.

90. Walter Mosley, "Black to the Future," *New York Times Magazine,* November 1, 1998, 34.

91. Ibid.

92. Greg Tate, "Ghetto in the Sky: Samuel Delany's Black Whole," in *Flyboy in the Buttermilk,* 160, 165–166.

93. Ibid., 165.

94. Ross Posnock, *Color and Culture: Black Writers and the Making of the Modern Intellectual* (Cambridge: Harvard University Press, 1998), 262.

95. Samuel R. Delany, "Afterword," in *Stars in My Pocket Like Grains of Sand* (New York: Bantam, 1990 [1984]), 384.

96. Samuel R. Delany, *Silent Interviews* (Hanover, NH: Wesleyan University Press, 1994), 199.

97. Gates, *Signifying Monkey,* 217–234.

98. Ishmael Reed, *Mumbo Jumbo* (New York: Simon and Schuster, 1972), 162.

99. Patrick McGee, *Ishmael Reed and the Ends of Race* (New York: St. Martin's, 1997), 16.

100. Ishmael Reed, cited in Reginald Martin, *Ishmael Reed and the New Black Aesthetic Critics* (New York: St. Martin's, 1997), 63.

101. Stephanson, "Interview with Cornel West," 277–278.

102. Delany, *Silent Interviews,* 38–39.

103. Huyssen, *After the Great Divide,* 168.

104. Patrick Boylan, *Thoth, the Hermes of Egypt* (London: Oxford University Press, 1922), 59. My discussion of the various facets and functions of the mythical Thoth are drawn from Boylan's book as well as from Rudolph Anthes, "Mythology in Ancient Egypt," in *Mythologies of the Ancient World,* ed. Samuel Noah Kramer (New York: Doubleday, 1961), 15–92; and Carleton T. Hodge, "Thoth and Oral Tradition," in *General and American Ethnolinguistics,* ed. Mary Ritchie Key and Henry M. Hoenigsweld (Berlin: Mouton de Gruyter, 1989), 407–416.

105. John Edgar Wideman, *Reuben* (New York: Penguin, 1987), 67.

10
The "Color Line" Then and Now

The Souls of Black Folk and the Changing Context of Black American Politics

Adolph Reed Jr.

The Souls of Black Folk is by far the most widely known of W. E. B. Du Bois's books. It probably ranks among a handful of the most broadly recognized titles in black American literature. From the standpoint of the historian of political thought, the very fact that the book has come to occupy such an iconic space is worthy of note and examination in its own right. After all, Du Bois published two books of nonfiction before and at least nine after *Souls,* including the posthumously published *Autobiography.*[1] Most of these books were written for popular, or at least nonspecialist, audiences, and most were noted, reviewed, and read at the time of their publication. *Darkwater* and *Dusk of Dawn* have been regarded as powerful analyses and commentaries on their times. And over the course of the sixty years between initial publication of *Souls* and Du Bois's death, his views on several core topics changed substantially. Yet it is *Souls* that has become the definitive Du Bois text, especially since the late 1980s.

No doubt *Souls* has attained recognition because of its literary qualities, as well as for other reasons that relate indirectly to its content. It is in this sense that David L. Lewis describes the book as "an electrifying manifesto," and many other commentators—at the time of the book's initial publication and since—have remarked on its expressive power.[2] Henry Louis Gates Jr. goes farther than most, insisting that the book's significance transcends its specific ideas, interpretations, and positions and is thus transhistorical. Extrapolating from J. Saunders Redding's observation, Gates asks: "How can a book be 'more history-making than historical'? It becomes so when it crosses that barrier between mainly conveying information, and primarily signifying an act of language itself, an object to be experienced, analyzed and enjoyed aesthetically."[3]

For most who have commented on it, however, the power of *Souls* is not so easily separable from its context and content. Most have found its force to lie in the text's project of, as Lewis describes it, "mobilizing a people for a bitter, prolonged struggle to win a place in history."[4] In Redding's own characterization, for example, *Souls*

> may be seen as fixing that moment in history when the American Negro began to reject the idea of the world's belonging to white people only, and to think of himself, in concert, as a potential force in the organization of society. With its publication, Negroes of training and intelligence, who had hitherto pretended to regard the race problem as of strictly personal concern and who sought individual salvation in a creed of detachment and silence, found a bond in their common grievances and a language through which to express them.[5]

Lewis's and Redding's formulations go to the heart of explaining *Souls*'s persisting resonance as a text bearing on black American politics. Du Bois crystallized a distinct sensibility, and articulated a critical voice for a point of view and social position, in black American political life at the turn of the twentieth century. Not only did this voice respond to historically specific challenges that confronted the black population at that time; it defined and responded to those challenges in terms that helped to convoke a programmatic node in black politics—indeed it even shaped what subsequently has been understood as the foci and boundaries of black politics. This understanding has been the foundation of popular as well as scholarly perceptions of the nature, content, limits, and possibilities of black political action throughout the twentieth century and into the twenty-first. To that extent as well, it has guided what has been considered the appropriate sphere of black political criticism and practice throughout this period.

The political perspective that Du Bois helped to articulate (notwithstanding claims to the contrary and the appearances they invent as common sense) was not the expression of a generic racial voice. He elaborated a perspective that was especially congenial to, and reflected the sensibility of, a particular stratum of the black American population. Redding's characterization indicates as much and gives us a picture of some of that perspective's politically salient, if typically unacknowledged, features. For instance, as Redding indicates through his unproblematized adoption of the formulation, the perspective Du Bois articulated posited the existence of a collective racial subject. Such formulations as "the American Negro," as the singular subject of a verb implying mental activity, beginning "to think for *himself*" (emphasis added) are not simply innocent figures of speech. They are a form of political synecdoche in which an element within a larger population is taken to represent the whole. If nothing else, more than three decades of feminist scholars' challenges to the claim that the generic "he" was only a neutral shorthand should sensitize us to formulations that subsume a larger population synecdochically into a smaller one.

Redding immediately makes this clear in his next sentence. He shifts from the generic, third-person, singular frame of reference to specify who exactly he means: It was "Negroes of training and intelligence . . . who . . . found a bond in their common grievances and a language through which to express them." The distinctive political accomplishment of *Souls* was to help galvanize members of this stratum, to fortify them with a rhetoric that both defined political goals and strategies for themselves and the race as a whole and naturalized collapsing the latter into the former.

As I have argued elsewhere, the political perspective that consolidated among black political elites during the first two decades of the twentieth century has largely shaped what has been recognized as black political discourse and practice—including the academic study of black politics—ever since.[6] There are reasons to be concerned about that fact. The political synecdoche on which this approach to politics rests is not simply a logical problem; it has implications for restricting legitimate political speech and practice and constraining the substance of political agendas, and it correspondingly constrains notions of legitimate lines of inquiry. Moreover, this politics formed within the context of specific political problems at a particular historical moment.

Despite some superficial rhetorical continuities, the political circumstances that spawned Du Bois's formulations and made them plausible have altered in ways that have important consequences for their usefulness as guides to political understanding and action. I shall discuss those consequences after specifying the historical particularities that ground the politics laid out in *Souls.*

THE FOUR CANONICAL THEMES OF *SOULS*

Appreciations of *Souls* have centered primarily on four of the book's substantive themes: the judgment regarding the color line, the image of the Veil, the critique of Booker T. Washington, and the double-consciousness image. Each of these themes emerged from historically specific circumstances and concerns. Examining those contexts and concerns should be an important element of assaying the political significance for our time of the arguments and perspectives Du Bois laid out in *Souls.* Doing so also helps to shed light on the conceptual and ideological dynamics that drove black politics through the twentieth century.

The imagery of the Veil that recurs in *Souls* has a straightforward, specific foundation. Except for one more mystically evocative instance in the book's first chapter—in the midst of the famous double-consciousness passage—every reference to the Veil is clearly, almost prosaically, a metaphor for racial segregation. That this would be so also makes perfect sense. Not only was separation of the races in daily life the unofficial norm all over the United States, so that, as Du Bois repeatedly laments, the better classes of whites and blacks were almost never in contact with each other. In addition, Du Bois wrote precisely during the period when codified racial segregation—the Jim Crow regime—was being consolidated all over the South. Many blacks of his class, for example, Homer Adolph Plessy and the Comité des Citoyens in New Orleans,[7] sought with little success to challenge the consolidating regime; others lamented in tones quite similar to Du Bois's the fact that their options were so artificially and unfairly limited by Jim Crow laws and social conventions.

In this sense, Du Bois's imagery was resonant partly because it expressed the sense of injustice commonly felt among his class peers at the limitations imposed by Jim Crow. His complaints concerning the Veil were all the more powerful because he articulated them as Booker T. Washington solidified his ascent in public life largely on the strength of having proclaimed black Americans' cheerful acquiescence in the segregationist order.

I have examined at length in *W. E. B. Du Bois and American Political Thought* the historical specificity of Du Bois's double-consciousness formulation and the shift in scholarly focus since the late 1980s on *Souls* toward centering the two-ness idea, as well as the increase in popular invocations of the notion during the same period.[8] From a historiographical point of view, these parallel shifts are interesting in two respects. First, the double-consciousness formulation dropped out of Du Bois's writing for the last two-thirds of his life. It is difficult to sustain a view that it was a pivotal notion in his thinking if it effectively vanished even from his reflections on *Souls,* not long after the beginning of a lengthy, prolific career. This leads to the second point of interest.

If there is scant basis to focus on the double-consciousness idea for making sense of Du Bois's politics and thought, the factors accounting for its popularity must be entirely presentist. I have laid out in chapters 8 and 9 of that book an argument that attempts to account for both academic and ideological sources of this presentist enthusiasm. In sum, I believe the notion speaks to problems of social milieu and political-economic imperatives that are distinctive to strata within the black professional and managerial classes in the postsegregation era. I shall not rehearse that argument here. Instead, I shall leave the matter for now, perhaps provocatively, with my concluding assessment that double consciousness is "the neurasthenia of the black professional-managerial class at the end of the twentieth century."[9] I would amend that judgment now to extend it to the beginning of the twenty-first.

The "Color Line" in Context

In contemporary intellectual life and political discourse, the "color line" image rivals the double-consciousness formulation in popularity both as an iconic condensation of Du Bois's text and thought and as a rhetorical device adduced in support of claims that stress the continuing significance of racial hierarchy in American life. Contextualist examination of Du Bois's formulation not only can help to ground and thereby clarify significant features of his political thinking and its evolution over time. Examining key distinctions between the context within which Du Bois initially made that claim and the contemporary period for which many commentators assert its pertinence can also help to illuminate features of black political ideology that give the color-line imagery its distinctive resonance and encourage its appropriation in commentary on politics even in the postsegregation era.

Du Bois's portentous observation concerning the color line is the first theme to appear in the book and perhaps its most familiar idea or phrase. The book's "Forethought" begins: "Herein lie buried many things which if read with patience may show the strange meaning of being black here at the dawning of the Twentieth Century. This meaning is not without interest to you, Gentle Reader; for the problem of the Twentieth Century is the problem of the color-line."[10] He reiterates and expands upon this observation in the book's second chapter: "The problem of the twentieth century is the problem of the color-line,—the relation of the darker and lighter races of men in Asia and Africa, in America and the islands of the sea."[11]

Du Bois made this assessment during a historical moment in which racial ideology was approaching its apogee as a frame of reference for understanding social life in the West, as a foundation for intellectual activity and government policy and a driving force in global politics. On the domestic scene, these were the years of the reactionary reconstructing of southern government and political life on explicitly white supremacist grounds and the expulsion of black people from effective civic participation. The culture of popular debate and participation in all sorts of political institutions that had developed among the freedpeople after Reconstruction was eliminated in one southern state after another as the Democratic Party, spearheaded by the violence perpetrated by its various paramilitary extensions, led white supremacist putsches. In addition to massive disfranchisement of black voters and consolidation of a regime of racialized terror, this period also, as symbolized in the Supreme Court's 1896 *Plessy* ruling, was marked by white supremacy's codification in the apartheid system of state-mandated racial segregation. Even boosterist proclamations of a postsectionalist, progressive "New South"—the first of several that dotted the twentieth century—were predicated on a foundation of codified white supremacy.[12]

Outside the South as well, elite anxieties about the influx of Eastern and Southern European immigrants spawned notions of Anglo-Saxon and bourgeois (the notions were hardly distinguishable) racial displacement or suicide, which drew from and reinforced the scientific racism that increasingly overtook American intellectual life in the last quarter of the nineteenth century. Uncertainties about how to regulate contact with presumed inferiors in the new public venues—mass transit, popular entertainments, department stores—in large cities exacerbated these concerns. Labor militancy and the growth in expressions of organized political radicalism seemingly raised the stakes of the presence of volatile races from Europe's margins. The rise of the ethnic political machine, real or imagined, further overheated these elite racial anxieties by suggesting inferior breeds' potential accession to political power. Even elites outside the South were little less inclined than their southern counterparts to find racial arguments self-evidently compelling as explanations for manifest inequalities. Although they eschewed the violent excesses and bloodthirsty rhetorical extremes that drove the southern offensive, they were also quite receptive to racialized views that characterized the franchise and political participation generally as a privilege rather than a right and, where possible, sought to restrict immigrant voting accordingly.[13]

Both American and European imperialist adventurism accelerated rapidly during that period and took on distinctly racial justifications and racialized the targets for conquest. British imperialism yielded Rudyard Kipling's infamous "white man's burden," and American expansionism was driven ideologically by an explicitly racialist rhetoric that drew on the dominant social science of the day. Both academic and informed lay wisdom of the time proceeded from the view that race was a crucial motive force in history, a motor of evolution. Weaker and less-developed races were thought destined to give way before the stronger and more advanced, as a natural law. The main line of debate was not whether race had a genuine foundation in human biology but whether extant racial differences were mutable over time, usually calibrated in thousands of years. Indeed, a decade and a half before *Souls* was published, the prominent French racialist Georges Vacher, Comte de Lapouge propounded a racial prophecy quite similar to Du Bois's color-line formulation, though obviously from the other side: "The conflict of races is now about to start. I am convinced that in the next century people will slaughter each other by the million because of a difference of a degree or two in the cephalic index."[14]

At the time of *Souls*'s publication Du Bois embraced the liberal race theories himself. In reflecting nearly four decades later on his views at that time, he noted that he had been "born in the century when the walls of race were clear and straight; when the world consisted of mutually exclusive races; and even though the exact edges might be blurred, there was no question of exact definition and meaning of the word."[15] He described his own view at the time thus:

> At Harvard ... I began to face scientific race dogma: first of all, evolution and the "Survival of the Fittest." It was continually stressed in the community and in the classes that there was a vast difference in the development of the whites and the "lower" races; that this could be seen in the physical development of the Negro.... Eventually in my classes stress was quietly transferred to brain weight and brain capacity, and at last to the "cephalic index."
>
> In the graduate school at Harvard and again in Germany, the emphasis again was altered, and race became a matter of culture and culture history.[16]

Given those options, it is not surprising that Du Bois would gravitate toward the cultural and historical view of race, which at least held out possibilities for improvement. "I could accept evolution and survival of the fittest," he recalled, "provided the interval between advanced and backward races was not made too impossible. I balked at the usual 'thousand years.'"[17]

Just as Du Bois changed his views about race and the primacy of racial difference,[18] he also amended his view regarding the primacy of the color line. In his preface to the fiftieth anniversary edition of *Souls,* he indicated

> I still think today as yesterday that the color line is a great problem of this century. But today I see more clearly than yesterday that back of the problem of race and color lies a greater problem which both obscures and implements it: and that is the fact that so many civilized persons are willing to live in comfort even if the price of this is poverty, ignorance and disease of the majority of their fellowmen; that to maintain this privilege men have waged war until today war tends to become universal and continuous, and the excuse for this war continues largely to be color and race.[19]

From the turn of the twentieth century, at a moment when race was a paramount metaphor in social theory and political practice, it easily could appear that race would be the force most significantly shaping social relations for the foreseeable future. This diagnosis would have been all the more likely if one accepted, as Du Bois did at the time, the prevailing wisdom that assigned race such a prominent role in world history and social organization.

Du Bois subsequently retreated from his famous color-line assessment in concert with his perception of changed historical reality and his own changing interpretation of that reality. His changed perception was influenced in part by his embrace of a more Marxian view of politics, but his turn toward Marxism also reflected a shift in the discursive center of gravity among reform-oriented intellectuals in the 1930s and 1940s, a shift away from racialist, culturalist, or other idealist understandings of the bases of hierarchy and exploitation and toward explanations rooted in political economy and class conflict.[20] Explicitly racial justifications for inequality or colonial domination became less fashionable after World War II, and by the end of the 1970s the victories of the civil rights movement in the United States and of decolonization struggles elsewhere had begun to show clearly both that challenging the color line could succeed and, poignantly, that doing so did not resolve anywhere near as much as was implied in Du Bois's early pronouncement.

The Status of the "Color Line" in the Twenty-First Century

Why, then, does the color line formulation seem so resonant under such substantially altered political and social conditions? As with the latter-day enthusiasm for Du Bois's double-consciousness formulation, answering that question requires investigation of features of contemporary black American politics and intellectual life to discern the sources of the notion's appeal. Examination of Thomas C. Holt's *The Problem of Race in the 21st Century* provides a useful starting point for that investigation.[21] The book's title evokes Du Bois's apothegm, and Holt opens with a discussion of it, affirming its soundness as a forecast of the last century and noting that "indeed issues of group difference—and especially *racialized* differences—have informed most of the major conflicts of the century."[22] Holt is clear, however, about the historical specificity of Du Bois's original claim and observes that Du Bois himself saw in the 1930s "that the fight against racism must deploy differently in the era of monopoly capital and the consumer revolution ... than it had in the world of his youth and coming of age."[23] Holt is also very clear that racial ideology and socially consequential racialist practices have evolved over time. The heart of the book is his account of the ways that racism has functioned and race has been conceptualized differently under what he characterizes as pre-Fordist, Fordist, and post-Fordist global regimes of capital accumulation. This is in service to his objective of "rethinking our explanations of race," which reduces to addressing the problem of "how we are to recognize racism and the racial, about what kinds of transformations are currently under way in the racial regime we inhabit, and thus how we are to fashion a response."[24]

What is somewhat less clear is that this formulation of the problem either may presume too much of what needs to be interrogated or, in a stronger form of the same criticism, may betray a deeper normative commitment to preserving the power of race or racism as a fundamental frame for making sense of inequality and hierarchy. Holt gives this away when he adduces Stuart Hall in characterizing race as "the modality in which class is 'lived,' the medium through which class relations are experienced, the form in which it is appropriated and 'fought through.'"[25] But what if instead of *the* modality, medium, or form through which class relations—as well as, in Holt's view, "other fundamental conflicts in the social system"—are expressed we approach race as *a* modality? That is, the more definite qualifier implies more than an assessment of the role that race plays, the work it does, in the reproduction of capitalist hierarchy; it also suggests a characterization of race's foundational significance in capitalism that approximates an ontological claim.

This is not a pedantic point. I believe we are better able to understand the ideological and institutional structures that reproduce inequality—including race—and to challenge them if, instead of seeing the complex of ideology and practice that constitutes racism as a sui generis medium expressing and reproducing capitalism's contradictions, we consider it more consistently as a species within a genus of narratives and relations of inequality based on ascriptive status. These relations and the narratives that sustain them form the basis of hierarchies of civic worth that "sort populations into categories of classification that are in principle set off from one another by clear, uncrossable boundaries" and thereby mediate and stabilize a system of social power and stratification rooted in capitalist labor relations.[26] The genus is partly captured by Holt's description: "Any ideology, any ostensible truth, any revered commonsense that stifles [people's] chances for self-realization because of who they are," though ascriptive status can also secure chances for self-realization or perhaps, though this is less likely, be neutral in relation to distributive outcomes. Holt concludes that such formulations are "likely to be racism, sexism or both,"[27] but those categories do not exhaust the actual, much less the possible, bases for politically significant ascriptive differentiation.

In contemporary American life race and gender are certainly among the most durable and broadly consequential and now the most familiar and recognizable metrics of ascriptive hierarchy. Ironically, one reason that racism and sexism stand out is that since roughly the 1950s the struggles against them have succeeded in denaturalizing them, in destabilizing their commonsensical quality, which is a necessary element of any ascriptive hierarchy's discourse of legitimation. However, they are by no means the only taxa of ascriptive status, either currently or in the past.

Although the race idea began to take coherent shape as a metric of hierarchy by the eighteenth century, in the ways we currently presume to understand it, both substantively and evocatively, race became fully delineated within a more general pool of discourses of ascriptive differentiation only in the middle to late nineteenth century. Moreover, for the first third of the twentieth century at least, during the period when race thinking's hegemony was at its apogee, feeblemindedness was a social classification equally arbitrary, equally considered fixed by heredity and immutable, and often as substantively life-determining as race or gender. For much of that period so also was classification as a habitual criminal. The latter status appears to be making a comeback, led by the classification of sexual predator. As a consensually commonsensical Other (who could even for a breath imagine not suppressing sexual predation, itself a usefully ambiguous and ideological category?), the image of the sexual predator is an utterly uncontroversial focal point for the diffuse anxieties, condensed as stigma and opprobrium, that can spearhead social panic and propel the steady advance of the public/private punitive apparatus and attendant political economy appropriate to neoliberalism, or what Holt characterizes as "post-Fordism."[28]

The urban underclass also may be well on the way to becoming a discrete race-like population as well and one that draws legitimizing verisimilitude partly from the ways that it does and does not overlap already marked ascriptive populations defined by racial narratives. Indeed, no less culturally authoritative a voice on this topic than Daniel Patrick Moynihan, capping a thirty-year career of concocting lurid, ugly fantasies about poor people, at his 1994 Senate Finance Committee hearing on welfare reform literally invoked "speciation" in characterizing the nature of inner-city poverty. "I have to think," he asserted, "because it is so new, I have to think we have to address [increased rates of nonmarital births] at the level of science. If you were a biologist you could find yourself talking about speciation here. There is no society in history with the levels that we are now dealing with."[29] As I indicate below, Moynihan's speciation imagery is not entirely discontinuous from his earlier characterizations of black, inner-city poor people.

At the broader generic level, I have described the work that ascriptive hierarchies do:

> These hierarchies mediate and manage this stratification system by defining populations and assigning them ascriptively to what come to be understood as appropriate niches of civic worth and entitlement. [They] evolve and are enforced formally through laws, public policies and quasi-official means—such as officially tolerated but unofficially enacted preferences and coercion—and informally through popular ideologies, social practices and normative sanctions. From this perspective, race appears as a social category that has evolved to denote an especially durable kind of ascriptive civic status in the context of American capitalism and the political and ideological structures through which it is reproduced as a social order.[30]

From this vantage point, the problem organizing Holt's rumination probably would need to be recast on the order of interrogating: the kinds of transformations currently under way in the universe of ascriptive ideologies that undergird and help constitute the regime we inhabit; the ways they are likely or unlikely to build upon and overlap the familiar racial categories grounded loosely on phenotypic narratives; how they may transform the content and significance of those familiar categories; and thus how we might hope most productively to fashion responses.

I am not suggesting that Holt should have written a different book or defined his topic differently. My point is to throw into relief and examine logical and interpretive premises that shape the book that he has done; this includes conceptual and normative presuppositions that guide his argument's trajectory and the ideological premises that support them. Specifically, positing that the task of "rethinking our explanations of race" should be linked fundamentally to the need "to recognize racism and the racial" under new conditions may foreclose possibilities for the outcome of the rethinking by concluding in advance that "race and the racial" will survive the process in more or less their familiar forms, or at least in forms that will be close enough to the familiar to leave them unproblematically recognizable.

But from that perspective, how would we classify, say, an underclass that has become: (1) understood as a discretely marked, degraded, and self-reproducing population in the ways that are now associated with undesirable and stigmatized racial groups, defined by essentializing narratives that hover opportunistically between biology and biology dressed up as culture; (2) by our current folk norms, multiracial in composition, albeit most likely including in perceptibly greater frequencies than the general population people who would be classified as black and Latino "racially," though as small enough pluralities to preclude assimilating the group ideologically as a simple proxy for nonwhite inferiors; and (3) separated in comparatively unambiguous ways rhetorically and perhaps even in quotidian recognition and the everyday public/private exercise of arbitrary police power from the larger populations that remain understood "racially" as black and Latino but have become normalized, perhaps on a model, *mutatis mutandis,* of the civic incorporation of those populations that became white "ethnics"?[31] That is, how would Holt's perspective handle the victory of the social vision and ideal according to which "racial" difference could be recognized without stigma or marginalization and in which levels of socioeconomic inequality and disparities disappeared between the familiar racially defined populations—not counting the relatively greater number of individuals offloaded, as it were, from the nonwhite racial populations to the underclass?

In this circumstance "race" would exist but arguably no longer in the same kind of politically significant way. The political and ideological work of stabilizing capitalist hierarchy that we now associate with race would be done by other categories of ascriptive differentiation that could appear all the more plausibly as natural because they had been shorn of a lexicon of race rendered less effective through successful contestation over time. This is not an entirely fanciful possibility. It would be a realization of an ideal and social vision that has underlain a strain of black civil rights activism since the consolidation of the Jim Crow regime at the end of the nineteenth century. That ideal—a regime of justice in which race has been supplanted by ostensibly natural, or morally neutral, hierarchies produced through the market and individual cultivation—can be seen within Holt's own account of the NAACP's argument in the Sweet case in 1920s Detroit, though he seems not to recognize this implication.[32] It would also be a fulfillment of the ideal of racial liberalism that emerged after World War II, expressed in both long-since clichéd "content of character" rhetoric and a strain of enthusiasm for Barack Obama's presidential candidacy and election.

Holt nearly acknowledges the possibility of this sort of transformation of race's meaning and significance in discussing the proliferation of class-insulated gated communities in the United States and elsewhere. However, he stacks the deck against confronting it by stipulation, setting it up for dismissal through a rhetorical question. If such communities have "at least a token black or other minority presence," he asks, "are they, by virtue of that fact, any less racial?"[33] Of course, if the minority presence is "token," the answer would have to be negative. That is true by definition. But what if the presence were *not* token? What if it were the norm, or at least common enough not to seem exceptional, that the occupancy patterns of gated communities approximated the familiar racial groups' demographic frequencies within the general population? The question then would no longer be rhetorical, and maintaining the negative answer would require more extensive argumentative gymnastics.

Holt or others might object that my question is unfair or absurd because the circumstance I propose is a facile hypothetical and a practical impossibility. That response would amount to acknowledgement that, even taking into account the power of the transformative processes they contend work on social formations macrohistorically, Holt, Hall, and others[34] who argue in this vein about race see it as sufficiently durable as to be ultimately impervious to essential transformation, either by dissolution or radical revaluation. That is, such a response would amount to an admission that, when the chips of actual historical possibility are on the line, they do accord race an ontological status.

Post-Katrina New Orleans and the Limits of Racial Interpretation

A portent of a more prosaic, yet no less chilling, version of the alternative racial future I have limned and processes through which it could emerge may be germinating in post-Katrina New Orleans. The horror and outrage crystallized by images of the mass of overwhelmingly poor and black people stranded in the Superdome and Convention Center and on overpasses in the days after the storm sparked considerable rumination and public hand-wringing about poverty, race, and their connection. Much of this pivoted on assertions as to the character and extent of race's significance in the society and whether and how it played a role in the fate of those vulnerable people who seemed to be victims of nothing better than callous neglect. In some views at least this neglect evoked comparisons to genocide.

As the city dried out, concern with the nexus of race and justice shifted to focus largely on whether blacks—especially poor blacks, though in practice this distinction typically was elided—would be encouraged to return to the city and would receive the material support necessary to do so and to reestablish themselves there. Suspicion grew that significant white interests—real estate developers, Republicans, and others who would benefit materially from elimination or reduction of the city's heavy black majority, generic racists who simply wanted black people gone (except when it was time to be served a cool, tropical drink or entertained with some music)—were contriving to limit blacks' return. Ample evidence sustained this suspicion, as displaced people languished for months and years in limbos around the country and public officials at every level, pundits, and "experts" stepped forward to urge rebuilding a city with a "smaller footprint" and to question the prudence of rebuilding the flood-prone, predominantly black Lower Ninth Ward and New Orleans East but never the equally devastated and flood-prone, predominantly white and affluent Lake View.

When Mayor C. Ray Nagin seemed poised to accept a proposal that called for an indefinite moratorium on rebuilding those two black areas, in the framework of a general recommendation of an approach that would target areas for recovery in descending priority based on pre-Katrina market value (which would have placed even many affluent blacks toward the back of the queue), opposition among black New Orleanians, both in the city and elsewhere, intensified and erupted in public debate and protest. Nagin, who had received less than 40 percent of the black vote against another black candidate in his first election, was facing reelection in a field featuring several potentially strong white challengers in a city with a much smaller black electoral majority—that is, a field in which he could no longer anticipate being the white electoral choice. This is the context in which Nagin made his notorious "Chocolate City" comment.

He and other black officials, as well as whites who did not want to inflame racial tensions, faced a quandary: How could black political fears of wholesale racial removal be quelled and blacks' demands for equitable inclusion in the calculus of recovery be reconciled with the larger imperative—exemplified in Nagin's resolute, almost boastful commitment to a "market-driven" approach—of letting market forces drive recovery according to the principle of rent intensification?

A two-sided political narrative helped to resolve the quandary. On one side, Nagin and others issued assurances that no neighborhoods would be excluded from plans for recovery and that all homeowners would be able to participate in the planning process. This formulation concretized the abstract "black community" as a set of discrete neighborhoods, geographically defined constituency groupings that are generally, though unevenly and unofficially, recognized as mapping demographically onto race. This construction of the black community underwrote an instrumental discourse of black interests and concerns anchored on advocating and mobilizing resources for specific subcommunities. It also affirmed those black neighborhoods' inclusion within a citywide universe of administratively incorporated constituencies—stakeholder groups—that in principle accords equal civic standing and voice for black and white subunits. This became the domain in which politics is enacted as an ongoing process of shaping and negotiating acceptable accommodations to an overarching program of recovery and the allocation of costs and benefits associated with it. Reading blacks into a universe of "homeowners," a category that overlaps "neighborhood" and in fact defines a boundary or threshold of authentic neighborhood voice, simultaneously established property ownership as a normative baseline of vested status in the recovery process in general and affirmed black owners' standing as legitimate stakeholders. Thus the interests and concerns articulated by an administratively stipulated stratum of respectable homeowners—a category sufficiently broad with respect to wealth, income, and other class indicators to seem plausibly diverse—were positioned, along with those advanced by a smaller stratum of more specifically interested functionaries and potential recovery contractors and subcontractors, to stand in for or become recognized as those of the "black community."

If assimilation to a pragmatic discourse of neighborhoods and homeownership could allay concerns about exclusion through affirming a version of black community compatible with a neoliberal framework of recovery, the imagery of a pathological urban underclass did so through negation, by providing a basis for accommodating the exclusion of a considerable segment of the nominally black population from this construction of a vested black community centered normatively on homeowners. The underclass narrative has been the unquestioned commonsense truth about poverty and inequality in New Orleans as elsewhere for at least two decades. In the aftermath of the flood the most lurid and vicious forms of this imagery propelled racist responses to suggestions that Katrina's dramatic exposé of poverty and neglect revealed the effects of racial injustice. However, the controversy sparked by a plan to raze the city's low-income public housing projects, in the midst of an extremely acute shortage of affordable housing and while thousands of former public housing tenants and others remained displaced, condensed an ecological articulation of the underclass narrative that melded the physical structures and the people occupying them into a singular, reified sociological entity—the "projects"—as site and source of poverty and a litany of social pathologies.

The ease with which this ecological narrative became implanted reflects in part the confluence of several larger intellectual and ideological currents bearing on poverty and inequality. Within social policy discourse, hegemonic Chicago school and New Urbanist arguments construe "concentrated poverty" and "neighborhood effects" as at least most proximately implicated in reproducing poverty and supposedly related social pathologies.[35] The twenty-five-year retreat from public commitment to provision of social support for the indigent has both exacerbated poverty's manifestations and more deeply inscribed victim-blaming explanations as common sense. The U.S. Department of Housing and Urban Development's HOPE VI program's focus—justified by the Chicago school/New Urbanist ideological consensus—on subsidizing privately developed "mixed income" housing projects encourages local officials and private developers to represent destruction of existing low-income housing as an antipoverty strategy.[36] And a class-skewed rhetoric of racial "self-help" that reinforces behavioral explanations of poverty has gained currency in concert with the general rightward shift in American social policy discourse and material incentives provided by devolution and privatization of social services. Barack Obama's reliance during his presidential campaign on denunciations of black poor people's supposed behavioral failings as a way simultaneously to reassure whites and to establish his racial bona fides among black elites is a clear testament to this rhetoric's hegemonic status.[37]

Each of these, more or less diffusely, has long since permeated constructions of poverty in general and low-income public housing in particular in news media and other opinion-shaping institutions. While the city was still underwater, Republican congressman Richard Baker of Baton Rouge exulted, "We finally cleaned up public housing in New Orleans. We couldn't do it, but God did," and scarcely two weeks after the storm a national grouping of more than 200 academics, mainly liberal sociologists and not a few with even sturdier left credentials, published a petition urging the federal government to take advantage of the tragedy's silver lining, that is, the opportunity to "deconcentrate" poverty from New Orleans and the affected Gulf Coast region.[38] Locally, black reactions to the developing climate were ambivalent, in part no doubt because the racial connotations of Baker's comments were clear and resonated with more openly and virulently racist calls for preventing poor blacks, and sometimes blacks in general, from returning to the city. However, two of the four black members of the City Council castigated public housing residents as "soap opera watchers" whose return would contribute nothing to the city's recovery, and black Housing Authority administrators expressed similar sentiments.[39]

As debate intensified over the place of public housing projects and their residents in the city's recovery, the ecological construction of low-income public housing as the cause, or breeding ground, of poverty and social pathology increasingly settled in as a commonsense baseline of discussion. This common sense united blacks and whites in defining, or at least acquiescing in elites' definition of, public housing residents as outside the universe of constituencies vested in the calculus of recovery. Several factors no doubt contributed to this interpretation's success. One was its familiarity, a reflection of the principle, most famously recorded and demonstrated by Josef Goebbels, that even propositions for which there is no evidence at all can become popular truth through incessant and emphatic repetition as self-evident. Everyone "knew" that housing projects were synonymous with pathology. Some whites "knew" so by definition, because the projects housed blacks who are by nature lazy, shiftless, and criminal. Others, black and white, "knew" that projects—through mechanisms most probably could not begin to describe—either were magnets that drew and exacerbated dependence and other forms of pathology, produced those behavioral effects themselves, or both.

Most significant, though, for what it suggests about possibilities for radical transformation in the meaning and significance of race as a metric of ascription, is that articulation of a notion of a politically authentic black community also contributed to successful demonization and exclusion of the overwhelmingly black and vulnerable indigent population. Although vested black homeowners were certainly more likely than their white counterparts to express empathy with the plight of the excluded poor, this empathy ultimately proved fleeting, as no significant voices among this stratum or the elected officials representing them emerged to challenge the framework and program of exclusion. Moreover, black homeowner–driven neighborhood associations in New Orleans East, Gentilly, and across the city have mobilized as insistently as whites to block location of smaller-scale, privately developed low-income housing in their areas. Indeed, the debate over public housing's place in the logic of recovery, in posing a sharp distinction between these two black strata, may have mutually reinforcing rhetorical consequences with important longer-term programmatic implications.

Incorporation of the respectable homeowner stratum as the repository of black political authenticity both legitimized a construction of corporate black political identity at least superficially compatible with neoliberal governing imperatives and undercut charges that racism motivated the public housing population's exclusion. Absence of substantial black challenge to the demolition proposal reinforced this effect. In throwing into relief the contrast between the black homeowner stratum and the demonized public housing population, the public housing debate also provided whites with an acceptable model of nominally equal black civic membership, one made more tolerable because of its explicit differentiation from another black population marked as the repository of long-standing pejorative stereotypes, a separately racialized, subordinate population that is available for containment and repression. This may suggest discursive and programmatic contours within which a post-Katrina biracial regime can be reconstituted. In practice, of course, these two black populations overlap considerably; that is one of the contradictions at the core of what I believe it is not a great overstatement to label an incipient process of improvised reracialization. Negotiating those contradictions practically—for example, through extension and contraction of opportunity structures in various domains and fine-tuning the targeting of police and other repressive power—is the dynamic through which, over time, ascriptive group boundaries are drawn, redrawn, and imposed. Already New Orleans has at least three different "public" school systems, drawing from and in the process creating different populations and skewed to reflect different horizons of expectation and projected social and occupational trajectories.[40]

The New Orleans case underscores just how plastic and context-dependent race is as an ascriptive status. New Orleans has as deeply entrenched a history of black/white racial hierarchy as any city in the United States, and race has been a principal metaphor shaping local political debate since the 1960s or longer. Since 1990, the city has witnessed several flare-ups of an explicitly white supremacist assertiveness that strains disbelief in atavism—most dramatically around former Nazi and Klansman David Duke's campaigns for governor and U.S. senator, as well as municipal efforts both to remove an obelisk commemorating the Crescent City White League's 1874 insurrection against the Reconstruction government and to impose a nondiscrimination provision on the elite krewes that sponsor Mardi Gras parades.[41] The demographic shock associated with Katrina precipitated another such eruption, as exuberance at the apparent opportunity to "take back the city" overwhelmed restraint and spilled over copiously into mainstream public discourse.

Yet even in this context, where race has so long been the default, if not sole, metaphor through which inequality and hierarchy have been justified, stabilized, and challenged, it is possible to see processes of differentiation and ascriptive labeling at work that could ensue in subverting that metaphor and reestablishing on different terms the pattern of social relations that it has condensed and legitimized. From this perspective, race may still be in New Orleans a default medium through which "fundamental conflicts in the social system" are expressed but that turns out not to tell us very much about either race, those conflicts, or even the relation between the two. Nor is it clear that it will remain so in the future. To that extent, the New Orleans case shows the inadequacy of Holt's assessment that the challenge for the twenty-first century concerns assessing "how we are to recognize racism and the racial." His perspective may impose a procrustean frame of reference that impedes understanding the dynamics of hierarchy actually at work. At best we would have to respond that in New Orleans the familiar constructions of race may now partly constitute a basis for some black people's inclusion in the domain of civic respectability and recognition as stakeholders and some others' exclusion. Moreover, while it remains meaningful in various ways—including ways bearing on stratification—racial classification no longer can be said by itself to confer life chances or social position on anyone of any racial designation.

The New Orleans case also suggests the limitations, despite Holt's and Hall's arguments to the contrary, of engaging the question of race's social and political significance without clarifying what race, and by extension racism, is and is not, both conceptually and pragmatically.[42] By this I do not mean to contend that race has some essential characteristics, or range of characteristics, that can be specified definitively across time. Holt is correct that racial ideology does not depend necessarily on claims anchored in biology or phenotype and that, as the social constructionist consensus has undermined strictly biological views of racial difference, culturalist arguments have gained more traction to buttress or supplant them.[43] As I indicate above, this is not a new phenomenon; hanging indeterminately between biological and cultural metaphor has been a feature of racialist ideology's apparent explanatory power for more than a century, indeed throughout its history as a taxonomy of human differentiation. However, ascertaining race's significance, being able in Holt's phrase to "recognize racism and the racial," requires as a precondition resolving at least tentatively how (and whether) race, and racism, can be identified conceptually as a distinctive kind of taxonomy within the universe of ascriptive ideologies. From that perspective Holt's—and Hall's—contention that, because race has no singular, coherent meaning, we should not attempt to specify its characteristics and conceptual boundaries more clearly and should focus instead on charting its operations over time, is a non sequitur.

It is possible conceptually to distinguish race among ideologies of ascriptive hierarchy without accepting either the taxa propounded in its name, the putative bases asserted for differentiating them, or the deeper philosophical claims that would justify sorting human beings into such classificatory systems in the first place. If not, then how could we know that "race" is the label that most appropriately applies to one ascriptive regime or another? In fact, Holt's failure, or refusal, to reflect on what distinguishes race as an ideology leads him, despite his expressed intentions, to reify it as a category. Thus even as he attempts to track its changing significance over time, he in effect treats racism, and thus race, as not merely transhistorical but suprahistorical.

This is most immediately a problem of analytical underdevelopment. Because he does not identify properties that would mark an ascriptive system as specifically racial, he has no basis for claiming that ascriptive regimes and ideologies in different "social formations" or "historical moments" are indeed best identified as race and racism other than that they appear to overlap categories of the familiar racial taxonomy. This failure to specify conceptual boundaries leaves little safeguard against two related problems. One is that in the absence of some clear sense of the boundaries of the racial it is not possible to determine whether that appearance might rest on anachronistic or otherwise contextually inaccurate perceptions. This heightens the danger of taking the notion of race's content and meaning that prevails at a given historical conjuncture in a specific society and projecting it inappropriately onto other contemporaneous societies or other historical moments. Such reifications, among other limitations, are likely to be naively parochial. Indeed, in the current context the tendency to project parochial American notions of race and its political significance onto other societies looks much like a reflex of cultural imperialism and all too conveniently converges with the program of undermining other states' sovereignty associated with imposition of the "Washington consensus."[44]

The other is conflation of folk and analytical notions of race. Race's cultural force, as with other essentialisms or categories of ascriptive differentiation, derives largely from its commonsensical quality, the sense of naturalness that places its foundations beyond examination and thus obscures its arbitrariness, and the fact that that apparent naturalness is, as I indicate above, produced and "enforced formally through laws, public policies and quasi-official means and informally through popular ideologies, social practices and normative sanctions."[45] Holt notes the problematic "fuzziness" of everyday and scholarly thinking about race yet curiously determines that engaging in efforts to "define the concept and to catalogue its substantive content" is part of the problem. This notion also may result from Holt's apparent failure to recognize that race can in principle have a categorical essence without having a natural or empirical one.[46]

In arguing that "the meaning of race and the nature of racism articulate with (perhaps even are defined by) the given social formation of a particular historical moment,"[47] Holt clearly wants to stress race's plasticity and historical contingency. He indicates that the logic of racial classification may change; different populations may become racialized or deracialized, presumably, in different ways. But even as he laments scholars' persisting "failure to historicize the problem of race," his perspective nonetheless naturalizes race and racism. He insists that "if race is socially and historically constructed, then racism must be *re*constructed as social regimes change and histories unfold," and he notes that what appears to be racism's "intractability" is more accurately "its reproduction."[48] However, in asking "what enables racism to reproduce itself even after the historical conditions that initially gave it life have disappeared" without considering what the "it" stands for, he implies that race has a monadic foundation that exists independently of social and historical context. His references to race's historicity are at odds with his metaphor:

> Implicit in this approach is the conviction that neither race nor racism can live independently of its social environments, the times and spaces it inhabits. By nature a changeling, it attaches itself to and draws sustenance from other social phenomena and from racist discourse itself, like one of those insidious monsters in late-night science fiction movies. The historian is left to examine the carcass it once inhabited before moving on to another social body, while the sociologist busily constructs diagnostic questionnaires after the disease has already mutated.[49]

This may be stylistic flourish, but his imagery is nonetheless of a discrete thing that adapts to its changing environment. And Holt seems to find this sort of decidedly ontological metaphor especially apt in characterizing racism; elsewhere he avers: "As for the thing itself—racism's powerful hold, its tenaciousness—it appears to rise not from some parasitic attachment on the surface of an otherwise healthy body politic but from viral growths within the living whole. Race yet lives because it is part and parcel of the *means* of living."[50] He all but acknowledges acceptance of this idealist and primordialist view in observing that "some of the same ideas and tropes have circulated through racist discourse from time immemorial, a fact that leaves us just a short step away from conceiving racism as a timeless or innate human quality."[51]

Holt's ruminations on race and racism are particularly revealing for two reasons. One is that *The Problem of Race in the 21st Century* is the most direct and extensive argument for the continuing applicability of Du Bois's early assessment of the importance of the "color line." The other is that Holt is among the more lucid and sophisticated of those scholars who endeavor simultaneously to follow out the practical intellectual and political implications of a constructionist understanding of race and to sustain a view of racism as an autonomous and transcontextual social and political force in the world. In contrast to Howard Winant, for instance, who engages the question of race's meaning and significance at a similarly high level of abstraction focused on historical "projects" and "formations," Holt more consistently asserts race's historicity and more consciously attempts to avoid explicitly idealist formulations, even to the point, as I have shown here, of seeming often to argue against himself. That he has such difficulty harmonizing the two positions suggests that they may be intrinsically incompatible. That he persists on pain of self-contradiction suggests an intensity of commitment to holding both positions that may be instructive in its own right.

Holt's persistence in what seems akin to attempting to square the circle is not an idiosyncratic conceptual lapse. It stems from an effort to harmonize competing intellectual and civic or political commitments. He has emphasized challenging conservatives who deny racism's persistence in the present as a crucial interest shaping his writing on race.[52] This perspective makes clearer the basis on which he rejects calls to "define the concept and to catalogue its substantive content." He believes that efforts to specify race's (and thus racism's) boundaries are either instrumental to conservatives' objective of denying the existence of racial inequality or at best unacceptably vulnerable to appropriation in support of that objective.

> Much contemporary commentary on race and racism seems directed at containing these concepts within relatively narrow and clearly recognizable frames. Indeed, some of these analyses appear more concerned to limit the scope of available legal remedies by narrowly (and anachronistically) defining what can legitimately be called racially "motivated." Others are well-intentioned efforts by careful scholars trying to get a clear "fix" on the object of study; for them, admitting all manner of invidious acts of distinction under a racial designation risks losing focus and analytic efficacy.[53]

Holt's stance is in this respect an ironic analogue of neo-Lamarckian race theory. As Stocking and others have noted, ambiguity as to whether race's essential foundations lay in biology, culture, or history made the notion a fluid, constantly moving target conceptually. Conflation of folk and analytic notions of race, by affirming a specious intuitive knowledge of what race is, imbued those fin-de-siècle understandings of race difference with a sense of everyday reality that made them all the more resistant to challenge. Therefore, an element of Boasians' and other egalitarians' strategies for combating notions of racial hierarchy required undermining their commonsensical character—defamiliarizing them—by fastening race discourse onto conceptually coherent, rigorous criteria that then could ground evaluation of racialist claims. This intellectual enterprise was no more responsible for defeating early-twentieth-century race theory than Charles Hamilton Houston's and Thurgood Marshall's legal arguments were for defeating codified racial segregation, probably much less so. Factors like the leftward shift in the domestic political climate in the 1930s and 1940s, the embarrassment that Nazi exterminism presented for racialist ideology, and cold war concerns with the United States's international image were undoubtedly more important. However, the intellectual struggle against race theory's commonsense reality played a significant role in disseminating an alternative, denaturalized notion of race that later would be known as social-constructionist.[54]

Where early-twentieth-century egalitarians sought to challenge the view that *race* explained everything about manifest inequality, Holt is intent on challenging a view that *racism* has little or nothing to do with contemporary inequality. Those earlier antiracists sought to specify race conceptually in order to demonstrate that it is without foundation as a scientific or natural category. Holt wishes to demonstrate that racism is a foundational (or as nearly foundational as one formally committed to a constructionist view of race might plausibly claim) element of American or Western society in order to argue against contemporary antiegalitarians who insist that unjust racial inequality was eliminated by the civil rights legislation of the 1960s. This commits Holt, as it does many others, to casting the net of racism much more widely than those conservatives would permit.

Postwar Racial Liberalism and the Foundations of Racism Discourse

Argument for a broader perception of racism's boundaries derives partly from recognition that patterned racial inequalities can exist and persist without conscious bigotry or discrimination. "Institutional racism" entered social science and policy discourse by the end of the 1960s, as egalitarians already struggled to articulate a notion of racial justice that could go beyond strict antidiscrimination or, more precisely, a notion of racism that included more than simple prejudice and overt discrimination.[55] Triumphant Reaganism, buttressed ideologically by the vast right-wing propaganda apparatus, has increased the pressure on scholars and others identified with the interests of racial equality to generate effective responses to claims that racial injustice is no longer a significant source even of inequalities that appear as racial disparities. A typical response to this challenge has been to propound more variants of the institutional racism thesis, among them notions like structural or systemic racism or narratives charting the putative legacies of slavery and Jim Crow in durable, racialized inequalities. Similarly, concerns to demonstrate the bases for a possessive investment in whiteness or the material workings of white skin privilege have sought to throw into relief ways that whites benefit from and may be materially committed to policies that sustain and reinforce racial hierarchy. These efforts have led to fruitful examinations of the complex ways that racial ideologies have been institutionalized in American political development, embedded in and shaping even ostensibly race-blind politics and policies, and scholarship in this area has contributed significantly to demystifying the account, once a standard of postwar racial liberalism, of racial hierarchy as an aberrant appendage on a fundamentally egalitarian American ethos.[56] In the political domain, however, the payoffs from this line of argument have been less successful from the standpoint of advancing egalitarian interests and objectives.

Unnoticed in the persisting debate over whether and to what extent manifest inequalities stem from racism is that both sides in effect acquiesce in the presupposition that only inequalities resultant from unfavorable treatment based on negatively sanctioned ascriptive distinctions like race qualify as injustice and warrant remedial action. This constraint, as well as the fact that it goes unnoticed, is both accommodation to and expression of the triumph of neoliberalism[57] as the commonsense ideological and programmatic framework for discussing inequality or injustice. Antiegalitarians and other conservatives argue that such racial inequalities as exist result from neutral workings of market forces and/or intrinsic failings—cultural, behavioral, increasingly once again biological—of the poor and economically marginal and therefore do not qualify as evidence of persisting racism. Antiracists respond by demonstrating that market forces are not neutral and are in significant ways racialized and that seemingly pathological or maladaptive behavior is often either a rational adaptation to unequal and badly constrained conditions, the product of past or current racially discriminatory institutional arrangements, or both. To that extent, neither side in the argument challenges the presumption that only inequalities resultant in some way from stigmatization of ascriptively defined populations are objectionable to the point of justifying political intervention. Unjust inequality thus construed becomes in effect a boutique phenomenon, applicable only to discrete population segments or categories rather than a tendency rooted in the core mechanisms that reproduce the social, political, and economic order in general. This is a view that, among other limitations, preempts strategies of popular political mobilization.

Debating inequality on those limited terms is in one sense only a pragmatic response to the fact that the neoliberal mind-set has become hegemonic truth in American politics. Inequality as such, even severe inequality, no longer seems to be a cause for public concern and action. The term itself is increasingly replaced in academic and policy discourse by "disparity," precisely because the latter term is held not to be normatively loaded—that is, not to connote injustice. Because of the civil rights and women's movements' legislative, judicial, and ideological victories, discrimination on ascriptive grounds is the most reliable basis on which objections to inequality can gain the standing necessary to pursue remedies in courts and legislatures. For example, when residents of the Cabrini-Green housing project challenged the demolition and relocation plan adopted by the City of Chicago and the Chicago Housing Authority, they found it necessary to do so on grounds of civil rights violations, stressing the disparate hardship the plan imposed on blacks, women, and children. Yet accepting that framework also affirms and reinforces the underlying normative principle that naturalizes—that is, removes from the realm of legitimate concern—inequalities that can be attributed without qualification to market forces or allegedly bad or irresponsible individual behavior. To put this perhaps yet more plainly, debate over *whether* inequalities stem directly or indirectly from racial or other discrimination backhandedly validates the view that only inequalities that result from some form of discrimination are unjust.[58]

Several features of the political and ideological landscape have combined during the 1950s or so to channel institutionally and culturally resonant notions of injustice into a narrower framework of discrimination. Cold War anticommunism exerted ideological and political pressure to sever formulation of racial justice vis-à-vis black Americans from programs of economic redistribution, which conservatives attacked as de facto evidence of subversive activity. During the nearly quarter century bracketed by the 1944 publication of Gunnar Myrdal's *An American Dilemma* and the 1968 Kerner Commission report, social scientists increasingly redefined the "Negro problem" as a matter of unfair inequality that stemmed most crucially or fundamentally from whites' attitudes. This had the effect of tying discussion of racial inequality to notions of prejudice or bigotry. The mythology of the "affluent society," also articulated and legitimized by social scientists and policy intellectuals (and likewise partly reflecting cold war ideological sensibilities), held that a perpetually growing domestic economy had obviated a politics centered on economic redistribution. A corollary of this view was that those obvious exceptions to the regime of growth-driven affluence suffered from exogenous or idiosyncratic handicaps, such as invidious and irrational discrimination or deficits of either preparation or individual capacity. This view no doubt strengthened the cultural and political force of civil rights discourse by defining discrimination as at odds with the precepts of the affluent society. At the same time, it provided commonsense nurturance for notions like "human capital," "cultural deprivation," and the "culture of poverty," which more or less subtly deflected social policy away from material redistribution and toward correcting supposed inadequacies among poor people.[59]

This is a very schematic, telescoped account of the trajectory of the pertinent tendencies in postwar political history, and it does not do justice either to the complexities and countertendencies at play simultaneously with those I note here or to how the tensions between those tendencies shaped and leavened the outcomes I indicate.[60] Nevertheless, by the 1980s these ideas and ideological dispositions had all become raw material for the Reaganite right wing to use in fashioning a new political common sense about inequality, government, and markets. Arguments about the sources of black poverty that in an earlier time would have employed the language of blacks' racial inferiority ever more comfortably substituted "culture" for "race," first under the rubric of the culture of poverty, then as the "urban underclass." Both characterizations resolved the problem of making fundamentally racialist justifications of existing inequalities in the context of postwar racial liberalism in which racism had become negatively sanctioned.

Ironically, however, it was avowedly liberal black sociologist William Julius Wilson's assertion in *The Declining Significance of Race,* midway through the Jimmy Carter administration, that "class" factors were increasingly significant in relation to racial discrimination in shaping blacks' life chances in the postsegregation era that most immediately provoked the pattern of defensive response on which the political discourse of black intellectuals and racial advocacy elites has pivoted ever since. The greater long-term consequences of Wilson's argument, though, did not follow from his contention that direct racial discrimination accounted for less of black inequality than in the past, which in any event is a more judicious claim than that implied in his provocative title. More significant was his conception of class, by which he meant "any group of people who have more or less similar goods, services, or skills to offer for income in a given economic order and who therefore receive similar financial remuneration in the marketplace."[61] This formulation, in the tradition of Chicago sociology, reifies and naturalizes the capitalist wage relation as the "marketplace." In this light his reference to "a given economic order" is either a simple absurdity or empty filler that functions only as a rhetorical garnish conferring an appearance of sociological generality on a naive shopkeeper's view of universal law.

In treating class as a category demarcating groups defined by possession of similar bundles of resources, including human capital, Wilson grounds it in purported attributes rather than location and functions in a system of social and economic reproduction or place in a hierarchical social order. He therefore in effect reduces class to culture, in the way the latter was typically conceptualized in postwar American social science. As Stephen Steinberg put it succinctly, the essence of human capital theory is "that most conventional of ideas—that success comes to those who possess the appropriate set of personal and cultural virtues."[62] Thus Wilson recast the terms of the race-versus-class debate, which historically had been centered in the political left, from its familiar focus on the extent to which black inequality stemmed from capitalist market imperatives or racism as an autonomous ideological force into a debate over whether black inequality derives from racism or impoverished and low-income blacks' cultural deficiencies.[63] From there, it was only a small step, as underclass ideology gained currency in the Reagan years, for those putative group deficits of human capital to be recast summarily as social pathology. Moreover, the notion that socially recognizable "groups" that significantly overlap racially and ethnically marked populations can be characterized on the basis of distinctive clusters of human capital is no more than a conceptual half step away from Victorian notions of race temperament.

Egalitarians' earlier cultural victory in establishing race as a biological category in order to make it a stationary target for demystification ironically created space for familiar racialist arguments to be repackaged respectably, as I elaborate below, in culturalist language. This is both a reminder that there are no technical or theoretical final victories in political and ideological struggles and an illustration that racialist ideologies—like all ideologies of ascriptive hierarchy—are not products of theories of difference so much as normative and practical commitments that lead to production and propagation of theories of difference. They are political programs, and those who pursue them seek, or at least gravitate toward, the most convenient and pragmatically effective theoretical justifications for them.[64] This logic extends beyond the opportunistic choice of biological or cultural metaphor. As Holt notes, race's content, and thus racism's content, is fluid. Stephen Jay Gould demonstrated wonderfully in *The Mismeasure of Man*[65] that both folk and scientific metrics of racial difference are typically improvised according to the needs of the moment. Early intelligence testers and racial anatomists, for example, were known to reverse their assessments of one or another trait's link to intelligence or advanced evolutionary development on finding that it was distributed in racial patterns different from initial expectation. In this sense, Holt is correct that it is a mistake to concentrate on determining race's specific content and meaning. But taking that reality into account only makes assigning priority to identifying "racism and the racial" seem all the more beside the point, if not counterproductive.

To return to the case of post-Katrina New Orleans, applying the racism label does not help us make sense of the complex material and ideological dynamics shaping the terms of recovery and renewing the social and political order there. It cannot capture the ways that those dynamics draw from, crosscut, overlap, revise, and supplant familiar racial narratives and categories in reestablishing a hierarchical regime that substantively restores the political and economic status quo ante. In that context the focus on identifying racism and the racial would lead—indeed has led—only to a second-order debate as to whether the inequalities that characterize the politics of recovery stem from racism or some other source. As so much of public discussion of Katrina's impact and responses to it has demonstrated over and over, that debate is an intellectual and political cul-de-sac. Intellectually, it cannot be resolved, particularly without clear delineation of the boundaries of racism. Politically, it redirects attention from the reality and substance of injustice to the name by which we should call it. And as the rhetorical stakes of classifying it as racism increase, the implication that what cannot be labeled conclusively as the effect of racism does not qualify as an injustice demanding corrective action becomes more deeply and surreptitiously embedded.[66]

In this respect as in others, New Orleans stands out only as a particularly intense condensation of more general tendencies operating in American politics. Debates over whether persistent inequalities should be classified under the rubric of racism have been markedly unproductive of anything other than more such debate. Whether racial disparities in income, quality of employment, and access to education, housing, or health care stem from racism—however, if at all, defined—does not tell us what the mechanisms are through which those disparities are concretely reproduced or suggest how they can most effectively be alleviated.

In addition to the pragmatic reasons I discuss above, habit of mind and its institutional equivalent also channel discussion of inequality into the familiar grooves of the discourse of racism, despite its interpretive limitations and lack of political payoff. This effect is likely exacerbated by the sense among advocates of equality and racial justice that prior victories have been eroded and remain under urgent threat. This sense disposes toward a defensive posture, particularly as dismissal and denial of racial injustice have figured so centrally in the right-wing juggernaut's rhetorical arsenal.

The institutional expressions of civil rights and racial advocacy are in general likewise habituated strategically and discursively. Before Reaganism's triumph, racial advocacy organizations could anticipate, whether or not their efforts routinely succeeded, winning incremental victories on behalf of their constituencies through a pluralist version of palace politics. Under terms of the framework of governance that prevailed in national politics from the New Deal through the 1970s, the civil rights movement's success translated into recognition and inclusion within a semiofficial interest-group system in which organizations—including others identified with social wage and social justice concerns, such as trade unions, and, later, environmental, feminist, and public interest advocacy groups—defined, articulated, and pursued formulations of their constituent groups' concerns through mechanisms of administrative negotiation, lobbying, and litigation.[67] A discursive least common denominator of what has amounted to a regime of race relations management, in keeping with the precepts of the dominant racial liberalism, has presumed that racial disparity constitutes prima facie evidence of racial injustice and that demonstration of disparities will trigger some sort of remedial response.

The right has long since successfully undermined these presumptions. Yet racial advocacy and race relations elites, rather like entertainers who freeze their personae at the moment of their greatest popularity, persist in a strategic discourse that has become obsolete. In part, this simply reflects a well-known difficulty in reorienting entrenched institutional perceptions and practices. Functionaries' commitments to accustomed ways of doing things congeal into a powerful inertial imperative, and that tendency is likely reinforced by the political reflex to defend the familiar language of advocacy in the face of explicit and aggressive attacks on it. Because their constituencies are typically diffuse and their programmatic objectives are typically minutely incremental, and often arcane to nonspecialists, advocacy groups are relatively free in defining their terms of success and failure. Thus, as the rightist offensive has advanced, groups enmeshed in the regime of elite negotiation have accommodated by steadily, almost imperceptibly, narrowing the scope of their expectation. This has meant gradually blurring the distinction between victory and defeat. Increments of victory become smaller and increasingly symbolic. Then success becomes recast as limiting the extent or slowing the pace of retrenchment.

I recall the late Paul Wellstone lamenting in the mid-1990s that liberals and progressives in Congress and the advocacy world had fallen into a practice of responding to Republicans' intensely reactionary initiatives by proposing and fighting furiously for slightly less reactionary alternatives—and then celebrating the "victory" that as likely as not had made things on balance somewhat worse than before. Of course, a material imperative operates in this regard as well. Electoral incumbents—including trade union officials—need to show victories to be reelected; advocacy groups need to show them to sustain fund-raising.

Being on the defensive can feed a tendency to hunker down into familiar rhetoric and practices. Inability to respond effectively to existing challenges often calls forth compensatory evocations, almost as if to conjure them, of earlier times when the organizations or movement had greater normative force and political efficacy. Commemorations of events associated with the high period of civil rights activism in the 1960s often seem to function as such gestures. In part they are placeholders for absent strategic responses to threatening conditions in the present, in part appeals for loyalty to conventional practices and narratives on the basis of reverence for their association with prior heroism and success.

This amalgam of habit, pragmatic imperative, deep structural logic, wish fulfillment, nostalgia, and pathological organizational inertia condenses and sustains a perspective, or sensibility, that posits race, or racism, as a sui generis form of ascriptive hierarchy. This perspective emerges from and reproduces the logical framework of racial liberalism—"race relations"—that evolved as a political and intellectual common sense over the second half of the twentieth century. It depends on moralistic but substantively empty formulations like the lament that racism is America's "original sin" or "national disease." The presumption of self-evident moral imperative underlying such formulations is partly what energizes flights—as in the New Orleans case—into hopelessly convoluted, tortured argumentation aimed at fitting travesties of justice and patterned inequalities into a language of racism that is simultaneously vaporous and procrustean. The conviction that race, or racism, is a unique form of social evil, stratification, exploitation, or oppression also underlies efforts, such as Holt's, to meld constructionist and ontological views of race that are fundamentally irreconcilable. The logical impossibility of that objective does not deter the effort because the interpretive impulse derives from ideological imperatives, not analytical ones. The point is to preserve racism's rhetorical centrality, itself a product of the postwar race relations regime, as at least a (if not the most) distinctively virulent and objectionable form of injustice. As that regime has adjusted in concert with the new social morality of neoliberalism, academic and other advocates of what in an earlier time was called the "race line" increasingly have seemed to elevate maintaining racism's status as uniquely egregious among forms of injustice over the goal of challenging injustice itself.

REPARATIONS: BEHIND THE MOMENT OF ENTHUSIASM

Nowhere is this tendency more clearly visible than in the emergence of the discourse of reparations for black Americans at the end of the 1990s. The moment of high enthusiasm for the reparations idea apparently has waned, but during the several years it held the political imagination of a considerable segment of the publicly vocal black professional-managerial class and allied identitarians, one striking feature of the reparations discourse was its utter lack of concern with political efficacy. Reparations talk has been unrestrained by strategic consideration of how it could be possible to build the kind of political force necessary to prevail on the issue. When pressed on this question, proponents commonly have taken refuge in a debater's trick that has been a staple of race-line politics at least since the Black Power era—a call for shifting the focus of the struggle for reparations to the international arena. Not only does this move only sidestep the problem of political agency by displacing it onto a vague, remote alliance; it also makes the basis for the reparations claim all the more diffuse by linking it to demands based on prior colonial and neocolonial exploitation.[68]

In place of strategic argument, the reparations claim has been driven by a fulsome and elaborate effort in making the case that black Americans *deserve* special compensation or public attention of one sort or another. This may partly reflect the appeal that the notion has for lawyers, as much of the activity around the issue has taken the form of preparation of brieflike arguments justifying the claim for either lawsuits or journal articles. This mind-set also reflects and reinforces elements of a class-inflected naïveté regarding how political change is made. These include the conviction that one's own commonsense view of the world is equivalent to what "reasonable people" think and the related presumption that what one perceives as good arguments will be transparently convincing and will convert automatically into political action. What makes these sometimes preciously parochial views seem sensible is a particular class-skewed understanding of politics, one linked to presuppositions about who counts in the world and, therefore, how policy decisions are made and implemented.

The latter understanding is perhaps less naive but no less class-bound. The principle of elite negotiation on which the postwar race relations regime was built was established partly as a preferable alternative to political mobilization. That fact was obscured by the eruption of broad, popular civil rights activism between the 1950s and 1970s; struggles over harnessing and channeling that political dynamism to fit regime imperatives were central to what has been recognized as the black politics of that period. Nevertheless, insider negotiation has always been the cornerstone of the race relations idea as a field of intellectual specialization and as a social management practice.[69] It is predicated on the assumption that black Americans' citizenship and practical concerns can or should be formulated through the lens of race and articulated, or brokered, through individuals or organizations recognized by governing elites as representative of the black American population as a singular racial collectivity.

This is the frame of reference in which the notion "black leader" makes sense, the only one in which it can appear plausible that discrete individuals or even organizations can automatically—that is, without open, deliberative processes, including provisions for official registration of dissent and mechanisms of recall—and legitimately speak for the large, diverse population labeled "black Americans" as a monolithic bloc. As Michael Rudolph West argues in his important study *The Education of Booker T. Washington,* "The idea of race relations is a form of analytic segregation."[70] It assumes that black Americans enact their citizenship as a corporate entity (initially characterized as "the Negro," later the black or African American "community") fundamentally distinct from the rest of the society (understood as "America" or "white America"). This regime is also the context within which the racism discourse has had its greatest strategic political meaning and force. It has been a key rhetorical device in the ongoing negotiation around policy increments and gestures of symbolic legitimation (e.g., displays of "respect" for Jesse Jackson or other stipulated black spokespersons or icons, use of the term "African American," etc.) that constitutes the race relations regime's routine politics of positioning.

Some reparations enthusiasts explicitly embrace a separatist politics in which succeeding in the demand is at best secondary to reinscribing the race line as the authentic discourse through which black Americans are to articulate their political aspirations. For some in this camp, indeed, the reparations demand performs a didactic function ultimately dependent on the improbability of its success. From this perspective, failure affirms the conviction that blacks have no recourse to justice or full membership in the United States. Others are less cynical in their support and believe that framing demands for equality in the language of reparations is important as a vehicle for establishing a normative foundation for affirmative action and other compensatory policies.[71] However, across the board, reparations talk eschews political mobilization in favor of petitioning governing elites, whether earnestly or not. Randall Robinson, former president of the racial advocacy organization TransAfrica, maintained in *The Debt: What America Owes to Blacks,* one of the texts that propelled the enthusiasm, "Until America's white ruling class accepts the fact that the book never closes on massive unredressed social wrongs, America can have no future as one people."[72] Moreover, Robinson makes clear that he has no quibble with inequality in general. "Lamentably," he avers, "there will always be poverty." His focus is on purely racial redistribution, a program that, among other limitations, makes all the less likely any possibility of broad public support.

I argued during the height of the enthusiasm that, as an approach to advancing egalitarian political interests, reparations talk is counterproductive, that in insisting on defining black Americans' disadvantage and exploitation as sui generis it is capable only of petitioning governing elites for special consideration.

> There's a more insidious dynamic at work in this politics as well, which helps us understand why the reparations idea suddenly has spread so widely through mainstream political discourse. We are in one of those rare moments in American

> history—like the 1880s and 1890s and the Great Depression—when common circumstances of economic and social insecurity have strengthened the potential for building broad solidarity across race, gender, and other identities around shared concerns of daily life. These are concerns that only the minority of comfortable and well-off can dismiss in favor of monuments and apologies and a politics of psychobabble, concerns like access to quality health care, the right to a decent and dignified livelihood, affordable housing, quality education for all. They can be pursued effectively only by struggling to unite a wide section of the American population that is denied those essential social benefits or lives in fear of losing them. Isn't it interesting that at such a moment the corporate-dominated, opinion-shaping media discover and project a demand for racially defined reparations that cuts precisely against building such solidarity?[73]

But even though mainstream opinion-shaping media were instrumental in projecting the reparations idea into popular culture and exaggerating the breadth of its support among black Americans, they neither created the enthusiasm nor kept it alive. Reparations talk and imagery clearly struck a responsive chord within the professional-managerial strata, among whom the race line has historically functioned as a social resource and form of political capital. Taking that social base into account suggests a practical foundation beneath agitation for reparations that otherwise appears incomprehensibly fanciful; it is a proprietary assertion of the discourse of race and racism as the default framework through which inequality or injustice at all impinging on black people is to be understood, explained, and addressed.[74]

Like the 1983 march commemorating the 1963 March on Washington for Jobs and Freedom, reparations fervor was partly a placeholder for a political agenda. With assistance from the public information industry, it created a simulacrum of political dynamism, a Potemkin insurgency mounted entirely through legal briefs and position papers, academic panels, and media events. Tellingly, the most visible attempt to demonstrate popular black support for the issue, the nationally promoted August 2002 Millions March for Reparations, failed unequivocally in that objective, with a turnout generally estimated as somewhere in the modest four figures.[75] These failures did not matter, however, because, despite representation of the demand for reparations as the racially authentic stance, for many advocates popular black support was at most a longer term goal of agitation. The deeper appeal of reparations talk for its proponents is that it is an instrument, even a prop, for assertion of a sense of racial peoplehood as the primary basis for political identity. This was always the agenda of the separatist nationalists who had nurtured the reparations idea on the fringes of black political life for more than a generation, as Martha Biondi, John Torpey, and other scholars have noted. And those nationalists have characteristically finessed the seeming conundrum that the programs they propound as racially authentic, including reparations, lack popular support from living black people by interpreting that absence of support as evidence of the brainwashing or psychological damage inflicted by American racism.

The contention that black Americans suffer from widespread and persisting behavioral pathologies originating from slavery and historical racism is a point at which nationalists and adherents of more conventional tendencies within the discourse of racial liberalism have converged in reparations advocacy. Indeed, assertion of links between the slave experience and contemporary inequality may suggest two pragmatic sources of reparations talk's appeal. First, in centering the "memory" of slavery as a formative experience that all black Americans share, the legacy of slavery formulation constructs a basis for racial "community" and solidarity that is at least superficially plausible (it is ultimately only idealist twaddle, after all) in postsegregation conditions. Second, to the extent that it locates the sources of black poverty most immediately in putative cultural or behavioral deficiencies, it is both consonant with and partly constitutive of triumphant neoliberalism.

FROM THE "DAMAGE" THESIS TO THE NEOLIBERAL RACE LINE

The notion that the experience of slavery left an intergenerational imprint on black Americans' patterns of social organization, behavior, and attitudes has been recycled in various iterations at least since E. Franklin Frazier's research on the black family in the 1930s. As Daryl Michael Scott argues, however, it was only in the postwar period that the view took hold that distinctively black family forms (more accurately, patterns of household and kinship organization that occur in greater frequency within the black population than among whites or the general population) have reflected and produced social "pathology."[76] Scott connects that turn to the emergence and consolidation of postwar racial liberalism and its focus on racism's putatively damaging effects on blacks' psyches and, eventually, culture. This approach, he notes, marked a new direction in racial liberalism as an ideology and social program, among other ways as a departure from "interwar racial liberals' economic approach to securing the civil rights of black folk."[77]

In the mid-1960s, in his incarnation as a functionary in Lyndon B. Johnson's administration, sociologist Daniel Patrick Moynihan tied this perception of pathological black family organization to another notion that had recently become a popular truism anchored in social science and social policy: the imagery of a self-perpetuating culture of poverty that impedes its participant victims' abilities to take advantage of opportunities for upward mobility. Moynihan's formulation underwrote a new liberal common sense about the sources of racial inequality, one that represented bigotry and discrimination, structural disadvantage, and black Americans' deficiencies as mutually signifying elements informing causal accounts of racial inequality and its nexus with social policy.[78] This made possible an essentially racial interpretation that avoided the postwar stigma attached to biologistic racism because it represented the supposedly self-defeating black cultural characteristics not as racially innate but as having been engendered by racial subordination. However, this narrative in effect racializes culture by representing it as a transhistorical, independently causal force (the substantive meaning of the cliché "takes on a life of its own") that confers upon a discrete, racially labeled population durable social and mental characteristics—values, attitudes, behavior—held to constrain its social capacities. So what appears to be an interpretation in which culture displaces race instead redefines culture substantively *as* race. That conceptual sleight of hand depended on the same sort of ambiguity about culture as a natural category that had underlain Lamarckian race theory.

Anthropologists and others sharply criticized Moynihan's account and other versions of the culture of poverty narrative, not least because of the naive, racializing notion of culture on which they rested.[79] Yet as Scott indicates, although these criticisms were able for a time in the 1970s to "push damage imagery outside of the mainstream academic journals," the notion never retreated from popular common sense, conservatively inflected opinion journals, or mainstream social policy discourse.[80] Its resilience reflects both the limits of the postwar egalitarian victory over race ideology and the reciprocal power of folk tendencies to construe racially labeled populations as natural groups. What the antiracist victory had won was negative moral sanction of "racism" as an ideology of hierarchy built on the assumption that racial groups have distinct and different psychocultural endowments and capacities fixed by biological inheritance. But this is only one form of racialist ideology. Rejecting it requires rejecting only that races' biological characteristics determine their social or mental capacities; it does not necessarily challenge the more fundamental assumption that they are in some way or other natural groups. In fact, prominent Boasians, including Boas himself, never abandoned the view of races as natural populations.[81] So it should not be surprising that everyday, popular understandings of the nature-like bases of familiar narratives of ascriptive differentiation have not been undone by that victory, particularly as the folk beliefs ostensibly seem constantly reinforced by observation of material differences.[82]

Much as egalitarians had succeeded in defeating only one strain of racialist ideology, critics of Moynihan's pathological black family thesis and other versions of the culture of poverty had only partial and temporary success in beating back the rhetoric of cultural determinism. In retrospect, only the phrase *culture of poverty* became sufficiently controversial as to lose rhetorical force; the determinist principle that underlay it survived, in both popular and scholarly discourse. By the beginning of the Reagan era, this racialized cultural determinism returned under a new label: "urban underclass." This formulation has been amply criticized and exposed as an ideological mystification, as nothing other than the old culture of poverty narrative in new garb.[83] Nevertheless, by the early 1990s the label and the associated imagery of a largely black, inner-city population mired in self-destructive and dangerous pathologies had attained the status of commonsense truism: As with race, people generally "knew" that there is an underclass, "knew" who makes it up and what its characteristics are. They "knew," that is, with unshakeable certainty but without evidence or experience, that poverty and inequality are rooted in the existence of a racially marked population that is alien to the rest of society in its values, norms, and behavior. I note above how this common sense has played out in the post-Katrina fight over demolition of low-income public housing.

Even liberals and many who considered themselves farther left politically blithely rehearsed this moralistic imagery as though it characterized a real population. Historian Jacqueline Jones, in a 1992 book expressly intended in part to counter mean-spirited rhetoric about poor people, nonetheless approached contemporary black urban poverty through the lurid fantasies that underclass narratives routinely projected onto economically marginal inner-city residents. Crack cocaine, she imagined, had created in inner-city neighborhoods "a world without culture, obligation, or larger meaning of any kind," one in which "young men on the street threatened to undermine the corporate ethos that had sustained the black community under slavery."[84] Cornel West expressed a perspective common among black commentators when he bemoaned the "nihilism that increasingly pervades black communities," which he characterized as "the major enemy of black survival in America." In this vein he also insisted that economically supportive policy interventions like jobs programs would not "fully address the cultural decay and moral disintegration of poor black communities . . . which are in need of cultural revitalization and moral regeneration."[85] Across the ideological spectrum the imagery of a population mired in social pathology became the default frame for depicting black poverty and privation. For the right, it was evidence of moral failing and liberal ineptitude, if not innate racial weakness. Liberals gravitated more toward accounts that defined the putative underclass's existence as a legacy of racial exclusion and discrimination. Those who identified with a more leftist politics might stress the underclass's origins in racism and capitalist economic dynamics.

William Julius Wilson provided a narrative that was instrumental—in no small part because of his status as a prominent black sociologist and self-described "social democrat"—in legitimizing the underclass idea as the consensual commonsense discourse frame about black poverty for those who did not want to seem racist or conservative. In *The Truly Disadvantaged* Wilson defined the underclass in behavioral terms, as "a heterogeneous grouping of inner-city families and individuals whose behavior contrasts sharply with that of mainstream America." He located them within a "ghetto-specific culture" marked by the standard litany of pejorative features: crime, drug abuse, teenaged pregnancy, out-of-wedlock births, female-headed households, and welfare dependency, all of which added up to a "tangle of pathology."[86] In tying the underclass's emergence to these factors, Wilson provided a formulation that could be adduced to insulate the pejorative imagery against charges of racism or victim-blaming. He also was usefully ambiguous on the crucial question of whether the pathological culture is durably self-reproducing and therefore would likely resist or undermine the effectiveness of interventions intended to broaden opportunity structures and provide income support. His definitive declaration on the issue was a waffle:

> If my concept of *social isolation* does not imply self-perpetuating cultural traits, am I completely ruling out the possibility that some cultural traits may in fact take on a life of their own for a period of time and thereby become a constraining or liberating factor in the life of certain individuals and groups in the inner city?

> It would be dogmatic to rule out this possibility, however ... as economic and social situations change, cultural traits, created by previous situations, likewise *eventually* change, even though it is possible that some will linger on and influence behavior for a period of time.[87]

This passage's meaning hinges entirely on its adverbs and other conveniently nonspecific qualifiers (e.g., "for a period of time"). It brings to mind the indeterminacy that made Lamarckian race theory more palatable to the young Du Bois than the alternative of immutable inferiority, though it makes no concrete claim like Lamarckians' assertion of a thousand-year lag in blacks' race development, which Du Bois rejected. It is not cynical to suspect that Wilson's formulation is strategically crafted in that respect: It proffers the oceanic assurance of the culture of poverty's commonsensical familiarity without the awful roar of its nasty ideological underpinnings.

Wilson also exhorted liberals to abjure concerns that the underclass narrative unacceptably blames poverty's victims. He did so partly by asserting that their prior reluctance to confront black pathology had enabled the rise of the more mean-spirited conservative arguments in the first place—in effect shifting the victim-blaming charge onto liberals themselves. He contended, erroneously, that "the controversy surrounding the Moynihan report had the effect of curtailing serious research on minority problems in the inner city for over a decade, as liberal scholars shied away from researching behavior construed as unflattering or stigmatizing to particular racial minorities."[88] Thus, he maintained, conservatives, who frame their arguments more harshly, had been able to reduce discussion of inner-city poverty to its expressions in pathological behavior because liberals had refrained from doing so. Wilson's own summation: "The liberal perspective on the ghetto underclass and inner-city social dislocations is less persuasive and influential in public discourse today because many of those who represent the traditional liberal views on social issues have failed to address straightforwardly the rise of social pathologies in the ghetto."[89]

Much as Booker T. Washington proclaimed surrender to the white supremacist regime's inevitable victory well before its consolidation, Wilson called for capitulation to right-wing hegemony in social policy discourse halfway through Ronald Reagan's second term. His view that liberals could best counter conservatives' arguments that invoked "different group values and competitive resources"[90] to explain poverty by adopting softer versions of those arguments was an expression of the reflex that Bill Clinton, under the rubric of triangulation, elaborated into a political strategy, the substance of which meant redefining the boundaries of liberal aspiration to fit within conservative programmatic and ideological hegemony.

At the same time, a new approach emerged on the right for discussing the nexus of race, culture, poverty, and social welfare policy, one reminiscent of the embrace of Black Power by Richard Nixon's administration. In Reagan's first term the administration's visible black advocates were combative ideologues like the economists Thomas Sowell and Walter Williams and flacks like Clarence Pendleton and J. A. Y. Parker, all of whom went out of their way to antagonize the black political and racial advocacy establishment, subjecting it to unremitting criticism or denunciation. In the second term, other black voices—most visibly Robert Woodson and that moment's incarnation of Glenn Loury—sought to, or to appear to, engage the black racial advocacy elite in dialogue. More important than the sincerity of their posture, which was and remains debatable, was its discursive content. The black neoconservatives, as they were often known, appealed to mainstream racial advocacy elites on the basis of a shared sense of special black middle-class responsibility to lead the moral uplift and rehabilitation of the underclass. Although the two camps continued to disagree sharply on issues like affirmative action, the rhetoric of special black middle-class responsibility for the underclass's rectification struck a responsive chord and, along with the associated patter that touted "self-help" as the racially authentic uplift strategy, by the early 1990s had become an all but universal theme in black political discourse, at least within the professional-managerial strata.[91]

This may help to make sense of black racial advocates' generally incoherent response to Clinton administration initiatives like welfare "reform" and punitive, racially invidious crime policy. By the time Bill Clinton ran for the presidency, underclass ideology already was embedded in the center of gravity of mainstream black political discourse. Clinton prominently sported both *The Truly Disadvantaged* and its author during his 1992 campaign, and he counted Wilson as an adviser and included him among the group of academics and black public figures he projected throughout his presidency. Cornel West, a self-described leftist and "freedom fighter," argued that structural interventions are inadequate to confront the "self-destructive and inhumane actions of black people," and black academics and pundits generally embraced some version of the social pathology–cum–special responsibility–cum self-help narrative about black poverty. In this environment there was not much conceptual or political space from which to mount a sharp critique of Clinton's regressive policies and rhetoric.

Clinton's perspective and initiatives had considerable support among the black upper strata whose pronouncements make up what is represented as black opinion. Henry Louis Gates and Oprah Winfrey may have been among the more blunt and caustic in expressing their views of black poor people's defectiveness, perhaps because neither has claimed to be a race leader. However, as Janice Peck notes in her magnificent study of Winfrey as neoliberal icon, they were hardly alone in their support for Clinton's policies. And many others at least quietly acquiesced, in effect accepting the sacrifice of black poor people—as they had accepted Clinton's sacrifice of Rickey Ray Rector early in the 1992 campaign—as collateral damage. Two years after Clinton's welfare reform debacle, Toni Morrison, another White House favorite, admiringly declared him "our first black president."[92]

In the social vision around which this new discursive strain in black politics coheres, the black American population consists most significantly of a successful middle and upper-middle class that remains vulnerable to racial discrimination and a growing black underclass primarily in need of moral and behavioral uplift, preferably led by black middle-class "role models." In between them are a gauzy, folkish image of churchly, generically hardworking, quietly heroic men and women who strive, in Clintonspeak, to "play by the rules" and struggle against the odds to live respectably and hold families and communities together and the socially liminal, politically disconnected "youth" category, which similarly functions as a prop for moralizing rhetoric. John Singleton's execrable 1991 film, *Boyz N the Hood,* illustrates the extent to which this cartoonish vision was by then already enshrined as popular cultural common sense. This image of the black "community," however, leaves out the working-class and lower-middle-class[93] citizens who constitute the largest segment of the black American population. There is no room for them in this picture of a black community because: (1) they clearly and publicly assert self-conscious political agency and therefore cannot plausibly be represented as incapable of formulating and pursuing their own interests directly or as needing middle-class tutelage or spokespersons; and (2) they are fundamentally like other working-class Americans in their central daily concerns—decent jobs, housing, health care, education, economic security for old age, and the like.

Even granting its substantive denial of the existence of the significant bulk of the black population, however, a fundamental analytical tension remains at the core of this discourse. If the social positions of the groups held to constitute the black community are so dramatically different, how—without resort to racial essentialism—could they reasonably be assumed to share a political perspective and agenda? This question raises problems of intellectual respectability and interpretive consistency, because embrace of openly essentialist notions contradicts the discursive conventions among liberal and leftist academics that race is a social construction, and the academy is a primary domain for the new black political discourse's production and circulation. Pressure to address this tension has underlain appeals to conceptual dodges like "strategic essentialism" (which supposedly enables a suspiciously Protestant stance of embracing essentialism in practice but not in principle) and "intersectionality," as well as the elaboration of academic subfields like critical race studies and black cultural studies. These all seek to resolve the contradiction on the plane of high theory, through flights onto a level of abstraction high enough to blur the intellectually and politically messy distinctions of concrete life, such as the complexities disclosed through close examination of the nexus of race and politics in post-Katrina New Orleans.

Concern with negotiating that contradiction was also reflected in political scientists' efforts to assess the proposition that increasing economic stratification among black Americans in the postsegregation era had accelerated interest-differentiation within the black population. Studies by Michael C. Dawson, Katherine Tate, and Carol M. Swain addressed the issue most directly. This scholarship defined its objective as ascertaining the extent to which differentiation by economic status or other criteria affected black adherence to race-conscious politics.[94] But each prejudged the conclusion by positing a category of collective or generic racial interests as the baseline from which deviation should be measured and by treating the legitimacy of the nominally race-conscious political agenda as given. That is, their approaches did not interrogate the foundations of what they characterized as the racial agenda, whence it was derived, or how its actual or potential benefits are distributed across the black population. Dawson's finding of a racial "linked-fate" politics and Tate's finding of high group cohesion around the racial agenda could just as easily result from asymmetrical subgroup power in agenda-setting in the name of the race, particularly in the absence of clear, public processes for agenda formation. Indeed, each found that race consciousness, expressed as commitment to the racial agenda, seemed to increase, not decline, with education and income. Each treated this finding as anomalous because each ultimately proceeded from a simplistic model that assumes a version of forsaking one's roots—a point where postwar social science's narrative of modernization meets the notion of racial authenticity as "keeping it real"—as the driving force of black interest-differentiation. That is, neither scholar at all considered the possibility that this finding could say more about the class basis of the "linked-fate" agenda than about the persistence of an abstract norm of group solidarity. To that extent, it seems as if these scholars, with or without intention, raised the possibility of political differentiation in order to refute it.[95]

Emergence of the conveniently amorphous category of celebrity commentators known as "black public intellectuals" also was partly a response to the challenge of crafting a rhetorical basis for a politics of black racial solidarity in the postsegregation, neoliberal political world. The modal posture of the public intellectual is a freelance racial voice, a sage who is enmeshed in the articulate and successful strata but is also a conduit to the sensibilities of the black mass that lives outside national civic life and whose thinking and aspirations are alien and obscure to the society at large.[96] The black public intellectual career path also runs disproportionately through faculty employment—so much so that it has become increasingly common to encounter graduate students whose desired career trajectories openly envision pursuing a doctorate as a step toward becoming a public intellectual at least as much as preparation for an academic career. Left-of-center academic audiences are a primary market for the consumption of public intellectuals' products—books, lectures, and journal and magazine articles. Black public intellectuals' claims to insider knowledge and evocations of popular political engagement, combined with access to visible platforms in mainstream communications media, provide a pontifical cultural authority that buttressed common stereotypes and give them an aura of immediate veracity by imbuing them with the rhetorical intimacy of firsthand experience, which at times approaches voyeuristic titillation. This is why I have characterized the role of the black public intellectual as akin to that of the trusted native guide and interpreter in colonial lore.[97]

Attentiveness to the challenge of articulating a narrative of racial solidarity's foundations compatible with the sharply class-inflected new black political discourse may help explain the eruption of public calls for coming to grips with the impact of slavery's legacy on blacks and other Americans. This fixation arose and spread like a Great Awakening among academics, activists, and the increasingly visible public intellectuals in the mid-1990s. Perhaps some of this enthusiasm was inspired by the comparably evanescent call—issued initially by Lani Guinier and others, then taken up cynically and retailed by the Clinton administration—for a national "conversation" about race.[98] Whatever its proximate sources, the assertion that black

Americans of all strata—from the most successful and accomplished to the least—in some way or other are afflicted with the "trauma" of ancestral enslavement also attained the status of commonsense truth that attaches to formulations incessantly rehearsed in the various outlets of the public information industry—newspapers and magazines, broadcast networks, public opinion polls, and the like.[99] The successful, in this view, face the trauma arising from direct or indirect discrimination manifest, for example, in glass ceilings, susceptibility to racial profiling and police brutality, real estate redlining, disparities in health outcomes (often seen as partly somatic expressions of the trauma itself), wealth, income, and other, more finely parsed markers of economic security and status, as well as difficulties in hailing cabs or being buzzed into boutiques. Slavery's long hand among the poor appears more crucially in patterns of pathological, self-destructive behavior. However, underlying this distinction is a presumption that the generic experience of trauma originating in slavery constitutes a substantive bond of shared racial history and sensibility linking all black Americans (and, in some more expansive constructions, all black people everywhere).

At the time, the patter about remembrance of slavery and its heritable trauma, which often veered into pure psychobabble or worse, seemed to be a curious popular hysteria that gripped a segment of the black middle classes, a moment of collective emotional catharsis. It seemed also perhaps partly an artifact of the ambivalent relation between black and Jewish group advocacy elites, which occasionally descends into rhetorical competition over the extent of comparative historical suffering. It was noteworthy in this context that the upsurge of slave-trauma discourse was coincident with the moment of heightened public attention to the Nazi extermination of Jews, reflected in and propelled by the popular film *Schindler's List* and the proliferation of Holocaust museums and public memorials around the country. And a common refrain in that discourse characterized the transatlantic slave trade as the black Holocaust.[100] In retrospect, it is not difficult to see how that moment of middle-class agitation also became the immediate rhetorical precursor from which the reparations enthusiasm grew, particularly given the contemporaneous precedent of the movement for reparations to victims of Nazi exterminism.

With respect to charting the forces shaping contemporary black political discourse, however, it is more significant that both the fixation on the trauma of slavery and the moment of reparations fervor also overlap and express a deep ideological commitment to racial metaphor as the sine qua non for discussion of black Americans' status and aspirations in American politics. This insistence on the primacy of the race line—the narrative of racism or racial disparity—as the interpretive frame for any inequality or claim for justice involving black people became increasingly prominent as slave-trauma rhetoric morphed into reparations talk. It is also at the root of the contemporary attractiveness of Du Bois's "color line" apothegm.

In invoking Du Bois to buttress claims that race continues fundamentally to define black Americans' political, economic, and social conditions, Holt and others seek to annex his cultural authority in a debate over whether "race" (i.e., racism) has declined in significance in determining black Americans' life chances in the postsegregation era. Instructively, Holt refers to Du Bois's modification in the 1930s of his earlier prediction regarding the color line's significance but does not acknowledge Du Bois's yet sharper move away from the notion in the 1950s, when he observed, "I still think today as yesterday that the color line is a great problem of this century. But today I see more clearly than yesterday that back of the problem of race and color lies a greater problem which both obscures and implements it ... the fact that so many civilized persons are willing to live in comfort even if the price of this is poverty, ignorance and disease of the majority of their fellowmen."[101] Contrary to Du Bois, Holt asserts in his concluding assessment that racism, although often camouflaged, "permeates every institution, every pore of everyday life. Justice in the courts, earnings on our jobs, whether we have jobs at all, the quality of our life, the means and timing of our death—all form the stacked deck every child born black must take up to play the game of life."[102]

I draw this contrast not primarily to suggest that Du Bois's 1953 view was right and Holt's is wrong. (However, given the historical trajectory of the intervening half century, if Du Bois's judgment was correct then, Holt's is most likely incorrect now.) My point is to underscore that Holt's engagement with Du Bois, like that of many other contemporary scholars, is shaped by a specific presentist political and ideological agenda—vindication of the race line as the nonnegotiable frame of reference for addressing black Americans' political and policy concerns. As I have argued, this is a distinctly class-inflected political agenda. From this perspective, the polarity commonly posed between race-based politics and class-based politics is miscast.

The race line *is* a class line. It is rooted in a commitment to a politics of racial elite brokerage or racial representation that, as indicated in the increasingly tortuous and convoluted formulations required to argue for funneling any problem or issue affecting black Americans into the discourse of racism and racial disparity, is ever more contradictory and inadequate the farther we move from the Jim Crow era in which it was born and evolved. There are several reasons that the race line nevertheless persists as the hegemonic framework for black political discourse. The institutional and ideological pressures I have described give it the force of habit and the verisimilitude that reassuring familiarity confers. It is anchored within a political economy of race relations that delivers material and symbolic benefits disproportionately to members of the professional-managerial strata who occupy the status of brokers or representatives and who insist on it as the default language of black political aspiration. In endorsing behavioral narratives of inner-city poverty and in shifting the language of racial justice's normative foundation from pursuit of equality as an ideal to pursuit of diversity and racial parity, the discourse constituting the race line has accommodated and reinforced consolidation of the neoliberal regime in American politics.[103]

Taking this into account also provides perspective on the bases of the iconic appeal of *The Souls of Black Folk,* which Du Bois wrote virtually at the beginning of a career that spanned nearly the totality of the segregation era, as well as the specific appeal of the color line and double-consciousness formulations. Du Bois wrote *Souls* during his most politically conservative period, and it is also the text in which he most clearly adopts the voice of the race spokesman.

THE LONG HAND OF BOOKER T. WASHINGTON

In this context it is instructive that Du Bois's challenge to Booker T. Washington now is the least noted or discussed among the four canonical elements of *Souls*'s content. (David L. Lewis's chapters in the first volume of his Du Bois biography are a more than welcome exception.[104]) From the perspective I have laid out here, Du Bois's critique of Washington has the most direct bearing on contemporary black American political and ideological life. The debate over Washington's legacy provides a revealing window into the ideological and institutional relations and processes out of which grew the form of political debate and action that defined the universe of racial action throughout the Jim Crow era and beyond.

The form of elite brokerage politics that was the essence of Washington's program assumes that black people do not function as full citizens and that structured relations of accountability need not mediate relations between putative leaders and led. This view, as I have shown, persists into a post–Jim Crow environment in which there is no longer any credible justification for it and in which its limitations and inadequacies are all too clear. The discourse of racism and the postwar racial liberalism from which it emerged are lineal descendants of the synthesis that Washington helped to craft at the dawn of the twentieth century, a discourse and practice of "race relations," which, as Michael Rudolph West argues eloquently, was predicated upon positing the black American population as a corporate entity separate and distinct from "white America" and represented by generic race leaders or spokesmen. West argues that the race relations idea appealed to white elites in Booker T. Washington's day—and since—because it sidesteps questions of equality and establishes discussion of black Americans' status and condition on a plane "isolated from the normal contest and conflict of American society."[105]

This politics is also the framework within which the role of generic race leader or race spokesperson emerged, with Washington as its initial embodiment. It is a testament to the power of ideology that this notion has persisted as a commonsense category for so long and has provoked so little skepticism or critical scrutiny. For more than a century even radicals have accepted it and the principle of unitary, racially authentic politics that it assumes. This discourse's commonsense power in black politics stems from its deep resonance with the worldview and matrix of political, social, and economic interests of a social stratum that is embedded, directly or indirectly, within a political economy of race relations. For this stratum, *The Souls of Black Folk,* which Du Bois conceived partly as a condensation or assertion of a collective voice and a rallying point for a similar, albeit more idealized, stratum of race-conscious elite black Americans at the beginning of the twentieth century, has become an icon of ideological legitimation.

I can anticipate objections that my argument here denies the existence of racial injustice and inequality or diminishes their significance in American society. I want to make clear that there is no question that advantages and disadvantages, social benefits and harms, opportunities and constraints, and everyday civic regard are distributed in American society asymmetrically, in a general pattern in which black people tend to be represented in significant disproportion on the more precarious, more exploited, less privileged end of the distribution. That is clearly true. Nor are those outcomes the product of random or neutral processes. Individual cases may be more ambiguous, but at the societal level those inequalities stem from the often complex dynamics that produce, enforce, and contest political, economic, and civic hierarchy in the United States, dynamics that are generative in their outcomes and to a substantial extent have been and remain shaped partly through the metaphor of race.

The problem is that the discourse of racism or racial disparity, as the New Orleans case illustrates, does not help either to identify the precise mechanisms through which even many decidedly racialized inequalities are produced or to guide development of strategies for challenging them. Analytically, its taxonomic impulse abstracts away from the discrete characteristics of relations and phenomena to extract whichever of their features can be construed as generically racial. To that extent it privileges category over content, labeling over description. Politically, as I have argued, racism discourse points in no direction other than calls to combat or compensate for racism or racial disparity. The scope of strategic imagination it allows is limited—and has been since its origination with Booker T. Washington and the emerging stratum of race men and race women in the early twentieth century—to petitioning ruling elites for consideration on behalf of a black population presumed to be civically mute.

As left political engagement in other domains eroded with the advance of Reaganism, academic black studies became more prominent as a site for articulating the race line and projecting it as an insurgent political critique. Influences of postmodernism and interpretive postures such as cultural studies supported reformulation on more theoretically elaborate and professionally respectable bases the inflection toward political engagement that has been associated with black studies as an academic practice since its creation in the ferment of the 1960s. This is the academic environment that gave rise to the black public intellectual. It is also the context in which Holt and others revisited black intellectual history as a field of study, in the spirit of authenticating the race line in contemporary politics by associating it with a venerable tradition.

The halo of apparent association with Du Bois, however, does not eliminate the crucial questions concerning claims of *Souls*'s pertinence for our time: Does the color-line apothegm, the Veil metaphor, or the double-consciousness formulation shed light on the content, mechanisms, or trajectories through which existing inequalities—even those that are most clearly racialized—are reproduced? What programmatic insight can any of those formulations provide to assist in combating inequality and injustice in the present? What affirmative vision does any provide of a more just world, not to speak of strategies for pursuing it? I believe that I have demonstrated here that those questions have a single answer: None worth mentioning. Nor could Du Bois's formulations have more to say to our times and the problems facing us. His perspectives and concerns were oriented toward events and perspectives, problems and debates, that made up *his* contemporary world. The belief that "greats" can speak across the ages is either a hortatory political device or naive idealism. Timeless verities are the province of fortune cookies.

By contrast, I submit that the most intellectually and politically productive approach to texts from the past involves trying to locate them as nodes within an evolving pattern of political debate, in which possibly controversial interpretations, arguments, and positions advanced at point A can, if successful (and success may depend only secondarily on truth content or intellectual elegance), become the commonsense understandings that form the baseline for debate and practice at point B. This approach, which I discuss more extensively in the "Introduction" and "Conclusion" to *W. E. B. Du Bois and American Political Thought,* presumes that the enterprise of the history of black American political thought should be approached pragmatically as the history of ideologies—that is, with an assumption that authors in the past were primarily motivated by trying to understand and do things within their contemporary worlds and that their thinking was largely shaped by the discursive networks available to them and the challenges and options they faced. Moreover, the character and sources of their perceptions of those challenges, including perceptions of their relative weight and urgency, must be part of the focus. How one conceptualizes and assesses the social and political landscape and defines and orders its dangers and possibilities is likely to be shaped significantly by one's own social position, and insight into the often complex relation between social position and social perception is a necessary element of making sense of the thinking of an individual or a discourse community. If it is reasonable to talk about a tradition of ideas, I believe that tradition lies in the generative debates that have culminated in making the world as we know it.

NOTES

1. The books published before *Souls,* of course, were *The Suppression of the African Slave Trade to the United States of America, 1638–1870* (1896) and *The Philadelphia Negro: A Social Study* (1899). Those published after include *John Brown* (1909); *The Negro* (1915); *Darkwater: Voices from Within the Veil* (1920); *The Gift of Black Folk: The Negroes in the Making of America* (1924); *Black Reconstruction: An Essay Toward a History of the Part Which Black Folk Played in the Attempt to Reconstruct Democracy in America, 1860–1880* (1935); *Black Folk Then and Now: An Essay in the History and Sociology of the Negro Race* (1939); *Dusk of Dawn: An Essay Toward an Autobiography of a Race Concept* (1940); *Color and Democracy: Colonies and Peace* (1945); *The World and Africa: An Inquiry into the Part Which Africa Has Played in World History* (1947); *In Battle for Peace: The Story of My 83rd Birthday* (1952); and *Autobiography: A Soliloquy on Viewing My Life from the Last Decade of Its First Century* (1968).

2. David Levering Lewis, *W. E. B. Du Bois: Biography of a Race, 1868–1919* (New York: Henry Holt, 1993), 277. For a sampling and summaries of these reactions to *Souls,* see Arnold Rampersad, *The Art and Imagination of W. E. B. Du Bois* (Cambridge, MA: Harvard University Press, 1976), xii–xvi;; Henry Louis Gates Jr., "Introduction" to Du Bois, *Souls of Black Folk* (New York: Bantam, 1989), 13–16; Herbert Aptheker, "Introduction" to Du Bois, *Souls of Black Folk* (Millwood, NY: Kraus-Thomson, 1973), 14–15; David Levering Lewis, "Introduction" to Du Bois, *Souls of Black Folk* (New York: Modern Library, 2003), xi–xii.

3. Gates, "Introduction," 16–17.

4. Lewis, *Du Bois,* 277. Also see Lewis, "*The Souls of Black Folk,* A Century Hence," *Crisis* (March/April 2003): 17–21.

5. J. Saunders Redding, "Introduction" to Du Bois, *Souls* (New York: Fawcett, 1961), ix.

6. Adolph Reed Jr., *Stirrings in the Jug: Black Politics in the Post-Segregation Era* (Minneapolis: University of Minnesota Press, 1999), 18–52. See also Adolph Reed Jr., "The Study of Black Politics and the Practice of Black Politics: Their Historical Relation and Evolution," in *Problems and Methods in the Study of Politics,* ed. Ian Shapiro, Tarek Masoud, and Rogers M. Smith (Cambridge and New York: Cambridge University Press, 2004).

7. For a recent, popular discussion of this node of black opposition to encroaching Jim Crow, see Keith Weldon Medley, *We As Freemen:* Plessy v. Ferguson (Gretna, LA: Pelican, 2003).

8. Adolph Reed Jr., *W. E. B. Du Bois and American Political Thought: Fabianism and the Color Line* (New York and Oxford: Oxford University Press, 1997), 127–130 and 163–186.

9. Reed, *Du Bois,* 176.

10. W. E. B. Du Bois, *The Souls of Black Folk: Essays and Sketches* (Chicago: McClurg, 1907), vii.

11. Ibid., 13.

12. On the consolidation of the white supremacist order in the South, see Rayford Logan, *The Betrayal of the Negro: From Rutherford B. Hayes to Woodrow Wilson* (New York: Macmillan, 1965); C. Vann Woodward, *Origins of the New South, 1877–1913* (Baton Rouge: Louisiana State University Press, 1951) and *The Strange Career of Jim Crow* (New York: Oxford University Press, 1966); J. Morgan Kousser, *The Shaping of Southern Politics: Suffrage Restriction and the Establishment of the One-Party South, 1880–1910* (New Haven, CT: Yale University Press, 1974); Stanley P. Hirshson, *Farewell to the Bloody Shirt: Northern Republicans and the Southern Negro, 1877–1893* (New York: Quadrangle, 1968); Charles A. Lofgren, *The Plessy Case: A Legal-Historical Interpretation* (New York: Oxford University Press, 1988); Jack Bloom, *Class, Race, and the Civil Rights Movement* (Bloomington: Indiana University Press, 1987), chap. 1; Glenda Gilmore, *Gender and Jim Crow: Women and the Politics of White Supremacy in North Carolina, 1896–1920* (Chapel Hill: University of North Carolina Press, 1996); Helen G. Edmonds, *The Negro and Fusion Politics in North Carolina, 1894–1901* (Chapel Hill: University of North Carolina Press, 2003 [1951]); and Henry Grady, "The South and Her Problems," in *Joel Chandler Harris' Life of Henry W. Grady, Including His Writings and Speeches,* ed. Joel Chandler Harris (New York: Cassell, 1890), esp. 97–108.

13. On non-southern-elite whites' racialized concerns about immigrants, see Kenneth W. Warren, *Black and White Strangers: Race and American Literary Realism* (Chicago: University of Chicago Press, 1993); and John Higham, *Strangers in the Land: Patterns of American Nativism, 1860–1925* (New York: Atheneum, 1981). Clear statements of this racialized anxiety abounded among northern WASP elites, characteristically focusing on the supposed problem of assimilability—that is, whether immigrant "stocks" could ever, by racial temperament, function effectively within American institutions. See, e.g., Edward A. Ross, "The Causes of Race Superiority," *Annals of the American Academy of Political and Social Science* 18 (July 1901): 67–89. Du Bois's "The Relation of the Negroes to the Whites of the South" appeared in the same issue of *Annals* and was reprinted in *Souls* as the ninth chapter, "Of the Sons of Masters and Man." See also John R. Commons, *Races and Immigrants in America* (London: Macmillan, 1907). Even otherwise progressives such as Charlotte Perkins Gilman and Margaret Sanger expressed their concerns about the effects of immigration in those terms. See Charlotte Perkins Gilman, *The Living of Charlotte Perkins Gilman: An Autobiography* (New York: Ayer, 1935); Margaret Sanger, *The Pivot of Civilization* (New York: Brentano's, 1922), 125–138; on Sanger also see Edwin Black, *War Against the Weak: Eugenics and America's Campaign to Create a Master Race* (New York: Four Walls Eight Windows, 2003), 127–144.

14. See, in addition to Ross, "Causes of Race Superiority," William I. Thomas, "The Scope

and Method of Folk Psychology," *American Journal of Sociology* 1 (January 1896): 434–445; Dorothy Ross, *The Origins of American Social Science* (Cambridge: Cambridge University Press, 1991); and George W. Stocking Jr., *Race, Culture, and Evolution: Essays in the History of Anthropology* (Chicago: University of Chicago Press, 1982). Lapouge's statement is cited in Jonathan Peter Spiro, *Defending the Master Race: Conservation, Eugenics, and the Legacy of Madison Grant* (Lebanon, NH: University Press of New England, 2009), 116.

15. Du Bois, *Dusk of Dawn,* 116.

16. Ibid., 98.

17. Ibid., 99.

18. See Reed, *Du Bois,* 123–125.

19. Du Bois, "Fifty Years After," in *Souls* (Millwood, NY: Kraus-Thompson, 1973), xi. This introduction appeared in the 1953 edition of *Souls* published by Blue Heron.

20. Du Bois himself was challenged sharply in the 1930s by a group of younger black activists more inclined than he toward a working-class politics. See, e.g., Reed, *Du Bois,* 67; Jonathan Holloway, *Confronting the Veil: Abram Harris, E. Franklin Frazier, and Ralph Bunche, 1919–1941* (Chapel Hill: University of North Carolina Press, 2002), 118–119, 167–168; David Levering Lewis, *W. E. B. Du Bois: The Fight for Equality and the American Century, 1919–1963* (New York: Henry Holt, 2000), 320–348. Nikhil Pal Singh discusses these critiques from a concern to vindicate Du Bois's view, in *Black Is a Country: Race and the Unfinished Struggle for Democracy* (Cambridge, MA: Harvard University Press), 70–84.

21. Thomas C. Holt, *The Problem of Race in the 21st Century* (Cambridge, MA: Harvard University Press, 2000).

22. Ibid., 3.

23. Ibid., 22.

24. Ibid., 7.

25. Ibid., 27, 112–113; also see Stuart Hall, "Race, Articulation, and Societies Structured in Dominance," in *Black British Cultural Studies: A Reader,* ed. Houston A. Baker Jr., Manthia Diawara, and Ruth H. Lundeborg (Chicago: University of Chicago Press, 1996). Hall's statement appears in a paragraph characterizing the "structures through which black labour is reproduced," which, he contends, are expressed as race relations. In this essay Hall generally, like Holt, in practice seems to treat race as a sui generis or foundational form of ascription. However, at this moment in the text he is referring specifically to how race functions in the "constitution of [black labor] as a class" (55). In this instance, he may not be making the broader, more ontological claim; he may be commenting only on how race functions in the specific context of reproduction of a racialized labor system. Holt extrapolates from the more restricted context of Hall's statement to propound a more general, at least implicitly ontological claim about race's singular importance in capitalist society. I do not suggest that Holt adduces Hall improperly; as I indicated, in most of the essay Hall seems also to conceptualize race as a singular form of ascription. The potential for confusion here may be exacerbated because both Hall and Holt engage the question at a level of conceptual and historical generality that distills race so cleanly from its specific contexts of constitution and reproduction in the complex dynamics of given social orders that it can be difficult to ascertain when a claim is intended to be contextually bound or not. Hall's essay was published originally in *Sociological Theories: Race and Colonialism* (Paris: UNESCO, 1980), 305–345.

26. Adolph Reed Jr., "Unraveling the Relation of Race and Class in American Politics," *Political Power and Social Theory* 15 (2002): 271. Rogers M. Smith describes ascriptive status designations as those that "stress the significance of involuntarily acquired traits that differentiate people." Rogers M. Smith, *Civic Ideals: Conflicting Visions of Citizenship in U.S. History* (New Haven, CT: Yale University Press), 508. Smith correctly singles out "race, ethnicity, religion, gender and sexual orientation" as key ascriptive markers in U.S. political history. As his broader

characterization indicates, those do not exhaust the universe of categories of ascriptive differentiation that have been, or have the potential to become, politically significant in American life.

27. Holt, *The Problem of Race,* 119–120.

28. See, for example, James W. Trent Jr., *Inventing the Feeble Mind: A History of Mental Retardation in the United States* (Berkeley: University of California Press, 1994); Elof Axel Carlson, *The Unfit: A History of a Bad Idea* (Cold Spring Harbor, NY: Cold Spring Harbor Press, 2001); Nicole Hahn Rafter, *Creating Born Criminals* (Urbana: University of Illinois Press, 1997); Troy Duster, *Backdoor to Eugenics,* 2nd ed. (New York: Routledge, 2003), 132–145. Steven Selden, *Inheriting Shame: The Story of Eugenics and Racism in America* (New York: Teachers College Press, 1999), 127–157; Nicole Hahn Rafter, ed., *White Trash: The Eugenic Family Studies, 1877–1919* (Boston: Northeastern University Press, 1988).

29. Daniel Patrick Moynihan, U.S. Senate, Committee of Finance, The Work and Responsibility Act of 1994, July 13, 1994, transcript, 33.

30. Reed, "Unraveling," 266.

31. Walter Benn Michaels examines the fluidity of race, culture, and white identity in the Progressive era and 1920s in "Race into Culture: A Critical Genealogy of Cultural Identity," *Critical Inquiry* 18 (Summer 1992): 655–685, and *Our America: Nativism, Modernism, and Pluralism* (Durham, NC: Duke University Press, 1997).

32. Holt, *The Problem of Race,* 73–74.

33. Ibid., 105.

34. Howard Winant stands out as another proponent of this perspective on race and historical social formations. See Winant, *The World Is a Ghetto: Race and Democracy Since World War II* (New York: Basic Books, 2001), and *Racial Conditions: Politics, Theory, Comparisons* (Minneapolis: University of Minnesota Press, 1994), and Michael Omi and Howard Winant, *Racial Formation in the United States: From the 1960s to the 1990s,* 2nd ed. (New York: Routledge, 1994).

35. For critical discussion of the convergence between underclass ideology and New Urbanist urban design in an ecological narrative about poverty and its expression in federal and local housing policies based on displacement and dispersal, see Larry Bennett and Adolph Reed Jr., "The New Face of Urban Renewal: The Near North Redevelopment Initiative and the Cabrini-Green Neighborhood" in *Without Justice for All,* ed. Adolph Reed Jr. (Boulder, CO: Westview, 1999); and Charles Goetz, *Clearing the Way* (Washington, DC: Urban Institute Press, 2003).

36. David Imbroscio, "'United and Actuated by Some Common Impulse of Passion': Challenging the Dispersal Consensus in American Housing Policy Research," *Journal of Urban Affairs* 30 (2008): 111–130; Xavier de Souza Briggs, "Maximum Feasible Misdirection: A Reply to Imbroscio," *Journal of Urban Affairs* 30 (2008): 131–137; John Goering and Judith Feins, "Social Science, Housing Policy, and the Harmful Effects of Poverty," *Journal of Urban Affairs* 30 (2008): 139–148; and David Imbroscio, "Rebutting Nonrebuttals: A Rejoinder to My Critics," *Journal of Urban Affairs* 30 (2008): 149–154.

37. See Preston H. Smith II, "'Self-Help,' Black Conservatives, and the Reemergence of Black Privatism," in *Without Justice for All.* On Obama's castigation of black poor people, see Adolph Reed Jr., "Where Obamaism Seems to Be Going," *Black Agenda Report* (July 16, 2008), available at www.blackagendareport.com/index.php?option=com_content&task=view&id=697&Itemid=1. Also see Adolph Reed Jr., "Obama, No," *The Progressive* (May 2008).

38. "Moving to Opportunity in the Wake of Hurricane Katrina," New Vision: An Institute for Policy and Progress, September 15, 2005. For critical discussion of this call see: Adolph Reed Jr. and Stephen Steinberg, John David Arena, and Xavier de Souza Briggs, "Symposium: Katrina, Race, and Politics," *Political Sociology: States, Power, and Societies* 13 (Fall 2006). The Reed and Steinberg article appeared originally in the online publication *Black Commentator* 182 (May 6, 2006) at www.blackcommentator.com/182/182_cover_liberals_katrina.html.

39. The exact statement by then city council President Oliver Thomas was: "We don't need soap opera watchers now. We're going to target the people who are going to work. It's not that I'm fed up, but that at some point there has to be a whole new level of motivation, and people have got to stop blaming the government for something they ought to do." James Varney, "HANO Wants Only Working Tenants," New Orleans *Times-Picayune,* February 21, 2006. Black council member Reneé Gill Pratt seconded Thomas's comment, as did white council member Jackie Clarkson, who later succeeded Thomas as council president after he was forced to resign following a corruption indictment.

40. See Darran Simon, "Benjamin Franklin Names New Principal," New Orleans *Times-Picayune,* June 21, 2008; Steve Ritea, "300 Students Turned Away by N.O. Schools," New Orleans *Times-Picayune,* January 24, 2007; Paul Hill and Jane Hannaway, *The Future of Public Education in New Orleans* (Washington, DC: Urban Institute, 2006); United Teachers of New Orleans (UTNO) and American Federation of Teachers (AFT), *Reading, Writing and Reality Check: An Early Assessment of Student Achievement in Post-Katrina New Orleans* (October, 2007); UTNO, Louisiana Federation of Teachers (LFT), and AFT, *"National Model" or Flawed Approach: The Post-Katrina New Orleans Public Schools* (2006); William Quigley, "Fighting for the Right to Learn: Report on the Results of the Public Education Experiment in New Orleans Two Years After Katrina," New Orleans *Tribune,* May/June, 2008; Paul Tough, "A Teachable Moment," *New York Times Magazine,* August 17, 2008.

41. James Gill, *Lords of Misrule: Mardi Gras and the Politics of Race in New Orleans* (Jackson: University Press of Mississippi, 1997), esp. 221–283. See also Adolph Reed Jr., *Class Notes: Posing as Politics and Other Thoughts on the American Scene* (New York: New Press, 2000), 180–186.

42. Holt, *The Problem of Race,* 18; Hall, "Race," 50–54.

43. Holt, *The Problem of Race,* 13–15.

44. Bourdieu and Wacquant have criticized as an expression of cultural imperialism current tendencies to read notions of race distinctive to the United States, particularly the relation between race and politics, onto Brazil and elsewhere in the world. See Pierre Bourdieu and Loïc Wacquant, "On the Cunning of Imperialist Reason," *Theory, Culture, and Society* 16 (1999): 41–58; and Wacquant, "For an Analytic of Racial Domination," *Political Power and Social Theory* 11 (1997): 221–234. Wacquant ("Analytic," 221–222) also notes the problem that "a particular schema of racial division developed by one country during a small segment of its short history, a schema unusual for its degree of arbitrariness, rigidity and social consequentiality, has been virtually universalized as the template through which analyses of 'race' in all countries and all epochs are to be conducted." Also see Mara Loveman, "Is 'Race' Essential?" *American Sociological Review* 64 (December 1999): 893–894; Mahmood Mamdani, *Saviors and Survivors: Darfur, Politics, and the War on Terror* (New York: Pantheon, 2009), esp. 75–170; John R. Bowen, "The Myth of Global Ethnic Conflict," *Journal of Democracy* 7 (1996): 3–14; and John Mueller, "The Banality of 'Ethnic War,'" *International Security* 25 (Summer 2000): 42–70. And perhaps nothing illustrates the tendency toward reification and anachronism as clearly as the emergence and proliferation of ahistorical, ontologized notions of "whiteness." For critical discussion of the historical limitations of the "whiteness" idea, see: "Scholarly Controversy: Whiteness and the Historians' Imagination," with articles by Judith Stein, Eric Arnesen, James R. Barrett, David Brody, Barbara J. Fields, Eric Foner, Victoria C. Hattam, and Adolph Reed Jr., and a response by Arnesen in *International Labor and Working-Class History* 60 (Fall 2001): 1–92.

45. Reed, *Class Notes.* See also, on the conflation of folk and analytic notions of race, Ann Laura Stoler, "Racial Histories and their Regimes of Truth," *Political Power and Social Theory* 11 (1997): 197–201; and Wacquant, "Analytic," 222–224.

46. Holt, *The Problem of Race,* 8.

47. Ibid., 22.

48. Ibid., 19.

49. Ibid., 21. Like Hall and others, Holt's inclination to anchor interpretation in an idealist discourse influenced by Foucault and poststructuralism adds to the ambiguity surrounding formulations such as this. Strictly speaking, for example, race and other identities do not "attempt to 'interpellate,' speak to us or hail us into place as . . . social subjects" (Stuart Hall, "Introduction: Who Needs Identity?" in *Questions of Cultural Identity,* ed. Stuart Hall and Paul du Gay [Thousand Oaks, CA: Sage, 1996], 5). They are pure mental constructs, abstractions that are incapable of any such action. The language of "projects," which Holt also embraces, is similarly propelled by idealist formulations that are struck at a level of abstraction that renders conveniently ambiguous whether they are intended as metaphor or direct description of historical processes. Winant (*The World Is a Ghetto*) has perhaps most extensively employed this language of "projects," which collapses nuance and randomness into a linear account and imputes causality and motive to ideas—with or without acknowledging doing so—to drive an account of race and its history. This penchant for idealist formulations brings to mind Herbert Butterfield's caution against the "realm of specious generalizations and vague plausibilities, built up out of confusions of thought . . . characterized by the bold handling of concepts that do not represent anything capable of genuine concrete visualization—the whole issuing out of a process of too much argumentation upon abridged history." Butterfield, *The Whig Interpretation of History* (New York: Norton, 1965 [1931]), 98.

50. Thomas C. Holt, "Marking: Race, Race-Making, and the Writing of History," *American Historical Review* 100 (February 1995): 12.

51. Holt, *The Problem of Race,* 8.

52. Ibid., 5–12; Holt, "Marking," 18–20.

53. Holt, *The Problem of Race,* 8.

54. For examination of these developments, including their complexities and contradictions, see, in addition to Stocking, *Race, Culture, and Evolution,* Vernon J. Williams, *Rethinking Race: Franz Boas and His Contemporaries* (Lexington: University Press of Kentucky, 1996); Lee D. Baker, *From Savage to Negro: Anthropology and the Construction of Race, 1986–1954* (Berkeley: University of California Press, 1998); Elazar Barkan, *The Retreat of Scientific Racism: Changing Concepts of Race in Britain and the United States between the World Wars* (Cambridge: Cambridge University Press, 1992); and James B. McKee, *Sociology and the Race Problem: The Failure of a Perspective* (Urbana: University of Illinois Press, 1993).

55. See Louis L. Knowles and Kenneth Prewitt, *Institutional Racism in America* (Englewood Cliffs, NJ: Prentice Hall, 1969); Robert Blauner, *Racial Oppression in America* (New York: HarperCollins, 1972); and several of the contributions in Joyce Ladner, ed., *The Death of White Sociology* (New York: Random House, 1973).

56. See, for example, Smith, *Civic Ideals,* and "Beyond Tocqueville, Myrdal, and Hartz: The Multiple Traditions in America," *American Political Science Review* 87 (September 1993): 549–566; Desmond S. King and Rogers M. Smith, "Racial Orders in American Political Development," *American Political Science Review* 99 (February 2005): 75–92; Joseph Lowndes, Julie Novkov, and Dorian Warren, eds., *Race and American Political Development* (New York: Routledge, 2008); Michael K. Brown et al., *Whitewashing Race: The Myth of a Color-Blind Society* (Berkeley: University of California Press, 2003); Michael K. Brown, *Race, Money, and the Welfare State* (Ithaca, NY: Cornell University Press, 1999); and Ira Katznelson, *When Affirmative Action Was White: An Untold History of Racial Inequality in Twentieth-Century America* (New York: Norton, 2006).

57. Monica Prasad provides one of the clearest and most succinct characterizations of neoliberalism as a practical program as consisting in "taxation structures that favor capital accumulation over income redistribution, industrial policies that minimize the presence of the state in private industry, and retrenchment in welfare spending." Prasad, *The Politics of Free Markets: The Rise of Neoliberal Economic Policies in Britain, France, Germany, and the United States* (Chicago: University

of Chicago Press, 2006), 4–5. David Harvey also examines neoliberalism as a utopian ideological program, "a theory of political and economic practices that proposes that human well-being can best be advanced by liberating individual entrepreneurial freedoms and skills within an institutional framework characterized by strong private property rights and free trade." This translates into a logic of subordinating all other interests and values in society to the efficient functioning of markets (except when doing so hinders large corporate or investor-class interests; neoliberalism is, as Harvey also notes, a program for class power as well as a free-market utopia). Harvey, *A Brief History of Neoliberalism* (Oxford: Oxford University Press, 2005), 2–3.

58. My point is not to engage in what Wacquant ("Analytic," 225–227) characterizes as the "logic of the trial," i.e., to indict the use of the tools pragmatically available for pursuing protections, relief, and remedies for victims of inequality for the identitarian narrowing of the discourse of equality. In the absence of the kind of political power that can revise the rules of the game, there are few alternative ways in specific cases to fight for the immediate or short-term interests of people who are politically and economically vulnerable. However, the extent to which civically engaged scholars and others accept without criticism a frame of reference that naturalizes inequalities not attributable to invidious treatment on ascriptive grounds reflects and reinforces neoliberal ideological hegemony.

59. On the separation of class and economic inequalities from liberal antiracism in the postwar era, see Judith Stein, *Running Steel, Running America: Race, Economic Policy, and the Decline of Liberalism* (Chapel Hill: University of North Carolina Press, 1998), 69–120; Risa L. Goluboff, *The Lost Promise of Civil Rights* (Cambridge, MA: Harvard University Press, 2007), 217–270; Stephen Steinberg, *Turning Back: The Retreat from Racial Justice in American Thought and Policy* (Boston: Beacon, 1991), 21–49; Mary L. Dudziak, *Cold War Civil Rights: Race and the Image of American Democracy* (Princeton, NJ: Princeton University Press, 2000), 203–248; Walter Jackson, *Gunnar Myrdal and America's Conscience: Social Engineering and Racial Liberalism, 1938–1987* (Chapel Hill: University of North Carolina Press, 1990); Preston H. Smith II, "The Quest for Racial Democracy: Black Civic Ideology and Housing Interests in Postwar Chicago," *Journal of Urban History* 26 (January 2000): 131–157; Alice O'Connor, *Poverty Knowledge: Social Science, Social Policy, and the Poor in Twentieth-Century U.S. History* (Princeton, NJ: Princeton University Press, 2001), and *Social Science for What? Philanthropy and the Social Question in a World Turned Rightside Up* (New York: Russell Sage Foundation, 2007); Stephen Steinberg, *Race Relations: A Critique* (Palo Alto, CA: Stanford University Press, 2007); and Leah Gordon, "The Question of Prejudice: Social Science, Education, and the Struggle to Define the 'Race Problem' in Mid-Century America, 1935–1965" (Ph.D. diss., University of Pennsylvania, 2008). See also Gunnar Myrdal, *An American Dilemma: The Negro Problem and Modern Democracy* (New York: Harper and Row, 1944); Lee Rainwater and William L. Yancey, eds., *The Moynihan Report and the Politics of Controversy* (Cambridge: Massachusetts Institute of Technology Press, 1967); U.S. Commission on Civil Disorders, *Report of the National Advisory Commission on Civil Disorders* (the Kerner Report) (New York: New York Times Books, 1968); Michael Harrington, *The Other America: Poverty in the United States* (New York: Macmillan, 1962); Kenneth B. Clark, *Dark Ghetto: Dilemmas of Social Power* (New York: Harper and Row, 1965); and Oscar Lewis, "The Culture of Poverty," in his *La Vida: A Puerto Rican Family in the Culture of Poverty, San Juan and New York* (New York: Random House, 1966).

60. Recent examinations of the two decades or so after World War II that focus on the complex interplay of competing and conflicting tendencies are Howard Brick, *Transcending Capitalism: Visions of a New Society in Modern American Thought* (Ithaca, NY: Cornell University Press, 2006), and Wendy L. Wall, *Inventing the "American Way": The Politics of Consensus from the New Deal to the Civil Rights Movement* (Oxford: Oxford University Press, 2008).

61. William Julius Wilson, *The Declining Significance of Race: Blacks and Changing American Institutions* (Chicago: University of Chicago Press, 1978), ix.

62. Stephen Steinberg, "Human Capital: A Critique," *Review of Black Political Economy* 14 (Summer 1985): 68. On the general tendency in postwar American social science to reduce class to culture, see also Adolph Reed Jr., "The 2004 Election in Perspective: The Myth of 'Cultural Divide' and the Triumph of Neoliberal Ideology," *American Quarterly* 57 (March 2005): 5–7.

63. For discussion of the historical race/class debate in left politics, see Reed, "Unraveling"; Ellen Meiksins Wood, "Class, Race, and Capitalism," and Reed, "Rejoinder," in *Political Power and Social Theory* 15 (2002). For a representative illustration of the reformulated race/class debate, see Kenneth Clark, "The Role of Race," and Carl Gershman, "A Matter of Class," both in *New York Times Magazine* (October 5, 1980). As the Clark-Gershman exchange shows clearly, the terms of this debate had little in common with the historically familiar one except use of the words "race" and "class" as labels marking its poles. It is significant from the standpoint of the historian of ideologies and perhaps instructive politically that this clear distinction in meanings of the race/class debate has gone so largely unnoticed or remarked upon by even leftist intellectuals who defend, and often militantly, Wilson's subsequent embrace of underclass ideology as a "class" critique of inequality. It suggests a willful blindness that in one way or another (i.e., with or without direct material inducement) likely reflects the substance of ideological hegemony. See also Charles V. Willie, *The Caste and Class Controversy* (Dix Hills, NY: General Hall, 1979), and *The Caste and Class Controversy on Race and Poverty: Round Two of the Willie/Wilson Debate,* 2nd ed. (Dix Hills, NY: General Hall, 1989); Bart Landry, *The New Black Middle Class* (Berkeley: University of California Press, 1987).

64. Smith, *Civic Ideals,* examines the complex ways pragmatic objectives shaped the theoretical apparatus of ascriptive inegalitarianism in the United States from the founding through the Progressive era.

65. Stephen Jay Gould, *The Mismeasure of Man* (New York: Norton, 1996).

66. Instances of this sort of tortured race-first argument abound. Some representative versions include: Kristen Lavelle and Joe Feagin, "Hard Truth in the Big Easy: Race and Class in New Orleans, Pre- and Post-Katrina," in *More Unequal: Aspects of Class in the United States,* ed. Michael D. Yates (New York: Monthly Review Press, 2007), 79–93; Michael Eric Dyson, *Come Hell or High Water: Hurricane Katrina and the Color of Disaster* (New York: Basic Civitas Books, 2006); Eric Mann, *Katrina's Legacy: White Racism and Black Reconstruction in New Orleans and the Gulf Coast* (Los Angeles: Frontlines Press, 2006); South End Press Collective, *What Lies Beneath: Katrina, Race, and the State of the Nation* (Boston: South End Press, 2007); and Manning Marable, "New Orleans Reconsidered: Race or Class," 2 parts, available at www.manningmarable.net/works/columns.html.

67. For instance, the Urban League and Jesse Jackson's Operation PUSH attained inclusion as line-item accounts in Carter administration budgets.

68. For one scholar's sustained endorsement that retails several of the stratagems aimed at finessing the political impracticality of this pursuit in the United States, see Martha Biondi, "The Rise of the Reparations Movement," *Radical History Review* (Fall 2003): 5–18.

69. In overlapping but distinct ways James B. McKee and Stephen Steinberg examine the intellectual genesis and foundations of this regime. See McKee, *Sociology and the Race Problem: The Failure of a Perspective* (Urbana: University of Illinois Press, 1993), esp. 256–330; Steinberg, *Race Relations: A Critique* (Stanford: Stanford University Press, 2007), esp. 5–40; and Steinberg, *Turning Back,* 21–93. In Steinberg's view the race relations framework's greatest deficiency has been its aversion to examining the structural sources of racial inequalities, although his contention that more race-specific policy interventions are needed to address them does not follow necessarily from that criticism.

70. Michael Rudolph West, *The Education of Booker T. Washington: American Democracy and the Idea of Race Relations* (New York: Columbia University Press, 2006), 16.

71. John Torpey, "Paying for the Past? The Movement for Reparations for African-Americans," *Journal of Human Rights* 3 (June 2004): 179–181; and Torpey, *Making Whole What Has Been Smashed: On Reparations Politics* (Cambridge, MA: Harvard University Press, 2006), 123–125.

72. Randall Robinson, *The Debt: What America Owes to Blacks* (New York: Dutton, 2000), 208.

73. Adolph L. Reed Jr., "The Case Against Reparations," *The Progressive* (December 2000): 17. I examine the recent reparations "movement," its origins, and significance in contemporary black politics more extensively in Adolph Reed Jr. and Kenneth W. Warren, *Culture/Politics: The Present(ism) of Black Studies* (Boulder, CO: Paradigm Publishers, forthcoming).

74. Reed, *Stirrings,* 199–121; Reed, *Du Bois,* 163–176. See also Michael K. Brown and Steven P. Erie, "Blacks and the Legacy of the Great Society: The Economic and Political Impact of Federal Social Policy," *Public Policy* 29 (Summer 1981): 299–330.

75. Torpey, "Paying for the Past?" 183, and Chris L. Jenkins and Hamil R. Harris, "Descendants of Slaves Rally for Reparations," *Washington Post* (August 18, 2002). Some proponents object that, because the march was called by a rump faction of reparations activists, its low turnout should not be taken as indicative of lack of popular support. However, the fact remains that no other evidence has been adduced to buttress the claim that reparations is a significant issue among black Americans broadly, and similar local events have been no more successful at generating turnout. Adamma Ince, "No Masses, No Movement: Black Boomers Shout Reparations in the Court—But Go Silent in the 'Hood," *Village Voice* (May 21, 2002); and Torpey, *Making Whole,* 125–126. It is likely that one reason many activists failed to endorse the 2002 rally was suspicion that it would not generate substantial attendance; NAACP member polls between 2001 and 2004, for example, reported responses ranging between 56 percent and 71 percent in opposition to the reparations idea (*Making Whole,* 127). Indeed, one justification commonly advanced for reparations activism is a supposed need to *generate* popular support for the idea among black people.

76. Daryl Michael Scott, *Contempt and Pity: Social Policy and the Image of the Damaged Black Psyche, 1880–1996* (Chapel Hill: University of North Carolina Press, 1997), esp. 41–119. Also see E. Franklin Frazier, *The Negro Family in Chicago* (Chicago: University of Chicago Press, 1932), and Frazier, *The Negro Family in the United States* (Chicago: University of Chicago Press, 1939). For another view that distinguishes Frazier from subsequent proponents of arguments for black cultural pathology, see Anthony Platt, *E. Franklin Frazier Reconsidered* (New Brunswick, NJ: Rutgers University Press, 1991). Scott's argument distinguishing the basis of Frazier's characterizations of black family structure from subsequent proponents of theories of cultural or behavioral pathology also is an illustration of the importance of contextualist sensibility in intellectual historical interpretation.

77. Scott, *Contempt and Pity,* 97.

78. See Rainwater and Yancey, *The Moynihan Report.* Programmatically, this melded imagery made it possible to translate concerns with alleviating poverty into initiatives aimed at correcting individual deficiencies. In the same year, black social psychologist Kenneth B. Clark's widely read *Dark Ghetto* also identified black social pathology as a central social problem. However, unlike Moynihan, Clark attributed its sources to discrimination and inequality in the present, not slavery's legacy.

79. See, for example, Charles A. Valentine, *Culture and Poverty: Critique and Counter-Proposals* (Chicago: University of Chicago Press, 1968); Eleanor Leacock, ed., *The Culture of Poverty: A Critique* (New York: Simon and Schuster, 1971); William P. Ryan, *Blaming the Victim* (New York: Random House, 1976); Stephen Steinberg, *The Ethnic Myth: Race, Ethnicity, and Class in America* (Boston: Beacon Press, 1981), 106–127; and essays by William P. Ryan, Frank Riessman, Laura Carper, Bayard Rustin, Whitney M. Young Jr., and James Farmer in *The Moynihan*

Report. Herbert Gutman, *The Black Family in Slavery and Freedom, 1750–1925* (New York: Pantheon, 1975), was a similarly visible, systematic refutation of the "legacy of slavery" argument concerning the "black family."

80. Scott, *Contempt and Pity,* 192. Black Harvard sociologist Orlando Patterson's oeuvre illustrates the staying power across the decades of the "damage thesis" as an explanation of black American poverty and inequality. See Patterson, "The Moral Crisis of the Black American," *Public Interest* (Summer 1973): 43–69, and Patterson, "Toward a Study of Black America," *Dissent* (Fall 1989): 476–486.

81. See Robert Miles and Malcolm Brown, *Racism* (New York: Routledge, 2003), 44. Also see Stocking, *Race, Culture, and Evolution,* 192–193; Franz Boas, *Race, Language, and Culture* (Chicago: University of Chicago Press, 1940); and Ruth Benedict, *Race: Science and Politics* (New York: Viking, 1943), 3–21.

82. For a useful discussion of the tendency to see social categories as natural kinds, see Myron Rothbart and Marjorie Taylor, "Category Labels and Social Reality: Do We View Social Categories as Natural Kinds?" in *Language, Interaction and Social Cognition,* ed. Gün R. Semin and Klaus Fiedler (Newbury Park, CA: Sage, 1992), esp. 18–21. In an observation that bears directly on the limitations of the postwar antiracist consensus, Rothbart and Taylor note that "a belief in essentialism could remain intact even if no expert was able to describe the essence of a particular category, because the possibility exists that there could be advances in science relevant to its discovery" ("Category Labels," 19). This is one reason that each seeming advance in techniques of genetic measurement becomes a platform for reassertion of claims to have found objective bases for essential differences in human populations.

83. See Reed, *Stirrings,* 122–128 and 179–196, for both arguments and references to an extensive critical literature debunking the underclass idea. As early as 1986, Richard Nathan, then of Princeton's Woodrow Wilson School of Public Affairs, called for shutting off debate on whether a distinctive urban underclass actually existed and who comprised it, instructively proclaiming that *journalists* had already demonstrated its existence. See ibid., 182. Also see Mimi Abramovitz and Ann Withorn, "Playing by the Rules: Welfare Reform and the New Authoritarian State" in *Without Justice for All.*

84. Jacqueline Jones, *The Dispossessed: America's Underclass from the Civil War to the Present* (New York: Basic Books, 1992), 283–284. Also see Adolph Reed Jr., "Parting the Waters (review of Jones, *The Dispossessed* and Raymond S. Franklin, *Shadows of Race and Class* (Minneapolis: University of Minnesota Press, 1992)," *Nation* (November 23, 1992), and "Exchange: Reed All about It" (letters by Jacqueline Jones, Mark Naison, Michael F. Paris, Robert J. S. Ross, and Martin Fass, and my reply), *Nation* (March 15, 1993).

85. Cornel West, *Race Matters* (Boston: Beacon, 1993), 14–15, 58. See Reed, *Stirrings,* 272, n. 19, for an illustration of the extent to which pronouncements of widespread social pathology among poor black people had become hegemonic among the black pontificating strata.

86. William Julius Wilson, *The Truly Disadvantaged: The Inner-City, the Underclass, and Public Policy* (Chicago: University of Chicago Press, 1987), 6–7, 20–21, 137. Also see Adolph Reed Jr., "The Liberal Technocrat (review of *The Truly Disadvantaged*)," *Nation* (February 6, 1988): 167–170, and "Exchange (letters by William Julius Wilson and Martin Kilson and my reply)," *Nation* (May 14, 1988): 662f.

87. Wilson, *The Truly Disadvantaged,* 138. Wilson's apologists typically insist that the quoted passage demonstrates his rejection of this crucial element of the culture-of-poverty formulation. His awkward and oblique prose style, including frequent use of passive voice, creates considerable ambiguity in his arguments. Nevertheless, his attempts to distinguish his account that centers on the emergence of a "ghetto-specific culture" as a consequence of "social isolation" from the culture of poverty (*Truly Disadvantaged,* 55–56) can be read as specifications or elaborations within a culturalist account of poverty just as plausibly as they can be held to constitute a

critical rejection. Even his qualifications that (1) "concepts such as *social buffer, concentration effects,* and *social isolation* are used to describe the social and institutional mechanisms that enhance patterns of social dislocation originally caused by racial subordination but that have been strengthened in recent years by such developments as the class transformation of the inner city and changes in the urban economy" and (2) "the significance of increasing social isolation is not that ghetto culture went unchecked following the removal of higher income families from many inner-city neighborhoods, but that the increasing exodus of these families made it more difficult to sustain the basic institutions in these neighborhoods in the face of increased joblessness caused by the frequent recessions during the 1970s and early 1980s and changes in the urban job structure" are arguably only specifications of the historical process through which the putative "ghetto-specific culture"—by which he defines the underclass—came to exist. He continues, immediately before the passage I quote in the text, "As the basic institutions declined, the social organization of inner-city neighborhoods (sense of community, positive neighborhood identification, and explicit norms and sanctions against aberrant behavior) likewise declined. This process magnified the effects of living in highly concentrated urban poverty areas—effects that are manifested in ghetto-specific culture and behavior." It is worth recalling that Oscar Lewis consistently argued that the culture of poverty was rooted in structural subordination and that even Moynihan's version of self-perpetuating black pathology supposedly originated in slavery and racial oppression. Why, after all, does Wilson feel it necessary to explain that his formulations of an inner-city underclass and its ghetto-specific culture differ from culture of poverty theories? It is because they are so obviously similar. Wilson, like Lewis, Moynihan (whom he defends against liberal critics), and others, defines urban poverty as a problem in fundamentally behavioral terms and anchors his account to claims that tie it to the existence of a discrete population characterized by behavioral pathologies. The logical structure of his narrative of the pathological underclass—including his claims regarding the impact of the stable middle class's departure from ghettos—leaves a strong implication of inertial reproduction of the pathological culture. The notion of "social isolation," which he asserts as a substantially causal factor in his tangle of pathology, is in fact only a "just so" story propped up by specious statistical inferences with no basis in the facts of how people actually live and experience their worlds. What work, then, does that notion do in his account? Rhetorically, it evokes an evolutionary imagery that is consistent with the culture-of-poverty narrative as well as with common folk residues of Victorian notions of cultural evolution and the formation of "historic" and "true" races. In this light, Wilson's "social isolation" is embedded in the same web of associations as, and indeed is logically precedent to, Moynihan's invocation, seven years after publication of *The Truly Disadvantaged,* of the language of "speciation" (Moynihan, Work and Responsibility Act of 1994, n. 164) in his Senate hearing. From this perspective, Wilson's waffle on the issue of cultural self-perpetuation seems more likely to be a moment in the incremental advance of an ascendant ideology via semantic infiltration; it smacks of an attempt to harmonize structural and behavioral arguments by absorbing the former into the latter while denying that is what he is doing. To that extent, his defense, in fact his entire narrative about the "underclass," looks like a cosmetic attempt to reconstruct a version of the culture of poverty acceptable to liberal sensibilities. This reading is certainly consistent with Wilson's contention that liberal social policies can be pursued successfully only by accommodating them to the right-wing's behavioral discourse. He made a similarly cosmetic move in suggesting that the term "underclass" perhaps should be replaced by something like "ghetto poor" because the former term "has become a code word for inner-city blacks [and] has enabled journalists to focus on unflattering behavior in the ghetto." "The Name of the Game," *Time* (August 27, 1990). Wilson indicated, though, that he "would probably continue to use underclass in his own work." It is, of course, not the word that is the problem but the concept loaded into it, which Wilson in no way intended to modify. For another attempt to rescue the underclass idea from left-egalitarian criticism by changing its name, see Jennifer Hochschild, "Equal Opportunity and the Estranged Poor," *Annals of the American Academy of Political and Social Science* 501 (January 1989): 143–155. Hochschild proposes to resolve the underclass debate by calling it the "estranged poor."

88. Wilson, *The Truly Disadvantaged,* 4. On the empirical and historical falsity of Wilson's claim that castigation of Moynihan had counterproductively stifled research on black urban poverty, see, in addition to the substantive rebuttals of that claim shown in Valentine, *Culture and Poverty;* Leacock, *The Culture of Poverty;* Ryan, *Blaming the Victim;* Steinberg, *The Ethnic Myth;* Gutman, *The Black Family;* and the various contributors to the *Moynihan Report,* Sanford F. Schram finds that a "tabulation of articles on topics related to the *Moynihan Report* (e.g., female-headed families, teen pregnancy, unmarried mothers) and listed in the *Social Sciences Index* between 1960 and 1990 indicates that rather than scholarship being silenced on the issue it continued along at a rather low rate, just as it had before the Moynihan report appeared (e.g., 10 articles in 1966), only to peak at much higher levels in the mid-1970s (20 articles in 1974), and then again in the last half of the 1980s (37 articles in 1988 and 55 articles in 1990). If there is any trend," he concludes, "it has been upward, and was increasingly so by the 1980s." Sanford F. Schram, *Words of Welfare: The Poverty of Social Science and the Social Science of Poverty* (Minneapolis: University of Minnesota Press, 1995), 197, n. 73.

89. Wilson, *The Truly Disadvantaged,* 12.

90. Ibid., 5.

91. See Smith, "'Self-Help,'" and Willie M. Legette, "The Crisis of the Black Male: A New Ideology in Black Politics" in *Without Justice for All,* 291–324.

92. Henry Louis Gates, "Two Nations ... Both Black," *Forbes* (September 14, 1992), 132–138; Toni Morrison, "The Talk of the Town, Comment," *New Yorker* (October 5, 1998), 32; and Janice Peck, *The Age of Oprah: Cultural Icon for the Neoliberal Era* (Boulder, CO: Paradigm, 2008), 150–170. Also see many of the contributions in DeWayne Wickham, *Bill Clinton and Black America* (New York: One World/Ballantine, 2004). On Rickey Ray Rector, see Marshall Frady, "Death in Arkansas," *The New Yorker* (February 22, 1993), 105–133.

93. By *working class,* following Michael Zweig, I mean to refer to all those who as a rule work under conditions in which "they have relatively little control over the pace or content of their work and aren't anybody's boss." By *lower-middle class* I mean those working people who may have some limited managerial or supervisory authority in their jobs but not substantially greater autonomy or security than other workers. Michael Zweig, *The Working Class Majority: America's Best Kept Secret* (Ithaca, NY: Cornell University Press, 2000), 3–4. I want to clarify my usage partly to distinguish it from the prevalent tendency to construe class in cultural terms rather than as a category related to location in a system of social reproduction anchored in political economy. I have given a schematic account elsewhere of how class became defined as the equivalent of culture in postwar U.S. intellectual and political life; see Adolph Reed Jr., "Reinventing the Working Class: A Study in Elite Manipulation," *New Labor Forum* 13 (Fall 2004): 18–26, and "The 2004 Election."

94. Michael C. Dawson, *Behind the Mule: Race and Class in African-American Politics* (Princeton, NJ: Princeton University Press, 1994); Carol M. Swain, *Black Faces, Black Interests: The Representation of African Americans in Congress* (Cambridge, MA: Harvard University Press, 1995); and Katherine Tate, *From Protest to Politics: The New Black Voters in American Elections* (Cambridge, MA: Harvard University Press, 1994).

95. Dawson, *Behind the Mule,* 67, 87–88, 211–212; Tate, *From Protest to Politics,* 25–27. I discuss these three studies more extensively in Reed, "The Study of Black Politics," 123–134, and *Stirrings,* 38–47.

96. See Reed, *Class Notes,* 77–90, and Dubey, Chapter 9 in this volume. Fashions in black studies scholarship also reflected and reinforced this view of a politically opaque black community. The focus on "everyday resistance" that became fashionable as part of the cultural

studies turn presumes and insists that private or indirect acts are the authentic domain of black political expression. To that extent, despite a superficial rhetorical populism, this interpretive tendency also posits as its default object of investigation a black population that is civically mute and requires specialized interpreters to render its perspectives and concerns comprehensible in American public life. Robin D. G. Kelley, "'We Are Not What We Seem': Rethinking Black Working-Class Opposition in the Jim Crow South," *Journal of American History* 80 (June 1993): 75–112, reflects in both title and content the central trope in both the public intellectual stance and this turn in black studies. For a critique of this turn in black studies scholarship and its implications, see Kenneth W. Warren, "The End(s) of African-American Studies," *American Literary History* 12 (Autumn 2000): 637–655.

97. Reed, *Class Notes,* 77 et seq.

98. See Adolph Reed Jr., "Yackety-Yak About Race," *The Progressive* (December 1997): 18–19, and "*America Becoming*—What Exactly? Social Policy Research as the Fruit of Bill Clinton's Race Initiative," *New Politics* 8 (Winter 2002): 165 et seq. Also see Claire Jean Kim, "Clinton's Race Initiative: Recasting the American Dilemma," *Polity* 33 (Winter 2000): 175–197, and "Managing the Racial Breach: Clinton, Black/White Polarization and the Race Initiative," *Political Science Quarterly* 117 (Spring 2002): 55–79. Clinton's embrace of the "conversation" came in the wake of his support of the travesty of welfare "reform" and his having abandoned Guinier's nomination as U.S. assistant attorney for civil rights.

99. See, for example, the following from the *New York Times* alone: Charisse Jones, "Bringing Slavery's Long Shadow to Light," *New York Times* (April 2, 1995); Samuel G. Freedman, "Laying Claim to Sorrow Beyond Words," *New York Times* (December 13, 1997); Bob Herbert, "In America; Renewing Black America," *New York Times* (July 4, 1995); and Eric Foner, "The Crisis Is Within," *New York Times* (February 14, 1999). Foner's essay is a review of sociologist Orlando Patterson's book *Rituals of Blood: Consequences of Slavery in Two American Centuries* (Washington DC: Civitas/Counterpoint, 1999). It is not accurate to attribute Patterson's version of this narrative entirely to the immediate political moment, as he had been recycling it in different packages—popular policy journals and magazines, op-ed essays and books—for nearly three decades.

100. Some have proposed applying the Swahili word *maafa*—which apparently translates as "unspeakable horror"—to designate this black Holocaust. See Jones, "Bringing Slavery's Shadow," and Freedman, "Laying Claim." Also, on the dynamics of relations of black and Jewish group advocacy elites, see Cheryl Greenberg, *Troubling the Waters: Black-Jewish Relations in the American Century* (Princeton, NJ: Princeton University Press, 2006), and Adolph L. Reed Jr., *The Jesse Jackson Phenomenon: The Crisis of Purpose in Afro-American Politics* (New Haven, CT: Yale University Press, 1984), 88–105. On the significance and role of Holocaust imagery as an element of Jewish-American interest-group politics, see, for example, Peter Novick, *The Holocaust in American Life* (New York: Mariner Books, 2000), and Norman Finkelstein, *The Holocaust Industry: Reflections on the Exploitation of Jewish Suffering* (London: Verso, 2003).

101. Du Bois, "Fifty Years After," xi.

102. Holt, *The Problem of Race,* 121.

103. Walter Benn Michaels provides a provocative critique of the general displacement of equality by diversity as an ideal of social justice in neoliberal America in *The Trouble with Diversity: How We Learned to Love Identity and Ignore Equality* (New York: Metropolitan, 2006), and *The Shape of the Signifier: 1967 to the End of History* (Princeton, NJ: Princeton University Press, 2004), 19–81.

104. Lewis, *Du Bois,* chaps. 10 and 12.

105. West, *Education of Booker T. Washington,* esp. 14–19, 45, and 222–224.

Conclusion

Adolph Reed Jr. and Kenneth W. Warren

The academic practice of intellectual history is itself a historical phenomenon. Questions and topics take on interest for scholars because they connect with contemporary concerns and perspectives. Interpretation is enmeshed in evolving cultural and ideological dispositions, "ways of seeing" that generate discrete patterns of discourse, which in turn yield distinct questions and concerns, distinct focal points for investigating events, ideas, and relations in the past. Although thematic and focal shifts in intellectual-historical interpretation do not track ideological currents typically in intentional or self-conscious ways, scholarly discourse is at least as likely to follow broader ideological conventions and trends as to shape them. The questions that scholars ask, and where and how they seek answers to them, are refracted more or less obliquely through the wakes those currents leave as common sense—the baseline of premises and propositions whose validity is assumed without reflection, as self-evident. This is true not only of historical scholarship but also of intellectual life in general, and the intellectual history of black Americans as a field of study is not exceptional in this regard. Neither are this volume and its authors.

Renewing Black Intellectual History represents a discrete interpretive orientation, one that proceeds from the assumption that understanding ideas, formulations, stances, and debates in the past requires examining them first of all within the practical milieu—the contexts of discourse, debate, and action—within which they were embedded. From this perspective the individual chapters are case studies exemplifying how a historicist approach can illuminate significant features of black American thought in particular historical moments. They examine either the thinking of individuals or the *mentalités* of discourse communities in ways that emphasize their historical specificities—their sources and foundations within the matrices of material conditions and ideological forces that constituted their contexts of interpretation and action. Warren's two chapters are illustrative. His chapter on Douglass shows that reading *Life and Times* in relation to contemporaneous liberal reformers' concerns about democracy, popular politics, and the ambiguities of representation broadens our perspective on that text in its time. This account also deepens our understanding of the origins and emergence of the notion of black leadership as spokesmanship for a presumably mute population in the fin-de-siècle political and ideological context.

Similarly, the chapter on Du Bois's *Dark Princess* situates the novel in relation to Du Bois's shifting, ambivalent relation to notions of democracy, oligarchy, and revolution in the decade after World War I. That chapter reads the novel's romantic notion of revolution, with its simultaneous embrace of imagery of technocratic rationality, mass jacquerie, and putschist conspiracy, as indicative of tensions in Du Bois's evolving political thinking in the environment of the late 1920s, in which militant, racialized anticolonialism and a revolutionary Marxism were gaining traction within the discourse of leftist intellectuals and reformers. In exploring how Du Bois formulated notions of popular revolution that harmonized with long-standing elitist political commitments, Warren also sheds at least suggestive light on persisting contradictions within black American thought regarding notions of collective racial voice.

The historicist approach we advance here necessarily presumes continuities between intellectual history and social, cultural, and political history, as well as the history of political economy. Jones's chapter on black popular culture and Reed's on the Educational Alliance and Urban League exemplify, respectively, the confluence of cultural, political, and institutional history with intellectual history conceived as the history of ideologies. Stein's chapter is in this regard a classic text, a foundational example of the interpretive depth and richness that such a supple materialist approach to the history of political thought can generate. Mitchell's chapter on the linked roles of gender ideology and race theory in shaping Garveyite ideology and practice, Smith's examination of influences of Chicago school human ecology on black elite reform discourse in the 1940s and 1950s, and Robinson's chapter on Black Power–era nationalism all similarly ground their analyses in the broader ideological currents and political dynamics of the time.

An implication of this perspective on intellectual history as the history of ideologies is that scholarly construction of the field is itself an ideologically laden endeavor. This is particularly clear in the practice of black intellectual history. Throughout its existence this specialty area has been understood among practitioners as well as others to be linked more or less overtly to normative political commitments. Interpretation of the history of black political thought was a significant venue for strategic political debate outside the academy well before calls for black studies programs arose in the ferment of the 1960s. Argument from racial authenticity has been a common (if not standard) trope in black political debate, and attempts to establish continuity with foundational traditions has been a normative touchstone of political argument. Scholars' accounts of the historical trajectory of black thought, therefore, frequently have been linked to extramural political agendas, or at least have been seen as having implications for them. Black studies' consolidation as an institutionally recognized field of study only fortified those connections.

Indeed, as black studies evolved since the 1970s coincident with the atrophy of black political debate outside the academy, academic constructions of black

American thought have become even more significant politically. Emergence and normalization within the academy of the "black public intellectual," a category of public figure occupying a rhetorical space usually associated with political activists and agitators, throws into relief the extent to which academic black studies has melded seamlessly with the world of political commentary. At the same time, largely under the rubric of cultural studies, a central strain of black studies discourse has come explicitly to define scholarly practice in the field as political action, thus redefining the boundaries of the political to fit within academic practice. Hence both chapters on the post–Jim Crow era focus in part on the role of black studies discourse as an element in the constitution of contemporary black American thought. Dubey's chapter on the postmodern moment in black literary studies examines the ideological and class imperatives that have shaped the discursive terrain of postsegregation-era black literary criticism. Reed's chapter assays the sources and bases of the appeal of Du Bois's "color line" apothegm in contemporary intellectual life, arguing that it is an expression of a class-based insistence on the primacy of a discourse of race and racial disparity for discussing matters bearing on black Americans.

Although this volume was conceived several years ago, there is no avoiding the fact that it appears at the moment when Barack Obama has, for many, become the cynosure of all commentary on black politics and intellectual life. On the one hand, it would be a willful act of blindness to pretend that the readers of this volume will not be tempted to assess the interpretive orientation represented by these essays in light of the Obama phenomenon, for as we say above, concerns about the past necessarily "connect with contemporary concerns and perspectives." Yet on the other hand, to present these essays as if the texts, debates, and discussions they analyze were merely prolegomena to the Obama presidency would be fundamentally to repeat the error that this volume criticizes, as well as to view black history as having a telos that can be discerned if one only brings to bear the right interpretive apparatus. To succumb to such a tendency would in effect make the only issue of the moment that of assessing how effectively or fully the Obama presidency "represents the needs and interests of black America," a formulation that not only presumes a corporate black entity but also begs the question of how the needs and interests of those presumably constituting this entity are formulated and developed in the first place. In fact, to make the Obama presidency the sole, or even the primary, point of articulation between black Americans and politics is less an analytical than a political or normative move that defines the bounds of feasible political engagement as congruent with the imperatives of the Obama administration. To be sure, one feature of the present moment—and a factor in the success of Obama's candidacy—is the way that candidate-centered politics has come to dominate public discussion and understanding of what politics is. But it is one thing to acknowledge this fact and altogether another thing to acquiesce in its entailments, particularly when one's primary concern is not political prognostication, or even political legitimation, but rather clarifying the terms and assumptions that can help guide intellectual inquiry within an academic field of study.

Index

About the Authors

Adolph Reed Jr. is professor of political science at the University of Pennsylvania. He is editor of *Race, Politics, and Culture: Critical Essays on the Radicalism of the 1960s* and *Without Justice for All: The New Liberalism and Our Retreat from Racial Equality* and author of *The Jesse Jackson Phenomenon: The Crisis of Purpose in Afro-American Politics, W. E. B. Du Bois and American Political Thought: Fabianism and the Color Line,* and *Stirrings in the Jug: Black Politics in the Post-Segregation Era* as well as *Class Notes,* a collection of his popular political writing.

Kenneth W. Warren is the Fairfax M. Cone Distinguished Service Professor of English at the University of Chicago. He teaches courses that reflect his interest in genre, the politics of race, and the relation of culture to politics. He is author of *Black and White Strangers: Race and American Literary Realism* (1993) and *So Black and Blue: Ralph Ellison and the Occasion of Criticism* (2003) and has written numerous articles in publications including *American Literary History, boundary 2,* and *New Literary History.*

Madhu Dubey is professor of English and African American studies at the University of Illinois–Chicago. She is the author of *Black Women Novelists and the Nationalist Aesthetic* (1994) and *Signs and Cities: Black Literary Postmodernism* (2003) as well as essays on twentieth-century African American literature published in journals such as *African American Review, American Literary History, The Black Scholar, differences, New Formations,* and *Signs.* Her areas of research interest include African American literary and cultural studies, feminist theory, postmodernism, and science fiction.

William P. Jones is associate professor of history at the University of Wisconsin–Madison. He is author of *The Tribe of Black Ulyssses: African American Lumber Workers in the Jim Crow South,* and his articles have appeared in a number of journals including *International Labor and Working-Class History, Labor History,* and *The Nation.* He is currently writing a book about black trade unionists and the civil rights movement.

Michele Mitchell is associate professor of history at New York University. She is the author of *Righteous Propagation: African Americans and the Politics of Racial Destiny after Reconstruction* (2004) and the coeditor of *Dialogues of Dispersal: Gender, Sexuality, and African Diasporas* (2004). Mitchell served as North American coeditor of the international academic journal *Gender and History* from 2005 through 2008. Her work has also appeared in *Cuban Studies, The Public Historian, Remembering Jim Crow: African Americans Tell about Life in the Segregated South* (2001), and *Elizabeth Cady Stanton: Feminist as Thinker* (2007). Mitchell is currently working on a new book manuscript that is tentatively entitled *Idle Anxieties: Race, Gender, and Idleness during the Great Depression.*

Touré F. Reed is associate professor of Afro-American and U.S. history at Illinois State University. He is the author of *Not Alms but Opportunity: The Urban League and the Politics of Racial Uplift, 1910–1950* (2008). He is currently engaged in research for two books: *New Deal Civil Rights: Class Consciousness and the Quest for Racial Equality, 1933–1948* and a documents reader titled *Civil Rights and the Fight against "Social Disorganization": Underclass Ideology and Liberal Activism and Policy, 1933–2008.*

Dean E. Robinson is associate professor of political science and public policy at the University of Massachusetts–Amherst. His work focuses on black politics and the political determinants of racial health inequalities in the United States and elsewhere. Robinson is author of *Black Nationalism in American Politics and Thought* (2001) and articles on race, inequality, and health in the United States. He is working on a comparative study of governmental response to health disparities in the United States, Australia, and New Zealand and a book titled *Does Conservatism Make Black People Sick?*

Preston H. Smith II is associate professor of politics and African American studies at Mount Holyoke College. His research interests include postwar black politics, black and Latino coalitions, nongovernmental organizations, and community economic development. Smith has written on black self-help, racial democracy, and housing policy. He is currently working on a manuscript titled *The Quest for Racial Democracy: Black Civic Ideology and Housing Policy in Chicago, 1940–1960.*

Judith Stein is professor of history at the City College and Graduate Center of the City University of New York. She is the author of *The World of Marcus Garvey: Race and Class in Modern Society, Running Steel, Running America: Race, Economic Policy, and the Decline of Liberalism,* and the forthcoming *Trading Factories for Finance: The Politics and Economics of the 1970s.*